FIVE GOLDEN RINGS

By

Judy Burr

ISBN: 978-0-9897788-1-7

Dedication

For my wise son, Charles True,
who believes a universal shift is occurring.

Contents

Acknowledgments

Many people participated in this adventure, but I would like to offer a special thanks to the authors who bravely created their thought-provoking books.

You helped me discover myself, and for that I will forever be grateful.

Special thanks to Sheila, my Sedona friend.

Prologue

I THOUGHT MY SAGA BEGAN when I picked up the phone and flirted with the man who had dialed a wrong number, but it was long before that fateful night.

I remember it vividly, like it was yesterday. Pat, my husband, came home with a pamphlet about the swinging lifestyle. This surprised me, because I was happy sexually, but the brochure made me realize my mate needed something more. I was a modern woman, and a hippie at heart, so I listened while he talked about the benefits.

It would strengthen our marriage, he had said, and it would be fun.

We did try it, and the lifestyle was interesting, but when Pat planned a camping trip with another woman, it ripped at my jealous side. I would have enjoyed the excursion, so why her? Why not take me? Of course, I didn't tell him how I felt. Instead, I planned a trip of my own. My sister, Jana, and I flew off to Las Vegas, the giant gambling mecca.

I met Lance that weekend, and he became my knight in shining armor. He wooed me with fervor, and he eventually convinced me to leave my husband. I divorced Pat to marry my hero, a man who would never consider sharing me.

Unfortunately, Lance was a controller, and after a year I was fed up with his crushing love. I left him and went to work for Pioneer Enterprises. That's when my adventure began. Taking that job secured my fate and caused my arrest.

Pioneer Enterprises was a telemarketing company, an industry I'd never heard of. They were selling advertising items over the phone, and people were giving up their credit card information in hopes of winning one of the five grand prizes. This was unfathomable to me. I couldn't imagine buying something sight unseen, but it was happening on a grand scale.

I was hired as their accountant, but eventually I oversaw everything except sales. My official title was Chief Financial Officer, but my bosses called me the "glue." I held the company together, and with my systems in place they became wildly successful.

I stayed with that firm for seven and a half years, but in the end, I left to start my own company. Being an owner in a male dominated industry was satisfying, but what I really wanted was a nest egg. I wanted out of the industry, and I needed money to fund my next project. I was nearly a debt free millionaire when the feds made their move. They wanted to prosecute my former bosses, and they needed my cooperation to make it happen.

The arrest shocked me because my company was squeaky clean. We had complied with every regulation, and we had done so from day one. Still, they effectively shut me down, and they seized every dime. I was able to retain an attorney, and he managed to secure a monthly allowance for me, but it wasn't enough. To make ends meet, I took on a roommate, and that man led me into an entirely different world.

Rod was an entrepreneur, and his company was based on compassionate capitalism. His wealth would come only after his associates succeeded. The concept was intriguing, and his business plan was brilliant. I secured a second on my home and became an investor. In return, he hired me to be his accountant, and our relationship grew.

This new job pleased my pre-trial supervisor and the federal investigators. I had not yet agreed to become a government witness, but work meant stability, and that was important to the FBI. For me, it meant a secure financial future. I fully expected Rod's company to flourish, and when it did, my investment would pay off.

I finally agreed to become a witness for the government, but by the time I surrendered, I had another problem. Rod and I had become lovers, and being a born-again Christian, he was determined to convert me. He wanted us to spend eternity together, which wouldn't be possible if I didn't accept Jesus Christ as my savior. Though I did not believe and was not interested in converting, I allowed him to perform the ritual and lay hands on me, but only because he was engulfed in paranoia. He had suffered through a hostile takeover attempt of his company, and he no longer trusted his business associates. He needed someone he could trust, someone who believed in him.

PART I

The Magic Returns

CHAPTER 1

My Saving Sister

I LEARNED A POWERFUL LESSON that winter, the second winter following my arrest. I realized that surrender was necessary and submitted to my circumstances not to save myself, but to save my friend. It was the only way. Not giving Rod what he needed would have meant that everything we had both worked for would be lost. Trusted colleagues had betrayed him in a hostile takeover attempt, and he was teetering on the brink of mental collapse. If he didn't stabilize, his company, Global Enterprises, would never recover.

To make matters worse, the group, the Seattle Hawks, as I came to call them, had solicited my help. Ultimately, they hoped to unseat him as president, and they needed someone close to make that happen. I had a huge financial stake in the company, and as the accountant, I was the woman in the know. If anyone could help them, it would be me, and I was a sensible person. I would want to protect my investment, wouldn't I?

Certainly. At least, under normal circumstances, I would. It was true I had often questioned the business practices of Global's young dynamic president. In fact, I'd taken Rod to task on many of his decisions, but there was a problem, and it was bigger than money. I was in love with the man.

At the time our affair was not public knowledge, so when the Hawks approached me, I listened. I did not agree, and eventually, I told Rod everything, but it was too late. My lack of faith had attracted these doubters, and in Rod's mind, that made me the ultimate enemy. If only I had believed in him, then everything would have been fine.

Rod was a born-again Christian who had been trying to convert me since day one, but he was so enamored with me, he decided I must be a sorceress, otherwise, he wouldn't have fallen so hard. He was a married man—married to an angel, in fact—who was carrying his third child and waiting patiently at home with their two boys. I knew this bewitching idea was his way of dealing with the guilt, for how else could a man of God justify an affair?

No doubt Rod felt conflicted, so when he finally laid hands on me, I allowed it. I submitted to his belief system, even though it went against every grain of my being. I did it for him. As he was trying to "save" me, I attempted to "save" him.

Rod did stabilize. This didn't happen overnight, but the immediate shift was remarkable, and I was convinced he could lead again. He made me promise to never leave him, saying with me by his side, he could do anything. I felt the same way.

Rod was a charmer, and he charmed me. Most of the time, I was completely taken by him. His dark eyes were enrapturing. They seemed to see things others could not. I grew to love his intuitive awareness, and I was even fond of his over-sized nose, which he distracted successfully with dark-rimmed glasses. He was tall and wiry, but very strong, and I wanted to be in his arms. He made me feel safe, which was amazing, considering my circumstances.

I had a whole host of enemies by the time I met Rod, and some of them had threatened my life, so it was easy to embrace him as a friend and protector. If I hadn't joined him in business, things might have been different, but I did, and Global Enterprises became our demise. He wanted full control and I wanted respect, something he couldn't give me. I was twenty-two years his senior, but my wealth of professional experience counted for nothing, not when it came to compassionate capitalism.

"Success only comes if your subordinates prosper," he had said. "If you want to be wealthy, you must first help others."

"Yes, but you also need financing and a good business plan," I had argued.

Finally, the day of reckoning came, and I gave up. I fully submitted, realizing all the while it was his demons we were facing, not mine.

Still, that day changed my life.

In my desperate hour, I called out to God. Tired of going it alone, I wanted Jesus in my life. I prayed for redemption, and thankfully, my words were heard. I was internalizing a new kind of awareness and happily called myself a Christian.

Now, if only I could make my family understand. They would not be pleased to know I had returned to Rod, but as much as I needed him, I needed them. I especially wanted my sister's support, so with that in mind, I called her.

"Hi, Jana. Miss me?"

"Sure do! Your honey-do list is still hanging here on my bulletin board. Funny, but none of the chores are checked off." She was giving me a hard time, but I sensed a smile.

"Well, sis, you had better hire a contractor to paint those walls, because I have work to do."

"Are you coming home?" she asked. Since her home had been mine during the recent weeks, I knew she was asking if I was returning to Colorado Springs.

"Only long enough to pick up my car. I've got to get

back here as soon as possible."

"You've decided to live in Vegas then?"

"Yes, Jana. I need to be here for Pam. I can't miss the birth of my second granddaughter."

This made sense to her. She knew how attached I was to my first granddaughter. Marie was my dream come true, and as much as I hated admitting I was old enough to be a grandmother, being one was something I truly enjoyed. My daughter and her husband, Jason, would soon receive a second blessing, and I couldn't imagine living away from them. I especially wanted to be near their little girls.

"Well, at least Rod is letting you out of his clutches long enough to retrieve your Lexus. I was afraid I'd never see you again."

I cringed. It wasn't exactly that way. I had to qualify the good news. "I'm bringing him with me, Jana."

"No!" Her response was exaggerated, but not unexpected.

"Don't panic. It's not as bad as you think. In fact, things couldn't be better."

I got a harrumph.

"Please trust me on this one, little sister. I need your support. I promise, everything has changed."

"Judy, you always say that when you fall back into the arms of an abuser. Will you ever learn?"

"Rod's not an abuser!" I defended. "He was out of his mind with worry when you met him. It was those Seattle Hawks. They were trying to steal his dream. If he had lost control of Global, it would have destroyed him."

"You're not planning on living with him again, are you?"

I swallowed hard before answering. "Yes, Jana. I love Rod."

"Judy!"

"It's going to be fine. We've just had the most amazing week. I swear, I know why we're together. Truly, Rod and I are meant to do this. I absolutely know it."

"How? What happened?"

"I'll explain when we get there. It's really complicated, but the good news is, I'll be able to visit often. We're opening the Denver market together. I'll be in the Mile High city every other weekend."

"What, with your master manipulator?" she said facetiously. My sister was, most definitely, not happy.

"No. At least, not for the entire time. We'll fly in together for the Friday night seminars, but then he'll go home to Eugene, and I'll stay with you or Shirley. Isn't that terrific? I'll be able to see my sisters, and maybe even my son. He's bound to be in town occasionally. I think his dad is coming in as a partner, so that should bring Charlie around more."

"Pat is joining Global?" This was over-the-top for Jana. She couldn't imagine why I'd bring my ex-husband into the enterprise.

"Yes! He needs something different. Global is a great opportunity and Pat is eager to talk with Rod about becoming our local field coordinator. Charlie has always envisioned joining me in business, and now his dad will lead the way. I've told Chas he has to finish college first, though."

"I sure hope you know what you're doing."

"I do, and I can't wait to see you. I'm going to blow your mind. I can barely believe what happened, and it happened to me. Jana, I recognized Rod from another lifetime. We truly are soulmates."

"Are you sure you're alright?" Her voice resounded with alarm.

"I promise, I am. I'll explain Friday. Can you leave the door unlocked? The plane gets in at 11:00 p.m. I don't want to wake you."

"Okay," she said, relenting. "I'll see you then. Love you."

"Love you, too," I said.

After hanging up, I thought, *what a relief.* I had expected resistance, but Jana had been tolerant. I was pretty sure she wasn't happy about opening her house to my young lover, but she had done it. Now Rod and I could pick up my car in the Springs, open a new corporate franchise in Denver, then begin life anew in Las Vegas, the place where it all began. I couldn't wait, and I felt optimistic about the future. Even if the judge ruled against me—God forbid—I felt certain I would return to the free world abundantly rich.

The success of Global Enterprises meant everything, for him and for me, and, of course, for his family. I especially wanted the company to succeed for his wife's sake. Mary Ann had been my one true ally during the takeover fiasco, and I felt deeply connected to her. It was a most uncommon partnership, and I believed we were all part of the same soul family.

"Where's your car?" he asked after we deplaned.

"In that far corner of the lot." I pointed across the blacktop.

Rod asked me why I had parked so far away.

"Well, I would have left my coupe in Jana's garage and taken a cab if I knew my trip was going to be two weeks, not two days. The lot was packed when I got here." I shot him a look with this comment; it didn't miss the mark.

"I missed you, Judy. I needed you," he defended.

"Well, I'm glad, and I have no regrets, but my Lexus better not be damaged. I'll hold you accountable for any dings."

I got his quirky smile. "I've got your ding, Ms. Burr. Hope your sister's asleep when we get there."

"Me, too. I'm exhausted, though. I can't wait to curl up with you." I was asking for a break, but Rod didn't care. He had a voracious appetite for sex, and he rarely took "no" for an answer.

He quickly changed the subject. "There it is," he said, spotting my car.

My coupe had weathered its extended stay in the

airport lot, and the engine purred with the turn of my key. It was a comfort to be behind the wheel again, kind of like throwing on an old pair of jeans—it simply felt good.

At Jana's we found the front door unlocked, but as soon as we were downstairs, she came to greet us.

"Hi!" she chimed happily.

"Jana!" I ran into her open arms. "How's everything? God, I've missed you."

"I missed you more," she said and quickly turned her attention. "How are you, Rod?" It was more than a casual question. Jana was searching. She had seen Rod at his worst and now needed assurance. Was her sister safe with this man?

"Fine. Much better, thanks. Sorry about Christmas. Not a very good introduction, was it?"

"Nothing like a first impression," she said sarcastically. "So, what's going on? What happened between you two? And how come you're suddenly opening a market here?"

I looked at Rod and then back to Jana. "You want to hear the story now? It's after midnight."

"Sure. I took the day off, but if you're too tired ..."

I was suddenly alert and talking sounded better than sex. More than anything, I wanted to tell my sister how Rod had saved me. I wasn't sure she'd like the reason for my new attitude, but I intended to convince her it was real. At least, I wanted to try. She was my best friend and she loved me. I wanted nothing to change that, not even Rod, not even the fact I now considered myself a Christian of sorts.

"No, I'm not too tired. Make us some tea, and we'll talk. Is that alright with you, Rod?" I asked my partner.

"Sure! I'll just change into some shorts. Meet you girls in a minute."

"He seems harmless tonight. Nothing like that crazed lunatic we were locking out at Christmastime," Jana said after we were alone in the kitchen.

"He's fine, Jana. Rod Steersman is a good man. His genius makes him fragile, but he's recovering. I was afraid he'd never break that streak of paranoia. I also saw my chance for financial independence slipping every day."

"Did you invest all your money in Global?" she asked.

"Every last penny and more. I'm in debt up to my eyeballs. Luckily, I had enough sense to buy a second home. If I hadn't done that, I wouldn't have a roof over my head."

"When can you move into the new house?"

"My renters leave tomorrow. That's the biggest reason I can't stay. Jason and some of his friends are moving my furniture in there on Sunday. Thank God for my son-in-law. By the time Rod and I get back on Monday, we should be able to go straight home. I'm so excited. It's like getting a new lease on life, a fresh start, and it feels good."

"Well, I'm happy for you, but I will miss you."

"I'll miss you, too. It's been great staying with you. Thanks so much, Jana. I don't know what I'd do without you. You always provide a haven."

"I just wish you never needed one."

I laughed, recalling how far back the pattern went. "Me, too! I hate it. Remember the first time?"

She didn't, but then there were so many pages to tumble through.

"I was only eighteen, and I kept running away from my first husband. Trouble was, Dad would never cover for me. He always told Gene I was there. I finally got wise and started sneaking in the back door. I'd tiptoe downstairs, and you'd let me hide out in your room."

"Oh, yeah. I was excited you trusted me."

"That's when we really got to know each other. Five years is a big difference between kids, even teenagers."

"Sure is," she said.

"I thought you were too cool, Jana. I can still picture

your bulletin board. You had all these articles about famous women tacked up, a bunch of clippings on career women."

I received my sister's wise smile. Jana was sensible in every way. She was a pretty girl, but she wore no makeup, not even a hint of mascara, and she dressed accordingly. She purchased top of the line, but nothing trendy or chic. The items in her closet could be worn until they were threadbare. Her shoes were purchased for comfort, not flair. You would never catch Jana in a pair of high heels, absolutely no way. Too bad, I often thought, because she was rather short, only about five-foot two.

Over the years, she hadn't changed much. She had beautiful thick dark hair when she was thirteen, and on this day, it was the same, only shorter. Of course, the cut was utterly practical. Her waves hung casually to her shoulders, and it was healthy, never having been damaged by any kind of chemical or hot iron. Jana was simply a classic, as beautiful on the inside as she was on the outside.

"You were only thirteen years old, and you already had role models," I said. "I couldn't believe it! All I ever wanted was a husband and the cute little house, complete with a white picket fence, two babies, and a dog. That was the extent of my dream."

She laughed. "You fell for the indoctrination. I, on the other hand, felt a need for independence."

"Don't you ever get lonely?" I asked.

"No. Not really. I'm happy single. Sure as heck wouldn't want to go through what you have."

"It hasn't been all bad. I need a man in my life. I love being in a relationship."

"Well, just don't get married again."

"Never. That's the furthest thing from my mind."

She knew this was true, and obviously so, since my lover was already hitched. She was about to say more, but at that moment Rod walked into the room.

"Hi, ladies," he cheered.

"You look better," my sister said in her offbeat, slightly antagonist kind of a way.

"Is that one of those back-handed compliments?" he retorted with a wry smile.

I tried to soothe out the tussle. "It's been a trying week," I said, heaving a sigh.

Rod looked at Jana. "How much have you told her?"

"Nothing yet. We were waiting for you," I said.

Rod and Jana were looking at me, so I closed my eyes and stepped back in time.

"Jana, do you recall anything about those last days at church, that final summer at St. Luke and St. Stephen's?"

She stared.

"How about that last summer at choir camp?" I prompted.

"I can see the bunk beds. I remember singing in a circle at night after dinner. Not much else, but I know all three of us went together that last year. Why?"

"Well ..." I paused. "I think something might have happened to us girls when we were little. I also think it might have something to do with that church."

She said nothing, so I continued. "You know how I haven't been able to recollect much about my childhood."

She nodded.

"Before age twelve, everything is pretty much a blank."

"I know. That's so strange," she said.

I was encouraged. "Maybe not; maybe Shirley's stories about having been molested are not so farfetched."

Jana's shock was evident. She resented our sister's insinuations about our dad. I needed to stem her rising anger.

"I'm not saying she was right. Certainly, Dad wasn't involved, but I'm convinced something sinister happened at that church. Don't you recall anything about that 'speaking in tongues' thing?"

"No!"

"I guess you were too young. You were about seven, but there was a huge scandal over the practice, and Father John was thrown out of the parish over it."

"Is that what happened to him? I always wondered, cuz I really liked him."

"Me, too, but I'm telling you, there was an uproar over the issue. It divided the entire denomination. Today there are two different Episcopalian groups, and that's why."

I had her attention. "Well, what happened?"

"I'm not sure, but I intend to find out. Something tells me Mom knows more. Did you ever wonder why she stopped going with us to Sunday services?"

"I never thought about it, but now that you mention it ..."

"Yeah, she used to sing in the choir and everything. Then she just quit. Remember, half the time she wouldn't even get up to drive us, and it was a long walk."

"Oh my gosh! And up that hill. That hill was a killer." Jana was engaged.

I laughed. She had been a peanut butter kid. That and macaroni and cheese were about all she'd ever eat. Consequently, she had been a bit pudgy. No doubt that hill had been a killer to her. "Sure was, baby sister; I'll bet you were glad when we stopped tackling it."

"Not really. I was finally old enough to participate, but then it was over. I missed St. L & S. Why did we stop anyway? Suddenly, there was no more camp, no more choir, no nothing. What happened?"

"What happened was the congregation got involved in a bunch of devil stuff, and I got tripped out."

More surprise. I looked toward Rod for reassurance. He was listening intently, so I continued. "That year, Jana, there was all kinds of talk about demons and devils."

"Really!"

"Yes, really. You were too young, but I was smack dab in the middle of the whole thing. That summer, I saw something going on at the tiny chapel near the woods and asked one of the counselors about it. She said they were expelling demons!"

"You're kidding."

"No, I'm not; I swear I could see them. I remember watching a red ring of dancing lights that went all the way around that little church. I accepted her answer matter-of-factly and went on about my business. I really believed they were casting out demons, and I wasn't the least bit bothered by it."

"No way!" she said incredulously.

"Yes, way," I emphasized. "It wasn't until later, after the adults started bringing the kids to the altar, after we were back home, I started to trip. They were speaking in tongues, and I didn't know what to think."

"When was that?"

"That same year, right after camp, back at St. L & S. I watched Father John lay hands on the kids, and then the jabbering would start. It was oddly fascinating, but I never wanted to do it myself."

"Was Shirley there?"

"I can't remember, but I don't think so. She says her memories go farther back, but I'm beginning to believe something did happen to her. I'm starting to flash on the same kind of memories. She no longer thinks Dad had anything to do with her troubles, but she still swears something happened. Jana, don't you wonder why Mom had a nervous breakdown?"

"I haven't thought about that in forever."

"Neither had I, but I'm telling you, things are coming back, and whatever was going on, I think it finally ended when we stopped going to that church."

This was too much for my sister. She was far too down-to-earth to internalize something so bizarre. She looked at my lover.

"Jana, think about it," I said, distracting her. "Shirley has had problems most of her life. Mom had a nervous breakdown when we were kids. I lost most of my first twelve years, and not one of us has ever been in a successful long-term relationship. What's up with that?"

She had no answer. Rather than acknowledge the insinuation, she went back to the camp. "You were really told they were casting out demons?"

"Swear to God, and I could see them, too. I still can. I see them dancing all around that cute little chapel. At that time, I just couldn't figure out why they were so happy."

"No wonder you wanted out of there."

"But I didn't. I loved St. L & S. I didn't want to leave until they started pressuring me. I didn't care if the other kids spoke in tongues. I just didn't want to do it myself. When they tried to make me, I left. I left and never went back."

"So, that's why we quit," she said calmly.

Rod interjected, "They were trying to save Judy. They knew she was possessed, and they tried to help her, but she ran away."

Jana shot him a silver bullet — silent, but deadly.

"It's true." I said, coming to his rescue. My interpretation was different, but at that moment, I was not inclined to explain. "Rod recognized it long ago, and he's been trying to get me to accept Jesus Christ ever since. Last week I finally did."

"Judy, what are you saying?" She was baffled. I was the queen of hostility when it came to Christian dogma. She couldn't understand why that had changed.

I needed something plausible. So I told her about our

intimate week, said how I recognized Rod as my soul mate. With the background established, I explained how we had finally prayed together, asking for deliverance. When I was done, she didn't have much to say, but she did believe I was sane. My methodical, logical presentation had stood on its own.

"Well, I'll be interested to see what Mom knows about this," she finally said.

"Me, too. I'm sure she can tell us something. I remember one day she drove over to Father John's house. I was in the car, but she wouldn't let me go in. I asked her why he was no longer our priest, but whatever she said didn't make any sense—something about him having been institutionalized. She wouldn't get into specifics, and she got mad at me, because I wanted to talk with him. Now, I'm wondering if he did something scandalous. I can remember sitting on his lap, but that's all. Shirley was always around him, too. It gives me chills to think about it."

"Yuck," she said.

"Yuck is right. Anyway, I feel bad for having always accused Shirley of being a liar. I think maybe she was a victim after all. In her confusion, she lashed out at the folks, but I'll bet something really happened, and maybe more than once."

"It fits," Jana said.

"Sure does, all too well. How awful."

"So, what are you planning to do?" She was speaking to me, but she was staring at Rod.

"For starters, I'm going to apologize to Shirley. I'll let her know she's not the only one with strange memories. She's been doing well but maybe knowing someone is truly empathetic will further her healing. After that, I'm going to talk with Mom. I can't wait to see what she has to say."

The atmosphere was beginning to thin. Finally, she

quizzed me, but in a humorous way. "So, you're a born-again Christian?"

I smiled. "I do feel different. Happier somehow."

"And you think Jesus Christ has something to do with that?"

"Absolutely, Jana! I'm telling you, it's like the weight of the world is off me. I can't exactly explain it, but I do feel different somehow."

"Are you going to church?"

"Not yet, but we probably will. Don't get me wrong. I'm not going to start evangelizing or anything. I'm still the same ole Judy Burr. I just lean on Jesus now. He's my rock and when things get tough, I call on him. Maybe it was crazy to believe I had a direct link to God. Maybe that's why things got so messed up. One thing I do know is nothing ever comes easy. My life has been a bowl of cherries, but I always end up with the pits."

This made both of us laugh, but Rod seemed upset.

"Just kidding, babe. You're my cherry on the top, but you know what I mean. I wouldn't be facing the possibility of a prison term right now if I had chosen a different life path. If I had been able to return to the church, I might not be in this mess."

Jana agreed, but with some reservation. "Maybe," she said.

"Well, whatever. One thing I know is I'm exhausted. What do you say we call it a night? It's almost 4:00 a.m. Don't you think we should get some rest?"

For the first time since our arrival, everyone agreed. Each of us wished the other a good night, and we went to bed. As I drifted off, I gave thanks the first hurdle had been conquered. My sister had patiently listened, and she wasn't judging, at least not in so many words. *Thank God for family.*

CHAPTER 2

The Merging

MY MIND WAS OFF in a distant land when a herd of thundering horses jolted me from my incubus. I tried to ignore the charge, but suddenly they were upon me, four monstrous hoofs. I opened my eyes, barely in time to ward off the cold nose as it pressed toward my face. Then came a second attack. Four more feet, but these were softer, seeking my attention gently. I smiled and pushed the covers off me, motioning for my dogs to get down. Gus and Buster, my buddies, had slept upstairs with my sister, but when she opened her bedroom door, they rushed to greet me.

Gus had bounded down the hall, the noise above my head stirring my dreams. He was the youngest and knew no manners. Although he was almost five years old, he was still a puppy and always would be. Buster, his father, was much wiser and a very sophisticated Schnauzer. He was a gentle soul, but he had missed me, and now he wanted my affection. I wrapped myself in a robe, slipped on some warm fuzzies, and took the monsters outside. Jana soon joined us. In her hands she carried two steamy mugs of gourmet coffee, and at her feet tagged her two dogs, long-haired Lhasa Apsos, naturally dressed for the cold.

"Sleep well?" she asked, handing me the welcome brew.

"Like a rock. I'm going to miss my cozy basement apartment."

"I'm going to miss you," she said.

"Well, at least I'll be back more often," I encouraged.

She pulled one of the heavy patio chairs toward me and sat down. "How did that happen? I thought the management team at Global's headquarters in Las Vegas was trying to keep you away from Rod. How are you opening franchises together?"

"They don't know. I'll be traveling incognito."

"Oh," she said flatly.

"Actually, they believe I'm still living in Colorado. I think they suggested the Denver market just for Rod. They don't want me publicly acknowledged as a business partner, but they know he cares about me. I'm sure they believe it's a sex thing, and this is their way of saying boys will be boys."

"Sounds like a male attitude."

I chuckled. "Yeah, little do they know, instead of seeing each other every other weekend, we'll be living together in Vegas and traveling to San Diego and Denver. We'll sell out the markets so fast, it will make heads spin. Our revenues will put the company back in the black, and when that happens, Rod will be the hero of the day."

"But what about you? What about your book?"

"This is perfect for that; don't you see, Jana? When Rod's at the office, I'll be free to write, and then on Friday we'll hop on a plane together to San Diego, and I'll be home the next day. After a Denver gig, I'll stay here, and he'll fly back to Oregon to spend the weekend with his family."

"That sounds good. At least Shirley and I will have some time with you. So, your first orientation meeting is tonight?"

"Yes. I hope we have a record crowd. I'd love to start off with a bang."

"Well, you'd better leave early. There's a storm coming. It's supposed to hit this afternoon, and the highway between Colorado Springs and Denver can get treacherous."

"You're right, and I've got to take the dogs to Shirley's place before checking into the hotel."

"Are you spending any time with her? She's not going to like it if you don't."

"Oh, we are. We're going to stay with her tomorrow night. We'll head back to Las Vegas from there on Sunday morning."

"Quick trip," she commented curtly.

"I know, but I'm anxious to get back. I can't wait to unpack—the sooner, the better. Once the house is set up, I can get into my writing."

"Too bad you don't have a PC."

"I know, but I'm supposed to be getting mine back from the Feds. Hopefully, by the time I'm ready to write, they'll be willing to release it. There's nothing on it they could possibly want, anyway. All the company records were on the mainframe."

"What a fiasco," she said as a shiver hit her. "It's freezing out here. We'd better get inside."

"One thing for sure, I won't miss the winter storms," I said.

"Oh, you'll still be dealing with a fair share of them. Just be careful on the way home, will you? Don't forget, you don't have snow tires."

"I know, baby sister, I know. I'll be driving, too. I want Rod to take in the view."

Mentioning Rod silenced her, so we slipped into the house to get dressed. I woke His Highness, and while he visited with Jana, I packed for our trip. The first of the snowy flakes began to fall even before my car was fully loaded.

"Guess we'd better get going," I said to Jana.

"It doesn't look too bad, but better be safe than sorry." She was holding back tears.

Rod gave her a hug, and I was pleased by their body language. They seemed to be more accepting of one another. The few hours spent together had worked wonders, or maybe Rod had worked her in his own special way. He was seductively charismatic. At least, he could be if he was so inclined.

The first part of our drive was relatively uneventful, but the downy flakes picked up speed and were soon coming down sideways in sheets of ice. The traffic slowed, and I plowed through it methodically. Then we hit rush hour and were caught in a bumper-to-bumper blizzard, with no end in sight.

"Oh my gosh, Rod, we're never going to make it. I'll have to drop you at the hotel and then take the dogs to Shirley's."

"Not to worry, Ms. Burr, we've still got plenty of time."

Amazing. The man could be a maniac one day and a soothing saint the next. His voice carried affection and his demeanor was comforting. God, I loved him. I glanced over to see him calmly petting Buster. Clearly, they were content with each other. *One big happy family*, I thought.

"Jana seemed positive," he said. "She's sure an intelligent lady."

"My sisters are bright. Jana graduated from CU with a double major in mathematics and economics. She can't add without a calculator, but she's a whiz on the computer. I really admire her. Shirley is the artist of the family, and she's a musical savant, but her manic-depressive nature impeded her talent."

"I didn't know she was artistic. You never told me."

"There's lots of things I haven't told you, Mr. Steersman. In case you never noticed, we've always paid more attention to your world. Really, you know very little about mine." I was teasing, but there was a hidden message.

"Well, what does Shirley do?" he asked, ignoring my dig.

"She sings like a bird and plays the piano, too. She also taught herself guitar. I thought she might do something with her talent, but after losing custody of her two sons, she lost the heart for most everything. Thankfully, she now has Michael, who keeps her going."

"Poor kid." He was reflecting, remembering the history. "She's coming around. I could tell she was healing when I met her last winter. Shirley will be fine, Judy. She has Jesus in her life, and that's all any of us need."

His words made me happy. It was nice to hear something positive about my sister. Most people were highly critical of my second-born sibling. Few understood her and many were quick to judge. Rod, on the other hand, patiently heard her out one afternoon at my house. Afterward, he helped her delve deeper, and in his own way he assisted in her healing.

"Won't she be surprised to find out I've accepted Jesus?" I asked.

"Oh, I doubt it. I bet she fully expected your turnaround." The words came casually and rang true. Just like Rod, Shirley had unshakable faith. In my mind, they were out in left field, but I admired the strength of their convictions. I also knew Shirley was praying for my return to the church, and I was open to the possibility. With Rod at my side, I might waltz through those doors. After all, stranger things had happened.

The intensity of the storm was growing, but my mood remained quietly contemplative. While Rod listened to music, I imagined him on stage. Tonight would be the night. Tonight he would step into those preacher shoes to reclaim his world, and I would be there. Thank God. The conspiracy had not separated us and now, God willing, the magic would return.

I wished more than anything for a full share of the credit, but Las Vegas would never publicly acknowledge me. As far as they were concerned, I could be the wind beneath his wings, but no more. Well, that would be enough. I would watch him shine and wait in the wings, pretty much like his wife had done. I would, that is, if I could get back to the hotel before he took the stage. Finally, I pulled into the parking lot, but we had less than two hours. There was no way to get to my sister's house, drop off the dogs, and get back in time.

"Come in with me," he said. "Let's see if there's any way to sneak in the dogs."

"What?" I exclaimed. "You're crazy!"

I wanted to object further, but he took off. I jumped out of the car and followed him. Inside the hotel, I waited in the lobby. He was jubilant when he returned to my side.

"There's a back door, and it's right by the elevator. I'm sure we can do it." As soon as the words were spoken, he was gone. Once more I was on his tail. It was one of those times. He was most definitely in charge. My heart began to pound with anticipation, or maybe it was the espionage, but point in fact, I was tickled he was willing to risk getting thrown out for the sake of my puppies. Of course, his motives were not purely unselfish. He wanted me at the seminar. He needed me, actually. My friendly adoring face did wonders for his ego.

After putting our bags in the room, Rod took my rollaway and emptied the contents onto the bed. "This should work," he said. "Let's go."

"You're going to put them in a suitcase?" I cried.

"Sure. Can you think of a better way?"

I had expected to walk them in on leashes, but Rod was halfway down the hall. This time I grabbed my coat and caught up to him at the elevator.

When we got to the car, the door was icing shut from

the storm, and so were my dogs. They were shivering from the cold. Looking into the airborne drifts, I knew better than to risk the highway. It would be foolish to go out again. We needed to settle down for the night, dogs included.

"Hold Buster, Judy," he said, unzipping the bag.

I did as he asked, then cautiously placed my papa puppy upright in the case. He was standing above the wheels, and that somehow reassured me. At least he wouldn't be upside down or sideways or something. "We'll have to take them one at a time," I said. "They won't both fit in there."

Rod looked up at me and laughed. "I didn't realize they were so big."

Poor Buster. He looked pathetic as the case zipped shut. Then we were off. Rod rolled through the lobby with me behind him, and when we were safely on the elevator, we looked at each other and started laughing.

"Only with you, Mr. Steersman," I said. "Never a dull moment."

"Only for you, Ms. Burr. Never for another would I act such a fool."

The door opened and a stranger stared at us. We checked our mirth, and the mission continued. Buster was unloaded and the process repeated. Gus was not so easily contained. He panicked in the bag and tried to wrestle free. We finally zipped him in, then moved faster than ever. Fearing a bark of protest, we launched down the hall and into the elevator. When both pups were safely in the room, Rod and I fell howling onto the bed, and the dogs jumped in the middle of our merriment.

We ordered room service, had our fill, and I made beds for the dogs in the bathroom. I left them with plenty of food and water, hoping they would be quiet while we were at the orientation.

As I greeted our guests at the conference room door,

my positive attitude set the tone for the show. Global Enterprises was offering a once-in-a-lifetime opportunity, and surprisingly, several interested entrepreneurs had braved the elements. After Rod's speech, they were ready to brave his world as well. About twenty-five percent of the group signed up that first night, and we knew there would be more. In two weeks, we would be returning to another exuberant crowd. Prospective independent contractors were on the horizon.

"I love you, Mrs. Global," Rod proclaimed back in our room.

"And I, you, Mr. Global. You were great tonight."

"No, Judy. You were great. You had them sold before I ever got there."

"Well, we make a dynamic team. Who could resist us?" I teased.

"Not these dogs," he said, as they jumped around the room. "Why are they so excited?"

"They need to go out. We'd better bundle up and sneak them out the back way."

"Okay," he said, enjoying our little conspiracy.

Midnight was approaching, and in Denver the carpet rolled up about ten, especially on a stormy night. Knowing we had little to fear, we snapped on their leashes and paraded them proudly down the hallway.

Outside the wind had quieted, and huge flakes of snow drifted gracefully from a luminous sky. When I turned our charges loose, they pranced joyfully. Rod and I sauntered through the land of enchantment. Tall cottonwood trees lined the parking lot, and the branches bent obediently to the weight of fresh-fallen snow. It was a beautiful sight, enhanced more so by the moon's twinkling light.

"Nice night," my partner said. It was a veritable covering of snow over metal. The cars were nearly buried, and it felt like we were surrounded by small numinous mountains.

"Yes, I'd say it's an exceptional evening."

Rod wrapped an arm around me and pulled me close. Looking deep into my eyes, he said, "I'll never let them separate us again, Judy. I'm going to be the best thing that ever happened to you. I'll treat you like a queen for the rest of your life." Then he kissed me. It was one of those mystical kisses, and even in the frigid air, my body was warming. Rod became aware of my heat. "Let's go take a bath," he said suddenly.

"You took the words right out of my mouth, my love. Besides, my toes are freezing."

After calling the dogs, we headed back to our room. A few people saw us, but nobody objected to our companions. The dogs got nothing but smiles, which added to our euphoric mood. It was a perfect night.

We slept late the next morning, and Rod ordered room service again. This time I did not try to hide the dogs. When our coffee and eggs were delivered, the waitress delighted in our stowaways. She cooed to them and received a substantial tip for all her oohing and aahing. After she retreated, we relished in the moment, and while nibbling on toast, Rod said, "It's back. The magic is back."

"Thank God," I spoke.

"Judy, I know we can do this. Together we really will ground Global in profitability. Did you see that crowd? I could feel the decibel of hope—it was rising all evening—they loved the program."

"I know, and I'll bet every one of them will be back next week. They'll be bringing their friends and neighbors, too. It will be a great meeting for Pat to attend. He really is a hard worker, Rod. He'll be our best field coordinator."

"I'm anxious to meet him. Does his wife support Global?"

I swallowed hard. Rod believed husbands and wives should work as a team. He did not like it when one spouse opposed the program. Knowing Pat's wife was extremely frugal, I did not know how she'd react to the small investment required. "I really don't know, but if he can get her to the presentation, I'm sure she'll be inspired."

"Well, be sure to tell him to bring her. How many other people do you think will be interested?"

"Lots," I said matter-of-factly. "I can't wait to tell my friends we're opening a market here. It's a great opportunity, Rod. I'm so glad the board agreed to open this section of the country. It couldn't be better for us or for the company."

My meaning was obvious. The coordinators had played right into our hands, and after all we had been through, it was a welcome relief.

"God works in mysterious ways, Ms. Burr."

I sighed. Yes, I had returned to a spiritual path, but I had no intention of becoming a crusading Christian. Sometimes I found Rod's God-talk exasperating, and I still hated the church dogma. *Give it a rest, Mr. Steersman.*

He must have read my mind, because he set down his coffee cup and picked up my hand. When I was solidly in his grasp, he led me back to bed. I was pulled in close, and then he reached for the phone. He called the desk and asked for a late check-out.

"We'll travel the whole world together like this, Judy. I'll soon be renting the penthouse suite for you, and if you want, you can order caviar for breakfast."

The picture was nice, but I didn't want him to get carried away. "Rod, I don't care about caviar. I only want you to be happy. My plan is to take care of your needs and be there for you. If you want me to travel with you, I will. We'll get these new markets going, and then you'll be on your way. More than anything I want to see your vision realized, but for you, not me. My dream is to write. I love you, Rod, but we no longer share the same goal."

He did not like hearing from my independent side, but he had the means to quiet me. He spun silk threads over my body, and with mellifluous fingers, captured me in his web. We made long, luxurious love that day. I hadn't enjoyed that kind of innocent affection in quite some time, and it truly felt miraculous. There were no fantasies, and nothing, absolutely nothing, got in the way. The Do Not Disturb sign was hung on our door and even the dogs were in full compliance.

~

My nephew, Michael, saw us as the tires spun and the car slid up the driveway. Jana had been right. My Lexus was not properly outfitted for the icy Colorado roads.

"There's Michael," I said, trying to steer into a parking space.

"Good. He can help me unload," Rod said.

As soon as I opened the door, the dogs clambered across my lap. They were racing to stretch their legs.

"Hey, I didn't know you were bringing them," hollered my nephew. Quickly, he forgot about us and headed up the snowbank behind Buster.

"So much for your helper," I said with a giggle.

Rod's eyes followed Michael with affection. "Guess you're elected," he said happily.

Inside, Shirley was ready for us. Her place was tiny, but tidy. It was also nice and warm. We had barely said "hello" and taken off our coats when the dogs came charging back. They were covered with snow, and behind them Michael was stomping his feet.

"Oh, no!" cried Shirley, looking at the damage. Ice crystals were quickly fading into the carpet, and water spattered all over her tiled entryway. I looked at Rod and we giggled. It would have been impossible to break our good mood, at least on that afternoon.

"Hey, you wanna throw snowballs?" my energetic nephew asked. His question was directed at my lover.

"Sure." Rod slipped on his coat.

Before I had time to blink, they were gone, and I was left alone with Shirley.

"Just like in Las Vegas," she said. "There they shagged softballs. Here it's snow, but still, it's no different."

"Gotta love it," I said. "So, how are you?"

"Really good. I'm doing super. Everything's been going great. And you? What's happening with you and Rod? I thought it was over between you two."

I hadn't planned on telling her, at least not so soon, but we were alone, and there could be no better time. Without hesitation, I opened my heart and told her the story. I covered most of what happened between us and discovered Rod had been right, Shirley wasn't surprised. In fact, she took the whole thing in stride.

"Well, cool," she said. "So, are you hungry? I'm making pork chops."

"Sure. Can I help?"

She wouldn't hear of it, so I crashed on her couch. Right after stretching out, the boys came back. They shook off more snow and then entered the little living room. Michael flopped on the floor and turned on the television. Rod tugged at me until I made room for him. When he was comfortable, I lay against him. He wrapped both arms around me, and we merged into each other. The dogs were at our feet, the TV was blaring, my sister was singing to the popping chops, and amidst the clatter I felt a great sense of contentment.

"Isn't this cozy?" Rod said, echoing my thoughts. "I'm so comfortable."

"Me, too." My words fell softly, and after a few minutes, I acknowledged the peace.

Thank you, God, I thought. *Thank you for restoring my Rod.*

I had missed him so. Now, I couldn't imagine letting him go. Indeed, the magic had returned, and I was sure the merging would carry us to far distant places.

CHAPTER 3

The Crying Coyote

INTERSTATE 70 WAS TREACHEROUS, but as we crested Floyd Hill, an incline dreaded by most seasoned truckers, the highway cleared and so did the mountain sky. Only wisps of clouds remained as we rose above the expanse.

"It's beautiful," Rod said.

"Isn't it? This is one of my favorite views."

I breathed deeply and settled into the drive. As I wove through the Rockies, Rod took in the panoramic sight with each curve providing a new feast for his eyes. The dogs slept lazily in the back seat with the music playing softly as a mild distraction. When a favorite Annie Lennox tune came on, I broke the silence, saying, "I don't feel that way anymore."

He had no idea what I was talking about, "What?"

"The song," I said. "This is the one about a little bird falling out of its nest. I used to believe that little bird was me, but no more. I don't feel lost any longer."

Rod smiled, but his look was smug. His expression said, "I told you so," meaning I was no longer lost, because I had accepted Jesus as my savior.

Maybe, I thought, but it feels like love. I was deeply in love with my man and we were together again. That was why

I was happy. Maybe Christ had united us somehow, but I didn't care to analyze. I preferred to roll with the flow, to let it go. Sinking deeper into my leather, I pressed the pedal to the metal. I watched as the speedometer needle climbed, then set the cruise at a hundred miles an hour. Rod didn't seem to notice, so I threw my mind into the high-performance maneuvering. Moving through the mountains at that pace was exhilarating, and I did not let up until we approached Vail.

Rod broke my trance when he broached the subject of food. "How about we have lunch in the valley?"

"Sure," I said. "I know a good place on the west side. It's right off the highway, and the locals frequent it. We used to hang out there when we came here to ski. Pat's brother practically lived within walking distance of the restaurant."

"Great," he said, allowing me to act as travel guide.

I took the familiar exit, but when I pulled into the parking lot, nothing looked the same. "This is totally different. The last time I was here there was no hotel and that shopping mall didn't exist either."

"The Crying Coyote," Rod said. "Well, it looks good. Let's try it."

"That's a new name, too, so it must have different owners. Too bad, the previous owner was a local. His son was a champion downhill skier and a bit of a celebrity around here. They ran it together, and the atmosphere was terrific. Progress. Guess it changes everything."

"The almighty dollar runs it all," he said knowingly.

We entered by way of a deli door and I pointed to the right. "The main dining area must be that way. At least it used to be. This part was a pub."

He led the way to the hostess station where we waited about five minutes. There were plenty of empty tables. What could be causing such a delay, I wondered? When the hostess finally led us toward a table, her attitude was curt.

Minutes passed, and Rod put down his menu. "I'm going to find a restroom. Order me a club sandwich if our waiter ever shows," he said and stood up.

"Sure," I said, wishing we hadn't stopped at the place. So much for a nice local pub.

I was seriously annoyed placing the order. The server acted worse than the hostess. The only thing we received were gruff shoulders, frowns, and curt, crisp words. I looked around the room and was amazed by the negativity. Most of the customers were alone, buried in newspapers or books, sipping at what appeared to be gloomy cups of coffee. The ambiance was dismal.

Our food came shortly after my partner returned, and about halfway through my sandwich my stomach felt queasy. "I don't feel good, Rod," I said, looking up from my plate.

"Why? What's the matter?"

"I don't know. I just feel weird."

He stood up for the second time. "Come on. Let's get some air."

There was a side door leading to a patio, so we went out that way. He stood near the railing and took in the fresh mountain crispness. Watching him, I followed his example and my stomach began to settle.

"I'm okay now," I said after a few minutes. "Let's go back inside."

"You sure?" he asked.

"Yes, I'm sure. I need to finish my lunch. We won't be eating again until late tonight. I have a full day planned for us in Glenwood Springs."

I had reserved a room in Glenwood Springs, not because it was halfway to Las Vegas, but because it was one of my favorite Colorado towns. The large hot springs swimming pool was always a delight, but the resort also housed world-renowned therapists. I had booked a couples' massage, and I could hardly wait. Hopefully, magical fingers would dispel the restaurant negativity.

Rod hadn't initially been receptive. He wasn't a massage kind of a guy, but he eventually warmed to the idea, and now he seemed happy about it. Maybe, he too, was simply anxious to get out of Vail. "Okay, let's go," he said.

While I waited as Rod paid the cashier, I looked at a painting on the wall: The Crying Coyote. At first glance, I liked it. It looked like a whole party of dancing dogs gathered around a campfire serenading the moon. *Well, that's cool.* They must have painted it especially for this restaurant.

As I stared at the canvas, my eyes took in the gyrations of the group. They were dancing alone, in pairs, and in small groups. Some of the curs were on all fours and some were standing erect, but they seemed to be paying homage to the wild raging fire in the center of a glen. The flames illuminated their faces, and looking closer I realized their teeth were bared. Their eyes stared ominously, but it was the blood dripping from their mouths that captured my attention. I saw no signs of the carnage they had feasted on, but their nasty expressions were revolting. The sinister grins suddenly reminded me of the night I had seen dancing demons. My choir camp experience came tumbling back, and once again I felt sick. This was a picture of devils, no doubt about it. They were worshipping their Fire God.

I couldn't look at the picture again, so I turned and focused on the diners. What I saw increased my uneasiness. My mind swirled in silence. Oh my God. These people are evil.

Never in my life had I seen evil manifest, not in humans anyway, but in this restaurant, the ugliness was evident. I could see demons working in people's eyes and on their tormented faces. It was in the body language and extended to the way they reacted toward one another.

What in the world, I wondered?

I was still staring when Rod came up behind me. He gently took my elbow and tried to steer me out the door, but I stopped him. "Wait," I said. "I have to show you something." I turned back to the wall. "Look at this picture. Tell me what you see."

It didn't take long. One glance was enough. "Let's get out of here," he said.

The fresh air hit us like a blast of purity, but we remained silent until we were out on the highway again. I was the first one to speak. I couldn't wait. I had to ask, "What was that, Rod? What did you see in that picture?"

"That was the evilest thing I've ever seen," he admitted. "That picture was a nasty piece of work. The Crying Coyote, my eye. That painting and the restaurant resembled something sinister."

"That's what I thought. The ugliness hung in the air like a thick block of fog. No wonder I started to get sick."

"You are with Spirit now, Judy. The whole world will appear different."

"Oh, Lord. I had no idea. Those poor people; they looked so lost."

"There are lots of lost souls roaming this earth. Now that your eyes are open, you'll see them more often."

I had no response, and he instinctively knew silence was golden. I was in a state of shock and needed time. Reflecting on the situation, I found myself thanking God for touching me. Nothing else could explain my experience. It was far too profound to pass off any other way.

CHAPTER 4

A Hint of Doubt

I DID NOT EASILY SHAKE OFF the memory of what happened in the quiet valley of Vail, Colorado. The experience rocked me to the core. I didn't understand. If this kind of thing did occur in the world, why hadn't I seen it before? After all, I believed in God, and I never doubted the existence of evil, but I had never seen it manifest before my eyes, either. So why now? Why was I suddenly witnessing this phenomenon? Had Rod been right ...? Had he seen in me what I had just seen in those poor tortured people at the restaurant? The thought was unnerving.

I found myself staring at every gas station attendant, every cash register clerk, and all the fellow travelers in the rest areas. None of them carried the look of those Crying Coyote patrons, so by the time Rod and I arrived at our home in Vegas, I had pretty well shaken off the incident. We settled in quickly and he returned to work. I threw myself into the task of unpacking.

Making a fresh start in a new house was cathartic, and working away from Rod had its benefits as well. We had been stuck like glue for almost three weeks, so I did a serious reality check during those first few days away from him.

The week in the mini suite had opened my heart, and because of Rod, I was a more sensitive person, nothing more. One night, after Rod returned from a hard day at the office, I started to share my thoughts. I was grateful we were still together, and more than grateful for my new clear vision. I was about to tell him this when he distracted me with news of his own.

"I've secured another major investor, Judy, so the pressure is off."

I looked into his eyes to see if trouble was brewing, but I saw nothing. "Really, who?"

"George Johnson."

The name sounded familiar. "Do I know him?"

"His son is one of our Salt Lake City coordinators."

Mentioning the town jogged more than my memory. "More Mormon money? How many shares did he buy?"

"Two points."

That didn't leave much. If Rod wasn't careful, he would seriously jeopardize his position as majority shareholder. "At what price?"

"Fifty thousand. He cut me a check right on the spot."

My partner was at it again. That was half the value. "Fifty thousand, that's a steal. Why did you sell so low?"

"He wanted to come in at half a point for twenty-five thousand, but I told him I'd double the ante if he would. He's thrilled to own two percent, and banking the money will make a huge difference."

That made sense, but I had another question. "Rod, whatever happened to your Puerto Rican investors? The couple who made the million-dollar offering? Timmy's friends. What happened to that deal?"

Obviously, the deal had gone south, but not before spending thousands of dollars. He and our other partner, Timothy Base, as well as a high-priced consultant, Dustin

Drake, had boarded a plane to secure the funds for Global. Rod had wanted me to go, but it was one of those times I was running away. Now the Puerto Rican memory was unpleasant, so he dismissed it.

"They wanted too many shares," he said casually. "Besides, if I had brought them in, it would have given Timmy too much power. This is much better. George is a great guy. He's loaded, and all he wants is for me to look after his son."

"He's buying a future for his boy then?" I questioned.

"I suppose, but he has no intention of joining corporate. He'll sit on the board but vote by proxy. He believes in Global and he trusts me. He knows I'm a man of God."

The divine validation. I truly hated it. I especially hated hearing it from Rod. Though I believed Rod had a good heart, and most definitely he believed in Jesus Christ, he was far from perfect. I felt a wave of disrespect, and I also felt fearful of the Mormon money.

Many of Global's investors were members of the Tabernacle Temple, and Rod's board was heavily loaded with Mormon influence. In fact, a senior Elder of that church had changed the entire marketing strategy. He filmed Rod's presentation, and for a time Rod didn't speak to a live audience. Would that happen again, now that there was money in the bank?

"Well, great, honey," I said. "That's wonderful, but does this mean our plans change? Are we still going to work together on the Denver and San Diego markets? Or will you go back to the infomercial strategy?"

"No. No more premieres. I want to stick to basics. In fact, I've already booked us a flight to San Diego. I can't wait to knock off their seaside socks. I wish we could stay there for the weekend, but I can't. I'm too busy and need to get back as soon as possible."

Relief. "That will work for me. Pam's coming over on

Sunday, and she's bringing Marie. We're spending the day at the clubhouse, and I'm sure the baby will love the warm kiddy pool. Pam says she keeps trying to jump in at their house, but the water's still freezing. Suppose you could join us? Maybe for lunch?"

"Maybe ... is anyone else coming?" he asked.

Being around my family was something Rod tried to avoid. His approval rating wasn't the best, and my mother was especially put off by the fact we were together again. Still, he and Pam had been friends. "Nope, and you're welcome. It would be nice to break the ice with Pam. Why don't you make a special effort to spend an hour or so with us?"

"Okay, I will. Sounds good. How about next weekend? Are you coming home with me? Or do you need to spend the weekend in Denver?"

I was surprised by the question. The new business plan included one weekend night in San Diego, the next weekend would be a Denver Friday night seminar. Afterward, I would stay over in my home state, and he would go home for the remaining weekend. What in the world? What now?

"You're not flying on to Eugene?" I asked, wondering if he sensed my disappointment. Returning routinely to his family and spending time with his boys was important, and I certainly needed time away from him, time to settle in, time to do my own thing.

"Nope," he said. "I can't yet. There's too much to do."

Inwardly, I sighed. Too many excuses. So many reasons to avoid facing his wife. Would he ever renew their relationship? I was perfectly happy to be the "other woman," but I knew Rod's guilt would soon overwhelm him if he didn't mend things with Mary Ann. Still, it was his decision.

"Okay then, I'll fly back to Vegas with you. I've got plenty to do around here. Moving is a big job. Tons of boxes are still in the garage. It seems like the never-ending story."

"The place is looking great, though. It feels so homey. How about a little atmosphere? Where are the matches? I'll light us a fire."

"That sounds nice," I said, taking some out of the drawer. "Care for a glass of red wine?"

"You're reading my mind."

After striking the gas, he dimmed the lights and I curled up with him on the couch.

"I love you, Mrs. Global. It feels so good to be with you every day."

Mrs. Global was his term of endearment for me. "Me, too, and I'm happy about the prospect of being in Denver every other weekend. That's going to be such a good market for us, Rod. I know a gang of people there; so does Pat."

"Umm," he muttered, slinking away from the business talk. He had started to rub my neck. A moan escaped me.

"Take off your shirt. I'll give those stiff shoulders a rubdown." His voice was sultry, and I rarely got such an offer, so I quickly obliged.

"Oh? You want to be my personal masseur?"

"I saw how much you liked it," he said, with a cutting edge. "You really got into it when we were in Glenwood Springs."

I raised an eyebrow before turning over. "Jealous, my love?"

"Actually, I was," he admitted.

"No way! Really? You were right in the room, and you still got jealous?"

He tried to laugh, but I could tell he was painfully serious.

"I almost went crazy knowing another man had his hands on my girl. Your oohing and aahing made me want to jump off the table. More than anything, I wanted to throw that masseur out the window."

"Rod! You're kidding," I said, sitting up.

"No, I'm not. It was torture for me."

"Then why didn't you let me have the female masseuse?"

"I didn't want a man. I couldn't lie still for that either. It would never happen," he said.

"Well, that's silly. They're professionals. They'd never do anything to compromise their jobs."

"Judy, I know that, but massage was new to me. I didn't know how to deal with it. We were stark naked, in the same room, and two strangers were manipulating our bodies."

Suddenly I got suspicious. "Rod, did you get a hard on?"

He did not answer, but his silence said everything.

"You bad boy. Did you blaze your glory for that woman? You're wicked. I may have to punish you. Maybe I'll give you one of my famous spankings."

"You want to take me to the barn, Judy Burr?" he teased. "I don't think so, little girl. I'm bigger than you."

"Yes, but I'm better. You know you can't resist me. You will submit if I tell you to, Mr. President."

My tone was playful, and he loved my modus operandi. I had never threatened to give him a whipping, and indeed he knew it was not something I would do. On the other hand, I could weave a wonderful fantasy, and he was more than ready to hear one.

"Finish your wine, Ms. Burr. Let's go to bed."

"I thought you'd never ask," I said, getting up.

He turned off the flames and followed me like a puppy, after which he received what he desired. It was a fun night, one I fully controlled, which was no surprise. The bedroom was one place where I could have my way. It was about the only place, but at least I had that much. Men are so vulnerable when it comes to sex. It is the easiest way to gain power over them. I learned that long ago, and over the years I had refined my techniques. I also learned to enjoy myself, and before our bedtime antics were over, I forgot about Puerto Rico, the Mormon money mongers, and Rod's wife.

Let it go, Judy, I thought, curling into my lover. *Don't let it haunt you.*

I didn't hear the doorbell the next morning, but my dogs did. They were barking even before jumping from the bed. As they ran down the stairs, I glanced out the window to discover the source of my wake-up call.

"It's the telephone company," I said to Rod, when he looked up. "You better hop in the shower. I'm having a jack installed up here."

"What for?" he asked.

"So I can have a phone in my office. I expect to get my computer back any time now."

"Really? Well, that's good news. What's going on with your legal situation, anyway? Do you know when the trials are set to start?"

"No, but I haven't talked to my attorney for a while either. I haven't talked to anyone except Pam, for that matter. Maybe I'll make some calls today."

He had no comment, so I grabbed my robe and went downstairs.

My legal situation was a subject Rod preferred to ignore. Not speaking about my upcoming day before the judge was his idea of willing it away. It was all about mind over matter; at least it was for him.

I was a positive person, but more pragmatic. One simply could not wish things away. You might wish something into existence, like a self-fulfilling prophecy, but once something was real, you couldn't make it disappear by ignoring it.

I heard a story once about an Indian guru who told his disciples he could manifest a Bengal tiger. The devotees believed in their mystic leader and gathered around him one evening to meditate. Quietly the group contemplated while the master went into a deep trance. When he emerged the next morning, there stood before him a most exquisite creature, a giant queen of the Bengals, fully marked, regal in her striping.

Here the story ends, and the author asks, "So, what did the mystic do with his queen now that she stood before him?"

The question is a good one, and it begs an answer. You cannot make something go away by pretending it isn't there, but that's exactly what Rod tended to do. I preferred meeting my challenges head on, but in my case, the federal prosecutors held the power, and they were moving at a snail's pace. I could not take my tiger by the tail, at least not on this day.

I was on the patio having coffee when the dogs went off again. I thought the ruckus was probably because of the same man, so I didn't even peek before opening the door.

"Sandy!" I said in shock. Sandy was one of Global's key players. Rod had moved him from Seattle to head up the customer service division. He was a good man, but he did not approve of our affair. To see him at my front door rather stunned me. "What are you doing here?" I asked after a few seconds.

"I came to get Rod. Is he ready?" Obviously, he wasn't happy either.

"I don't know. I'll have to check. You want some coffee?" I asked, trying to be polite.

"Sounds good," he said.

I led him to the kitchen, pulled a mug from my cupboard, and poured the brew. Remembering he liked it black, I handed it to him straight. "There's patio furniture in place if you'd like to sit outside. It's a beautiful morning."

"Thanks. This is nice," he said, looking around. "Looks like you're getting organized."

"Only in the kitchen, Sandy. Believe me, I've barely started. Moving is a big job."

"You said it! I sure don't want to do it again for a while."

"I hear that," I said. "How's your wife? Does Nancy like being office manager?"

"Yes, she likes it, but the books are still throwing her. I think we're going to hire a computer consultant to help set things straight."

"That should have been done months ago. Whatever happened to Aaron Clement? Isn't he still director of finance?"

"No, he went back into real estate. Guess he got tired of waiting for the proverbial payoff."

"Well, you can't blame him. He does have a family to feed. Make yourself comfortable, Sandy. I'll go tell Rod you're here."

I thought about the office as I headed up the stairs. No doubt they were hopelessly disorganized. There hadn't been a systems expert in place since I had left, which was months ago. I was more curious about something else, though, and I confronted Rod about it. "You told Sandy we're living together? Do you think that was wise?"

"I had to tell somebody. How else am I supposed to get back and forth to work? I can't take a cab every day. Besides, he's sworn to secrecy, and so is Nancy. I think Sandy is really pleased I confided in him. He feels like he's on the inside again."

Sandy was most definitely on the inside. Rod had seen to that by confessing our affair, but was he pleased with his situation? I had to wonder, and I suspected he might be regretting his move from Seattle. He and his wife picked up stakes and burned bridges to be a part of Global, but when the conspiracy went down Rod turned on Sandy. Because the takeover attempt originated in Seattle, Rod assumed Sandy was part of the coup and verbally battered the man. Sandy endured Rod's abuse because he didn't have much choice. Like me, he was fully invested in Global, with nothing left in his personal bank account. With nowhere to turn, and no means of leaving, he had stayed, but ... how much allegiance could possibly remain? It seemed like a dangerous situation.

"I just hope you can trust him. This had better not backfire."

Rod made a face, and I got the eyes. He was not happy. We hadn't quarreled since our week in the mini suite, but this morning he was aggravated by my attitude. Obviously, he didn't expect me to question him, at least not about Global. I needed to be the perfect companion, quiet and obedient, like his wife.

Not going to happen, Mr. Steersman, not a chance. You may have "saved" me, but that doesn't change the fact that I am an intelligent, independent woman with a mind of my own. *Get over yourself, Rod*, I thought, as he left without kissing me goodbye. I watched him walk away and wondered if I had made a mistake. God, I hoped not. His attitude had been most unpleasant, but again, there was nothing I could do. I decided to shake off my worry and get busy. I had my own work now, and I could not afford to get lost in his. Stay focused, I told myself. Don't start doubting yourself. Finish unpacking and follow your dream.

CHAPTER 5

The Glue

LATER THAT MORNING I called my attorney.

"Judy!" she said. "When did you get back?"

"Monday night, late. I've been unpacking. They installed my phone this morning, so I thought I'd better give you the number. What's going on? Is anything happening?"

"Yes, as a matter of fact. James Dominio called me yesterday. They want you to testify in one of the Pioneer trials next week."

"And so it begins. When exactly?" I asked.

"Thursday, I think."

"That will work. I'll be out of town on Fridays from now on. My job has changed, which will require some traveling."

"Have you told your pretrial supervisor?" she asked. "You're going to need permission in order to go anywhere."

"I haven't told him, no, but could you file the motion right away? We go to San Diego this weekend, so I won't need to notify them for that. Since the case originates from there, it's the one place I'm allowed, but next week and every other week after I'll need to be in Denver."

"What will you be doing?"

"I'm going to work the circuit. I'll be assisting the

president and helping to open new markets."

"That sounds like fun."

"I think so. I've also been commissioned to write the Global Story. That's exciting, because I've aspired to be an author."

"Judy, that's great. I'm glad things are working to your advantage."

"Thanks, Karen. I still get depressed occasionally, but I know wallowing won't do any good. I just keep hoping and dreaming. What do you think at this point? Does probation remain a possibility?"

"Absolutely. The FBI wants you to work with them on a regular basis. They're having trouble sorting through the files. Seems they bit off more than expected. The reams of records from the Pioneer raids have them confused."

"I can understand why. The company was huge. Before I resigned, Chris and Rich employed more than twelve hundred people. They were one of the biggest telemarketing conglomerates in the world. It's no wonder the Feds can't make sense of things. There must be a ton of information."

"That's an advantage for you. As you were their VP of Ops, they know how valuable your testimony will be. This is the first of many trials, but it's a chance for you to demonstrate your worth."

"The only thing I can do is talk about procedure. It's not like I have a secret weapon or anything. I just understand the inner workings, that's all."

I heaved a sigh at the thought of what was to come. I found no pleasure in testifying against my former business constituents. It wasn't that I was innately loyal, for truly I owed them nothing. In fact, they had treated me rather shabbily during the last year of my employment. For years I had recommended procedures that would fulfill the legal parameters, and we did things other "boiler rooms" did not, like ship actual product and randomly select participants for the giveaways. Pioneer's promotion included thousands of dollars in awards, one of which was a car or $25,000, that we gave away every year. I made sure of it.

"Why not?" I asked Rich one day. Rich was my boss, and the 'people person' of the company. He was also a handsome Italian, and girls swooned over him. Telephone customers swooned, too, for he had a winning voice and a charismatic personality. He was a consummate salesperson who did well as a telemarketer.

Chris was his colleague, and before they formed an alliance, they worked at the same company. He, too, had the gift of gab, but he was far better over the phone than he was in person. Chris could be downright rude one-on-one, but he was intelligent enough to understand what made the business work. He and Rich had partnered up, and as their business started to take off, they hired me. I was their office manager and accountant, and my responsibilities increased as the company grew. I became VP of it all, and my systems were appreciated.

"Why wouldn't you give out those awards?" I asked Rich. "God knows, you're making enough money. Distributing fifty grand won't mean diddly to you, and if you do it, you'll remain legal. Run this thing right, and you might stay in business a hell of a lot longer."

Rich presented my idea to Chris, who was wise enough to agree. We did it, as well as other things, when new legislation passed. Life was good, and the money flowed. I rolled right along with the numbers, and as my responsibilities grew, so did my knowledge.

One day Chris surreptitiously approached my desk. "Judy," he said. "We need to get a life insurance policy on you."

I looked up from my work and quietly choked. On first impression the man was not imposing. He was short and slightly balding, but his sweet baby face was deceiving. Chris could be ruthless, and he always looked after his own interests.

"No, really," he continued, speaking more emphatically. "What would we do if something happened to you? The transition would cost us a fortune."

He was serious! Oh my God. The last thing I wanted was to have my life on paper. Somehow that seemed threatening. I tried to reassure him.

"Chris, I've got good managers in place. You'd be fine. You'd only need to open channels of communication. Really, just trust your people."

On that day he walked away, but he must have talked to Rich about it, because his good-looking counterpart started saying things about my value. We were in Buffalo, New York, and I was assisting with the installation of a new high-tech telephone dialing system. This device was the latest and greatest invention for our business, and Pioneer always pushed the envelope.

"This is Ms. Judy Burr, everyone," he said, introducing me. "She is the GLUE, as you all know. Without her, none of us would be here today."

That nickname stuck, and most of my team used the title affectionately and often. Still, I had a very strong sense regarding the insecurities of my bosses. Rich and Chris didn't understand the complicated network of specialized departments. Under my leadership it worked, so what would happen if I stepped away? They didn't want to find out, and they started to make changes, just in case.

Under the guise of "proper management techniques" they restructured the corporate pyramid. Rather than have everything funnel up line through me, they established a broad leadership tree. First, I was asked to train a chief financial officer, which I did willingly. I was glad to shed the responsibility. Then came sales. My power was diverted there by hiring a general sales manager. Previously I had branch managers at each office, and when there was a question, they'd simply pick up the phone and call. It worked, but I didn't see any harm in establishing an overseer. Besides, it would certainly make my life easier.

Again, I willingly assisted with the transition.

Everything was fine until these two power-hungry men started to change my long-standing policies. The sales manager especially wanted to make changes, and he'd been able to convince Chris and Rich that my rules were too rigid. If things were done another way, it would mean more money. Money became the creed of the day.

For months I ran around trying to correct the chaos that ensued. My system was a well-oiled piece of machinery that moved efficiently, but small changes on the sales floor affected everything.

I tried to run interference, but my voice was not heard. Profits were up, so I was told not to worry. The two fresh corporate fools needed to run their own departments, so let them straighten out the mess.

To say I was frustrated would be an understatement. I had given my heart and soul to Pioneer Enterprises, and the owners had amassed fortunes. Effectively, they set me aside for the almighty dollar. I resigned in protest.

Sadly, they let me go. Sad for them, I thought, because I was pretty sure they would fall to the heavy hand of government authority. I, on the other hand, would start my own business, and my company would adhere to the regulations. I might not make millions, but surely the company would do well. I had also found someone who wanted to partner with me and was willing to put up the seed money. *Not too shabby*, I thought, walking away.

No, I didn't owe Chris and Rich anything. They had abandoned me, so when the Feds threatened me with eighteen to twenty-five years, it wasn't a difficult choice. I surrendered and became a witness for the government.

"What about my computer, Karen?" I asked. "Do you think I could get that next week? I'm going to need it to write the book."

"That seems reasonable," she said. "How long have they had it now?"

"More than a year. Certainly long enough to copy the hard drive," I said sarcastically.

"That long? Boy, the judicial cogs sure move slowly, don't they? I'll call James right now. I'm sure he'll make it happen."

"Thanks, Karen," I said. *One down, one to go.* I still needed to call my mother, and she would be tough. I hadn't spoken to her since returning, and I dreaded it. Mom was a Scorpio, a skilled grudge-holder. She was not happy Rod was back in my life. I picked up the receiver and punched in her numbers.

Thankfully, she was not home. I listened to her recorded greeting and then left a message of my own. "Hi, Mom. Got my phone. Call me. I miss you. Love you. Talk to you soon."

That gave me some breathing room. If she called when she was ready, she'd be less judgmental and more apt to listen. I said a little prayer of thanks and went back to my boxes. Those hard-nosed Feds had best be giving me my PC. They'd better give up something. *Please, please, I begged.* Just give me my PC. I'll survive this nightmare if I can write.

CHAPTER 6

Einstein Revisited

SUNDAY PROVED TO BE a perfect day for pool activities, so Pam, Marie, and I took full advantage. Once the baby wore herself out and was asleep in her playpen, my daughter and I were able to catch up.

"How was your trip to San Diego, Mom?" Pam asked.

"Oh okay," I said, recalling the incident vividly.

"Just okay? I thought you were stoked about the new market."

"I was, but before we left Las Vegas, a couple of coordinators confronted us."

"What? How'd that happen? I didn't think they knew you were in town."

"They do now. Cody Daniels and Nelson Balding paid Rod a surprise visit. They came right to the gate just before we left. I was standing next to him and there was no place to hide." This would never happen today, but this was before 9/11, before airport security.

"Well, that can't be a good thing," she paused. "How did Rod handle it?"

"I think he's okay, but I'm worried. The gossip mill could do some damage."

"Why should any of his team care? If Rod's paying your expenses, how can they complain?" she asked innocently.

"They shouldn't, but it's that judgment thing. Most of them still blame me for what happened."

"Why?"

"Because I'm the woman, that's why. It's always the woman's fault. Even when I divorced your dad, everyone blamed me. No one had a clue what really transpired between us, but because I ran off to Las Vegas, they assumed it was my fault. I was the wicked witch then, and it's happening again."

"Oh, Mom, I'm so sorry. I know how happy you were about the idea of traveling, especially since the seminars were going to take you into Denver."

"Thanks, but I'm not losing hope, not just yet. I am angry, though. You know what that jerk Cody Daniels said to me?"

"Jerk? I thought you liked Cody. Weren't you pals? Isn't he the one who helped you with the newsletter?"

"Yes, but Friday he called me a whore."

"WHAT!" she said, sitting up. "I can't believe it."

"Neither could I, but he walked right up to me and whispered in my ear, so Rod couldn't hear. He acted friendly, and I thought he was going to say something nice, but he bent down and said, 'I think you're a whore.' I was shocked! Too shocked to talk. He simply rejoined Rod and Nelson. I left to go the restroom. Can you imagine?"

"No! What did Rod say?"

"I didn't tell him."

"Mom! Are you crazy? Why not?"

"Because I have no intention of returning to the office, and I don't want to make things worse. It sounds like Global still has problems, so I'm trying to forget it happened."

"So, you plan to continue as before?"

"You bet. I want Rod to succeed. He's also paying the

bills here, so how can I complain?"

"Rod's paying?" She was surprised.

"Yes, he said he'd take care of everything. He must because I'm broke."

"Well, it's about time! How are you two getting along?"

"Better than ever. It's so good, I can't believe it. I swear we are soulmates. That week we stayed at the mini-suite I had an incredible experience. Pam, I recognized Rod from another lifetime. He was my husband before."

"Oh, please."

"I'm telling you. Something clicked between us. He may be Albert Einstein reincarnated."

"Mom," she scolded. "Rod may be brilliant, but he's crazy. I think Albert Einstein was a together kind of a guy. He wouldn't have returned as a paranoid schizophrenic."

My daughter—she never minced words. This label hit my funny bone, and I giggled. Through my laughter, I attempted to convince her, but as the story unfolded, her expression said it all. She thought I was wacked, even more wacked than my partner.

Finally, I was saved. His looniness walked up to greet us. "Hi, ladies. Enjoying yourselves?" he asked.

We were tickled to tears. "Rod," I started. "I was just telling Pam about that day I yelled at you for breaking the lead in your ever-sharp pencil. Remember how I stood up and told you that's why I always had to be the teacher?"

"Oh, yeah," he said, pulling up a chair. "Your mother told me I broke the chalk on the chalkboard, too. She said I always pressed too hard."

Rod's attitude was light, which kept our giddiness going. Pam glanced at the baby, who was still sound asleep, then laughed and said, "But Einstein? She thinks you were Albert Einstein!"

He smiled. "Now who's crazy, I ask you? Her or me?"

"But Rod," I defended. "It happened. All that was real. How else can you explain my insights?"

He didn't answer the question, but rather, he had a surprise of his own. "I can't explain it. But it is interesting I had just bought a huge poster of the genius. I saw it in a bookstore and had it framed. It's hanging in my office."

"Rod, you're kidding!" I said, "You never told me that."

"Well, I didn't want you to get carried away with this reincarnation thing. I couldn't add fuel to your Einstein fire."

"Oh my God," I said, staring at my daughter.

"Oh my God," she echoed.

After Rod left, and while we finished repacking the cooler, I asked, "Can you believe Rod has a picture of Albert Einstein on his wall?"

"That's too weird," she said, holding her belly and sitting down.

"You look good preggers, Pam. How are you feeling?"

"Terrific. This has been an easy pregnancy. I'm carrying the baby out front. The girls at the office tell me I don't even look pregnant from behind."

"You don't, and your legs look great. How's the job anyway?"

"It's good. I'm so happy, Mom. Getting on at the water district was the best thing that could have happened to me. At least I have job security."

Poor Pam, she needed job security. Her husband, Jason, had recently been indicted. They were using him to pressure me, and being my employee, he was targeted. It was a sordid affair, and my attorney was working on a deal for him, but the government had not offered a plea. I didn't have anything positive to say, so I changed the subject.

"Does your benefit package cover the baby?" I asked.

"Everything. It's the best coverage in town. Speaking of coverage, have you covered the bases with Grams?"

"Oh, yes," I said with exaggeration.

"Tough, was she?"

"Very. We're having lunch next week. I told her I'd explain everything then.

CHAPTER 7

Crisis Number One

THE WEEK STRETCHED OUT, and on Wednesday I was called downtown for a debriefing. The prosecuting attorneys questioned me for the better part of the day, but my computer was never mentioned. Finally, before I was dismissed, I addressed the issue. I did not ask James Dominio, because a postal investigator had no real power. Rather, I turned to the man in charge.

Conrad Baker was from Washington, D.C. His tall, angular body, combined with his chiseled face, reminded me of Abraham Lincoln. We had met before, but today we developed a relationship of mutual respect. I impressed him with my knowledge, and he treated me like an entrepreneur, not a criminal. I decided to brave my question. "Mr. Baker, what about my PC? Can I pick it up today?"

He didn't know what I was talking about. He turned to Dominio.

James Dominio gave me a cheeky grin—a very irritating expression. "They've copied the hard drive. At least I think they have, and the judge has ordered it released."

"Is it here?" Conrad asked.

"Should be upstairs," Dominio said with a shrug. He

didn't seem to think it was very important.

I pleaded to Conrad. "They've had it for almost a year and a half, and I've been asked to do some writing for the company that employs me. I need a word processor, and I really cannot afford to buy a new one."

Conrad seemed perturbed. He addressed Dominio again. "Let's find out where it is and get it down here for her. She can take it home tomorrow. Judy, can you be here by nine o'clock?"

"Yes, of course. Thank you very much."

"A year and a half," he stated more than questioned.

"Yes, this has been going on for a long time," I said. "I'll see you in the morning. Thanks again."

I was thrilled, and that night I tried to share my elation. Unfortunately, Rod was in one of his moods, and he rather effectively tuned me out. Were our gate greeters Cody Daniels and Nelson Balding stirring up trouble again?

Hang on baby, hang on, I thought, going to bed without him. *Keep those wolves at bay. Don't let them beat you down.*

~

"They've all taken a plea, Judy," said the lead prosecutor the next day.

"Really, Conrad?" I deliberately used his first name.

"Yes. All five co-defendants have pled guilty," he said proudly.

I was shocked. Those men were some of the upper-level salespeople at Pioneer. Two of them had been Richie's loyal friends and refused to cooperate. No way in hell would either of them go against their good buddy, their boss, their mentor. They were loyal to the core, or so I had been told. In fact, one had threatened me personally. I had been warned, "Testify and you die." Now they were turning state's evidence. A plea would not have been offered otherwise. I would not be the only one cooperating. What a relief.

"Wow! That surprises me. I thought they were adamant about going to trial."

"Their attorney convinced them it was a no-win situation. We offered them a package deal, and they took it—begrudgingly—but they finally signed. You won't have to testify after all."

I heaved a great sigh. "Am I free to go then?"

"You are, and we'd like to thank you. You really helped us. Understanding the inner workings of the industry was very beneficial."

I smiled knowingly. "It's quite complicated, isn't it?"

"It sure is, amazingly so. The other trial will be even worse. We've got rooms of records. You're not planning any trips or anything, are you?"

"No, Mr. Baker," I said, getting formal this time. "I'll be at your disposal. Just let me know the day before, so I can work it out with my employer."

"Are you having any problems with them because of this?" he asked.

"No, my boss is completely supportive," I said. "That reminds me, can I pick up my PC?"

"Sure. In fact, I'll bring it down for you. Where did you park?"

"In the garage. Do you want me to drive around front?"

"That would be good. I'll meet you out there in a few minutes."

That night was more of the same. Rod still refused to take me into his confidence, which worried me. I saw no signs of paranoia, but something was going on, and I did not want him to unravel. I decided to communicate without words. He was sitting on my overstuffed couch watching TV, so I came up from behind and began massaging his neck. He caved in my hands, and after working on his head for a while, his upper torso went limp.

Thank God, I thought. At least I can reach him this way.

Now that he was putty in my hands, I reached further. I stopped the scalp massage and reached into his shirt. Tweaking his nipples exacted a moan, so I climbed over the back of the couch and fell into his lap. Then I kissed him. He was mine, and I eased his pain in the best possible way.

The next morning Rod rose in good spirits. We were heading to Denver, and since he had no reason to stop at the office, nothing happened to dampen his mood.

The crowd at the presentation was large, almost twice the size as the first. We worked late into the evening, answering questions and signing up new dealers. Finally, we returned to our room, but Rod was not done talking about business.

"Why wasn't your ex-husband there? Where was Pat?"

I didn't know, but I hadn't called Pat either. Rod had scared me with his sullen mood, and fearing the worst, I had deliberately not made the call. "I have no idea. I could call him. It's only eleven, and he's probably still up. Would you want to meet with him in the morning before we leave?"

"For breakfast? Sounds perfect."

I extended the invitation, and Pat accepted. He did not say why he hadn't attended the meeting, nor did I ask.

Rod stared at me when I hung up the phone. "Why didn't you ask why he pulled a no-show?"

"I didn't think about it. I'm sure he'll tell us tomorrow. He'll be here at eleven."

My partner was aggravated, and his eyes turned steely cold. "Judy, don't you want Pat involved?"

"Of course I do. He'll be great for Global, and I know he's looking for a good business opportunity. It's a perfect match."

Rod did not buy it. He was keenly intuitive, and he knew I had a problem of some kind. Truth was, a small seed of doubt had taken root. I was worried about Rod, and consequently, I was concerned about Global. Did the company have a future in Colorado? Should I encourage my friends to invest? I wasn't sure, but those thoughts would remain silent. When he repeated the question, I continued the sham.

"Are you sure? Because if you don't think it's a good idea, now is the time to tell me. Are there issues with his wife? Do the two of you get along?"

"We're fine with each other. Really, Rod, it's okay. You'll see. Pat is a good man. You're going to like him."

Thankfully, he believed me, and I soon fell asleep, but somewhere in the night my alarms went off. When I rolled over, my partner was gone. Something was amiss, and Rod's disappearance meant trouble.

Searching the darkness, I could see a light coming from the bathroom. The door was slightly ajar, so I waited. I expected him to come out, but when he didn't, I got up. I slipped on a nightshirt and went to see what he was doing.

Rod was sitting on the floor next to the bathtub, surrounded by piles of paper. "What are you doing?" I asked, recognizing the spreadsheets. He was studying Global's market reports.

"Searching," he said, flatly. "Look at this."

He handed me a recap of the Phoenix market and I knew most of the names. I also knew what franchises belonged in which down-line, but the report was not accurate. "Who gave you this?" I asked. "This is totally messed up."

"I had Cody Daniels run it off for me. Can you believe it?"

Cody Daniels! The man who called me a whore! No wonder Rod was upset during the week. Cody was up to no good. Why, though? Why would he deliberately sabotage the volume reports? I plopped down on the floor and began to study the sheets. None of them were right. "Oh my God, Rod. These are all wrong!"

"Now do you believe me? I told you someone was trying to undermine my leadership. How can I possibly run the organization without accurate information?"

He had cried foul play before, but everyone thought he was delusional. Now I was staring at a good solid reason for his paranoia.

I think you're a whore.

The memory of Cody's words hit me again, but the secondary shock was stronger than the first.

"Rod," I said, sinking into the carpet. "I have to tell you something."

Rod maintained his cool as I revealed the information, and his calm was disturbing. Why wasn't he reacting? He'd wanted to throw my masseur out the window. How could he sit there and not react to the fact that Cody had called me a whore? Why wasn't my information causing an explosion? I stared at him blankly. When he finally spoke, his words hit me with an aftershock of great magnitude.

"Judy, how could you say such a thing?" he asked quietly. "You can't possibly expect me to believe Cody called you a whore. He's a God-fearing Christian, for heaven's sake."

I was livid, barely resisting the urge to ram my fist down his throat. I tried to speak, but it was impossible. Instead, I got up. If I had been dressed, I would have left the room, but I wasn't, and really, there was nowhere to go. I stormed away but only went back to bed. Then I sat there and wondered what to do. What was the fastest way to get away from this asshole?

He followed me. "Judy, I love you. It's okay. Just tell me the truth. Who set me up?"

Oh no! It was the who-done-it routine. That meant he was lost in paranoia. Again! As quickly as my rage hit, it disappeared. It was instantly replaced by fear.

"Rod," I said, trying to reach him. "Think about what

you just said. What could possibly be my motivation for lying? And who could have jimmied those reports if it wasn't Cody?"

Not enough. He was losing it. "I know how smart you are, Judy Burr. You could easily have accessed our computer via the internet. This is your work, isn't it?" he hissed.

"NO! I'd never do anything to hurt Global or you. Rod, I'm on your side. I'm your best friend. You've got to trust me."

"Trust you? How can I trust you after you said something so vicious? Why did you do that?"

"I said it because it's true! And because Cody was the one who gave you the reports. Think about it, Rod. He knows I'm around again. He's afraid I will uncover his dirty little deed."

Rod's expression was empty. I had no idea what to do, and speaking was not an option. Saying anything at this point could send him careening. Finally, after an infinite stream of seconds, he returned to the bathroom.

For a while, I left him alone, but my curiosity overpowered me. I wanted to get another look at the reports.

"Check this out," he said as I sat down on the floor next to him. He handed me the master tree. It was the complete corporate hierarchy, the down-line structure so far from accurate it was pathetic.

"Good grief. How long has this been going on?" I asked.

He dug in his briefcase and handed me another stack of papers. "I got this last week."

They were better, but they were still wrong. "Rod, do you have any of the reports from last November? The ones I left with you?"

"Not with me. They are back in the office."

"Well, you better lock them up. You're going to need them to fix this mess."

"Judy, you've got to help me. You're the only one who can."

Inwardly, I groaned. He needed me back in the office, which was the last place I wanted to be. I didn't mind helping him, but only from a distance. Still, this was another thing I wasn't willing to confess, at least not right at that moment. "Of course, I'll help you. You know I'm here for you."

This time I got sad puppy-dog eyes. Poor Rod, he really was in trouble. I tried to reassure him. "I'm still your Keymaster you know, and I made you a promise, remember? I vowed never to leave you alone in the field, and Rod, I never will. As long as you want, I'll stand by you. Besides, I want Global to succeed as much as you do, and I know you are the Gatekeeper. Without you, the company will fail."

My petition was to his ego, and finally, I started to get through. "Let's go back to bed, Rod, please."

"You go ahead, Judy. I'll be a few minutes."

That meant no, but I was exhausted. I was twenty-two years older, after all, and I needed my rest. "Alright, Rod, but don't stay up too long. I love you."

"I love you, too," he said.

Thank God, I thought. Somehow, we had muddled through, but what next? I couldn't think about it. I slipped into the darkness and prayed the morning would bring us some light. God help us. God help Rod. Please, don't let him fall again. Please, Lord, I can't lose him now. Not after everything I've been through.

I slept late and woke to the sound of running water. Rod was in the shower which was a good sign. It meant he had left the reports behind.

"Good morning." I said, entering the steamy room.

"Good morning, Mrs. Global." He said, sticking his head past the curtain. "Join me?"

"Better not," I said. "It's late and if I don't get ready, I'll miss our breakfast meeting." I turned to leave, but he pulled me into the enclosure, silk robe and all.

"I'll be on time, and I'll even save you a seat," he said. "Right now, there are more pressing matters."

The pelting water startled me, but before I could object, his mouth closed over mine. After a long, lingering kiss, he apologized. "Judy, I'm sorry about last night. I almost lost it, and I feel terrible." His words were serious, but his mind, his smaller, thinking brain, was much more playful. "What would I ever do without you?" he said. "You truly bring me balance. I'd be lost without you."

His breath was hot, and it had the desired effect. "Yeah? Do you appreciate me?" I asked, stroking him with more than words.

Rather than answer, he used his powerful arms to pull me upward. He lifted me above his waist and held me firmly, while I wrapped my legs around him. Then he lowered me slowly until I moaned with pleasure. "Does this show my appreciation?"

It was a challenge, a very sultry, sexy challenge. I arched backward to increase the pressure. "Almost," I said. "But I think I deserve better."

Rod set his sights high and gave me the reward I richly deserved. When he left the shower for a shave, I sank to the floor to recover. Most definitely, I would be late for breakfast.

Oh well. It will give the boys time to get acquainted.

CHAPTER 8

Leader at Large

WHEN I APPROACHED THEIR TABLE, Rod and Pat were deeply engrossed in conversation. "Good morning," I said, interrupting.

Pat was immediately on his feet and gave me a hug. "Hi, Judy. How are you?"

Not to be outdone, Rod stood to pull out my chair. Naturally, he expected me to sit next to him, and of course, I did. "I'm fine, Pat. You're looking well. I see you two found each other."

"Pat's not difficult to spot in a crowd," joked my escort.

I laughed at his flippant remark. It was true. Pat was impossible to miss. His healthy stock of red hair beckoned all. Not only did he stand out in the crowd, he captured an attentive audience besides. He was a tall man, extremely well-built and perfectly proportioned, with a beguiling smile. With his gentle demeanor, his easy mannerisms attracted friends. I watched him as he interacted with my partner, and I enjoyed my ex-husband's smooth reserve. He was curious, but cautious, and most definitely was not blown away by my seductively charismatic business associate. On the other hand, he wasn't defensive either. I could tell he was interested in Global's program.

The subtle comment about his hair caused no offense. Pat moved matter-of-factly right back into the discussion.

"It's a good solution for me," he said. "My renters are behind two months right now. I can easily evict them. How soon will you be ready?"

I was surprised. They were already negotiating a deal, and since Pat owned a large building in one of Denver's prestigious business parks, that was obviously part of it.

"It won't be long," Rod responded. "We broke records last night. This market is expanding faster than any of the others. If we continue at this pace, we'll be ready to set up the team showcase real soon."

"I can make it available in two months. Will that work for you?" Pat asked.

I stared at my partner. It seemed like they were moving awfully fast. Pat hadn't even been to an orientation meeting. That was no hindrance, however, at least not to Rod. His leader persona rose without hesitation. With the ease of a seasoned executive, he said, "Two months will be fine. I'll arrange for the deliveries when I get back to Vegas."

Pat smiled. He was gleaning a brighter future. "How many spas will you be sending?" he asked.

"Twelve," returned Rod. Then using a direct tone he explained, "We'll set up one of each color for display. The other ten will probably be sold even before they arrive, but you'll need to build twelve racks. They'll be trucked in by the dozen. It's the most economical way to deliver. I want to send our gazebo, a pool table, and a mini-jet boat as well. The dealers won't be able to order the boat until summer, but by the time we announce the release, they'll be primed."

"Rod, what mini-jet boat?" I asked. "You never mentioned a watercraft."

"I don't tell her everything," Rod said, knowing he had Pat's attention.

Pat enjoyed this immensely and joined the male camaraderie. “She’ll definitely run things if given the chance.”

I shot him a look, but Rod continued his two cents. “Judy is more than capable, but there can only be one leader.”

This line of reasoning was not to my liking. “All right, you two. That’s about enough.”

It wasn’t, though. Pat was having too much fun. “So, you have her under control then?” he asked. “She’s mighty headstrong.”

Rod empathized with loving eyes, eyes I wanted to tear out with my fingernails. “I’d say Judy is in full compliance. Right, Miss Burr?”

I did not appreciate the public stripping. “You’re the president, Mr. Steersman. It’s your world.” The effect was dramatic. My comment created a pause, and I sensed it wasn’t healthy. I decided to make a peace offering. “Actually, I’ve retired. I’m tired of the trenches, and I’ve backed away from the administrative end of the business. The only thing I plan to do now is help Rod with the seminars. I’m going to write the book, ‘The Global Story,’ but I’m leaving the leisure business to my partner.”

This seemed to restore the mood. Since Pat was satisfied my role was well-defined, he pursued another avenue. “So, what would my responsibilities be, exactly? As field coordinator, what would I be doing?”

“Basically, you’d be responsible for this entire market. You’ll receive commission on your own franchise activity as well as the others. You’ll also schedule the deliveries and most of the repairs. Global pays a flat rate for service, but you can job it out. It’s possible to earn a nice profit from that end of the business, too. We’ll bring you to corporate to train, but then the rest is up to you. It will be your enterprise, but you’ll have corporate backing. Global will fund your growth, and the sky’s the limit.”

Pat was intrigued. "I like it. It takes the multi-level marketing concept into the big league. What other products do you plan to distribute?"

"Besides what I'm sending you, we've got a jet ski and an all-terrain vehicle. Those items have moved slower, but we haven't promoted them either. The all-terrain vehicle might be big in Colorado, but our next corporate push will be the barbecues and patio furniture. After that, my eye is on a motorcycle. Basically, Global is interested in the 'big boy' toys. Any leisure item now reserved for the well-to-do will become affordable to all. We'll be providing an avenue for the 'good life.'"

Pat was entranced. "My wife and I are members of a multi-level marketing company, but it certainly doesn't offer this kind of opportunity. It took us years of hard work to generate a decent income, and even now, we must network constantly to keep the business going."

My partner was on cue. He worked his magic and captured my estranged spouse. Rod was fully present while explaining the theory of compassionate capitalism, then shifted into an entertainment mode. Leveling off into his presidential interpretation of the mastermind concept got us laughing. The illustration he used to demonstrate its effectiveness was hilarious. He conceptualized team cooperation with cartoon characters, and when we were rolling, he went in for the kill. He became the Preacher personified and revealed his Five Golden Rings. Global's key principles closed the deal, and when Rod was finished, Pat couldn't wait to sign on the dotted line. Finally, my ex had to go, but when he left us, it was with a great deal of enthusiasm. He was armed with excitement and promised to return with a parcel of interested prospects. No doubt our next meeting would break more records.

I marveled at Rod. He truly was inspiring, having won

the heart of a great skeptic. Knowing I was proud of his performance, affection was in the air. "Shall we go pack, Mrs. Global?" he asked. "It's almost time for us to catch a plane."

"Lead away, Mr. Global. I'd follow you to the ends of the earth."

When we were back in the room, he embraced me. "Pat is a good man, and I can tell he's trustworthy. That will make all the difference in the world. I'm glad you brought him to me. What would I do without you?"

I ignored the question but encouraged his observation. "He's also a hard worker, Rod. Truly you couldn't find a better person for the job."

"Never leave me, Judy," he said, refusing to be deterred.

While he was powerfully serious, he was also in need of reassurance. That was Rod's way. He was an amazing leader, but a lousy loner, and I was under no illusion. My loyalty meant everything to him. Momentarily, I flashed on the night before, but that crisis had passed without either of us losing control. If only we could maintain that kind of equilibrium.

"Hey, don't even think about it," I said. "Remember, I'm a sure bet. I made you a promise, Mr. President, and I intend to keep it."

That was enough. He threw back his shoulders and went to call the valet.

I had created the tiger, and now he stood before me, tall and powerful.

Rod's every movement was regal. He packed his possessions as though they were jewels, and he treated me the same way. When we went to the elevator, it was arm-in-arm. I was under his protection, and his adoration was obvious. He tenderly opened doors and swiftly closed them. Only when he knew I was comfortably seated would he join me in the cab. In the airport waiting area, on the plane, even at home, he doted on me, and I relished the attention.

It was so good to be back with him, so wonderful to be in sync. There was no question in my mind that his leadership abilities were larger than life. Whatever mischief Cody and Nelson were up to, Rod would get to the bottom of it. The reports would be corrected, and with accurate and up-to-date information, he would move Global onto solid ground.

PART II

THE SPLINTERING

CHAPTER 9

Little Boy Lost

THE NEXT WEEK, after Rod returned to the trenches, he became oddly reticent. I was curious about the reports, but since he didn't volunteer any information, I decided not to ask. I had promised not to interfere, so I busied myself with the house. Finally, with the boxes unpacked, I began to decorate the walls. Most of the pictures were easy to hang, but I was saving the best for last. I wanted to showcase his Christmas present in our living room, but the painting was so large, I could not manage it by myself. I was waiting for Rod, and thought he'd be happy to see his gift receive center stage. I was wrong.

He came home that evening in a state of agitation, and when he passed his Christmas present, he stopped to stare.

Without even looking at me, he drove nails into my backside. "You really did buy that picture for yourself, didn't you, Judy? It was never meant for me, was it?"

I was caught off guard. "What?" I said, "Are you nuts? That's not funny, Rod."

But he wasn't trying to be funny and he didn't appreciate being called "nuts."

"You were upset with me then," he said. "You didn't

believe in me. You bought the painting to spite me."

His words snapped like a whip. "No!" I cried. "I might have disagreed with your management techniques, but I never stopped loving you. I thought you were confused, that's all. Rod, I wanted you to have something special for Christmas."

The meanness left him, and a strange shift occurred. He looked like he might cry, and in a little boy voice, he said, "Really, Judy? Did you really buy it for me?"

"Yes, baby. I did. Of course, I did."

"It is beautiful," he said.

As I watched him staring, I was struck by his posture. It was no longer regal, but rather, it made him look young, lost.

A lost little boy, I thought.

"Yes, it is. You have fine taste, the best in fact. It is a very special piece."

His demeanor cheered. "Can I take it with me to the office?" he asked.

It sounded like he wanted permission to show-and-tell the item, and his next comment confirmed my suspicion. "I want everyone to see it. I want the guys to know you gave it to me."

His request upset me. "Well, Rod, it is yours. I suppose you can take it anywhere you please."

My sarcasm went unnoticed.

"Cool," he said, turning toward the stairs. He leapt like a young adolescent, taking two steps at a time.

Take your picture and go hang yourself.

I sat down on the couch and sank into the pillows. What was happening? Was Rod unraveling again? His recent behavior had been strange, and I recalled the afternoon Pam called him a schizophrenic. Her comment had struck me as funny, but now I wondered. Was Rod truly ill? Did his problems go deeper than paranoia? And if so, why hadn't I recognized the signs?

I realized I wore rose colored glasses. Our relationship had started at my most vulnerable time. I had lost everything, my business, my wealth, my friends, and every inch of control over my life. It had all been seized by the Feds. To say I was a lost soul would be an understatement, but Rod's friendship at least restored my spirit.

Continuing my train of thought, I decided Rod needed two things, well, three things really.

First, he needed his wife and family. As far as Rod was concerned, his wife, Mary Ann, and their kids were there for the duration. She was devoted to him and his dream, and was willing to wait, no matter what that meant. She even accepted me and told Rod she understood our partnership.

Second, he needed me, and I had already left once. When he won me back, he made me promise to never leave again, but my independent nature was a constant source of irritation.

Third, he needed his empire, Global Enterprises, but having had one hostile takeover attempt, he worried constantly about a second conspiracy.

Of all those things, number three concerned me most. His systems were a mess, and not one person in the office could set the records straight. He needed my help, but he wasn't asking. That meant trouble. I decided he had probably tried to bring me back, however temporarily, but had been met with too much resistance. Now he was lost, and I feared for Global. If he didn't find his way, the company would most definitely fail, and that would end the dream, his dream, my dream, and the dream of so many others.

Oh God, this can't be happening, I said silently. It just can't. I can't take any more.

When Sandy picked him up the next morning, I watched as they loaded my gift. Rod came back to say goodbye, and I received a conciliatory peck.

What the heck?

Rod was in trouble, deep, deep trouble. He was no longer a self-assured business executive, but rather, he had reverted to that little boy from the day before. He didn't even walk like a man. His legs were slightly bowed, and his hips had a bit of a swing to them.

"Definitely not the man I know and love," I said "Lord, help us."

On Friday our trip to San Diego was canceled, and then the next week a convenient storm blew into Colorado to provide a Denver excuse. I didn't ask why we weren't going to San Diego, and I tried to act nonchalant about these delays, but my concern was growing.

Rod wasn't completely remote during this time. He told me he had fired Cody Daniels and Nelson Balding. Unfortunately, this caused some dissension. It also caused George Johnson to step forward.

As Rod's most recent major investor, George suddenly wanted to be involved. He started to question the chief executive's business strategies, and he vocalized concern, saying Mormon money was on the line. This fact was nothing new, and Rod might not have cared if George had stayed out of his business, but he didn't. He started flying in from Salt Lake City, intimidating Rod. He did not like having a watchdog at headquarters.

Then, too, there was the problem of his elected travel companion—me. I was pretty sure his team was lecturing. 'Your affair is an abomination.' 'You need to honor your wife.' 'Lose your girl, or else.'

Rod's situation was not good, but giving in was not a solution. More than anything, he needed to start leading again, but could he? With the mounting pressure, I wasn't sure, and I wondered if this wasn't the plan. If the company was forced into receivership, it would unseat Rod. In fact, the other investors might sue him, and if they won, his shares could default to them.

Fools, I thought. *Can't they see how good he is? Can't they honor his dream? Doesn't he deserve a reward for taking the company this far?*

Apparently not, and as Rod's world started to collapse, he called my loyalty into question.

"Judy, when exactly did I lose you? When did you stop believing in me?"

It was late at night, and I was tired. "Rod, I never stopped believing in you. I still have great respect for your leadership abilities."

"But you talked to Chance that day. You talked about taking me out."

This was old news and dangerous territory. "No, I listened to Chance. He was concerned about Global's solvency. We discussed options, that's all."

"But you guys wanted to unseat me, didn't you?"

You guys. Here we go again. "No, Rod. We've discussed this a hundred times and I refuse to go there again. Get over it."

"Get over it?" he said, raising his righteous voice. "How can I get over it? My best friend wanted me to lose control. How can I get over it? Tell me, Judy, whose idea was it? You suggested Global should be ruled by majority vote, didn't you?"

I turned to leave. I was sick to death of this track.

"Where are you going?" he asked as I headed up the stairs.

"To bed. I'm tired, Rod. I am not having this conversation."

He chased after me. "But tell me, Judy, tell me when I lost you. When did you stop trusting me?"

I was pulling off my clothes. "I don't know, Rod," I said, crawling under the covers.

He stood above me, looking down, and I rolled over, so my back was to him. I could feel his confusion, but I wouldn't talk to him. Instead, I moved over. It was a signal for him to join me, which he did. After undressing, he climbed into bed and curled into me. I softened my body against his and reached backward. My touch elicited a moan, so I turned to kiss his soft, young, little-boy lips. He forgot about the altercation and got lost again. This time he was safe in my arms, and by taking full control, I brought out the man in my lover.

CHAPTER 10

A Beast is Born

TIME PASSED and Rod seesawed. He never talked about Global and I did not ask, but we didn't leave town either. I made excuses to my ex-husband for a while, and then I gave up.

"I'm sorry, Pat, but the company is reorganizing. There are new investors and they're making changes. The expansion has been postponed, but as soon as they're ready, I'll let you know. I'm sure Denver will be the first market they reopen."

"I hope so," he said. "I have at least a dozen people interested. They're just waiting for the word."

"That's terrific!" I said, quietly sighing. "I'll call you as soon as I know."

I played the role of sycophant, saying the words he longed to hear. I wanted them to be true, but I had my doubts. Rod was not stabilizing, and each day my patience grew thinner. One day I caught Rod flipping through my Rolodex. What the hell?

"What are you doing?" I asked.

"Looking. Just searching," he said defensively.

"For what?" Whose phone number could he possibly need from my index files?

"Is this your friend?" he asked, pulling out a card and pushing it in my face.

I looked at it. Mason. It was my other young lover, whom I hadn't seen for months. I looked at Rod in disgust. "Rod, you know that's over," I said, turning on my heel.

He chased after me. "Then why do you still have his card?"

"Why not? He's a friend. Why shouldn't I have his number?"

"Do you still talk to him?"

None of your business, I thought. Speaking my mind, however, could be dangerous, so I grabbed my swim bag instead. "No, I haven't spoken with him for some time now. I'm going to the pool. Care to join me?"

I headed down the stairs, leaving him holding the damn index card.

Rod's jealousy never settled after that day, and he continued to forage. I caught him in my drawers, but I had nothing to hide, so I controlled my temper. He was too fragile, and I did not want to tip the scales.

He also started to cling. He went to the office later and later and called more often once he got there. He wanted to know my whereabouts. Again, I tried to reassure him, which wasn't difficult, because I was usually home. I wouldn't write while he was there, but as soon as he was out of my hair, I'd head for my computer. No doubt, he was checking those files, too, but I was smart. I did not set up a password on my PC, which gave him access, but I hid the manuscript. Rod didn't know how to navigate a computer, so he'd never find my story. I was also writing his story, 'The Global Story,' which I made easy to find. It was a positive reflection of him and his company, so if he did open the document, the results would please him.

Even with all that, there were times he needed more. When he'd come home unexpectedly, I'd usually be sitting at my desk, though with my workspace right in front of the window, I always knew when he was approaching. This gave me ample time to close my files and turn off my computer. By the time he'd come upstairs, I'd usually be in the bathroom getting ready for the day, or for the night, or for whatever was approaching.

When he "surprised" me like this, he'd further reassure himself by making love, and I always felt like he was sniffing me out. Still, I didn't object, and my silence was usually enough to satiate him.

He truly believes I'm seeing Mason, I thought. *Well, you're wrong, Rod. The last thing I need right now is another man in my life. You are enough of a handful.*

On rare occasions, I couldn't control my anger, but I didn't stir up a fight either. Instead, I'd extrapolate a fantasy, and the scenarios were wild. I especially liked taking us to the mountains, where we'd explore abandoned mines. At some point, we would encounter a stranger, or possibly another couple, and I would order Rod to submit. I was exceedingly careful to use "made up" characters, so he couldn't attempt to read into any of my fantasies. I wanted no one to be accused of anything.

One late afternoon he came home with a driving need. I had seen Mandy, his secretary, drop him off, and I knew he was lusting for her. I excused myself to go to the bathroom, and when I came out, I was clad in a G-string bikini. Rod's eyes went wide, for this was not my usual attire.

"You like?" I asked, turning my back to him.

"You have no idea," he panted.

I bent over straight legged and offered a better view. He fell backward onto the bed. "Judy!"

"What?" I asked innocently, standing erect. "Is this something Mandy likes to wear?"

Shock.

I approached him, pushed him so he was lying flat, and

straddled him. "Or maybe she doesn't wear anything underneath."

Nothing. Rod was entranced.

"What's the matter? Cat got your tongue?" I crawled forward, and when my knees were around his shoulders, I pulled the thin strap aside and said, "Kiss Mandy, baby. Give her a sweet licking."

He obliged, and I remained poised for the caress. When I pulled away, he grabbed my buttocks.

"Let go, Mr. President. I have something for you."

He obeyed, and I turned so he could have his favorite view, my backside. Then I unbuckled his belt and released his burgeoning package. I took him swiftly, without hesitation, and he cried with the release. When I was finished, I dismounted and stood back down on the floor, then bored into his dark hazel eyes and said, "If you ever fuck her, I will slice them off. Do you understand?"

He nodded.

"I tolerate Mary Ann, because she is your wife and the mother of your children, but if you dare to have your cake and eat it, too, you will lose me. Is that clear?"

Again, he indicated he understood.

"I will not have it, Rod, not for a split second."

He had been breathless, but he started to collect himself and gave me a smile. "Don't worry, Judy. You are all the woman I need."

A flippant remark. I walked away, went downstairs, threw on my swimsuit, and went to the pool. I needed to swim. The session had left me wanting, and I needed to work off the frustration.

Another day, he dallied so long, I finally decided he might not go to the office at all. His presence was suffocating and I needed some fresh air. "I'm going down to the clubhouse," I said. "I want to get some sun. Care to join me?"

"Sounds good," he said. "Why don't you go ahead. I'll be there in a few minutes."

"Okay," I said. "I'll see you soon."

I lounged for some time, but he did not show up. When I started to overheat, I jumped in the water and swam a mile. Still no Rod. Again, I went to bask, but I wasn't a lounging kind of a person. I got restless, and I was hungry besides. I gave up waiting and went home to make a sandwich. When I got there the house was quiet, and I could not find Rod anywhere. I didn't see a note or anything, which was odd, but I decided something must have happened at the office. Probably Sandy picked him up, I thought, digging into the fridge.

As I was putting everything on the counter, a noise startled me. It seemed to be coming from the back of the house. Cautiously, I went down the hallway, and as I approached the back door, I heard it again. Someone was in my garage! Momentarily I panicked, but then I remembered my curious roommate. Was he snooping again? I opened the door, and this time I startled Rod. Apparently, he was so engrossed, he had not heard me come home.

"What are you doing?" I asked.

He was in my files, going through my four-drawer cabinet. "Looking," he said, as though it were an everyday occurrence.

"Looking?" I cried. "Looking for what? Rod, get out of there! That stuff is none of your business!"

"Judy, you're my girl! Everything about you is my business. I had no idea you owned and operated a school here in Las Vegas."

Rod was a master manipulator. In his own way, he was complimenting me, but he knew his comment would draw me away from the invasion. The school had once been a pet project of mine, and the memories were good. I had created a curriculum to train and motivate salespeople, and I personally led the class through the section on ethics. It was a fun and satisfying experience.

"When did you do this?" he asked.

"After I left Pioneer Enterprises, but before we opened the telemarketing firm. We were trying to bring credibility to the industry."

"What happened?"

"The school wasn't making money fast enough, and the space we were renting was perfect for a telemarketing firm. We acquired the necessary licensing and switched gears. Come on, Rod. If you want to know something, ask me. Don't disrespect me by invading my privacy."

"Alright, I'm sorry," he said sheepishly. "Just let me put this stuff away, and I'll be right in. Amazing, Judy. You are an amazing woman. You really are sharp. Too bad you didn't use your talents to help people, instead of scamming them," he added with emphasis.

Rod was on my last nerve, and this remark cut deeply. I had done everything humanly possible to meet, or exceed, the state mandates, and Rod knew this. Now he was throwing me into a pot of rip-and-tear schemers. I did not appreciate being tossed into that black kettle, but I didn't want to argue either. I simply sighed and turned to leave.

I went back to the kitchen but had lost my appetite. I put everything back in the frig and went upstairs to have a soak. Still damp from my swim, I started to shiver. I thought it was the air conditioning, but I decided it was my partner's comment that sent my body quivering. His behavior had been frigid, and not a bit Christian-like, at least, not in my opinion. Not even close. All I saw was an unforgiving hypocrite. The man I had allowed to lay hands on me was now standing in judgment, and his posture was bestial.

Look inside, Rod. Best be taking a really good look at

your own mistakes before you go talking about mine.

My cynicism was growing, and my intuitive warning system was on full alert. The trouble was I had no idea what to do about it. I was still trapped; leaving Rod was not an option, at least not right then. My pretrial supervisor had no idea I was no longer working, and I didn't want to tell him. How would I pay the bills without Rod? I had no reserves, and with my sentencing date looming, I was pretty sure a job wouldn't come easily. Besides, I didn't want to work; I wanted to write.

It was those blinders. Rod was going down the rabbit hole, and he was taking me with him. There seemed to be no escape, and I had no one to blame but myself.

Another day I returned from the pool to find him boldly sitting at my computer. "Get away from there, Rod," I said.

"Why?" he asked innocently.

"Why?" I attacked. "Because that is my PC. That is where I work. You belong at Global. You need to take care of business there, not here."

"Judy, just let me play," he said in the little boy voice. "Please. Please, show me how to navigate this system."

"No, Rod," I said, and turned in disgust. "No, I won't. You've got computers at the office. Go play on your own time."

My abruptness pushed him into action, and he lunged from the chair. I ran down the stairs, but he caught me by the arm. "What are you hiding?"

"Nothing." I jerked out of his grip.

When he took hold of my shoulder, I winced. "Ow! Rod, get your hands off me."

He forced me to turn, and when I was facing him, his eyes drilled into me. "Show me your files, Judy."

"Fuck you," I spat, tearing away. I sat down in front of the TV, clicking the remote while trying to quell my fear.

His frustration was apparent, but he left me.

You'll never get access to those files, I said to myself, listening to the clicking keyboard.

Eventually, Rod gave up, but the incident was frightening. I was finding it more and more difficult to communicate with him on any level, even carnal. Rod had become a selfish and demanding lover, and I lost all desire. I might try to spin a fantasy, but he'd ruin it trying to take over.

"Stop that, Rod!" I exclaimed one night.

"Stop what?" he asked.

"Stop changing my direction. I can't do that."

"Yes, you can, Judy. You can go anywhere you want to. You are the best."

"Not when you put words into my mouth. It disrupts the creative process."

This was the problem. He was trying to go back to our days of sexual transmutation, to the days when he tried to discover his enemies by means of my subconscious. I was done with that, and I wasn't willing to give him a fantasy, unless it was harmless. I felt safer this way, but sometimes he insisted. If he did, I'd simply shut down, and he'd conjure his fantasy. Unfortunately, this left my libido in limbo. It was a negative cycle, and it was alienating us on a grand scale.

"What's this?" he asked one day, pointing to one of my software instructions.

"That's the operating manual for my computer," I said.

"And these?"

"My discs?" I said. "They have all kinds of programs and records on them, basic stuff."

"Oh," he said, but apparently my explanation was not satisfactory. The next day I found him loading them into a box.

"What are you doing?" I asked again, only this time it was with alarm.

"Don't worry, I'll bring them back," he said.

This shook me. I had spent a year and a half without my PC, and the Feds had finally given it back. Now I was losing my programs and instruction manuals to a lunatic. "Rod!" I screamed. "I don't deserve that."

"Then you have nothing to worry about, do you, Ms. Burr?" he said in his condescending way. "If there's nothing on the discs, then everything will be okay."

"No, ROD! Everything will NOT be okay! I want you out of here. I want you out right now!"

I was furious, and it seemed I might get my wish. He was walking away. I watched as Rod carried my precious cargo out the front door where Sandy was in the driveway waiting for him. I flashed on calling a locksmith. I wanted to lock him out, to key him out of my life forever, but it was not to be. He must have known I'd take drastic action, because he took steps to prevent it. After offloading the box, he turned and came back into the house. My mouth dropped open, but he ignored my evil eye and headed up the stairs. This time I followed him. To my horror, he went into my office, sat down at my computer, and clicked on the system.

"Get away from there," I said. "Have you lost your mind? There's absolutely nothing in those files that would interest you."

"What files, Judy? Show me everything."

Maybe he hadn't found 'The Global Story.' Maybe he was more ignorant than I thought, but I still didn't care. I was not about to help him, not in any way, shape, or form. "Forget it." I walked away.

He flashed after me. Grabbing my arm, he forced me back into the room. "Sit down, Judy," he said, pushing me into my reading chair.

I looked up and knew not to move. His eyes were crazed, and his emotions were raging. The innocent, lost victim was gone, and a beast had been born. *Just how dangerous was this man?*

Remaining in my recliner, I stared. Rod was fixated on the machine, and he continued to explore. After a few minutes I brought my knees up to my chin, wrapped my arms around my legs, and dropped my head. In this position, I hid from him, and as I sat there, the tears began to trickle. Where was my hero? The man who saved me was gone. He had disappeared into the computer system, pecking one key after another. When I looked up, he glanced my way. The tear streaks softened him. I could tell by his expression, but in no way did my sorrow stop his plodding. Finally, I stood up.

"Where are you going?" he asked.

"To the bathroom, Rod. I have to pee."

He let me go, but when I came out, he was standing in the hallway. I saw a man hanging on the edge who was not about to let me go. "Come back in here, Judy," he said.

"I have things to do, Rod."

He was shaking and he took my hand. "You can't leave me, Judy. Not now. I need you right here." He tugged and pulled me back to the chair.

"Rod," I objected, but it did no good. I sensed his position, and recalling those hands around my throat, I sat back down. Satisfied I was compliant, he resumed his keystrokes.

Five minutes passed, then ten, and somewhere around the half-hour mark, I was finished with his shenanigans. I rose slowly and went quickly down the stairs. Amazingly, he let me go. I was searching for my purse when I heard him push away from the desk. I did not want him to know I was trying to leave, so I rushed to the couch and clicked on the television.

"Judy, come back upstairs," he said, blocking my view.

"No."

"Please, come open the files."

I had no response.

"What kind of code did you use?"

"Fuck you," I said flatly.

He picked up the remote and clicked off the TV. "Come back upstairs."

"Get out, Rod." I countered, but his reaction astonished me. Without a second's delay, in one powerful motion, he heaved the electronic gadget from his hand. It slammed into a picture on the wall. The impact shattered the glass into tiny smithereens that fragmented all over the sofa and the floor. The world around me fell in slow motion, and as everything crumbled, I bolted. I came out of the soft cushions and braced my hand on the back of the couch. Then I lifted my body over the velvet and landed on the floor behind it. Quickly, I moved toward the front door, but I was not fast enough. Rod's agile, young body caught me halfway across the living room, and when I felt him, I fell to the floor.

"Don't do this, Judy. Don't fuck with me," he said.

I curled into a ball. I wanted to avoid a frontal attack, and I knew if he sat on me, he'd probably wrap those huge hands around my neck. "Don't hurt me, Rod," I cried. "Please, don't hurt me."

Miraculously, my words reached him. I could hear the tears in his voice. "Why, Judy? Why do you provoke me this way?"

"I don't! I didn't do anything!"

"You always make me crazy," he continued pathetically. "Why?"

"It's not my fault, Rod. I've never done anything to you. Why can't you see that?"

I was crying now, and the tears were working.

"Get up," he said.

I balled tighter. The fetal position felt safe to me.

"Judy, just let me into your system. I won't damage anything. I promise."

Over my dead body, I thought. *Not a chance in hell.* I wailed even louder.

Finally, he backed off and went to the kitchen.

Thank God, I thought.

I remained deadly still, while he paced. Then I heard the bashing.

What in the world?

Again, a slamming and a splintering of wood. I held my breath, but when it happened a third time, I knew he was completely out of control. He was ramming his fists through the cupboard doors, and I envisioned my face getting in the way. When I heard the coffee maker hit the floor, the crash resounded through my brain. It brought me to my feet, and again, I made a dash for the door. He was coming for me, but I turned the brass knob and jerked hard. The sidewalk was cold on my feet, and he was hot on my heels. I started to scream.

"HELP! HELP!" I hollered to anyone who could hear.

The neighbors across the street were outside, and their presence stopped Rod in his tracks. Not me, though. I ran for my life, my naked feet carrying me all the way to the clubhouse. I crashed into the reception room out of breath, probably looking like an absolute lunatic.

"Call 911!" I cried. "There's a crazed man in my house and he's breaking everything!"

CHAPTER 11

The Madonna Returns

IT TOOK TWO MORE CALLS and thirty-eight minutes for a squad car to respond. When they did arrive, I was amazed to find Rod still at the house. The officers told me to wait while they questioned him, so I remained in the squad car, fully expecting them to haul his crazy ass to jail. While I sat wondering, another vehicle approached from the opposite direction. It slowed and parked two houses down and across the street. I strained to see the driver and couldn't believe my eyes. Rod had not called his trusted pal, Seattle Sandy, but rather, he'd summoned his secretary, Mandy.

Oh, great, I thought. *The damsel rescues her hero. Isn't that nice?*

Rod and his women. He did have a way with them. Well, you can have His Highness, little Miss. I am done with him.

"Ma'am?" The officer tapped on the window. "Would you come check the house, ma'am," he said. "Your friend seems docile, but my partner is holding him outside."

I dreaded passing Rod, but I had no choice. "Okay."

Proceeding past my attacker and through my front door, I was once again amazed. I could find no further damage. He must have regained control right after I left. Figures, I said to myself, walking around. He had to know I'd call the cops, probably was afraid to wreak any more havoc. In fact, he had cleaned up the coffeepot, and most of the glass from the picture was gone as well.

"I can't find anything else, officer," I said shakily.

He nodded and went outside to talk to his partner. It was a day of surprises, and this time I was truly shocked. I watched Rod smile, turn on the charm, and after entertaining the two public protectors, he walked away. He rode off with the long-legged brunette who had provided curbside service.

"Why didn't you arrest him?" I asked when they returned.

"He didn't assault you, ma'am."

"Well, he would have if I hadn't gotten out of his way. What about the damage he did to my property?"

"He told us he lives here. He said the two of you have been together for more than a year, and we found his clothes in the closet upstairs with yours. The damage is a civil matter. That's between you and him."

"What? How about the threats he's made to me personally? The man is dangerous, and I want him out of here."

The officers looked at one another, and I sensed they thought I was the lunatic. Rod had won. He had appealed to their male egos, and they related to him. Their attitude toward me was condescending.

"We can't force him to leave his own home. Legally, he has as much right to be here as you."

"But I own this place. Are you telling me I must let him back in here?"

"You can evict him, ma'am, through the sheriff's office."

"That takes time," I said. "What about right now? What happens tonight?"

They could have cared less. I was reminded of the time I'd asked the police to help me find my sister, Shirley. She had been out of control with heartbreak and was on the run. I was desperately afraid for her, but I had been told unless she hurt herself, or someone else, they could not intervene. This was more of the same, but now it was my life on the line.

Public servants, my eye.

As usual, I took refuge in the mountains. It was the one place I felt peace. No matter what calamity occurred, the impact always diminished by breathing fresh, high-altitude air. On this day, the effect was no less profound, and my anger lessened as I hiked toward Bristle Cone. I let go of the fear and began to merge with the earth. It was early spring, and there were signs of God's birthing. Tiny buds were knotting on the branches, with bursts of color here and there.

"This is what matters," I said out loud. "Rod needs to get out of that business world, and into this one. He's losing touch with nature. He's losing touch with everything, including his God."

I walked and I thought. My friend was in trouble, but I was done trying to rescue him. "The wrath of Rod," I said to the trees. He's failing and blaming, and I'm his target. Why can't he see the light?

Rod's personality was most definitely splintering, visibly so. He might struggle back, but even if he did, I could not take a chance on him. It was far too dangerous for me. I had to face the world without him.

I came out of the hills and checked into a hotel back in town. Ironically, I went back to the place where we had reunited and requested the Einstein mini suite.

Once I freshened up, I looked around, the familiar surroundings bringing back memories. After a beautiful San Diego weekend, Rod and I had returned to Las Vegas, where we spent nearly a week together, acting like honeymooners. We were in love, and I was sure we would live happily ever after, but Rod still needed one more thing from me. He needed me to accept Jesus Christ. As a born-again Christian, and the alpha-male leader, it was practically his duty; otherwise, how could we spend eternity together? For his sake, I acquiesced. Now I knew my sacrifice meant nothing. It had only stalled off the inevitable.

"That's it!" I said suddenly. I was talking to the walls, but walls or trees, I didn't care. "Oh my God, that's it!"

Rod could no longer use me as an excuse. He had saved me, and he had told everyone this. Since I was a "born-again Christian," he could no longer claim I was a sorceress. I couldn't cast a spell, so what did that make him? The "man of God" was an adulterer, a first-class sinner.

Good Lord, I thought. *No wonder he's troubled.*

I spent an awful lot of time thinking along these lines, and the more I did, the more it made sense. Rod did love me, but he could no longer justify our affair. The guilt was overwhelming, and his ensuing confusion was causing chaos at the office.

I wished for the umpteenth time I could help him. If only I was allowed in. If his team only realized I was not the problem, but the solution.

If only. It was the story of my life.

I had believed in Global, in Rod, and in what we were building. His wife believed, too, and she had become my greatest ally. She supported me when no one else did. I couldn't explain it, but I believed we were soulmates. Rod, Mary Ann, and I were part of the same heavenly family, bound by an "Uncommon Partnership." If only our love had prevailed. Another "if only."

Now what? I wondered. What would happen to Mary Ann and her children?

Maybe if I left him, maybe if I completely removed myself from the picture, maybe then Mary Ann would have a chance. And maybe—just maybe—if Rod wasn't torn between two loves, he might heal. If he recovered, then maybe his company would also survive.

I called him. It was almost 1 a.m., but I knew he'd be up. I also knew he'd be at the house.

"Hello, Rod," I said.

"Judy!" he exclaimed. "Judy, are you alright? Oh my God, I was so worried. Where are you?"

"It doesn't matter, Rod," I said. "You have to move out."

"I know," he said.

I could hear the sadness and the compliance. My shoulders heaved with relief. "How much time do you need?"

"A few days. I'll rent a weekly. That way I won't be tied to a lease."

I was hit by the finality of the whole thing and I could barely talk. Before breaking into sobs, I said, "Just do it as soon as possible, Rod. I can't afford to stay in a hotel for long."

"You took a room? Where are you, Judy?"

"I've got to go, Rod."

The moment I cradled the receiver, tears came. I could not hold them back, nor did I try. I'll miss you, Rod, I said to myself. I'll miss you so much.

I was wallowing in loneliness when the phone rang. *No*! I thought. *It must be him.*

I had made a mistake. He had used the 'star sixty-nine' feature, and now he knew where I was.

"Hello," I said timidly.

"You have a call, Ms. Burr." It was the operator. I breathed a sigh of relief. "Do you want us to put it through?"

Thank goodness I had requested privacy. "No, I do not want to take any calls."

"Yes, Ms. Burr, just ring the desk if you have any problems."

"Thank you," I said, hanging up. Knowing Rod would come after me, I began to shake.

"I'll be safe until morning," I said out loud. "Thank God he doesn't have a car."

I slept very little that night and left early the next morning. For the next three days, I cooled my heels at another hotel, but I grew impatient. I braved an attack and went to see if he had moved. Nothing was different. Not even his toothbrush was gone. The dogs had been well cared for, however, so that was some consolation.

This isn't going to be easy, I thought. It never is.

My men never wanted to leave, and Rod was no exception. I wasn't surprised by this, but I felt certain he wasn't leaving not because he loved me, but because he didn't trust me. He wanted to keep an eye on me, and he was afraid I had ulterior motives.

NOT. I had no intention of undermining either him or his company, and truthfully, everything about that business and the people involved was a source of aggravation. Of course, I still wanted the company to succeed. If it did, I would recover my investment, but I had psychologically abandoned my attachment to the money. That break occurred the year before, on day five of the marathon. I had lost my temper and threatened to sue him for breach of contract. I had the power to do it and threw that fact in his face. His reaction was instantaneous, and he went down hard. He sank into an abyss, which was frightening. I decided in an instant no amount of money was worth that kind of pain, and I stopped caring about everything except him. I didn't care if I lost every penny, and I decided if he failed, or if his company failed, it would not be because of me. No, I had no ulterior motive, not then, and certainly not now.

Whatever, Rod, I thought. *Some things are just more important than money, and your world no longer holds allure for me. As far as I'm concerned, you can have it. Take it all, baby. Just do it without me.*

I left the house promising my puppies a quick return, but this time I did not take a room. The loneliness had become crushing, and it was time to tell my daughter.

"Can I come over?" I asked.

"Mom! Of course you can. I was just making dinner. I'll set another plate." Then she enticed me further. "We're having beef stroganoff."

It was one of her specialties. "Yum. I'll be right there."

That evening, I unloaded my heart. When I finished my story, Pam was astounded.

"Oh, my God," she said. "I had no idea he was violent."

"I know. I didn't tell anyone except Jana. I kept thinking he'd be okay, but the takeover took its toll. He thinks everybody is his enemy, especially me."

"That's ridiculous."

"He's not well, Pam. I've tried to help him, but I'm the wrong person to do it. In his mind, this began because I didn't believe in him. I wouldn't follow him blindly, and he says my doubt caused the conspiracy. Now, any time something goes wrong, I'm the first one he attacks."

"But your investment got him started. Without you, his company would have closed long ago."

"I'm not so sure about that. He may have found another investor, but that's beside the point. Right now, I must stay away from him. Unless Global gets back in the black, it's over for us."

"Well, Mom, you can stay here as long as you want. What are you going to do, anyway? You know he'll never leave, not willingly."

"I'm going to help him."

"But how?"

"I'll rent a place and then pack him up."

"You'd better get a restraining order. He'll be mad as hell."

"A restraining order will only aggravate the situation. I'll just change the locks. I can't do it. though, until he has a place to go. Right now, he believes I'll return."

"Promise me you won't, please, Mom," she begged.

"Oh, I promise, Pam. Believe me, I value my life, and I do not want to lose it, at least not at the hands of that maniac."

She was satisfied and so was I. My strength was returning, and that night I slept like an innocent child. I was breaking the tie, cutting off the constricting knot.

I rented a place for Rod and paid the deposit plus the first week's rent. The place was nice, and the location was central. I was sure he could do no better. Content with my choice, I stocked the cupboards, made the bed, and hung fresh towels. I even bought him a shower curtain.

Before leaving, I wrote him a note, a letter, a rather lengthy dissertation, in fact. I told him how grateful I was for our connection and said I would always love him. Our time had come, however. Destiny brought us together, but our mission was done, and it was time to move on. I would be fine, and I wanted him to be happy as well. I left my goodbye on the counter and closed the door behind me. Good luck, my love, I said. May your dreams come true.

Now I only needed to get his personal items out of my house. That would be my greatest challenge.

I arranged to have the locks changed and went to the house with my son-in-law's truck and a bunch of empty boxes. Then I waited outside for the locksmith and together we ventured through the front door. My dogs were frantic, but I let them bark at the sliding glass door. They could wait. I had to check for Rod. He was gone, thank God, but his things were still in place. I had to work fast.

"All clear," I hollered down the stairs. "I'll be packing. Call me if you need anything." The locksmith said he would, so I turned on my heels and went to the closet. I grabbed Rod's clothes and personal items. Knowing he could do without everything else, I loaded them first. Then, I drove to his new home and unloaded, hangers and all.

I was shaking, but I returned to the house knowing someone would be there. I finished packing Rod's belongings, and since the locksmith was also finished, we made a final sweep of the house and left. I left a note taped to the outside of the garage door. It contained an address and a key, but that was all. I didn't expect Rod to be back before me, but I was taking no chances.

This last load of Rod's things brought the tears, and I let them stream down my face. Just like a woman, I said to myself. I'm still taking care of your sorry ass.

I did not immediately go home. I was afraid to, but I exchanged Jason's truck for my car, and drove aimlessly, ending up on the scenic loop of Red Rock Park. The twists and turns were a distraction, and as I pushed for speed, the fear diminished. Courageously I turned my direction homeward.

I approached the house cautiously and the note was gone. Thank God, I thought, hitting the automatic door opener. When the huge piece of aluminum lumbered up, so did my stomach. My eyes saw chrome and I gasped.

"ROD!" I screamed, backing out of the driveway. I expected him to be racing for the front door, so I moved as fast as possible.

"He's there!" I exclaimed, letting myself through my daughter's front door. She was standing in the kitchen. "Oh my God, he must have broken a window!"

"What?" she screamed heading toward the couch where Jason was feeding the baby.

"There's a truck in the garage. It must be Rod! Now what

am I going to do?"

Jason stood up, baby and all. The sight of Marie calmed me, but his words did not. "Judy, you're going to have to get nasty with this guy. He's obsessed with you. You need a restraining order. Better yet, let me go over there. I'll take care of him."

"What will you do?" I asked.

"I'll hit him upside the head with a baseball bat, that's what. I'll take him out. He has no business acting like such an asshole. He needs to be a man and get the hell out."

Pam must have told her husband the gory details. "Then you'll be up on assault charges, Jason. Wouldn't that be great? Don't you have enough problems?"

"I don't give a damn. I'd like to break every bone in his body. No man should treat a woman like that. There's no excuse for it."

"Settle down. This is my fight. I won't have you arrested on my account, not twice in the same lifetime."

My meaning was clear. Jason had been indicted because of me, and I'd die before it happened again.

"Let me have that little girl," I said. My affection soothed him, and he handed her to me. "So, what do you think, baby girl? What would Marie do?"

My cooing brought a smile, which was all I needed. I forgot about my invader and concentrated on my granddaughter instead. Pam and Jason nestled into the sofa, and for the next hour we were distracted by the TV. Finally, the baby was asleep, so I tucked her into bed, then went into their bedroom where I could make a phone call — a very private phone call — to my archrival, Rod Steersman.

"What are you doing, Rod?" I asked, without offering the cursory greeting.

I heard a cough and then a scratchy voice. "I'm sick. Judy, please come home."

"No, Rod. You go home. You don't belong there anymore."

"I can't. I can't move. I'm really sick, Judy." He was pleading, but I was not fooled.

"Damn it, Rod. I'm not falling for your subterfuge. Your place is set up. The drive is less than two miles. Get in that fancy truck of yours and get out of my life."

"I will. I promise, but not tonight. I've got a temperature and can barely lift my head off the pillow. I'm sorry, there's just no way I can drive."

He did sound awful, and I was beginning to wonder. "Then call Sandy. Or call your girlfriend, Mandy. I don't care who you call but have someone take you over there. Rod, the frig is stocked and so are the cupboards. Everything is ready. You don't even have to unpack."

"One day, Judy. Please, just one day." It was a whisper, and I could no longer doubt he was ill. Rod would not beg in such a fashion.

I was weakening. I could feel it, but my mind was also racing. How in the heck did he gain access? Rod didn't have a garage door opener. It hadn't been necessary, since he rarely drove, and I had paid dearly to have those locks changed. What the heck?

"How did you get in?" I asked, trying to use my last remaining shred of anger. I needed to make sure this never happened again. No more Rod surprises.

"The latch on the den window wasn't secure. I was able to pull up the window, and I took the screen off to get in. Judy?" He left the question hanging.

"What?" I responded, trying to stay angry. I checked all those windows. They all seemed secure.

"Could you bring me some 7-Up, or maybe some soup, or something? There's nothing here."

Well, that was too bad. "No Rod, I can't. I'll give you twenty-four hours. I want my house back."

I left it at that and hung up the phone. Then I sat in the darkness. My heart was aching. He was ill, of that much I was certain, and I did not want him to suffer needlessly. I decided to take him a few supplies.

I went to tell the kids. Naturally, Pam had a fit.

"Don't worry," I said. "I'll just drop off some soda and some soup and leave."

"You'll come right back?"

"No, I need to be alone. I'll spend the night at his new apartment. He'll think I'm here, so it will be perfect. Thanks for everything, honey."

"Be careful, Mom."

"He's docile, Pam. I can tell. Believe me, I have nothing to fear, not right now."

She knew I was right. Pam had seen enough personality shifts to understand. Even she could not begrudge him a nice cool drink.

Rod needed a friend, and as far as I was concerned, I was a good one. I would tend to his needs. The Madonna in me could not resist.

CHAPTER 12

Demon of Death

THE HOUSE WAS DARK, but rather than pull into the garage, I parked in the driveway. I wanted quick access to my car, just in case. I did not think the situation was dangerous, but I was on guard, nonetheless. Rod was the most unpredictable human I had ever met, and, in some sick way, this was part of the attraction.

On this night, I intended to drop off some life-giving liquids and then leave, but I also wanted to see if he had summoned Mandy. She adored him, that was obvious. He cared for her, too, but only as a friend. He had never crossed that line. At least, I didn't think he had, but maybe tonight, maybe in his hour of need.

I sat the grocery bags on the counter and climbed quietly up the stairs. The French doors were open, but the room was dark. Not wanting to shock him with a flood of light, I flipped on the switch in the hallway. There was a mound in the center of the bed, and Rod poked out his head. "You did come," he said.

The eyes were glassy and barely open, but immediately I knew they were raging with fever. "Yes, I did," I said simply. I went to the medicine cabinet and pulled out a thermometer.

"Judy, please, I'm so cold. Do you have any extra blankets?"

"Yes, I'll get them. Now, put this under your tongue."

"Did you bring any soda? I'm so thirsty."

He was shivering. I put my hand to his forehead. Dangerously high, I thought. "I've got 7-Up downstairs, but let's check your temperature. Can't get an accurate reading after a cool drink."

His lips parted, but barely. "Rod, under the tongue," I commanded, as though he were a child. He was unable to hold the glass-encased mercury, and it slipped down at an angle. "Hold it, Rod," I said, impatiently bringing up his fingers. He was overdoing it, a little too much of the poor pitiful me routine. I pulled a huge, heavy quilt out of the closet and laid it on top of the pile.

"Thank you for coming," he said.

"Don't talk, Rod. Remain still, and I'll be back in a minute."

He looked up desperately. "I'm not leaving, Rod. Don't worry. I'm just going to get you something to drink. Are you hungry? Could you eat some soup?"

He shook his head. Food was out of the question. The man was not well.

Downstairs I took my time. I put away the groceries, made some ice chips, and filled two large tumblers. Then I carried the glasses back upstairs. Rod was barely conscious, so I quietly placed the drinks on the headboard and removed the thermometer. He did not stir. I took the thermometer to the bathroom to read. 104° and climbing! Oh, my God! I thought. *He really is sick, deathly sick.* He had not been exaggerating. Truly, he would have been unable to lift his head off the pillow, at least not without help. Now he was practically comatose, and the ice-cold drink had not been touched. Leaving him was out of the question. I opened the medicine cabinet, put the thermometer away, and retrieved a bottle of aspirin. Removing two tablets as I moved toward the bed, I made up my mind to stay. I would be safe for now. In the morning, I'd see.

"Rod, sit up," I said. "Drink some of this and take these."

"No pills."

"It's only aspirin, Rod. They will bring your fever down. Now take them," I insisted.

Begrudgingly, he accepted my handout. "Drink some soda," I encouraged. "Get as much down as you can." Another swallow, but the glass was far from empty. He handed it to me, and I set it down. "It's right here if you get thirsty." He looked up, and I moved to the other side of the bed. A surge of strength lifted him, and he twisted to watch me. His eyes went wide with panic. I knew the liquids and heavy blankets would mean diddly if I walked out that door. The Madonna in me weighed the consequences and threw caution to the wind. It was a spontaneous decision, and a crazy one at that, but when I stripped off my clothes, he sank back into the pillows with a great sigh of relief. I climbed under the mountain of blankets and curled around his backside. His entire body was on fire, and it sank backward into my cool softness.

"Thank God," he said. "Thank you, Jesus."

"Quiet," I scolded. "Now go to sleep. I'll be right here."

This was assurance enough, and with my return he rested. I, on the other hand, did not. I was too worried, and I was too hot. Every time I tried to roll away, his hands would grab my arms. I knew he was sound asleep, but his subconscious was speaking. Hold me, Judy. Please hold me.

Hours passed, and nothing changed. In fact, I thought his fever was rising. I prayed for ministering angels and beseeched the heavens above, but my requests were answered only by his delusional cries. I couldn't understand him, but I felt his anguish. I tore away at some point and returned with an ice-cold washcloth. Placing it on his forehead brought him around some, and I took advantage by propping him up and forcing down some more aspirin. He gulped at the drink this time, so I was encouraged.

The vigil resumed and again, he would not let me slip away. As hot as he was, he still wanted my body pressed to his, so I tried to accommodate him. Finally, the medicine took hold. The shivers ceased and the sweat poured out. He drenched me, the sheets, and even the first layers of blankets covering him.

Thank God, I said to myself. Knowing the bedding had to be changed, I retreated from his side. This time I heard no objection, so I laid out some sheets, a pillow, and a few fresh covers. I made a makeshift bed on the floor and asked him to crawl down. It was like trying to roust a sleeping elephant, and he fell to the floor. Once everything was freshened, I attempted the reverse.

"Come on, Rod. Up you go," I said, pulling forcefully. "On the mattress, baby. You cannot stay down here on the floor." He rose slowly. "Here, put a fresh T-shirt on," I ordered. "Good," I encouraged him as he struggled. "Now, drink some more soda and take these."

"No pills. No thanks!" he emphasized stubbornly.

"Rod, you must take them. Your fever barely broke. It will rocket right back up if you don't."

"I'll be okay. No pills."

"Then I'm leaving," I said.

He sat up. "Judy, please don't leave."

"Then take your medicine. You want me to stay, do as I say."

He accepted the two little white tablets. What the heck? I wondered. Why is he being so funny about taking aspirin? That's weird. He swallowed them, and I stayed as promised. Thankfully, this time I was also able to sleep. It was a fitful night, but I did get some rest.

When I woke up in the morning, it was to the sound of running water. Rod was brushing his teeth. I was amazed. He splashed water on his face and came out with the towel still in hand. "He's alive," I joked.

"Oh my gosh, I feel so much better." He dropped the towel and crawled into my side of the bed. I skooched over some, but the huge pile of blankets kept me from going far. Rod wrapped an arm around me and closed the distance between us. "Umm, you feel good," he said. "I've missed you so much." Miraculously, his libido was alive. Indeed, he was recovering.

We nestled for a while, and when he lumbered off again, I got up to make him some soup. I played nurse that day while he stayed in bed, but that evening he was well enough to join me in front of the TV. It was like the old days, the good old days, and I had to remind myself not to regress. Tomorrow, I will send him on his way, I reassured myself. In the morning, I will tell him to go home.

He refused to take aspirin that night, but I made no fuss. I didn't believe, at that point, it was necessary, but later I felt his temperature begin to climb. Still, he remained stubborn. I could not sway him, so I left him alone.

Suffer then, I thought. *See if I care*.

I fell into a deep exhausted sleep. My body needed to catch up, but in the wee hours of the morning I became aware of hacking. Rod had started to cough. The flu was moving into his lungs. His repeated whooping would wake me, so finally I got up. Again, I went to the medicine cabinet. This time I brought back some cough syrup and aspirin. "Rod, sit up," I pried. "Take these."

"No. No pills."

"Then swallow some of this," I said, holding a spoon filled with the red elixir.

"No, Judy. I'm okay. Just come back to bed." He was

holding up the covers, and I was tired of fighting him. I dumped the syrup into a wad of tissues and slipped into his open arms. "This is all I need," he said quietly. "You will make me well."

It seemed I might. It was hours before his chest heaved again, but when it did, he wretched with convulsive force. It was no longer a tickle in his throat; his entire body spasmed with the cough. "Rod, please. Please take some medicine."

"No. Judy, lie down." He was pulling on me, and I thought he was being a stubborn fool, but I remained still, and presently, he began to pray. "Body, you are nothing more than a glove to house my spirit and soul. You have no dominion over my mind, and I command you in the name of Jesus Christ, release this illness."

He held me tight as another fit burst from his lungs, and then he resumed the crusade. "Leave me demons, you have no dominion here. By the authority of Jesus Christ, I bind you. This house serves God the Father, and I command you to leave. Be gone, NOW!"

I thought he was reaching, but I was wrong. He coughed one more time and then pulled me closer. I waited. I was ready to pounce, and I fully expected to make a stand. He was going to take medicine. He prayed again, but more quietly, and then he pressed his lips against my neck. "Goodnight, Judy," he said.

"Goodnight," I said, willing to wait. Time would set him to hacking, and then I would take care of business. I was wrong, though. That was the last of it. We fell asleep, and if he did cough in the night, I was unaware.

When Rod came out of his room the next day, his appetite was much improved. After a hearty lunch, I broached the subject of his move. "Do you want me to go with you?" I asked. "I mean, over to the apartment. It's nice, and I could show you around, help you get settled, stuff like that."

I was saying it's time to go, but he didn't want to hear it. "No, I can manage."

No words seemed appropriate, so I stayed silent and the day wore on. In the late afternoon, he began to cough again. "Want some cough syrup?"

"No, no thanks."

Here we go again. The sun faded, and the den filled with shadows. As the darkness deepened, so did the congestion in his lungs. He did not want to talk about the arrangements I had made for him, and the situation was exasperating. I was on edge, and finally his raspy bark broke my reserve. "Dammit, Rod, you're making yourself sick again. You don't want to leave, and you're allowing your body to fill with disease so I'll let you stay."

The implication was not appreciated. "Judy, I will go just as soon as I can. And you're wrong. I am not happy about this. Do you really think I enjoy being miserable with the flu?"

"You must," I said, standing up. "Otherwise, you'd take some medicine!" With that, I turned and stormed away. He was manipulating the situation and I wasn't happy. I went to bed and hid under the covers.

No way will he get away with this. And this time, I am not leaving. This is my house and I want it back.

He came to bed, but I refused to curl into him. My body was rigid, like my attitude. Somehow, he managed to keep the barking at bay, and we fell asleep. I began to dream.

My mind stretched and I reached for the stars. I wanted freedom, and presently, I found myself floating. Born on the tides of time, I traveled to the far reaches of the universe. I went through galaxies of radiant wonder, past planets dancing with light. Angels smiled as I went by, and I watched children gather flowers from fields of clouds. Peace encompassed me, but just when I was most happy, I felt a shaking in the wind. I lost my balance and began to fall. Speeding past eons, I saw blue and white approaching. I could not reverse my momentum. I recognized planet earth before smashing through the atmosphere. Fire! I was burning up! A scream escaped, and I sat up. Confusion rocked me.

Why wasn't I dead?

Then I saw him. Rod was lying in another pool of sweat. I touched him. His fever was raging. No wonder, I said in the dark silence. "Rod, Rod, honey, wake up. Your fever is peaking again. You need to take aspirin."

"No pills," he bullied.

"Well, at least move over to the dry side of the bed. I'm going downstairs. I want to freshen our drinks."

He did as I asked and I left him. I knew he wasn't faking it, but I believed his inner ego was working the circumstances. How convenient. How very convenient.

I shuffled around the kitchen for a few minutes and then poured some soda. After that I had a compulsion for a bath. I filled the tub, poured in some sandalwood and lots of bubbles, and lit candles. Music sounded good, but I was afraid it would wake Rod, so I sank into the warm caressing waves of silence. I started to drift, but Rod invaded my sanctuary. I felt his foot and opened my eyes as he slipped in at the other end.

"I'm dying," he said.

Not now, Rod, not again. I put my hand to his head. *Probably 103°*, I thought. "You're not dying, Rod. You just need some aspirin."

"No, Judy, I saw him. I saw the angel of death."

My delusional friend was trying my patience.

"Judy, cast him out. Please save me." He began to cough, and the spasm rocked his body. The shivering followed.

"Put your hands on me, Judy. NOW!" he begged.

I reached for him. I was no fool, but I wanted him well.

If he needed me to lay hands on him, then I would. "Look into my eyes, Rod," I said, cupping him above the ears. "Look directly into my soul. See my love."

His feverish pupils sought me out, and I saw red. His eyes were ablaze again, just like they had been at our mini suite. Another timeline, I thought. The conspiracy days revisited. "Look beyond what you can see and feel my heart. Know that I love you."

He nodded.

"Demon of death, you have no dominion here."

He looked down.

"Look at me!"

Cooperation.

"Good ... now hear me. In the name of God, and by the blood of Jesus Christ, I command you to leave. Satan, you have no dominion here. Be gone. Get out! Return to the bitter bowels from whence you came."

I saw a tear, and Rod sort of collapsed in my hands. Then he turned and leaned backward, falling against my breasts. His body was blazing, but in seconds it began to cool. I was astounded that his temperature dropped, and although it did not return to normal, it must have diminished by at least two or three degrees. I held him for some time, then whispered in his ear. "I love you, Rod. I will always love you. Remember that."

He nodded and hugged my arms, so they tightened around his chest.

"Let me go, honey. I'm going to put some crisp, cool sheets on the bed. Then we'll curl up together, okay?"

An approval. Pathetic, but at least it was something. Stretching the fitted percale, I marveled at what had occurred. *The man is filled with power,* I thought. If only he could learn to channel it. He truly might conquer the world.

"Hang on, honey. You'll make it yet."

Rod acquiesced to my need when he came back to bed. He took two aspirins, and then we spooned around each other. “No room for demons here,” I joked.

“Love conquers all,” he said. He was a bit too serious for me, but I allowed the thought.

Tomorrow, I will tell him. For sure, he must go. I was sad about the business at hand but determined. I had not come this far to get stalled again. I needed to move on, and that meant moving Rod out.

CHAPTER 13

A Card for Posterity

ROD'S EXIT WAS ANTI-CLIMACTIC. When the time came, he simply gave me a hug, promised to call, and told me to take care of myself.

What an enigma, I thought, watching him back the giant Dodge Ram out of the garage. A Dueley, I noticed. Two sets of rear wheels. Kind of like the driver. I laughed at the analogy and physically closed the garage door. Somewhere along the line, the automatic opener had stopped working. Then I found a huge screwdriver to secure the aluminum, wedged it tightly into the frame casing, and tested the door. It would not budge. I wanted no surprise visits, and this effectively locked out any intruding vehicles. Then I went to check the house. Rod had gained entry without a key and I needed to know how. I checked the windows. None were broken. I couldn't find a problem with the sliding glass door either. Maybe from the roof.

Upstairs all was secure. What the heck? Truly now, Judy, the man cannot walk through walls. Check the windows again.

I went back down to ground level, pulling at each opening. Finally, one broke loose and up went the window.

Checking the latch, I realized it had snapped off. *Those powerful arms*, I thought, *clipped it right in two*. Fortunately, the repair wouldn't be expensive, but urgency was required, as was extra security. I counted the windows and planned to buy gismos to lock them all down. I would not be surprised again.

Later, with my handiwork completed, I retreated to my office. I could not wait to log the recent events. A memorable journal entry, I said to myself.

I sat down at my screen and flicked the switch. Nothing. The drive whirred, but there was no display. "NO!" I cried. Damn you, Rod. Obviously, he had tossed my computer monitor in his fit of rage. I tried again. No luck.

Well, shit, I muttered, unable to adequately express my frustration.

"Rod! I cannot afford this!" I screamed. "You took everything else, but this is my dream. How could you?"

Now what? I had very little money, so what should I do? I went to bed and put my head on his pillow. I was beyond tears, so I stared at the ceiling. No recompense. The Federal raid flooded back, and I saw the agent walking out with my PC. Now it was gone again.

I should have let him die. Too bad I didn't suffocate the SOB while I had a chance, put him out of his misery. I was wallowing and knee deep in nasty memories when the phone rang. "I am not talking to you," I said angrily. "Never again."

The machine picked it up, and Mr. Pathetic came on. "It's nice, Judy, but it's not home. I miss you. Call me."

"Call you!" I jumped. "I'll call you alright. I'll call you every name in the book. You are truly a master, Rod Steersman, a master abuser. A dream-wrecker from hell, but you will not beat me! The Feds tried and now you. I hate you, but you will not win. Just watch and see."

I marched out the door. This time I made a trip to the electronics warehouse. I purchased a new monitor and hoped that would do it.

Praying with fervor, I clicked on to my world. "Please God. Please let it work."

Yes! I was in. I checked the files. All secure. Test print.

No! Not the printer, too. Oh, my God. That would be even more expensive. "I hate you, Rod!"

It was too late to go to the store, and I was too frustrated to work, so I shut off the system and went to relax. I made myself a powerful drink and sat down in front of the wide screen. Bring me relief, I begged the God of distraction. Take me away. My puppies pounced on me, and their cheery dispositions helped. I settled, but as I concentrated on the movie, something seemed wrong. The characters were slightly blurred. I stood up and examined the screen. It was cracked and further investigation revealed the top layer of glass was missing. There were three sections to the canopy, and one was gone! The other two were damaged.

"All right, Bucko," I said. "What else did you do?" Somehow, I knew there was more.

A few days later the lawn began looking dry. I went to check the clock for the sprinkler system. It was unplugged, but when I reconnected it, nothing happened. Playing with the mechanism caused it to shift on the wall, so I examined the back. The wiring had disappeared. Nothing was there to connect the timer to the system outside. Rod had ripped it off the sheetrock, and then cleverly covered his tracks.

Coy, very coy.

I also found battered kitchen appliances and more holes, holes in the walls made by angry young fists. Those thirty-eight minutes it took to rally a squad car had cost me dearly, and it was more than the money I lost. I was shaken with insecurity because all this time I tormented myself with the "whys" of what happened.

How could a relationship that was once so good have gone so bad? The story of my life. What is wrong with me?

I had no answer, so I went back to my work. I had a story to tell, and if I could do it well enough, it might get published. I needed to at least secure an agent or my pre-trial supervisor would soon insist I look for work, and so would my family. They were worried about my money situation. I had a mortgage, and now the responsibility was solely mine. *Money. The almighty dollar. What a merry-go-round.*

I no longer cared about earning a living. I wanted to live my dream, and if that meant selling my house and everything in it, I would do it. I was grasping the significance of Rod's fifth key. It was the element of sacrifice. He explained that if you wanted something bad enough, you must be prepared to give up everything. I understood the concept, but I did not believe in martyrdom, and Rod did. He used Jesus as the perfect example, and said if you died, but your dream lived on, then your sacrifice was worth it. I had no intention of dying, but my writing was so important to me, that without it I might not have wanted to live.

You were a good preacher, Rod. I'll give you that.

The calls came in, and I ignored them. Sometimes Rod would leave an "Everything's great" message, and then, usually late at night, I'd hear the loneliness. I rode those waves with him, for I, too, was lonely, but I refused the connection. I completed my outline and began the text. It was good, or at least I thought it was good. Whatever the quality, it was enough. I began to feel joyous, so I pushed further. I wrote a preface and then a legacy. "Search the legacy of a victim," I said. "In it you will find the key to trust. Trust holds the secret of hope which will end the pain that threatens to destroy all mankind."

The message was plain. I was writing "The Uncommon Partnership." It was my story about a love gone wrong, and it revealed the trauma and consequences of child abuse. Rod's pain had been uncovered, but his suffering was deep. The old wound continued to fester and ooze.

I was on automatic pilot when the phone rang, so without thinking I picked up.

"Judy. Judy, thank God."

"Hello, Rod," I said casually.

"I'm so glad you answered. How are you?"

"Fine. I'm just fine."

"What have you been doing?"

"Working. Just working."

"Really? You got a job?"

"No. I've been working on my book. You know, my dream come true."

"You're serious about this, aren't you?"

"What? You thought it was a joke?" My hostility resounded.

"No, I didn't mean that. I just wondered how ..."

"Whatever, Rod. I'll do whatever it takes. So, how are you?"

"It's going great, Judy. Everything is coming together. Even George Johnson is supporting me now. He's with me every step of the way."

"I'm happy for you," I said.

"Judy, can I see you? Will you have dinner with me? Maybe a movie?"

"No, Rod. I won't. It's out of the question."

"Then lunch. Just meet me for lunch. Please ..." He was begging. "Please, I have so much to tell you. It's my birthday, you know. Just meet me for a glass of wine, for old time's sake."

"Your birthday?" I glanced at a calendar. "Well, so it is."

"In an hour, then? At the Macaroni House?" he said,

assuming the sale.

"Alright, but wine won't do. I need to eat. I'm hungry."

"I'll buy you anything, whatever you want. I love you, Judy."

I ignored him. "Noon then ... twelve o'clock sharp."

"See you there," he said energetically.

He was on the patio when I arrived. Amazing! *He's on time.*

"Judy, you look great!"

"Thanks."

"Really. I've never seen you look more radiant."

"I am happy, Rod. I really am enjoying myself. I love writing. It's a gift from God."

"Well, it suits you. It's so good to see you. I was worried about you. Why wouldn't you take my calls?"

I rolled my eyes. My meaning was obvious.

"I'm sorry, Judy. Truly I am. I'm going to fix everything. Will you let me send someone over?"

"No, Rod. I've already taken care of most of it anyway."

"God, I'm embarrassed. I can't believe I was so out of control."

"You seem okay now. How are you doing? I mean really?"

He looked at me squarely, and I saw beyond the eyes to the seat of his soul. I knew he was healing. He confirmed my thoughts with words. "I'm going to make it, Judy. I really am going to be alright. And I'm going to save Global."

The warrior had returned, and I was glad he was in control. "I know, Rod. I believe you. Happy birthday."

"Thanks. Judy, please go to the movie with me tonight. Don't leave me all alone on my birthday."

"Rod, you're surrounded by adoring fans. Have one of your coordinators go to the show with you."

"I'm with them every day," he argued. "I want my best friend tonight."

I hadn't been out since he had left, and the movie sounded good. "I don't know, Rod. I'm not sure that's such a good idea."

"Well, think about it. Just consider it, will you? Now, what would you like for lunch?"

I ordered a salad and we chatted for the better part of an hour. When we were done, he walked me to my car. He did not try to kiss me or hold me or pressure me about the date. He simply said he'd call later and we parted.

When I arrived back at the house, my answering machine was blinking. The message was from Rod. He must have called as soon as I left him.

"Just wanted to say thanks. Thanks for seeing me. Your friendship means everything to me. Judy, when you think of your dream, remember the keys. Remember the Five Golden Rings. They will never let you down. I'll call later. Love you."

The Five Golden Rings! I had been working on them. I rushed to my notepad. *Are there five here?* I asked myself.

"One, two, three, four, five. Oh my gosh, there are!" I couldn't believe it. Rod had inspired me. "Search the legacy of a victim and find The Five Golden Rings. They hold the secret of hope."

I was amazed. Even apart, our work continues. *Soulmate*, I thought. *Wait till you see this*. Suddenly, I wanted to share. I thought about calling him. No, it would be too difficult to explain over the phone. Maybe tonight, but I wasn't sure I wanted a 'tonight'. "I know," I said. "I'll make him a card." A card would make a terrific birthday present, and it was something I could afford.

I knew Hallmark had a computerized system to generate personal greetings, so I took my notes and went to one of their stores. I was forced to edit, and then edit again, but eventually I was able to contain the message within the allowed space. Finally, I asked a clerk to print it. She read it first and then said, "That's beautiful. Where did you get it?"

"From a friend, the birthday boy. The words came from me, but he inspired them. It turned out pretty good, didn't it?"

"Really good, and it fits the space perfectly. Let me read it back to you. We only print once, and I want to make sure it's right."

"Okay," I said.

She began slowly, and I listened to my message.

~

THE FIVE GOLDEN RINGS

HOPE for all mankind rests in the HEART,
and the heart is nourished by LOVE,
a love freely offered.
Such freedom is found in TRUTH,
but truth does not come easily.
There is a price to pay. A lesson must first be learned.
We must first learn to FORGIVE.
Without forgiveness, truth remains buried,
and the freedom to love cannot be found.
Without love, our hearts harden
and no longer have strength for hope.
Without hope, we will most certainly perish.
Learn the lesson of FORGIVENESS
and embrace truth.
The TRUTH will set you free.
In that newfound freedom, you will discover LOVE.
The HEART, nourished by love,
will grow strong and provide sanctuary for HOPE.
With a place of perpetual rest,
HOPE will finally Spring Eternal.
Learn the lesson of forgiveness.
Begin by forgiving yourself.
It is a small price to pay.

~

"That's it," I said.

"Sounds great," she said. "So, it's a print?"

"It's a print."

At home I decided to tell Rod I did not want to go out, but I intended to ask him to come by. I wanted to put my creation in the mailbox, so he would at least have the card. Otherwise, I thought it was best to stay away from him. I was missing him too much, and I did not want to fall back into his arms. I signed the card, A gift of trust, in hopes the world might hear. "To Mr. Global from Mrs. Global."

With that piece of business resolved, I opened the doors to the patio. It was a cool spring evening, and the light breeze was uplifting. *Music*, I thought. Something soft to suit the mood. I put on an easy-listening station. Then I poured a glass of wine and went outside. Buster and Gus were thrilled. I hadn't joined them in recent days, and my presence set them free, too free, as it turns out. They began to bark and then run to the back gate. I called them, but they did not return. Finally, I got up to see what was disturbing them. I rounded the side of the house and ran right into him.

"ROD!"

He grabbed me and pulled me into his arms.

"What are you doing here?" I asked.

"Came for a birthday hug," he said, holding me tight.

I broke away. "Rod, you can't come over here like this. You should have called first."

"Why? You got company?" He was on the move, and he went directly into the house.

I followed him. "No, I don't have company, but this is no longer your home. You need to respect my privacy."

He grabbed me again. "I will, but let's dance. I love this song."

Lady in Red was playing, and we swayed in each other's

arms. The romance captured us. "I've missed you, Ms. Burr. So much."

"I know, Rod. I know." I had missed him, too, but it was more like missing a tooth that had been pulled. The pain was gone, but an empty socket remained.

He was hoping for words of endearment, and he dropped his head back to meet my eyes. Then he kissed me. The world fell away, and my heart started to race. Still, we danced. When the song ended, we remained entwined, and I forced myself out of the trance.

"Look, Rod, I got you a birthday card."

He followed me to the kitchen, and I handed him the tiny Hallmark sack. I sat down and waited. He smiled before reading it, but when he saw "The Five Golden Rings," he looked up.

"It's my interpretation of your keys, Rod. I had them committed to paper for your birthday, for posterity's sake."

Reading on, I watched as his expression changed. He was moved, and I knew he appreciated the gesture. "This is the most precious gift I've ever received. Thank you, Judy."

"You're welcome," I said. Trying to lighten the mood, I joked, "I couldn't afford much, but you can sure take this one to the bank."

"Words to live by," he said. "You really are talented."

"Thanks. Want some wine?"

"Sure."

I poured another glass. "Let's go outside. It's a beautiful evening."

The movie was forgotten. So, in fact was dinner, but he was not alone. I helped Rod celebrate his birthday. All night we celebrated, in fact, until the wee hours of the morn.

CHAPTER 14

The Assembly

RESPECT PREVAILED for the next couple of weeks, and Rod did not attempt to encroach on my space. He was calling, but not too often. He was bursting with creativity, and I enjoyed hearing about Global.

Two of his major shareholders, the Wentmores, practically adopted him, and Rod relished the attention. Mr. Wentmore coached him and Mrs. Wentmore coddled him. As Rod stabilized, his ideas grew exponentially. The board of directors met on a regular basis, and a certified public accountant was hired. Rapid progress was made, but there was a problem. The age-old problem—money. With a shortage of investors, it was tight. The president solicited support from his coordinators, and many rallied to the cause. Other devotees had no resources, but they worked for free. The team was solid, and the preacher sang his song.

"Let it be done right now."

I was happy for my friend, but then he tried to draw me in.

"No, Rod. There are too many painful memories."

"But everything has shifted, Judy. We're on a positive track."

"I'm glad, Rod, but I have a new career."

"I know and I respect that, but you should still be the one to write the book, The Global Story."

"Maybe one day, Rod, but not now. Besides, there are too many unknowns for me. What if I go to prison? I won't be any good to you behind bars."

"Judy! Don't think that way. Hold to the positive. If you lose faith, you'll lose everything."

"I haven't lost faith, not in myself, but I no longer share your vision, Rod. And I am not a member of the club. Your associates do not appreciate my expertise. They hate me, and until you tell them the truth, nothing will change."

He became defensive, and I found myself thankful our connection was across the wire. "The truth?" he interjected. "What do you mean? I've told them I was to blame. I publicly accepted responsibility for everything."

"I know, but you didn't explain why the conspiracy occurred in the first place. They still believe I'm the wicked witch who led their president astray."

"Judy, if you guys hadn't lost sight of our goals, we wouldn't be struggling right now."

There it was again. Whatever did he mean? You guys? "What guys, Rod?"

"You and Chance. You and the others," he said.

"I've got to go Rod ..."

"Judy, don't hang up."

"Really, Rod. I am not having this conversation. I'll talk to you later."

"Judy!"

"What?"

"Will you see a movie with me tonight?"

"Maybe ... call me later."

"Okay," he said. "I love you."

"I love you, too."

He's still stuck, I thought. Thank God we've separated. Once again, he had thrown me into the Hawks group, and I didn't appreciate it. Those people were his enemies. I was not.

You guys, I said to myself. *I am not one of the guys, Rod. Get over it.*

I plugged into my system and pulled up my journal.

Once you hand over your life, thinking someone is going to save you, you become nothing more than chattel. Your autonomy is gone, and you are reduced to slavery.

That's what I had done with Rod. Looking back, I could only blame myself. I had expected miracles from him, and most definitely, I was hoping he'd save me. Consequently, he gained power over me. Now I was on my own again, and I wanted it to stay that way. If I joined him at Global, the healing would never be complete. The 'you guys' had just proved it.

He never called me that night, and later I discovered he had taken Mandy to the movie. "You're an asshole, Rod Steersman," I said.

"I'm sorry. I got the impression you didn't want to go."

"Well, you were wrong. You could have at least called."

"You're jealous," he said flippantly.

"No, I am not jealous. I just don't like being stood up."

"Judy? You really don't care if I take another girl to the movies?"

He was hurt, and truthfully, I did care, and I was jealous, but Rod was a married man, and I had wanted him to get back with his wife. "No, Rod," I lied. "I don't care. You are free to do as you please but be careful of the lust trap. Mandy is very young and extremely impressionable. She'd love to get her hooks into you."

"It's not like that with us. We're friends."

"Whatever, Rod ... it's your life."

Mother's Day rolled around, and I thanked God for my

family. The companionship of my daughter and my mother always eased my loneliness. I had planned a family barbeque, but when Sunday arrived, my mother wasn't well. Pam told me to put away the burgers. She wanted to take me out.

"My treat," she said.

"Sounds like a deal. I haven't been out of this house for weeks."

At the restaurant, she broached the inevitable subject. "So, how's Rod?"

"He's struggling, but I think he's getting things back on track."

"Are you seeing him?" she asked with hostility.

"No, but we talk. I saw him on his birthday, but that's all."

"I hope that's true, Mom."

I did not need a lecture. I changed the subject. "You look like you've dropped. Have you been to the doctor recently?"

"Last week. He says everything is on schedule. I feel like I'm carrying this baby lower, though, and I must pee every twenty minutes or so. I'll sure be glad when she's born."

"I can't wait. What's your date again?"

"July 25th. Do you want to be there?"

"Don't you need me to watch Marie?" I asked. One live birth was enough. I had no desire to witness another.

"Would you, Mom? I wasn't sure how you'd feel, but it would be great if you don't care about being in the delivery room."

"I'd rather be with my granddaughter. In fact, why don't you plan to leave her overnight. That way Jason will have a chance to rest."

She was delighted, and I saw my Gemini turn into a little girl herself. "I'm so glad you're here. I would have died if you'd stayed in Colorado."

"Well, I didn't, and I'm not going anywhere. So, how's Jason's case coming along?"

"Oh," she said, turning down her smile. "Not good. He's refusing to cooperate, and he says he wants his day in court."

"He'll change his mind, Pam. They'll make it impossible for him. Let's just hope the DA offers a decent deal. If they want my cooperation for the Pioneer trials, they should help my son-in-law."

"Mom, what am I going to do? What if you both go to jail? How am I ever going to make it?"

"You'll be fine, Pam. You've got a great job, and you're a strong woman. You'll manage."

"But you're my best friend. I can't lose you and my husband, too."

"Honey, you're not going to lose us. We'll still be there for you. Besides, I'm optimistic. Karen told me the DA has given her every indication I'll get probation."

"Really?"

"Yes, really. That's why I decided to move back here. If I had thought otherwise, I would have stayed with Jana, rent free."

She was visibly relieved. "Oh my God, I can't believe it. That's the best news I've heard for a year. You have no idea."

But I did. I just didn't want her to count on it too much. I tried to squelch her excitement. "Well, we won't know until after the trials, but I am banking on it."

"Speaking of banking," she said. "How are you managing? Do you still have savings?"

"Nope. I've been living off credit cards. In fact, I'm behind on the house payment now."

"Mom! You can't lose the house. Not after everything you've been through."

"I won't. I've got a tax refund coming and when it gets here, I'll be able to catch up."

"Oh, good. How much?"

"Enough, Pam. It's substantial."

"Well, thank God for that."

Her words echoed mine. Thank God, indeed. I had always paid my taxes, and now I was waiting for the IRS to save my life. The government seized my assets as part of their civil suit, and effectively their action reduced my income for three years. A tax accountant had amended those returns, and now I considered it money in the bank. Please God, I said to myself later. Don't let this one stall. For once, let the wheels of justice roll smoothly.

Monday morning, Rod called. It was early, and I was surprised he was even up. "Judy, I could really use a friend. Could you come over?"

"Sure. I'll grab us some breakfast and be there in a few. You want anything in particular?"

"No. It doesn't matter. Thanks."

He didn't sound happy. What now? I wondered. When I arrived at the apartment, the door was open. I walked in, handed him the bag, and said, "Here, I got us egg sandwiches."

I received a blank stare for my efforts. "What's wrong, Rod?"

"I've lost Salt Lake City."

"What do you mean?"

"All of the Salt Lake City team is gone. They went home over the weekend, and they're not coming back."

"Well, they probably can't afford the commute. They have families to support."

"But this would make them all rich, Judy. We're just beginning to turn a profit again."

"Rod, I'm sure the guys believe in you, but by now their wives are probably pitching a fit. They miss their husbands, and the children need their fathers, too. Here, eat this," I said, unwrapping one of the muffins and handing it to him.

He took the nourishment but set it on the table. Not a good sign. "They want to take me down."

No! Not this, I winced. "Rod, no one wants to take you

down. It makes no sense. If Global fails, everyone loses. If you succeed, everybody wins."

"They're angry, and they want to hurt me."

"Why?"

"Why! Because I saved my wife and kids. If I hadn't bought them a decent vehicle, they would have drowned in the floods."

Oregon had experienced terrible flooding, and his wife escaped with her boys using the new four-wheel-drive vehicle. Rod had bought it for her around Christmas time, but apparently, he hadn't consulted the board before making the purchase.

I quaked inside. My choice to visit had been a poor one. Rod's victim persona was in control and this wounded warrior had a propensity for violence.

When I looked at the door, he grabbed my hand. "Judy, you can't leave. You're the only one capable of settling me. Please don't go."

"Okay, Rod, but you must calm down. Now, tell me what happened."

"That woman," he said, looking anguished. "I trusted her, and she turned on me."

"What woman?"

"The CPA. I thought she was sent by God, but it must have been a setup. She just showed up one day, and now she's told George Johnson I embezzled money."

"George? Surely, he wouldn't listen to such nonsense. He knows you have nothing to hide."

"Yeah, but he's disappointed, because his son is not on the circuit."

"A lot of people are disappointed, Rod. You made too many promises, promises you couldn't keep, but that does not make you a crook. George would never fault you for buying that car."

"They want to sue. They want to throw me in jail."

He was shaking now. I tried to reach him. "Honey, that simply won't happen. The numbers will speak for themselves. One bonus means nothing. When they realize how little you drew out over the course of a year, all this hoopla will go away. Just stand tall. You know your intentions were honorable."

"I loved them all," he wailed.

"Yes, you did, and they loved you, too, but they're scared. They do not want to lose their investments. Give it time, Rod. It will work out." He began to relax. Thank God.

"You're right, Judy. I have nothing to hide. In fact, my whole life is an open book."

I smiled. "Yes, but maybe you'll think twice about turning those pages next time. I'm telling you, Rod, people are quick to judge. They can be righteous fools."

"We all can," he said, echoing my thoughts. "Judy?"

I knew what was coming and more than anything I wanted to bolt. He had a good hold on me, however, so I waited. "Judy, I need you more than ever. I cannot do this without you."

"Yes, you can, Rod. This could be good for you. It will be cost effective to use the Vegas group. Just gather a few trusted coordinators. Form a local board of directors. Give them assignments and remain flexible. Until you can compensate them, you'll need to remember that they have to earn a living. Total commitment will come later, as the company grows."

He was deep in thought, probably reaching for some of that divine inspiration. "Yes!" he said suddenly. "I'll call it The Vision Quest Assembly."

"I like that."

"Judy, please sit on the board."

"No, Rod, I'll be there for you, but I do not want any

kind of official appointment."

"Would you at least come to the first meeting? I need you in my corner, please?" he begged.

"I don't think that's a good idea."

"Honestly, Judy. They all know how smart you are. It would really help if you demonstrated support. After all, you are Global's largest investor. It doesn't look good for you to step completely out of the picture."

"But I'm out of it, Rod. I care about Global, but only because of you. It's your dream, and for your sake, I'd like to see the company succeed. Other than that, I want nothing to do with the business."

This seemed unfathomable to him. "Your ten percent will make you a millionaire one day," he said defensively.

"Rod, I'll be a millionaire without Global. I've done it before, and I'll do it again." I don't need you, I was saying.

My assertiveness caused him to back off. "Alright, but at least attend the first caucus. If you want to step back after that, I won't argue. Just help me get over the hump. Judy," he said softly. "I know exactly how to save the company."

I was tiring. "You've always known, Rod."

"No, this is different. I have a plan that will blow your mind. I just need you in my corner. Will you be there? Just once?"

I looked up wearily and acquiesced. "Okay, Rod, but just this one time. Never again. Deal?"

"Deal!" he said and took a huge bite of his cold sandwich.

Wednesday afternoon, the call came. "The meeting is tonight at seven o'clock. Can I pick you up?"

"I'm having dinner with Mom. It's our late Mother's Day celebration. I'll have to meet you there."

"Will you be on time?" His concern was clear.

"Yes, Rod. She can't drive after dark. We're meeting early, so don't worry."

"Thanks, Judy."

"Hey, what are friends for?" I asked. What are they for anyway? I said to myself.

After hanging up, I thought back to the day Rod needed a friend. I agreed to go to his first meeting, he wolfed down the egg sandwich, and then a different alter ego emerged. I was practically dragged to the bedroom, and once there, he brazenly kissed me. His darting tongue was offensive. It was not familiar in any way. In fact, the probe into my mouth was pointed and driving. I did not like it, but the real turnoff came when he started licking my ear. No soft coos were emitted, but rather an urgent groan came forth, almost a growl. I fought him at first, but turning away only ignited his ardor.

He pulled my hair to trap me. I was about to object when he plowed down on my mouth. He bulldozed without mercy, and I couldn't breathe. I tore away, gasping for breath. I wanted to stop him, to somehow take charge, but it wasn't going to happen, not on that day. With a full body press, he took control, and I was caught in a wild fury fuck. My disgust shifted; it turned to lust. I bit his mouth. Not hard, but more like a love bite. Now I was on fire! His need was releasing mine, and I let him know by digging my fingernails into his back. He pulled off my jeans and shoved up my shirt. I tore open his robe and said, "Fuck me, Rod!"

"Like this?" he asked, holding himself above me so I could see. "Is this what you want?"

"Yes, inside me," I begged.

"You miss me?"

"Rod!" I cried, digging my nails into his buttocks. I had never wanted him more, but something was wrong. He was stroking himself and getting lost in his actions. He exploded all over me as I watched helplessly. Afterward he collapsed and I got up to wash off. When I put on my jeans, he objected.

"Don't go, Judy. Come back to bed."

"I have things to do, Rod. I'll talk to you later."

"Judy ..." he started, but I had managed to get outside, and I wasn't coming back, not ever!

~

"So, where's Boy Wonder?" I asked Sandy after walking into the den of wolves.

"In his office. He's talking to the Wentmores."

"Is everybody here?" I looked around, struck with nostalgia, missing the good 'ole days before the corporate takeover attempt.

"Aaron Clement hasn't showed, and we're not sure he will. He was pretty disillusioned the way things went down."

"Can't fault him for that." He was our greatest skeptic. A good man, smart, too, but he waited and watched for a long time. In fact, he only began to trust after we moved into this office space.

"How are you, Nancy?" I asked, turning to Sandy's wife sitting demurely in one of the side chairs.

"Exhausted. It's been a battle."

"I bet. How many hours are you guys working?"

She rolled her eyes and looked toward her husband. He tried to joke, but his voice was strained. "Oh, we sleep here. No time to go home. You look good, though. It seems like you keep getting younger. I, on the other hand, feel like I'm aging dramatically. Every day I look in the mirror, I lose a little more of this." He pointed to his bald spot and I laughed.

"Business can do that to you, especially when you work for Rod Steersman. I wouldn't come back for love or money. Never again."

Nancy seemed surprised. "You're not joining the assembly?"

"No, Nancy. I'm tired of business. I'm only here to demonstrate support."

"Really?" Sandy said. "What are you going to do now?"

"Write the book. It's one hell of a story, don't you think?"

"I never thought about it. Guess it could be," he said suspiciously. He had other questions, but before he could ask, Rod popped in.

"Hi, Judy. We're ready, guys. In my office, okay?"

"Okay," we chimed, rising for the occasion.

Extra chairs were brought in, and as people took their seats, I watched their faces. *Nothing pleasant about this reception.* No friendly greeting for me and certainly not for Rod.

Waves of negativity wafted in the air.

Well, now, I said to myself. This looks more like a lynching than a meeting of the minds. Rod had better be on cue tonight.

"Good evening," he began. "Thank you for coming. I've requested your presence so we can reorganize. As you know, we've lost Mr. Masters and the other members of the Salt Lake City team."

"What do you mean?" asked Rod's trusted right-hand man, Stuart Nicholson.

Stuart had been my archrival, and he didn't like the fact that Rod and I were friends. He methodically wooed his president, and the flattery and attention worked. He became Rod's confidant. Now this supposed "friend" was the first person to challenge him.

"What about George Johnson? His investment is substantial. Will he be a member of The Vision Quest?"

"No," Rod said, matter-of-factly. "For now, only Las Vegas associates will be invited. We must concentrate on this market first. Once revenues support expansion, our quorum will increase."

Rumbles. Under the breath grumbling.

"We've come a long way in the rebuilding process, but

our debts are large. It's imperative we stick together and focus our efforts. Global will, one day, make everyone in this room a millionaire, but perseverance is required."

Mr. Wentmore objected. "We've heard that before, Rod. I'm no longer sure we can recover. Wouldn't it be better to file bankruptcy and reorganize?"

"NO!" said the CEO and majority shareholder. "If we do that, people won't trust us. Everything Global stands for will be lost. No, I fully intend to pay all debts and honor all stockholder options. I want everyone to win. There can be no casualties in a spiritual war, and that is exactly what this is."

I heard a few "Amens." Rod was getting their attention. His preacher persona kicked into high gear, and he told us about his recent divine inspiration.

"God has shown me the way, ladies and gentlemen. I have a plan that will ignite small businesses across America. Global can no longer remain focused on the leisure industry. We need to penetrate the core of what made this country great. To restore the shattered American dream, and offer this land a real opportunity, we must make sure the mass merchandiser cannot strangle the average businessperson. Companies founded on a philosophy to serve need the backing of a Global network, our network, the one we've already got in place!"

My most unfavorite partner chirped in with his profound question. "How?"

"By providing an information connection, that's how," Rod said. "Think about this, folks. We have everything ready. We have the know-how. We are organized and we are skilled. The entrepreneur is getting squeezed out by big business, but we can unite them. We can create a chain of "small" businesses, and in turn, form a powerful Global hold." As he continued to explain the program, the energy in the room changed. Questions were asked, and Rod had the answers. Even I found his plan interesting.

The man has done it again, I thought. He really does know how to save his world. I sat quietly, waiting and watching when the buzz was interrupted.

The company's greatest skeptic walked through the door. His black face was a beacon of light, and I was first to greet him. "Aaron! Welcome. It's good to see you," I said, shaking his hand. I had not risen, but others did, and it was obvious he was well-liked.

"Sorry I'm late. I had to show a client a new listing."

Rod rose and offered a hearty handshake. "Good to see you, buddy. Have a seat." The room was crowded, but I moved over, and he squeezed in next to me. Rod reviewed, and this time the wolves supported him. It was Aaron with the questions, but they were answered by the team. Rod stood back and watched with relish. He had captured them. They were caught in his silk threads, and his plan became a grand design. I was silent, but a window was opening. I could see the perfect way to jumpstart the campaign. Finally, I tired of the drivel and spoke up.

"I think I know how to get this thing off the ground." All eyes turned to glare. The eyes of judgment were on the Jezebel, and truthfully, they did not want to hear.

"Really, Judy. What's that?" Rod asked in a slightly condescending way.

I gulped at the frigid air. Obviously, he was expecting a challenge, but I surprised him. I fully supported this new vision of his.

"Have one seminar, one mass meeting of the struggling entrepreneurs. No charge. Send out a series of flyers announcing the greatest opportunity for their fledgling enterprises, a chance to double revenues overnight. Pique their curiosity. Talk about the takeover of corporate

America, of Big Brother, and of Uncle Sam. Use the current statistics that cannot be denied. The mom-and-pop operations are dying. Small companies are being bled dry. Appeal to their sense of justice, and offer them the freedom to change, to take control, to compete. Show them how to stand together and reclaim their destiny. It can be done in one night. With you preaching the dream, Rod," I stroked. "I guarantee you'll have a seventy-five percent signup, maybe more. It will happen fast, and it will immediately put Global back in the black!"

When I finished, everyone was quiet. You could have heard a pin drop; even Rod didn't know what to say. Finally, Seattle Sandy ventured forth. "Judy, that's brilliant. How did you ever get so smart? That really is our answer."

Rod was not so sure. "Your idea has merit. I'd like to talk more about it later."

Later? Why later? What's wrong with now?

Someone else discounted my idea and offered a ridiculous alternative. The suggestions started buzzing again, and I stared. *No wonder they never get anywhere.*

Aaron finally silenced the room with yet another idea, a good one, but in my opinion, one that would take far too long to accomplish the goal. Rod liked it, though, and said so.

"That's exactly what I was thinking. Thank you, Aaron."

Damn you, Rod. Your mightier-than-thou attitude is going to kill everyone. It was useless, however. I left amid the uproar and drove home. Rod had sung his song. He had a golden dream, a pipe dream, in my opinion. Well, let it be done right now, Mr. Steersman. Steer your crew onto hell's forsaken shores. See if I care.

CHAPTER 15

Letting Go

THE PHONE RANG, but I ignored it. Then I heard the rumble. The roar of his diesel truck was headed my way. I flipped off the light in my headboard, put down my book, and grabbed the dogs. When the doorbell rang, they tried to race off, but I had them collared. "Quiet," I scolded firmly. Next, the phone. He was using his cell. Buster emitted a growl, and my heart jumped to my throat. Would Rod try the windows again? Would he break one to get in? I knew he would be angry. He hated it when I took off, but I didn't care. "Serves you right, Mr. God."

Finally, the vehicle moved away. *He's probably right around the corner*, I thought. Waiting and watching, wondering when I'll get home. I left the light off to continue my ruse. I also closed my bedroom door so the dogs would not start barking if he tried again. Thankfully, he did not.

"Guess he must have gone home after all," I said to the puppies the next morning. They were clamoring to get out, so I left the slider open while I made coffee. Since they didn't like to be outside without me, I went to keep them company while the java brewed. I had no sooner sat down than I heard a clinking at the gate. I knew it was Rod and there was no escape, so I waited.

"Good morning," I said, as he passed me and went directly into the house. I did not move. After a few minutes, he returned to the patio.

"Where'd you go last night?"

"What do you mean?"

"You left me. Who'd you go out with?"

"I didn't go out, Rod. After the meeting, I came straight home. I was here when you dropped by."

He was crushed. "I needed you last night, Judy. How can you run out on me that way?"

"How can you discount me that way?" I retaliated.

"I didn't. I said I liked your idea, didn't I?"

"In a breath, barely audible. You embarrassed me, Rod. It was more of the same, and I'm sick of it. Do me a favor and leave me out of your business."

"I can't! I don't even want it if you're not there. You're Mrs. Global, for crying out loud."

"Not anymore, Rod. Not anymore. What are you doing here anyway?"

This question made him wilt. I decided to ease up. "Sit down, Rod. Would you like a cup of coffee?"

"Please."

Returning with two steamy mugs, I made a peace offering. "I loved your idea, Rod. Looks like your first Vision Quest assemblage was a success."

"It doesn't matter."

"Why? How can you say that?"

"I've lost you. It's not the same."

"You haven't lost me, Rod. I'll still be here for you. I just don't want to have anything to do with Global."

"I'm broke, Judy. It's over."

Fatal words. Frightening words coming from Rod.

"How bad is it?" I asked.

"They're going to lock us out next week."

"What!" I exclaimed. My name was on that lease. "How far behind are you?"

"Two months."

"Well, that's manageable. Launch your new program, and you'll have it overnight."

"We need money for that, too."

"Not very much. At least not if you do it my way."

"Can you help me, Judy?"

I was aghast. He was talking dollars, and I couldn't believe he was asking. "No, Rod. You know I can't. I'm broke. I haven't even made a house payment this month."

"You haven't?"

"No! I'm tapped out. Money doesn't grow on trees, you know."

"Well, your book? How can you afford ...?"

"Rod. I'm holding on, because I expect an income tax refund, but right now I'm down to grocery money only."

He shifted in his chair. "A refund? How much?"

Dream on, darlin'. "Enough, Rod. Enough to continue my work, but I have no way of knowing when it will get here, or if it will get here. They could still pull an audit, but right now I'm willing to wait."

After talking about his circumstances, we decided he needed about twenty thousand dollars. It wasn't much, considering, but his situation was desperate, even more desperate than mine. Rod's assembly gathering had been his final attempt to secure funds, but his team refused to feed the till. They no longer trusted their leader. He was simply too unpredictable. One day he'd be fully present, and the next he'd exhibit the old paranoia. When this happened, progress was slow and profits trickled. *What a shame*, I thought. Rod was truly inspired this time. His idea was brilliant and cost effective, too, but it was too little, too late.

"Rod, surely you can come up with enough money to pay the rent. If you don't, the landlord will seize Global's property, and until you make good on the debt, you won't even have access to your records. The phones will go unanswered and so will your mail. Pretty soon your dealers and customers will start calling the Better Business Bureau and Consumer Affairs. Next the District Attorney will get involved and you'll find yourself under investigation. Honey, you can't let that happen. You must do something!"

"But what?"

"I don't know. What about your family? Can't they help?"

He didn't say and grew distant. Finally, he beseeched me. "Judy, please don't leave me."

"I'm not going anywhere, Rod."

"You promised. You promised never to leave me alone."

"And I haven't, and I won't. I'll always be your friend. I'll always love you. You know that."

He was extremely fragile. I could see it in every movement, in every breath, in the flash of his eyes, and in the quivering of his lips. Rod's world was crumbling, and this time there was no way to save it. Shaking from the realization of it all, he said, "Judy, I can't be alone right now. I need you by my side."

I remembered the broken cupboards, the shattered glass, the hands around my throat, and I was at a loss for words. I went into the house, made my way to the back bathroom, and changed into my suit. Then I came out and headed for the glass door. "Where are you going?" he cried.

"Swimming," I said, without emotion.

He followed me, and halfway to the gate, he grabbed me. "No!" he cried. "You can't go. Not now!"

"You're hurting me, Rod."

"How can you do this? How can you abandon me?"

"I'm not, but I cannot help you and trying to make me stay isn't the answer either."

He tightened his grip.

"Rod! Using force won't help! Don't you see, that's exactly what caused this whole ugly situation in the first place?"

The release was instant. "It is?" he asked in that little boy voice.

"Yes, it is," I said, and walked out the back gate.

He was gone when I returned to the house, but when he came back that night and rang the doorbell, I let him in and never asked him to leave. It was not the time.

"Will you come with me to the office, Judy?" he asked the next morning.

I stared.

"I'm only meeting Sandy and Nancy. We're going to discuss options, but we've already officially closed. Everyone has been notified, and the voicemail message effectively says we'll be reorganizing for a few days. Just be a friend and hang out with me, that's all."

After some more assurances, I agreed, and we left in his truck. I was trapped, but I also knew the support was crucial. As the day progressed it got a little scary watching Rod unravel when it became evident that he would have to pull up stakes. A move was his only hope. "I can't let these people down!" he cried.

Sandy tried to calm him. "You won't, but we must save the furniture and equipment. There's too much invested here and we can't lose it."

At one point, Sandy and Nancy left to get us some food, and I asked Rod to take me home. "NO! Judy, I need you."

"I have things to do, Rod."

He pinched my arm and pushed me down. "You're not going anywhere. If you leave, I'll lose my equilibrium."

The bully was back. I stood from the couch and confronted him. "I know no such thing. You've always managed before, and there's absolutely nothing I can do here. I want to go home."

A frightened angry boy emerged. "Why? Why do you always do this? Why do you want to destroy me? All I ever did was love you. Why do you keep running away?"

"I'm not running anywhere, Rod."

"Who are you going to tell? You guys did this, didn't you? This is what you wanted all along."

Danger. The eyes were darting, like black flashes of doom, twitching to and fro. I sat back down. Great tears welled in my soft baby blues, and my despair brought him around. "I'm sorry, Judy. I didn't mean that, but please, you can't go. You are my only hope. You are the one who brings me balance. Don't abandon me now. I'll never make it."

He was fiercely sincere. "Alright, Rod, I'll stay. I'll stay as long as you like, but I need something from you."

"What?" he asked, mashing his eyebrows together.

"I'll promise to remain by your side. I won't run away, or try to escape, and I'll submit to your wishes until you feel safe. When you think you are able to stand on your own, I need you to tell me, and then you must let me go. Promise me, Rod, when you're capable, you'll release me. I need to be free, honey. I have a dream of my own."

"Okay," he said simply.

I was appealing to Rod on a very deep level. Nothing was more important to him than pursuing his dream. So, I asked and then I gave up. I allowed him his whims, supported his every action, and never once considered running away.

We were stuck like glue, and Rod grew confident. He took charge when the movers arrived, and they packed with precision. A rented semi-truck was filled as well as two flatbed trailers, one of which was hooked to his Dodge Ram. It took two days to complete the job, and all this time he didn't know where he was going. Finally, he said, "Judy, I've got to get out of this town."

"Are you sure? You've got an awful lot of support here. I know you could set up shop cheaper. Just sell one of the spas, and you'll be on your way again."

"Judy, I need to honor my wife."

I was surprised. Surprised, but delighted. "Yes. Yes, you do, Rod. She deserves that."

"That and a lot more. I need my family, too. I miss my boys."

"I know, honey. And you'll soon have another child, probably a daughter, and it would be wonderful if she could know her daddy."

"I've just got to go. I can't do it again, not here."

I was trying to be supportive without jumping for joy. "Okay, Rod."

"I'll find the strength to restart if I get back into the mountains. I need trees. I need green."

"I can understand that."

"Judy, I'm going home."

He was excited, and I stilled. My heart skipped a beat. Would he really do it? I didn't know, and wasn't sure what to say, so I communicated without words. I simply kissed him. Softly, with no urgency, I leaned forward and touched my lips to his. He made no move, so I did it again. This time, I traced the inner folds of his mouth with my tongue. He lifted me into his arms and took me to bed. We united in mind, body, and soul, and for the rest of that night, nothing came between us.

"Hi, soulmate," he said sweetly the next morning.

He was holding two mugs, and the aroma warmed my senses. "What are you doing up?" I asked, reaching for one of the cups.

"Arranging. I just talked to Sandy. He and Nancy are with me all the way."

Still? He was still on track to leave. "Really? They want to go to Oregon?"

"They have family there. They're happy about it."

"Well, that's good. You'll need help, and at least they understand the system."

"Judy," he said, and paused.

Gulp. I knew what was coming.

"Judy, come with me."

"Oh, sure, Mary Ann would love that one. Honey, I'm home. I just brought my mistress along for good luck."

Rod was not amused. "I'm serious. I want you two to get better acquainted. I need someone to help me with the drive, and more than anything, I'd like to go into the hills with you. Mary Ann would understand. She'd even appreciate it. Come on, I'll fly you home from Eugene."

"Rod?"

"I'm not kidding. Mary Ann loves you, Judy."

"And I love her, but three is a crowd. Just who in the heck would you sleep with while I visited?"

He hadn't considered this, and I really didn't expect an answer. Knowing Rod, he'd want us both in his bed. Well, it didn't matter. I had no intention of doing such a thing. "No, Rod, really, I have got to get on with my life. I need to begin rebuilding for myself."

"Then come halfway. Go with me as far as Reno. We'll spend a few days, and then I can go on alone."

Somehow that sounded painful. "I can't, Rod. I just can't."

"Judy?"

"No. Honey, I'm sorry. It's impossible."

He was about to object when the phone rang. *Saved by the bell,* I thought, as he moved to my home office to take the call. I relaxed and sipped at the rich cup of gourmet coffee. It was delicious. When he came back, he did not ask again. He used the language of love, and we languished for a couple of hours. Finally, he got up to shower.

"Sandy and Nancy will be here about noon," he said, turning on the water. "Right after they pick up Mandy."

"Mandy?" What does she have to do with this?

"Yes. Mandy's volunteered to help me make the drive. She wanted a break before going back to work anyway. I told her I'd compensate her and buy her a ticket home. She's happy and it'll do her good to get out of town."

"Oh," I said as he closed the shower door behind him. I gulped again, but this time the brew tasted bitter. Still, I drank it and prayed for courage.

Downstairs in the kitchen, while we were having a bite to eat, Rod said, "Judy, do you have any extra cash? It took more than I expected to close the shop. I'm afraid I may come up short for the trip."

"Can't help you in the cash department, but I'll loan you my gas credit card if you promise to send it back as soon as you get there."

"You'd do that?"

"Sure. I wouldn't want you to get stuck halfway."

"Thanks," he said, but he seemed worried.

"If you really need cash, you could pawn your Rolex."

"My Rolex!" he exclaimed. "But you gave me that! My watch symbolizes too much, Judy. I could never part with it!"

I was irritated. "I didn't give you that watch, Rod. I financed it for you. You are still making the payments, aren't you?"

My question startled him. "Yes, of course, but I still consider it a gift from you. You made it possible."

"Well, you can buy it back. You don't have to lose it. Just use it to float a loan."

He thought about this, and finally decided he had no

choice. We left a note for Sandy, Nancy, and Mandy, in case they arrived before our return. Then we left to hock his precious showpiece.

"Down Rainbow and left on Charleston. There's one just past Jones, on the north side," I said.

"Know your way around Pawn City, do you, Ms. Burr?"

"Yep. Speicher was a gambler. When he ran out of cash, he'd pawn his gold. The guy was outrageous, never knew when to give up."

Rod was indignant. He could not fathom my marriage to such a renegade. "Well, God knew, and he stopped him dead in his tracks. That one got what he deserved."

"Didn't he though?" Speicher had recently passed. He had recovered from a hit and run, but the surgeries weakened his heart and it gave out. Knowing Speicher, I suspected his death might have been hastened by drugs, but that was speculation on my part. *Live by the sword, die by the sword*. Such is the life of an outlaw.

Finally, it was over. Rod had cash, a credit card, companions to help him, and a driver, too. They were ready, and I wished them well.

"I'll be out in a minute," Rod said to his traveling buddies. When they walked out the door, he turned to me. "Judy?"

Words were difficult. This was goodbye. "I love you, Rod."

"I love you, too. More than you'll ever know."

"Oh, I know, honey. I know. You take care of yourself, will you?"

"I'll be fine. And I will rebuild," he stated enthusiastically.

"I believe you."

"I'm going to honor all my commitments—yours, too. One day I'll make you a rich woman, Ms. Burr."

"You just enjoy your life, Rod. Forget about the eye of the tiger and go be with those kids. Be a good dad. Have some fun."

He brightened. "So, you think I'm going to have a little girl, do you?"

"I sure do."

"Judy, until I met you, I worried about being blessed with a daughter. Now I can't wait."

"She'll be good for you," I said smiling. "You give her a kiss for me, will you? And call as soon as she's born. I'll be anxious to hear."

"I will. You'll be the first to know."

"And Rod ..."

"What?"

"Take care of that partner of yours. Take care of Mary Ann."

"I'll honor Mary Ann as my wife, Judy, but you will always be my partner. You will remain Mrs. Global for the rest of my life. Nothing can ever change that."

"Well, okay then, Mr. Global. You go give them hell. One day we'll celebrate as soulmates, huh?"

"One day soon," he said, and kissed me. Then he left.

I didn't walk outside. I couldn't. My friend was pulling up stakes, and I didn't know how to feel. I closed the door and bolted the lock, then went out back. The dogs raced, but I barely noticed. It was that missing tooth again. The pain was gone, but an empty socket remained.

PART III

THE LION'S DEN

CHAPTER 16

The Flower of Creation

I DID NOT IMMEDIATELY RETURN to my keyboard. My creative flair was gone and typing felt impossible. I was out of sorts, oddly adrift, and wondered when I'd wash up on shore. I sat in front of the blurry television, and within days I managed to eat most of my meager stock of food. Necessity drove me to the grocery store, and although I was careful, when the clerk tallied me out, I was over. My check would bounce, and I had no means of beefing up my account. Action was required.

I remembered Rod's loan and decided to follow his example. I gathered my jewelry and made the trip. Down Rainbow and left on Charleston. Pawn city here I come. Like Rod, I was sorely disappointed by the wad of dollars, but it was enough for a while. Hopefully, the refund check would arrive. Feeling secure for the moment, I went visiting. I had been avoiding my daughter because I knew she'd question me about Rod. Now he was gone, and I needed to talk.

"Mom!" she said happily as I came through the back gate. She was on a raft, basking in the pool, belly up, wet blonde hair slicked back against her head.

"Hi! I see you're enjoying yourself. Where's Marie?"

"She's asleep," she said, climbing up the stairs and wrapping her burgeoning belly in a towel.

"That barely goes around you, Pam. Don't you have any beach towels?"

"Not many. What we do have are in the laundry."

I laughed. "Oh well, you'll soon need a blanket, anyway."

"Thanks a lot, Mom."

"Just kidding. You look great. That baby's sure out front!"

"Tell me about it!" she said, doing a walrus wiggle to get into a lounge chair.

I chuckled again. "Dang, girl, it looks like you're carrying twins."

"Better not be. Can you imagine? I swear, Mom, I'd die. I wouldn't even know where to put two babies. At least the girls can share a bedroom."

Girls. The word had a nice ring. My little girl was all grown up and had girls of her own. *The cycle of life*. What a miracle.

"So, what's up?" she asked.

"Not much," I said before giving her my news. "Well, he's gone."

"Gone? You mean Rod?"

"Yep. He packed everything up and left town."

"Everything?" She obviously thought this was too good to be true.

"Everything. Every stick of furniture, all the equipment, and the computers, too. Hauled it all out."

"What!" she exclaimed. "He packed out Global, too?"

"Yes, Global's gone. At least the Las Vegas hold is. Rod says he's starting over in Oregon."

"Really! That's amazing. He took it all? You let him do that?"

"None of that stuff means anything to me."

"But you bought it, Mom. It was your money!"

"Yes, but I'm glad to see the remnants of it disappear. Kind of feels good."

"Leaving it all behind, are you?"

"That's the idea. No more bad taste. Now the bitter past of Pioneer and Global can be forgotten. Out of sight, out of mind."

"Wow!" She was astounded. "Just like that he picked up stakes and moved? I can't believe it. I thought he'd never let go."

"It is his intention to rebuild."

"What a nightmare. He'd be better off filing bankruptcy."

"Not really. I think he's doing the right thing. Global is his dream, and he can't run from it. Besides, can you imagine the respect he'll gain by coming from the depths? Honoring those commitments will demonstrate his worth. When he does rise from the ashes, no one will ever doubt him again. Better yet, he'll never again doubt himself."

"Do you think that's possible?"

"I think if anybody can do it, Rod can. He's capable, but he needs to heal. Hopefully, his wife and children will help restore his sanity."

"Mom?"

"What?"

"How can Mary Ann welcome him back after all this? I could never forgive my husband like that. I'd hate him. I'd rake him over the coals. I'd take him for every penny."

"I'm not sure. I could never tolerate my man stepping out on me, but Mary Ann has a forgiving nature. She believes God has special plans for her husband. That's why she waited patiently. Just being the mother of his children has been enough for her. She's been the perfect submissive wife."

"Submissive? You mean she blindly looked the other way while he committed adultery?"

"Rod told me she hates the sin, but not the sinner."

Pam rolled her eyes.

"Think about it. She let him go, refused to judge, and now he's returning to her side. She was willing to wait, and he's on the way home."

My daughter was listening.

"I think she's an amazing woman, Pam. One night we were having a conversation about her wayward husband, and something she said made me laugh. I told her she was the smart one. She was out of the line of fire and simply waiting for him to grow up. I said, 'Rod's high maintenance. At least you have some peace while he gets his act together. Sowing his wild oats right now, that's all. One day he'll find himself, and then he'll make a fine husband.'"

"You said that?"

"I did, and you know what? She agreed with me! I'm telling you, Mary Ann's faith is remarkable. She really believes in Rod."

"Well, she can have him. I'm glad he's gone."

I ignored the comment. "Know something else, Pam. It wasn't until I agreed to stay with him that I finally got what I wanted."

"You went back with that man?"

"For a few days. He was losing his balance and barged into my life again. I didn't have a whole lot of choice, but I told him I'd let him come home on one condition."

"What was that?"

"I made him promise to release me as soon as he felt capable."

"And he did."

"Amazing, isn't it? I swear Pam, I was scared to death, but I decided to place my trust in God. I just gave up. Rod got what he wanted, and then so did I."

"What do you mean?"

"Don't you see? He's always believed the woman should

submit to the man."

"What a bunch of crap."

"I agree, but I did it. I gave up control, and in less than two days he set me free. I had to surrender before I could win."

"Now that's one for the books."

"Isn't it, though," I said.

"So, what now?"

"Funny you should ask. I guess that's why I'm here. I feel lost. I keep hearing this tune from Evita. Something about 'Where do I go now? So, what happens now?' I've got Madonna on my mind, and she's haunting me."

"Maybe you should go back to work. It would be good for you, Mom."

"I've thought about it, but I don't have the heart. I hate the idea of starting over. I'd have to take an entry level job and I can't imagine working for an hourly wage. Think about it, I'd probably regain my credibility, and then the judge would slam down his mallet. Maybe I won't go to prison, but thinking about the possibility dampens my desire. Besides, I'm a felon now. Employers don't like ex-cons."

"Any employer would be lucky to have you. You only need to get your foot in the door."

"Thanks, baby, but these shoes are stuck in wet cement. I'd rather spend this time trying to write. How else will I find out if I have any talent?"

"You could do both."

"Are you kidding? You of all people know how draining a full-time job is. Anyway, I'm sick to death of the business world."

"Mom, you've had a hard time. You'd grow to love it again. You only need to join the right company."

I was growing weary; all this conversation was convincing me to follow my original intention. "You know something, Pam. This is my opportunity to grow. I'm finally free. All the garbage of the last twelve years is gone, and now is the time. If I don't seize the moment, I'm a fool."

"Carpe diem," she said.

"You got it. Nope, I'm going home. I have a book to write, and right now it's my reason for living."

"Well, alrighty now. That's more like it, but how about some lunch first? I'm starving. Want a sandwich?"

"Love one, baby doll. Let's go chow."

~

Thank you, Pam, I said after returning home. I clicked on the computer and tried to remember my most recent thoughts. I was exploring the Five Golden Rings—Hope, Heart, Love, Forgiveness, and Truth—five keys leading to freedom, but something was missing. It was a cycle, as are most things in life. Without these elements one would perish, but what held the rings together? God? Well sure, but that was a bit too esoteric for me. I appreciated a more pragmatic approach, something more tangible. Love, Heart, Hope, Forgiveness, and Truth. Where did they lead? TRUST! Of course, I had known it all along. In fact, I had signed Rod's card, "A gift of trust." His five key principles were linked by trust, and where would we be without that element?

My work for the next few days felt inspired. I marveled at my insights, and at times I had to stop keying in the story to map out my thoughts with pad and pencil. Since I was exploring the intricacies of our "Uncommon Partnership," I drew out the inverted pyramid again, like I had done in our mini suite last winter. I labeled the corners, just like before. Rod was at the bottom and represented Wisdom. Mary Ann and I were above him, to keep him in check. She represented Truth, and I was Power, or the passion that drove us. My hold over Rod had been sexual, but he had feared my love, so much so he had accused me of being a witch. Truly, my love was unconditional, but he couldn't accept what I was offering. His belief system got in the way.

Originally, I thought his guilt stemmed from breaking his marriage vows, but the problem went back to his toddling years. A babysitter had set the nasty cycle in motion, then later his stepfather nurtured it, and so had his evangelic grandfather. Unaware a little boy was trapped in the cycle of abuse, no one extended a hand, but then, how could they? His secret was hidden well. He had lost trust, trust in others, and consequently trust in himself. Until he confessed the story to me, it riddled him with guilt, and the resulting fear was buried in the recesses of his mind.

My story was similar, but different. The Church had betrayed me. Hypocritical and controlling hearts sent me on the run. I tried to find a new place of worship, but there were too many mandates. I simply couldn't accept their doctrines. I remained spiritual and continued to believe in Jesus, but I gave up on organized religion.

Our third partner, Mary Ann, was the one who balanced us. She continued to believe in Rod and what he was doing, and somehow that trust of hers triumphed. Truly, the three of us were soulmates. Our Uncommon Partnership served a grand purpose, and something told me it wasn't so uncommon after all.

Still, there was more. Rod had taught me something else. To manifest a dream, one must believe, and before our belief system could solidify, a giant leap of faith was necessary. "Yes!" I exclaimed. "The cycle of life — it's not five keys, nor is it six. There are eight elements in all. It takes one ring to begin, six more to balance, and a final ring secures the domain. Love starts the process, Heart, Hope, Forgiveness, Truth, Trust, and Faith encircle Love, and finally, the outside circle of Belief binds them. It is the essence of completion, the essence of the divine."

I drew it out on paper, beginning with one circle, and

then expanding to the outside. When I finished, my creation contained a flower, and I remembered the image from my geometry days. I encircled the picture with one final ring, the ring of belief.

"The flower of creation," I said. "From start to finish." I knew I could make the image with a compass, and I vowed to pick one up at the office supply store.

I like that, I said to myself.

I thought about Rod and how our relationship had turned sour. The first time he became physically abusive I was appalled, not so much at him, but myself. I couldn't understand how I had managed to do it again. Why had I — once again — hooked up with a controller? What was wrong with me? Now, it was starting to make sense.

Rod and I came together to further our spiritual growth and to begin healing from old childhood wounds. Thinking along these lines made me feel more positive, and in fact, I felt enlightened somehow. Global was gone, but I was found. Thank you, Rod, I whispered. Thank you, Mary Ann. I closed my notebook and thought how intriguing it all was.

"What a joy it is to be alive," I said. "And all because I fell in love. LOVE is the beginning and the end, the alpha and the omega."

CHAPTER 17

Rape

I FLOATED ON A CLOUD for some time, my mental discoveries seemed to be coming from a source outside myself. Life would truly have been grand, except for one thing — money. I was short on cash.

After returning home from an errand one afternoon, I pulled into the driveway as usual. Since the automatic opener had long ago failed, I parked and got out of my car to open the garage door manually. I pulled on the aluminum, but it stuck midway. Now what? I wondered. Try as I might, I could not get the enclosure to open, so I gave up and pushed down. It wouldn't move in that direction either. The slider used to wedge out the world would not budge. I went through the house by means of the front door, and tried from the inside, but to no avail. Finally, I called a repairman.

"The casing is warped, ma'am. It needs to be replaced."

Naturally, I thought. I'm busted and this happens. "Well, how much will that cost?"

It turned out the entire door had to go. A new one was ordered, and I paid extra to have the job completed quickly. I did not feel safe with everything exposed, so I relinquished the better part of my cache to have it fixed. There were other things, too. I owed my mother money. When I'd needed funds to close on my big house, she helped me. My Lexus was used as collateral, but it was her name on the loan. I could not neglect that responsibility. Her Scorpio nature was too unforgiving, and of course, I had to pay my utility bills. I could not be without water, gas, or power. The mortgage payment I delayed. I'd pay that after the IRS came through, but I was still down to grocery money only. Again I was busted, and again I knew drastic action was required. But what? The 'ole tune returned. What happens now? Where do I go now? I cried because I thought the inevitable was at hand. I would have to get a job after all, and I hated the idea of giving up. Help me, my angels, tell me what to do.

The next morning, I had the answer. "Thank you," I said, as I dialed the newspaper classified section. This time I didn't advertise for a roommate; rather, I intended to sell my precious jewels. They were pawned, but if I released them completely, they'd carry me for a few more months.

"Anything else you'd like us to list?" the operator asked.

"Yes," I said. "A silver and gold Mariner Rolex, with a blue face." *If all else fails,* I thought, *at least the watch will sell. I can buy Rod another one when the time is right.*

When the ad came out, my phone rang off the hook. Unfortunately, no one wanted my five-carat diamond ring or my other jewelry. It was the watch that was coveted. I took names and numbers, promising to call back, but as the day wore on, I started to feel desperate. Maybe my diamonds wouldn't carry me after all.

The second day a man called. "Describe the ring for me," he said.

"It's a two-and-a-half-carat solitaire surrounded by another two-and-a-half carats of baguettes, truly beautiful."

"Can I see it?"

I explained it was at the pawn shop and said he'd have

to be a serious buyer to look at it. "I've got an appraisal for it and a picture, but I can't get it out of hock myself. You'll have to bring cash to view it."

"How about the Rolex?" he asked. "Do you still have it?"

"Yes, but it's pawned as well."

"That's okay. I know exactly what the watch looks like. When can I meet you?"

My heart leapt. "How about noon?"

"That's good for me," he said.

I hung up the phone, praying he would take the ring. "If only I can get by without losing Rod's watch," I said.

It was not meant to be. In fact, the gentleman didn't want my ring after all, at least not at my asking price. We haggled for a while, and I became stubborn. "Look," I said finally. "I need more money than that. I'm sorry, but I can't cut the Rolex loose unless you buy the ring as well." His wife was with him. She hadn't accompanied him into the store, but now he wanted to show her the diamond.

"Okay," I agreed. "I'll wait in my car. When you decide, come join me here." It was a calculated risk, as was telling him to meet me in my vehicle, but I was trying to trust. I had faith, and I truly believed I was doing the right thing.

"Judy," he said, taking the seat beside me. "You drive a hard bargain, but we'll agree to your terms. My wife feels certain we can sell your ring at our jewelry store."

"Great," I said. We exchanged cash for diamonds and gold and then parted company. I was back in business. Sorry Rod, but it was your turn to ante up. Besides, I justified, it was my watch anyway. No doubt you've defaulted on the payments. Probably the note will soon haunt me.

After that I felt like celebrating. I called my mother, "Want to do lunch?"

"Sure," she said. "Where do you want to meet?"

"I'll pick you up, Mom. Give you a chance to get ready.

I'm already out and about."

"Okay, see you in a few minutes."

When I arrived at her apartment, I counted out four one hundred dollar bills. "Here, Mom. Here's another payment."

"You don't have to do that, Judy. I don't need to make the payment for a couple of weeks."

"Thanks, but right now I've got the money, so take it. The way my life is going, there's no telling where I'll be in a couple of weeks."

"You sure?"

"Positive. So, what sounds good? Want to go for pasta? Or maybe Chinese?"

"Let's do pasta. I don't have much of a stomach for Chinese these days."

When we were seated comfortably, had placed our order, and were imbibing in a glass of vino, I said, "Mom, I've been curious about something."

"What?"

"Remember St. L. & S.?"

"Sure, what about it?"

"Well, do you know why Father John lost the parish?"

"Not really. He had a breakdown, I think."

"That's what I thought, but why did we go to his house that day? You made me wait in the car. What did you do in there?"

She looked up curiously and gulped at her wine. "That was a long time ago. I really don't remember."

"You sure? Try to think back. It was right after the church began to fragment, right after the uproar about speaking in tongues."

She contemplated briefly, and then said, "I really don't know why we went over there."

"Well, why did you stop attending services? You quit

going to St. Luke and St. Stephen's long before I did, and I remember having to walk up that hill with Shirley and Jana. You didn't even want to drive us to church."

"Guess I drifted away. Maybe I got lazy or maybe I wanted you to quit, too. I don't know. Those people were too hypocritical for me."

"But why? Were you involved in that devil nonsense?"

"That what?" she asked.

"The laying on of hands? The speaking in tongues stuff?"

"No. You told me about those services, but I never attended one."

"They were casting out demons," I said.

"Demons? You're kidding?"

"No, Mom, I'm not."

"Nothing like that was happening while I was there."

I was relieved for some reason. "It was awful. At first, I accepted the practice, but watching my friends speak gibberish was too much. I never wanted to try it."

"Thank God for that," she said, obviously grateful I hadn't been indoctrinated.

"I'll tell you, the whole ugly business sent me on the run. To this day, I'm curious. I wonder, were those kids really speaking a foreign language, or were they simply blathering nonsense?"

"I have no idea," she said.

I wasn't altogether convinced she didn't know more, but I felt like I shouldn't press the issue. I had another question. "Mom?"

"Hmm?" she responded absentmindedly. Just then the food arrived, so I waited.

"Mom, why did you have a nervous breakdown?"

"Judy!" she objected.

"I know it was a long time ago, but there's something

missing for me. I'm trying to fill in a few holes. Why do you suppose I can't remember my childhood?"

She wasn't a bit hostile. In fact, she was intrigued. "I have no idea. I've always wondered myself."

"Well, why did you experience a mental collapse? What happened?"

"Life was difficult, Judy. Three little girls were a handful and working full time was exhausting."

"I'm sure. I'll bet Dad wasn't much help, was he?"

"No, he was old school. I had to do it all. I guess I couldn't cope."

"That's it? You were institutionalized because you couldn't cope? You got tired?"

She stared. "Judy, your father had an affair."

If I had been younger, I might have balked, but I was a woman of the world. "Other men have affairs, but their wives don't end up hospitalized. Mom, is there anything in our background that would explain why all three of us girls are dysfunctional when it comes to men? Could it be possible Shirley was really molested? I'm not suggesting Dad. I would never believe such a thing, but maybe by some other family member, someone trusted?"

The question grieved her. "God, I really don't know. If anything did happen, I wasn't aware of it."

"Did you ever wonder?"

"No, can't say as I did. I was just extremely unhappy in those days. Guess I bailed out for a while. I needed a break."

It was time to ease up on my mother. "Well, I can understand that. I don't know how you did it. My kids were nine years apart, and I only had two of them. Three girls close in age would drive anyone crazy. So, you want dessert?"

Later, safely tucked away in my home, I reflected on the delicate human psyche. *So many shattered souls,* I thought. So much pain. But why? And why do people cope so differently? Some souls are healthy despite the worst conditions, more capable of handling stress. Others unravel in the face of adversity. My youngest sister had been one of those casualties, so had my most recent husband, and now there was Rod.

Many people and several circumstances contributed to Rod's breakdown, but the greatest of those was me. He fell in love with me and even told me he might be willing to sell his soul to share my bed. I thought he was joking, but he was serious, deadly serious. When word of our affair got out, and others started to judge him, he made excuses, saying he was bewitched. I must be trampling in the devil's playground, otherwise, he wouldn't be under such a powerful spell. Still, he loved me, and it was his Christian duty to save me. His delusions grew, and I allowed him to lay hands on me.

How ridiculous, Judy, I said to myself. What a fool you were. Your sacrifice accomplished nothing, absolutely nothing.

Rape. That's what it was. Or at least it felt like rape.

I looked up the word. "Rape: an act or instance of robbing or despoiling a person by force." Webster's dictionary was clear.

Rod had tried to force his beliefs on me. Why do Christians do that? What can they hope to accomplish with hell, fire, and brimstone? Power? Control? Certainly, the Church makes money that way. They use fear to bring in their flock, and they preach forgiveness to keep them in check. What a crock! What a trap!

Well, it didn't matter. Rod was gone and I was free. At least my mind was free, and for the time being, I still controlled my body.

Pondering my situation, I began to play with my circles again, but this time I used them differently. "History repeats," I said aloud. "What goes around, comes around."

I thought about Rod and wondered about his cycle of

destruction. He had a history of building up and tearing down. He had done it with Coastline, and now Global had suffered the same dismal fate, but why?

Success usually comes to those who feel worthy, and Rod's ego was fragile. As a young person, his mother failed to protect him and his father failed to validate his athletic prowess. No wonder he was clinging desperately to Jesus Christ. He had his wife, Mary Ann, but he was supposed to lead her, not lean on her. That's what he said. "It is a man's duty to provide headship for the family. If the husband can't do that much, he simply does not deserve to be loved."

That was what Rod believed. Without a doubt, he had swallowed the Christian dogma, hook, line, and sinker. And, wow, hadn't it taken him down! *Too bad he didn't learn the lesson of forgiveness,* I thought. "The rings, Rod. Don't forget the rings. Begin by forgiving yourself. It's a small price to pay. Hang on, baby. You'll make it yet."

CHAPTER 18

Devil in Disguise

HOW MANY DAYS OR WEEKS, I wasn't sure, but for a while life was good. I began to think Rod was doing well, since he hadn't called, and I was glad. Still, I missed him.

It's only that tooth, Judy. I reassured myself. There's a hole, but you'll get over it.

And I believed I would. Then one morning he showed up. Just like he had one time before, he came slinking through the back gate.

When the dogs raced away, I knew instantly that Rod had come calling. My mind flashed on the Rolex. He would not be happy. Maybe the panic showed on my face. I don't know, but when he rounded the corner that morning, his reaction was startling.

He came through the gate with purpose, and upon reaching me, demanded I go inside.

"No," I said defiantly. I could tell he was angry, and I had no intention of sequestering myself behind closed doors. At least outside I could scream, possibly getting a neighbor's attention.

"Get up, Judy. Now!" he emphasized.

"What are you doing here, Rod?" I asked.

He was indignant. "What are you doing, you mean? Now you've done it. Come on, I want to talk to him."

"Who?"

"You know who," he said, grabbing my hand.

Relief flooded me. Rod was obsessing about a man, not a watch. Thank God. My fear turned to anger, and I stood belligerently to follow him.

Without releasing his hold, he took me into the house and up the stairs. He searched each of the bedrooms and my office. Then we went back downstairs and checked that level and the garage. Eventually, he looked at me and appeared lost. "You mean no one is here? You don't have company?"

"No, Rod," I said, jerking my hand free. "I don't have company." I went back outside. Rod was obviously out of his mind. He had conjured up a lover for me, and this figment of his imagination would be tough to dislodge.

"I could have sworn Lou was here. I saw him so clearly," he said.

"Lou!" I cried. "Are you kidding?" Lou was one of Global's dealers, a nice enough guy, but not my type. Rod's paranoia had returned, and he was grasping at straws, focusing on the conspiracy. He had been unable to push the hostile takeover attempt out of his mind, and again, the betrayal was attacking his psyche.

"I'm out of line, aren't I? I've done it again," he said sadly.

I wasn't about to make the situation worse. "Rod, you're having trouble letting go. It's only natural. We shared too much. But believe me, there's no man in my life, not now and probably not for a long time. The only thing I care about is my work, and I want nothing to get in the way."

"Your book?" he asked timidly.

"Yes, honey, my book."

"Are you writing about me?"

He was a frightened young boy, and I knew this alter

ego. That splintered part of his personality could be unpredictable, and right at that moment, he was viewing me as the enemy. I might as well have been sitting there with a bat across my lap, because that's what my book looked like to him. I was the wicked stepfather threatening to beat him if he blinked. Unfortunately, Rod was no longer a helpless twelve-year-old boy. He was, in fact, a dangerously grown man, and I did not pretend otherwise.

"Well, of course I'm writing about you. You are my hero, Rod. You saved me, honey. Without you, I would have wandered aimlessly in the darkness. Now I have the light of Jesus Christ to guide me."

I reached him. The slant fell from his eyes and his brow softened. "Really, Judy? You're not going to discredit me?"

"How could I? I love you. I will always love you. You know that."

"You're not angry I left?"

"I miss you, Rod, but really, I'm happier now than I have been in a long time. In fact, I believe my writing is inspired."

Finally, a smile, a glimmer of hope. "Really?"

"Seriously," I said, getting excited about my recent revelations. "Sometimes I'm amazed by my thoughts. They feel like they're coming from somewhere outside of myself."

"You've stepped into the fourth dimension," he said knowingly.

The Rod I understood was coming forward. "I guess. All I know is I am content, and without a doubt, that's the message I intend to relay. Everyone is going to win in my book, and especially you — you and that angel wife of yours. How is Mary Ann, by the way?"

A shadow fell across his face. "She's okay, I guess."

"You guess! What do you mean, you guess?"

"Well," he said hesitantly. "She misses me. I haven't been home."

"What! Why not?"

The leader took over, and Rod threw back his shoulders. "I had to set up shop outside of Reno. We checked the state statutes and discovered there might be a problem if we tried to take Global's assets across the state line."

Somehow, I doubted it. I wasn't familiar with the relevant corporate regulations, but this sounded like one of Rod's convenient fibs, one that would justify his change of plans. "Well, Reno is nice and it's not too far from Eugene. Gosh, you can drive home to see the kids."

Without a reprimand, he continued. "Yes, and you can come up. You can visit too, Judy."

Trouble. "Maybe."

Not good enough. "Really, Judy, I wish you'd join us. At least come long enough to help Sandy, Nancy, and me get started. We've found a great place. It's in Lake Tahoe, sits on eight acres, and has a huge ranch-style house on the land. There's a cottage, too! It's big enough for everyone and everything."

I was not impressed. "How in the heck can you afford a place like that?"

"God works in mysterious ways."

Here we go, I thought. God had just led him down a wrong road to me, but now he was all righteous again.

"We needed money when we got there, so the first thing I did was go to one of the spa stores. I was ready to sell a unit on the cheap, but instead, the owner took an interest in me."

I knew the rest of the story. Rod had preached his dream and had acquired another loyal disciple. "So," I said. "You've opened a new market, one complete with a retail store, and lakefront property?"

"Exactly! It's the most awesome setup you could ever imagine."

"I can imagine, Rod. Believe me, I have a clear picture."

"Will you come then?"

I knew not to reject him. Saying no would only cause Rod to dig in. "I'd love to see it. When the time is right, and we can afford it, I would enjoy visiting. I do not want to get involved, though. I still want nothing to do with Global."

That was enough. "You can come and write," he said. "It's so beautiful, Judy. You'll really get inspired."

Get trapped, you mean. "I'm sure. I've spent some time in Tahoe. It is most definitely God's country."

Point in fact, the only thing I wanted was to get away, and while he went on about his exciting new headquarters, I mentally prepared a move of my own. *I'll rent this place and relocate to a secure apartment building. It is the only way to escape him. He'll never let go.*

Rod stayed that day, the next day, and then the weekend. I allowed him rest and gave him the attention he craved, but our passion failed to flower. It was more like a withering vine, and I wanted the leaves to fall quickly. Each time we made love, I plied my experienced fingers and satiated our cries. When our orgasms passed, I would profess fatigue. I did a lot of sleeping in those days, but all the while I kept wondering. When would he leave?

On Monday, we were hungry, but the cupboards were bare. "I need to go to the store, Rod. Do you want to come?"

"No. I'll hang out. Here, let me give you some money."

I had intended to ask and was glad it hadn't been necessary. I was also relieved to notice he didn't have a huge cache of cash in his wallet. He handed me two one-hundred dollar bills, and I left thinking there would be no mention of the Rolex, at least not on this trip. Thank God.

Shopping on that Monday afternoon felt good, and I took my time. I was free—or relatively so—free from my sidekick, or from the thorn in my side, depending on your point of view. I also had money, and I loaded my grocery cart with purpose. It was windfall, and I was glad to know the pantry would be full again.

When I got home, Rod was not around. I thought he was probably napping and decided to leave him alone. I breathed deeply and went back to the garage to retrieve my packages. Passing between his truck and my Lexus, I noticed the back of his vehicle was still loaded. There were numerous suitcases and several boxes. I even saw a computer.

That's funny, I thought. I wondered why he hadn't unloaded that stuff. A chill swept through me. Was Rod's ranch in Tahoe another fabrication? Why else would Global's goods still be in the back of his truck? I shivered with the thought. What if he really hadn't landed? What if he hadn't established a new Global hold?

Shaking with the idea, I put everything away. When I was done, I meandered around the kitchen, wondering what to do. Should I confront him? I was asking myself, but as it turned out, there was no need. Instead, he confronted me.

He stole down the stairs and surprised me from behind. "Where's my Rolex, Judy?"

My heart crashed to the floor as I spun around. "What do you mean?" I asked innocently.

He brushed by me and hit the playback button on my answering machine. "I saw your ad in an old weekly," the voice said. "If you still have the Rolex, please call me."

"Where is it, Judy?"

"Rod, I had some trouble. Your Rolex can be replaced."

He was horrified. His coveted Rolex was gone. It didn't matter that most of the money was used to cover the damage he'd caused. He wanted his watch, his damn jewel of validation. I was outraged. "I had to sell it. I had no choice."

I didn't see it coming, and the impact left my head spinning and my ears ringing. I had been slapped, backhanded hard across the face. Stars filled my head and I collapsed to the floor. I simply curled into a fetal-like ball and held tight.

Rod paced and raged, but I remained rigid. I was afraid to move, really. I was also afraid to speak, so when he began battering me with words, I sank deeper. He shook me, but I curled tighter. He screamed, but I locked out his cries. I could see my dogs behind the kitchen table. They were hiding in the corner and shaking.

I began to hate Rod.

He was a coward and a bully, but I had to reach him. I started to sob. “I’m sorry, Rod. I didn’t mean to hurt you. I’ll get you another watch somehow. I’ll find a way. Please don’t hate me.”

It worked. Of course, the groveling was effective. It gave him the illusion of power. *Big man,* I thought, coming out of my shell. Big, bad man hit little girl. You asshole! Adrenalin kicked in and my mind began to clear. I was in a dangerous situation, and caution would be required if I hoped to survive.

Rod was confused, pacing. “I have to think,” he said. “God, I can’t believe you did that, Judy. I trusted you. I should never have put you on the pawn ticket, dammit.”

You had no choice, jerk face. If you had a driver’s license it would have been different. Too bad, fool. My thoughts were malicious and vicious, but my mannerisms were soft and subservient. I kept my head down, my eyes tearing, and my mouth shut.

“Okay, write me a check. I want the money.”

I looked at him in disbelief but reached for my purse. I made out a check for twelve hundred dollars.

“That’s it! That’s all you got?” he screamed. “For my Rolex?”

I backed away, out of his range. “Well, after paying the pawn and the fee, that’s all that was left.”

"Judy! Write me a check for twenty-five hundred dollars. I won't take a penny less."

"Alright, Rod, but you won't be able to cash it. I don't have that much."

"What!"

"I've got about eighteen hundred, but that's it."

His eyes were flashing, the black dots twitching to and fro. I brought on more tears. "I was broke, Rod. They were going to shut off the utilities."

He approached me, but I backed off. "Okay, eighteen hundred dollars," he said, and then turned away. He went upstairs as I wrote the check. When he returned, it was with my CPU. "Okay, let's go. You're going to cash it for me."

My computer! He was holding my computer hostage. I glanced at the clock and knew I had him. It was after five, and that meant the drive-thru at my bank would be closed. We'd have to go inside to complete our transaction. When that happened, I would fuck him.

"Sure, honey," I said, dripping with sweetness.

He was settling, but barely.

Just as I expected, the drive-thru was closed, and true to form, Rod refused to let go. Believing I was under his control, he allowed me to park the car. Then he grabbed the keys and ordered me inside. He left the hostage hard drive on the front seat and went in with me. Fortunately, he did not accompany me into line but remained by the door next to the guard. He turned on the charm and chatted with the officer while I waited. When his body language began to slacken, I struck. Turning toward the man in uniform, I held up my check and raised my voice. "Sir! That man is attempting to extort money from me. He's threatened me physically and is forcing me to cash this check."

All eyes turned my way, and while the focus was on me, Rod made his escape. "Stop him!" I screamed, running after him. "He's got my keys. He'll steal my car!"

The guard moved but would not chase down Rod. Instead, he took my arm. "This is police business, ma'am. I have to call a squad car."

"It'll be too late! He'll destroy my house before they get to him. HELP!" I screamed. "That man is stealing my car."

Rod stopped in his tracks and returned to my side. He handed me my keys, gave the guard a shrug, and walked away. I raced to get a head start. Behind the wheel, I put pedal to the metal and sped toward home.

I parked on the street, locked my car, and went into the house via the front door, double dead bolting it behind me. Then I raced upstairs, grabbed his keys, and went to the garage. I needed to move his Dodge to the driveway. It was my only hope. Just as I was attempting to unlock the driver's side door, I heard the crash of glass.

Rod was breaking in! *He must have cut through the neighborhood and jumped cinder block walls*. His nimble lithe body is coming through a window! Fear! My fingers fumbled the keys and I dropped them. Cursing, I retrieved the ring and calmed myself. I managed to get inside, but the passenger window was open. I took time to roll it up. Then I pressed the locks down and started to turn the key. My escape was imminent, but something was wrong. In my confusion, I'd forgotten Rod did not have a garage door opener.

I was trapped.

I knew it was only a matter of minutes before he found me. I jumped out, propelled myself to the switch on the wall, and prayed he was upstairs. Then I raced to retrace my steps. The huge aluminum casing went up and the engine turned over. I slammed the transmission into reverse and was halfway down the drive before he came through the door. He stared, disbelieving, and I flipped him off before driving away. "Motherfucker," I muttered.

Once again, I headed for the clubhouse where I could call 911. This time the police response was immediate. They were already in the neighborhood, and they quickly followed me back to the house. Rod gave them a song and a dance. He told them we had been living together for more than a year and said he was trying to move out. I had made it impossible by taking off with his truck.

I attempted to set the record straight, but I was no match for the silver-tongued devil. They thought his story was credible. I was about to panic when one of the officers came to tell me he was leaving. Rod's girlfriend had arrived, and she had calmed him.

"Tell him I'm filing a restraining order. If he gets within ten feet, I'll have his ass arrested."

The message delivered, Rod left with Mandy. *Good 'ole Mandy.* If she only knew.

I cleaned up the glass, boarded up the window and climbed into the tub. The calming warm waters brought on tears, but attempting to wipe them away made me wince. The slap had been brutal and I knew it would leave an indelible mark. "Bastard," I sobbed. "Stay out of my life, righteous Rod! You're no Christian. In fact, you're a devil in disguise. I hate you!"

It was an emotional proclamation, but the words rang true. Rod really was beginning to look like the epitome of evil, at least to me he was. You tried to destroy me, but I don't fall easily. In fact, if you don't stay away, I'll destroy you, Mr. Rod A. Steersman. If you come near me again, you'll be sorry. I'll take your world apart, partner, and don't think I won't.

My words soothed me. I wanted to hurt Rod, and I did have the power to seize his assets. Trouble was, I didn't want them. Nothing he had was of any value, at least not to me.

All for a stupid watch. How shallow. How ridiculous.

As I vented, fear gave way to exhaustion. I was crashing from an adrenalin rush, so I moved from bath to bed. I knew Rod would not be back. He had Mandy. Sweet Mandy would love playing rescue and his "poor pitiful me" routine would not be wasted. She'd happily give him anything he wanted.

Well, better you than me, Mandy. You can have the president, honey. As far as I'm concerned, the man is demented.

CHAPTER 19

Murphy's Law

I NEVER MOVED FROM THAT BED. I couldn't; I was too depressed. When darkness fell, it mercifully took me with it. In the morning I awoke, but not happily. I was in pain. Turning my head was enough to send a bolt of lightning through my jaw. Rod's damage was extensive. Slowly I moved toward the medicine cabinet, but as I reached for a bottle of aspirin, I grimaced at my reflection. My face was beginning to discolor. *Oh great*, I thought. Now I'd have to hide until the bruising clears. I filled a glass with water and brought the pills to my lips. Another jolt. I could not open wide enough to take the medicine. God, I wonder if he broke my jaw.

Since I was no stranger to the procedure that would follow if there were shattered bones, I cringed at the thought. I shook the idea from my mind and pushed the broken pills through the small space between my teeth. *I'll wait and see*, I said to myself. God forbid I have to relive that experience.

It was the year I turned sixteen, and in those days, we knew how to have fun. We had wild, glorious parties, and there was always a band. Sometimes there were also parents, but for the most part, they left us alone. We were the spoiled suburban white kids, the kids with money and time to burn. Drugs were not yet indigenous to our culture, but we liked to drink and we loved to dance. On this night, the party was in Pinehurst, an elite development of homes, and the parents were there, so we began disbursing around midnight. Needing a new place to drink, we were out front discussing our options. I was standing with my boyfriend, Jim, and two of his friends, when we were approached. A Mexican gang of boys wanted to know which house.

"Where's the party?" one of them asked me. He looked nasty, and I was happy to let him know the bash was breaking up. They were only there to stir up trouble anyway. One of his buddies threw a punch and all hell broke loose. Standing there dumbfounded, I was slammed to the ground. That time a balled-up fist hit me and the impact was ferocious.

Someone screamed, "It's a girl! Let's get out of here!"

I was barely conscious, but I was aware of my boyfriend carrying me. He threw me in the back seat of a car, jumped in, and told his friend to take off.

"Follow them!" he ordered.

As we raced madly to catch those nasty North Denver boys, there was a screaming in my head. I wasn't sure if my companions were yelling or if it was something else, but when the car went screeching around a corner, I recaptured my senses.

"Stop!" I cried. "You'll kill all of us!"

Thankfully, the driver listened and pulled over. Jim asked me if I was all right.

"No! I'm not all right. Shit! The guy chipped a tooth. It hurts like hell," I moaned as the crisp air clipped my naked edge. "Jim," I said, turning to my friend, "I want to go home."

As soon as I was dropped off, I went to my parents' bedroom.

Flipping on the light, I said, "Dad, I got hit tonight. Some boys crashed our party and picked a fight. One of my teeth got chipped."

Groggily, he sat up. "Take two aspirins and go to bed. We'll see how it looks in the morning."

In the morning, I no longer had a face. It had been replaced with a basketball and my dad was gone. He had left for work, but my mother was still there. When I walked into the kitchen to present myself, she gasped at the sight of me.

"Mom, call the dentist. I have three chipped teeth and they hurt. I can't even breathe, they hurt so bad."

She raced to the phone, and when she came back, she said, "He'll see you now. Let me get dressed."

"I can drive myself," I said. I was angry with her for not paying more attention the night before. At that moment, I did not want her company.

"You sure?" she asked.

"I'm sure." I grabbed my keys and left while I had a chance.

My orthodontist nearly panicked when he saw me. "You need X-rays, Judy. You should be at the hospital, not here."

"My teeth hurt, doc. Can't you do something? The pain is excruciating."

He slapped some plaster against the exposed nerves and then called the hospital. "They're expecting you in emergency. Go have some pictures taken."

"Alright," I said begrudgingly. I didn't want to go. I was a mature kid, but I was still afraid. I did not like the idea of going to the hospital, but since he had already called, I figured there was no choice.

"Surgery!" I cried. "You're kidding!"

"No," the nurse said. "Your jaw is broken in four places. I'm surprised you can even talk. You need immediate attention. Better call your parents. You'll need an overnight bag and we need a signature since you're still a minor."

"An overnight bag! How long will I be here?"

"It could be a week," she said sympathetically, handing me the phone.

It was 'only' four days, but then I spent the next six weeks in wires. My jaw was clamped together with metal restraints; it was a horrific experience.

~

Now I wanted to cry again. The pain was different, but in many ways, it was worse. Again a man had hit me, but my assailant was no stranger. He was, in fact, someone I loved.

Why? I cried. Why, Rod? Was a watch so important? Was it worth a broken jaw, a broken heart? Certainly, even if the jaw was still intact, my heart was not. Rod's vicious blow had been earth shattering. In one swift movement, he had destroyed my self-confidence. I felt like a stupid fool and I wondered if he had ever loved me.

Mom was right, I thought. Rod was another scammer who had robbed me blind. He was after my money from the beginning. Well, I hope you choke on it, Mr. Rod Steersman. It was blood money anyway. It came from the telemarketing industry, from the spoils of war. Thinking about the source of my anguish, I began to settle. It's your karma, girl. It's come back to haunt you. Like Rod's cycle of destruction, I had one, too. I had made some poor choices, and now I was paying the price.

"Well, enough!" I said out loud. "This cycle has got to end."

Logically, I thought it should, but Murphy's Law was in play. My phone rang, and it was Mom. I didn't pick up but listened to her message. She wanted to remind me about our date for the following Friday night. We had planned dinner and a movie. I groaned but hoped maybe by then I might be able to eat. I wasn't worried about the bruising because her eyesight was poor. I was sure a good make-up job would provide adequate cover. My intentions were good, but the night came and went, and I never called her. I still could not eat and I could barely speak.

Pam called and left a message, too. "Are you okay, Mom? What's going on over there? I hope 'you know who' isn't there. Call me; I'm worried."

I rolled over, but not far enough to reach the phone. A few more days passed, and she called again. "Mom, if you don't call me, I'm coming over there. It's Marie's birthday party this weekend, you know. You are coming, aren't you? Call me!"

The bruise was yellowing, so I made the effort. I called her and made excuses for my neglect. "I've been working, Pam, working on my book. I'm sorry, but right now, I have a one-track mind. I have got to focus on this, don't you see? When the money runs out, so will my opportunity."

She bought it, but her grams didn't. At Marie's celebration, I tried to talk to my mother, but she was unforgiving. Her Scorpio nature would not allow me in. *Some things never change,* I thought.

Finally, I gave up and played with my granddaughter. When she wanted to swim, I sent her to her dad and went to get a burger. I still could not open wide enough to get a bun in my mouth, but bits and pieces of various foods made their way down my throat, and as my blood sugar rose, so did my desire to socialize. I spoke with friends, people I hadn't seen for ages, and the contact helped me feel human. When I returned home, it was with a much better attitude. Still, good ole Murphy was on the premises. I discovered an uninvited guest and much to my dismay, he was comfortably lodged in my bed.

CHAPTER 20

The Warrior Returns

"ROD!" I SAID IN DISMAY. "How did you get in?"

I walked toward the bathroom and looked at the window he broke the last time. Climbing on the cinder block fence, he gained access to the roof and came through the only opening possible.

"I've fixed it, not to worry." He grinned from ear to ear.

The board was back in place, but I was not happy. Still, I could see there was no reason to be afraid. Rod's warrior persona was in my bedroom, and this servant of God was harmless. He was the man who battled injustice, the man who always protected me. I had forgotten about this alter-ego, it had been so long. The proper body language was there, though, so I was greatly relieved.

Returning to the room, I said, "Rod, you can't just come barging in here any time you like. This is no longer your home."

"I'm sorry," he said, getting up. "Come here, you. Give me a hug."

"No, dammit. You need to leave."

"Judy, I'm crushed."

The man was clever, oh so clever. The look on his face

was pure innocence, as though nothing catastrophic had transpired between us. "Rod, you're not welcome here. Get out."

"Judy, please, I promise to call next time, but I had to see you. Now tell me, if I had phoned, would you have picked up?"

"No," I said matter-of-factly. "You hurt me, Rod."

He dropped his head and gave me the eyes. "I don't know what happened. I went crazy over that watch. I am so sorry. Are you okay?"

"Barely, I'm only barely able to eat."

"Please forgive me, Judy. I needed to lose that watch. It was the last link to the conspiracy. It's gone now, and I'm putting that ugliness behind me. Please, let me make it up to you."

He was reaching for me, and the wine from the party was clouding my judgement. I did not let him hold me, but I began to relent. I spoke a thousand words by lying down. "I'm tired, Rod. I had a few drinks this afternoon and I'm too tired for this. Really, I wish you'd go."

My response excited him, and I soon found out why. "I can fix that, Judy. Come on, roll over. Open those baby blues for me."

I turned to my side and looked up. He was dangling a small bindle of white powder. "Oh, my God," I groaned, turning my back to him. Rod was enticing me with crystal methamphetamine, an upper, a speedy mood enhancer.

"Come on, Judy, please," he begged. "I just want to talk. I can't leave you like this. I need for you to know how sorry I am, how much I love you."

"I know, Rod. I know. Now just go."

He tickled my ear and I brushed him away. He poked me in the ribs and I blocked him with my arm. "Come on, soulmate, for old times' sake. Just for tonight, please talk to me."

I felt like a little girl, a sad, lost little girl. *Here, sweetheart, have some candy. Come to daddy, he'll make you feel better.*

And it was tempting, too tempting. I had nowhere to go, no desire to do anything, and I knew my sidekick would be difficult to dislodge. "Okay, Rod," I said finally. "Lay it on me, baby. Lay out a nice long line, would you?"

He did not hesitate. The package was opened, a credit card was produced—my credit card. *Oh my God.* I forgot about my gas card. I'll have to cancel it after he leaves.

Rod tapped out a pile of yellowish powder and made two lines. "Ladies first," he said gallantly, handing me a rolled-up bill.

I snorted up one nostril, and then, before the burn could start, I switched sides and sucked the other line up as well.

"Whoa! What are you doing? One of those was mine!"

Of course I knew that, but I didn't say so. At that instant, it would have been impossible to speak—even if I had wanted to. The crystal hit my sinus cavity and burned a path to my brain. My eyes were tearing, and I held my face, waiting for the release. When the burning began to wane, I choked out a few words. "Sorry, honey. I told you I was tired."

"Well, not anymore, I'll bet."

He laid out a line of his own, sucked it up, and mimicked my expression of anguish.

"Nope, not anymore. Thanks, I needed that," I joked.

He settled, and so did our worries. Once again, I could see Rod as my friend.

"I've missed you, Judy," he said after a few minutes.

"I've missed you, too. Kind of like a bad tooth."

"What?"

I was giggling now. "You know, like after a dentist pulls it, when the pain is gone, but there's still a hole in your head."

Rod pretended to be insulted, but he was catching the

good humor buzz. "Hey, that's not very nice."

"Hay is for horses, honey. You are just an asshole."

No argument; in fact, he wholeheartedly agreed. "God, I am. I mean, I was. I am so sorry. That Rolex means nothing to me now. It was a ridiculous attachment and I needed to lose it. I really am sorry. Let me see." He touched my chin and I winced. "God, Judy, I feel awful. It's still kind of bruised. Has anybody seen it?"

"I don't think so. Today was Marie's birthday party, but it was well covered."

Later, I discovered Pam had noticed the yellowing, but she allowed my ruse. Thank God, she hadn't hit me with a guilt trip. If she had, I might not have been able to deal with my interloper.

Rod was in rare form; he did seem like an unwavering friend. He wanted to know all about my book, and although I refused him access to my computer, I shared some of my recent revelations. I drew out my flower of creation and showed him how it was seven rings, not five.

"And look, Rod," I said. "Finally, the whole thing is held together by Belief. Belief is the eighth ring. It binds the others."

He looked quizzically at the picture.

"It's what you've been preaching, Rod. Belief contains the flower. Belief is everything. It is the essence of the divine. See, you really are the son of a preacher man. You've been spreading God's word in your business message all along."

He smiled. "Yes, and now you're going to write it."

"You bet I am."

He was animated. "Judy, awesome things are happening. God really is working in my life. The Reno/Tahoe area is perfect for Global's headquarters. Support is coming from every direction. God, I want you to be there. Between my spoken word and your written word, we could reach millions."

"And we will," I agreed wholeheartedly. "Look, Rod, this flower even supports the Christian notion Jesus Christ is the true path to God."

Since I rarely supported this doctrine, he was surprised, but his eyes opened for an explanation.

"Look," I said again, drawing a fresh circle. "Where does it all begin?"

"With God. He is the beginning and the end, the alpha and the omega."

I frowned. "Yes, but what is God?"

His expression was blank.

"Rod, what is man's most basic need?"

"Love," he said knowingly.

"Exactly," I exclaimed, and labeled my first circle Love. "Aside from basic nourishment, man needs love. Babies die if they are not touched. Even an infant cannot survive without love."

"They die?"

"Yes. It's been proven."

Rod was surprised.

"There was an experiment, somewhere in London I think, and the results were dreadful. They stopped it too late and babies were lost. They had tested two different groups of orphaned babies. Some they touched and talked to, others they left alone in their beds. They even bottle fed them without any human contact, and the isolated babies just shriveled up and died."

"How awful," he said.

"I'll say, but it sure verifies our need for connection. We cannot survive alone. We require love."

"Speaking of," he said, reaching for me. He pulled me over on top of him, and I stared into his eyes. Yes, my warrior was there, and this man was a passionate lover, an adoring, unselfish lover. I felt a fullness staring into those saucers—no more holes.

"Hello, soulmate," I said.

"Kiss me, Judy."

And of course, I did. He kissed me back and held me softly against his chest. There was nothing rushed about our embrace, no driving hunger. We simply merged. I rested for a minute and then pushed off him.

"Anyway," I said. "As creatures of love, what happens? How do we grow up and find our way back to the source, back to God?"

"Tell me, Judy Burr. You're the expert; you show me what you've discovered."

"By loving, by receiving and giving love," I said happily. "Christ offers unconditional love, and if we accept him, if we love him back, we become one with God. Love makes the world go around."

That night I traveled into uncharted territory and Rod acted as my guide. We explored the Word of God and talked about our innate spirituality. I was reminded of the times we discussed different aspects of his business plan, but on this evening the focus was on me, and it felt good. My worth needed validation, and who better to offer it than the man who had taken it away.

Wasn't it like that with abuse? The victim always went back to the source, kind of like a dog returning to his vomit. No, that was too ugly, too unkind. I preferred to think about it as riding the winds. Sometimes, things were just out of your control. Sometimes, one had no choice except to roll with the flow.

We had ups and downs, and with them, we grew. Trouble was, I was addicted. I loved the highs in life, and I continually sought them out. This was one of those times. We talked all night, and the next morning we made love.

Finally, we slept for a couple of hours and then tried to eat. Eating was already difficult for me, but with crystal methamphetamine in my system, it was nearly impossible. I quickly gave up and asked Rod for another hit instead. The blast jumped our day, and fully energized, we went to the pool.

We talked about his family this time, and I discovered he planned to return to Reno on Wednesday.

"Mary Ann is due any day now," he said. "I want to be there when the baby is born. I can easily make the drive from Reno, and I'll be home by Thursday."

"Well, I sure hope that baby waits for you. They don't always cooperate, you know."

"I know, but God has told me Wednesday is good. I've already booked a flight for that morning."

"Umm, that's good," I said, languishing in my lawn chair.

"I'm roasting. Let's go for a swim," he suggested.

"Okay."

We walked to the shallow end and got in the hard way, one step at a time. The cool water was a shock, but it served as a wonderful distraction from Rod's home life. Reaching the deeper area, he swept me into his arms and began to carry me around. "Rod! These are my neighbors. What will people think?"

"I don't care what they think. I love you, Judy. I want you with me always. Will you move to Tahoe, honey? You could write there. I'd take care of you. I'd make sure you wanted for nothing."

He went on for a while, explaining how he planned to build a giant lodge. It would be both headquarters and home, and I would have my own private wing. I fell under his spell and in my altered state, I began to dream with him. Of course, Mary Ann and the kids were there. Somehow, we were functioning as one happy family. It was a beautiful vision, all filled with love, and we planned to lead by example, showing the entire world how to live peacefully within a soul circle.

"Yes!" I cried. "We'd be the epitome of the perfect Uncommon Partnership."

Rod laughed and dunked me. When I came up, he said, "Your book could be a 'how-to' manual."

"Oh, really," I shot back playfully. "And just how much instruction should I offer? How many of my secrets do you want me to give away, son of a preacher man?"

"None," he said, dropping me and breaking into a backstroke. "Some things are better left under cover."

I laughed and dove into the water. The rush was refreshing, and so was our comradery.

In my office the next morning, Tuesday, Rod listened to his voice mail messages on my speaker phone. One of the last messages was from his wife, which brought us back to the real world, and quickly.

"Looks like we'll be having a baby today," she said sweetly. "Better get home, Rod. This is a blessed event, honey. Daddy needs to be here." Her tone was kind and sympathetic. She was trying to gently draw her husband home.

It was difficult to get Rod on a plane that day. Like Mary Ann, I was tender, but he was reticent. At one point, he looked at me sadly and asked, "Do you want me to leave, Judy?"

"No, honey," I said, masking my true feelings. By then I was no longer high, and I only wanted him out of my hair. I needed sleep and nothing else. "Of course not, but you're going to have a baby. Don't you want to be there? Aren't you excited?"

Eventually he came around. He missed the first plane, but I got him to the airport in time for the second one.

"Call me," I said, kissing him goodbye. "I'll be waiting to

hear the good news. Hope you have a girl."

He smiled at the thought and rushed for the gate. I went home to sleep. I had refused a bump after hearing from Mary Ann. I did not want my thinking marred by chemicals. My body might have craved it, but my brain knew better.

Happy days are here again, I thought. Rod was returning to his earthly wife. That meant I'd be free to write, and I was anxious to get started. In the morning, I said. In the morning I'll climb back into my gold mine. Thank you, God. Thank you, my angels.

CHAPTER 21

Headed for Hell

THE NEXT AFTERNOON the phone rang, and anticipating good news, I picked up.

"We had a girl," he said.

"Wonderful, Rod. I told you. So, did you get there in time? Were you there for the birth?"

"No. I had to take care of some business, but Mary Ann understands."

The alarms, that nasty foreboding, hit me like a ton of bricks. "You mean you're still in Reno?"

"Yes. I had to stay. I needed to save the house, and there was an opportunity to liquidate some equipment. I'm picking up the check tonight, but at least this way, Mary Ann won't be forced to move."

He hadn't told me about the eviction notice. I asked for details.

"Well, thank God for that," I said, after hearing yet another explanation. "It would be awful if she was forced to move with a brand new baby."

My heart empathized with his angel wife. I, too, was worried about losing my house, but I was expecting a large refund check. There was hope for me, but Mary Ann was relying on Rod, and as of late, he was robbing Peter to pay Paul. To depend on her husband was probably a mistake. As it turned out, Mary Ann thought so, too.

At 9:30 a.m., as I was pouring my coffee, Rod appeared out of nowhere. His words startled me.

"I trusted you. How could you do this?"

I missed my cup and poured coffee all over my hand. "Ouch!" I said, trying to quickly dislodge the source of my pain. Turning to face him, I calmed myself. "What's wrong?"

"Come on, I'll show you what's wrong."

He took me upstairs — again — and again he conducted a search. When he found nothing, he stared.

Very gently I said, "Honey, there's no one here. I promise."

He groaned and went outside. I watched him carefully and knew something was wrong.

"Rod, what happened?"

"I had the money, and I wired it home, but our landlady wouldn't accept the payment. The eviction stands, and now Mary Ann is furious. She wants a divorce. The bitch says she's done with me."

Rod had just called his wife a bitch. That was a first. "How awful," I countered. "Can't you get someone to intervene? Remind your landlady about the children. If she relents, then so will your wife."

"You're right. I'll call my brother."

Rod was extremely distraught, but in my opinion, he was getting exactly what he deserved. Mary Ann had reached her breaking point and was no longer a compliant wife. That was scary enough, but Rod was also sleep-deprived. That meant he was still using the dangerous drug. I had no idea what to do, so I went on about my business.

About an hour passed, and finally he came to me. He was smiling, thank God.

"Okay," he said. "What did you do with it?"

"With what?" I asked.

"You know what. Come on, Judy, now is not the time."

"Rod, I don't know what you're talking about."

"My stash, Judy. Where is it?"

"I haven't touched your stash, Rod."

He grimaced. "Come with me. I must have dropped it."

"Find it yourself," I said flippantly.

Wrong. I had made a grievous error. He grabbed my arm and took me with him on the search. Every stair was scoped, his carpet tracks were retraced, the medicine cabinet was examined, every nook, corner, and cranny was examined, but we found nothing. Finally, he gave up.

"Call your friend, Judy. You have got to make a buy."

"No! You need to chill. The last thing you need is more dope."

Rod's anguish increased and he began to pace. "Judy, I can't do this. I'll fall apart. There is too much at stake. Do you want Mary Ann and the kids to lose the house?"

A low blow, but better verbal than physical. I knew it would be impossible to reach him, so I made the call.

After leaving the house, he made me stop at a drugstore. I did not ask why. I simply did as I was told. Reason was out of the question. We completed his mission and headed home. I was about to turn into my driveway when Rod hollered, "Stop!"

I hit the brakes and looked at him.

"Back up," he said, looking behind us.

I put the car in reverse.

"Slowly. Okay, stop." He got out and picked up something from the pavement.

"What is it?" I asked when he was back in the car.

He opened his hand and revealed a twisted baggy.

"How did that get there?" I asked.

"I must have dropped it when I got out of the cab."

I groaned. "Well, now you know."

"Let's go," he said, barely acknowledging the fact.

When we reached the house, I stayed downstairs while he returned to my office. I heard him on the phone and he sounded calm. *Thank God,* I thought.

After a half hour or so, Rod called me. I did not want to partake. He became more insistent, and finally, I decided to tell him in person.

"I don't want any, Rod. I'm done with that stuff. You do what you must, and I'll be here for you, but I do not want to get high."

The victim emerged. "Why did you stop the credit card, Judy?"

I gulped. "I figured you forgot to send it back, Rod, that's all. I didn't want it floating around out there."

"Please, do this with me, Judy," he said, changing track.

I looked down, trying not to meet his gaze, and my eye caught a flash. "You're shooting it? Are you crazy? No way!" I cried. "I am not into needles."

He grabbed me. "But you're into Rolexes. You're into destroying people's lives. If I had the money from the watch, my kids wouldn't be facing the prospect of becoming homeless."

Homeless? This was hopeless. I had to bring on the tears.

Rod panicked. He started moving toward me. I fell to the bed and curled up.

"I'm sorry," he said. "Judy, please. This will make you feel better. It will put us on the same wavelength. It's mellow, really."

I sat up and sadly looked at him, then extended my arm.

He put the handkerchief tourniquet around my arm and held the needle high. A drop of translucent liquid squirted from the top. I felt the prick, but it didn't hit me until he untied the knot. FEAR! My eyes went wide with shock.

"It's okay, Judy," Rod reassured. "Just relax, breathe deeply."

My stomach turned and my solar plexus wrenched. The pressure on my rib cage caused my heart to race. Spinning wildly, I flashed on his rage. Was he trying to kill me? I tried to move, to put some distance between us, no matter how slight, but I was rigid.

"Breathe, Judy," came the voice.

I gasped.

"Slowly."

Another breath, this one was easier.

"Go with it," he instructed.

With it? You son of a bitch! How can you go anywhere this way? How could he function? I wondered.

At some point, I decided I was not going to die, but my body remained comatose. I was aware of Rod making phone calls, but I also knew the news was not good. The thought of escape crossed my mind, but driving wasn't even a remote possibility.

When he finally came in to talk to me, he was irate. Thankfully, his anger was not directed at me, and by then, high as I was, I was in survivor mode.

I took up his crusade, and together we raged against the bitch refusing to help his children. With me as Rod's witness, he began to plan. He talked about ways to make his lady landlord pay, and I added to her punishment. The imagery made him sweat, and he tore off his shirt.

I was shocked, but the look on my face didn't stop him. His shorts came off. Sex wasn't something I had entertained, but Rod had a raging erection. He pulled off my pants and without so much as a kiss, spread my legs and positioned himself between them. My body shuddered when he entered me, and within seconds I was in orgasm. The euphoria was exquisite and continual. It simply didn't end, and Rod drove on madly and passionately, permeating every crevice of my being. I started to think we might both expire before obtaining the final release. I tried to slow things down, but he would not have it. He quickened the pace, and he wrapped one arm around my head for leverage, pushing harder, harder, and deeper.

"Come with me, Judy," he cried. "Let it go."

A guttural scream came from some creature deep inside and a wave of bright light washed over me.

"Now, Judy. Fuck me now, baby. GO!"

He was pulling on my hair and pushing with his hips. The orgasmic waves peaked and rocketed from my groin, traveling through my belly, up my spine, and out the top of my head. I was gone. I passed out from the shock of the whole thing.

Rod must have lost consciousness too, but before he did, he fell slightly to the side. Grateful for the breathing space, I began to recover. That orgasmic experience was new to me, and it affected me in a profound way.

I was putty in Rod's hands. We fixed again and talked quietly. I helped him make sense of things, but he decided he simply couldn't go home a loser. He would have to rebuild first.

I told him that was understandable, thinking all the while he would soon return to Reno, but that wasn't what he had in mind. Instead, he wanted to come back to Vegas. He needed my help, and he was sure the dealers would be pleased to know he had returned.

I tried to reason with him, but my arguments were taken as a rejection, and the victim returned. Each time he became fearful, the drugs came out, and I obligingly accepted my share. Days passed, and as they did, I became sick, hopelessly addicted to his chemical love.

When he booked two reservations for us to fly to Reno, I cringed. He wanted me to return with him to get his truck and pick up some necessary equipment. Then we were to drive back together to reestablish Global's Las Vegas hold.

I agreed, but he didn't trust me. My long-time habit of running away was in the forefront of his mind, and so, too, I speculated, was my substantial tax refund. I no longer trusted Rod, not even remotely, and I knew he was capable of anything.

We began a game of cat and mouse.

Rod started following me around the house. If I went downstairs to get us drinks, he would be there before the glasses were filled. If I wanted to use the restroom upstairs, I'd find him on the bed when I came out. I'd roll my eyes but that was all, and eventually he granted me bits of freedom. I took full advantage.

I managed to back up my computer, hiding the disc under the bed downstairs. I also hid my wallet and an extra set of car keys there. My purse was left in full display on top of the kitchen countertop. That could not disappear. I did some laundry, claiming I needed a few things for our trip, and put an extra set of clothes under the bed.

When Monday morning came, I dutifully packed an overnight bag, leaving it on the bed. After breakfast, I asked for a fix. This was a first, so Rod was reassured. He believed I was his, or if nothing else, I was hooked on his chemicals. He gave me a fleeting glance before heading up the stairs, but my face was buried in the newspaper. I had not a care in the world, or so he thought.

I gave him a minute, and then quietly called my dogs. My schnauzers followed me down the hall, and I grabbed my overnight escape bag. I was scared, sleep-deprived, and weak from starvation, but I stole away. The hallway door to the garage opened, my dogs were prompted, and then I stealthily put them in the Lexus. After they were secured, I joined them. I put the key in the ignition and prayed.

Please God, protect me. I hit the button and waited for the lumbering door to roll up. I was able to back out, and the door was halfway down again before he came out. He crouched into a deep-knee bend, opened his arms wide, and mouthed one word before the huge aluminum casing closed him out of my life.

"WHY?"

His anguish was heart breaking, but it did not stop me. I did not want to die, and without a doubt, we were on a one-way track headed for hell.

I went straight to a phone booth, and I tried to explain my reason for running away. I didn't want to be a drug addict, and I knew unless I made a break, it was hopeless for me.

He begged me to come home and promised we'd clean up.

I said I was confused and needed time to think. I promised to call him later, but my next call was to purchase a small bag of my own. The drive would be grueling, and I did not want to fall asleep at the wheel. Finally, I called my sister. "Jana, I'm coming for a visit. I've had some trouble, and I'll probably drive straight through. Please, don't tell anyone. I'll explain when I get there. See you tomorrow."

It was an ominous message, but I knew her arms would be open. *Thank God for Jana.* What would I ever do without her?

CHAPTER 22

Kicking the Habit

THE DRIVE TO COLORADO was no pleasure cruise. I made sure to take nourishment and went as far between stops as I possibly could, but my purchase was inadequate. In the foothills outside of Denver, I pulled over and scraped the baggy. Two hours later I turned down Jana's street, and she was right there. She was already out walking her dogs. "Hi!" I said, pulling curbside. "Want a ride?"

"Judy!" she exclaimed. "You're here already?"

"Yeah, I drove straight through."

"Well, what happened? Why the rush?"

"It's a long story. I'll fill you in at the house."

"I'll meet you there in a minute," she said, pointing to my packed backseat.

Since I had my own puppies, it would have been crazy to add hers, so I nodded and took off. I was waiting on her back porch when she got home.

It was only 5:30 a.m., so she joined me bearing two steamy mugs of coffee. "Thanks," I said, wondering if the caffeine could even remotely touch my fatigue.

"You look terrible, Judy. God, you're thin."

"I haven't eaten much in the last few weeks. That's why

I'm here. I came to recover."

"Recover from what?" she asked suspiciously.

I pulled up my shirt sleeve and showed her my bruised arm. It was blue and yellow all around the crux of my elbow.

She gasped. "Oh, my God! Have you gone loco?"

"Almost," I said. "I've been through hell, Jana. I'm really sorry. I just didn't know where else to go."

The tears rolled, and her heart went out to me. "It's okay," she said. "We'll get you through this. You're safe now; don't worry."

After I gave her a brief rundown, she went off on Rod. "You're going to have to take legal action, Judy. He'll never leave you alone. He's manipulated you in every way possible, but this is unforgivable. Enticing you to slam drugs is as low as it gets. It's the ultimate form of control."

"I know, Jana, I know, but I have to get well first."

She agreed, and we had breakfast together. After she left for work, I had a beer and prayed it would calm my inner trembling. It did nothing for me, however, so I mixed a drink. Finally, my blood sugar began to rise, and I was able to relax a little—not enough to sleep so I watched some TV.

Jana was surprised to find me alert and well that evening.

"Crystal doesn't leave your system all that quickly, Jana. You crave it as soon as the initial high subsides, but afterward it flows more smoothly. Believe me, I'll crash hard tonight and then tomorrow will probably be hellish. Really, I have no idea what to expect, since I've never shot the stuff. I just hope the withdrawals are manageable."

The next morning, she brought me a cup of coffee. "Come on, Judy. Walk the dogs with me."

I looked at her like she was crazy and rolled over.

"Come on," she coaxed. "You can go back to bed when we get back. Get up now."

I wanted to die, but I got out of bed and made the six-block walk, which seemed like six miles.

The following day she let me sleep in, and I was more than grateful. On day three, she tried again.

I had a horrendous headache and begged for aspirin. She left me a bottle and went to work.

Day four came, and I made the trip. It was much shorter, maybe more like two miles, instead of six. I thought there might be hope for me, but that afternoon the depression hit and I cried for hours. When Jana returned, I hid my anxiety, and she managed to get me out for an evening bike ride.

By day five, I was beginning to function. I did not get up at the crack of dawn, but when I did rise, I took my own dogs for a walk. I drove to the Garden of the Gods and parked, then chose an easy paved loop. The national park was a beautiful place, and communing with nature made me feel human again.

The weekend passed and Jana pushed, so did I. I even called my daughter.

"Hi, Mom," she said carefully. "What's up?"

Apparently, she hadn't missed me. Relief flooded my psyche. "I'm in Colorado Springs," I said casually.

"What!" She was shaken. "Mom, what are you doing there? What if the baby comes early? I need you here."

"I'll be back, Pam. Don't worry. I had some problems with Rod and I had to get away."

"Again! Can't that man take a hint?"

"Obviously not," I said.

"Where is he now?" She asked.

"That's why I'm calling. I'm not sure. Do you suppose Jason could go by the house?"

She said he could, of course, and promised to ask him when he returned home. I filled her in but left out the part about the needles. During our conversation, she told me she had seen my bruised chin. Now she was just happy to know I was making my break.

"I'll call you later after Jason checks out your house."

"Thanks, Pam," I said, and hung up.

When the phone rang a couple of hours later, it was Pam. "Mom, I'm scared. Jason left with a baseball bat. He said he's going to bash in Rod's head. I couldn't calm him."

"Oh, my God."

"Mom, what if Rod's there? I'm so worried. Should I call the cops?"

"Shit, I don't know. I never should have told you, dammit. I should have dealt with it myself." I was really upset. What if somebody got hurt or killed? What if Jason got in more trouble because of me?

"It'll be okay, Mom. Jason's not stupid. I'll give him a few minutes, then I'll go over there myself."

"No, Pam! Don't do that. Whatever you do, promise me you'll stay home. Honey, you're pregnant. Think about the baby."

"Okay. I'll call you in a few minutes."

"Okay," I said dejectedly.

Twenty minutes passed, and when the phone rang, I nearly jumped out of my skin. It was Jason. Thank God.

"Judy, that man is a mess. I've never seen such a poor excuse for a human being."

"Oh God," I groaned. "Do you think he's using?"

"No. He's coming down hard. I told him to get out and he started to cry. I actually felt sorry for him."

"What's the house look like?"

"It's a mess. Dirty dishes are all over the kitchen."

"That's a good sign," I said. "At least he's eating. Obviously, he's trying to clean up."

"Well, I couldn't throw him out, Judy. I'm sorry."

"It's okay, Jason. Thanks. I'll deal with it when I get home. I'm going to file a restraining order. It won't happen any other way."

Jana had been watching me. When I hung up the phone, she said, "You're not thinking of going back there, are you?"

"I have to, Jana."

"Let someone else deal with him, Judy. You're not strong enough."

"God, I wish it were that easy, but I went through this with Speicher. The family services division won't issue an order for anyone but me."

"You're not ready," she said flatly.

"Maybe not, but I don't think there's a whole lot of choice."

"There's always a choice," she lectured. "You know from experience you have to stay out of that man's reach. You told me yourself when you broke the addiction to Lance, it took ninety days. Your counselor said that was a minimum. Getting away from a controller is harder than kicking a drug habit. No contact of any kind for at least three months, not physical, not by phone, and certainly not in court. You know the drill."

"I don't think he'd ever show up for the hearing. Once I file the restraining order, he'll leave town. Maybe he'll finally go home."

"Don't bet on it. The man does not know the meaning of no."

Jana was wise, and I had tremendous respect for her, but there were other issues. "He's stubborn, but more than anything, he does not want to go to jail. For that matter, neither do I, and I'm violating a court order by being here."

She raised an eyebrow.

"Jana, there wasn't time to get permission to travel. If my pretrial supervisor discovers I've left town, he could have me picked up for contempt."

"Would he do that?"

"I don't know, but I have to report in soon. My regular appointment is in two weeks. Between now and then, he could stop by my house at any time."

"What about the trials? Are they scheduled yet?"

"So far, everybody has accepted a plea. I'm still working with the Feds, though. That's another thing. What if they call me?"

"How would you know?"

"I could call my attorney, but I'd rather not tell her what's going on. I prefer taking my chances."

"Judy, how do you live like this?"

My lifestyle was a constant conundrum for her. She simply could not understand how I tolerated the stress. "I don't know, baby sister, but I will tell you this, I am tired, dead tired. I want this to end."

"Well, thank God for that, but still, Judy, you need more time. You'll be tougher emotionally and physically in a couple of weeks. How about we go to the mountains for the fourth of July? We could spend four days riding mountain bikes. That would help strengthen your resolve."

I liked the idea, but I believed it was cutting things too close. "It will be too crowded. How about we go this weekend? Can you take a day or two off before the holiday? That way I'll make it home before the baby is born."

The compromise satisfied her, but before she said good night, she brought me a book. "Have you read any of Scott Peck's stuff?" she asked.

"No, but I have some of his audio tapes. I think he's a brilliant psychiatrist, and I agree with his religious views, too."

"Good, then you should like this."

"People of the Lie, The Hope for Healing Human Evil," I said, reading the title. "Really, Jana! Evil?"

"Not that I necessarily believe in 'evil' per se, but Rod

is definitely ill, and he sure fits the bill. This book helped me understand what I was feeling because of Shirley. I think it's got some good insight for you, too."

"You read this because of Shirley?" I asked incredulously.

"Yes. She traumatized me the same way Rod traumatized you."

"Really? You feel that strongly about our sister? I had no idea."

"I guess nobody did. It sure seemed like no one wanted to listen, least of all Mom and Dad. She made my life a living hell, Judy. Why do you think I moved into the basement when we were kids?"

"I thought you wanted your own room."

"I did, but it was because I was afraid of Shirley. I thought she was going to kill me."

I was shocked. "God, Jana. I am so sorry. No wonder you can't deal with her now."

It was an emotional moment, and my little sister began to cry. I put down the book, stood up, and wrapped my arms around her. "It's okay, honey. It's over. I'll protect you from Shirley. Don't worry, I can deal with her. I'll deal with Rod, too."

"I know," she said, trying to contain the flow. "Just promise me you'll read the book. Will you read the book, Judy?"

"Yes. I'll read it," I said, before we separated.

When I was in bed, I looked at the text again. I was amazed Jana had given it to me. She was more of a 'mind-over-matter' kind of a girl, extremely pragmatic. *Okay, little sister,* I thought. *I'll give it a shot.* Maybe 'ole Mr. Scott can help me kick the Rod habit.

CHAPTER 23

Evil and its Enabler

THE NEXT MORNING my dogs were dancing. Buster and Gus had grown accustomed to our morning walks, so when I grabbed their leashes, they raced for the doggie door. Loading them into the car, I laughed and happily whisked us away. My endurance had increased, so I passed the paved looped area and took to a trail in the hills. Once the highway was out of sight, I set my puppies free, and they ran ahead of me, but they never went far. They were my watch dogs and liked having me in their sight. A bend in the path would always bring them back, and their return would lift my spirits. With each new curve offering a different panoramic view, I drank in those red mountain cliffs until they became a part of me. The park was perfectly named Garden of the Gods.

When I crested the hill, my mind flashed back to Rod. Our partner, Timmy, had once said Rod is "high maintenance," which was an understatement. Being in Mr. Steersman's presence was enervating. He had a way of stealing one's soul and he was shrewd. People in his circle rarely realized they were being used, at least not until it was too late. Many of his disciples had been bled dry, but when they complained,

Rod simply cast them from his inner circle. He'd renounce them as "nonbelievers" and call them selfish fools. Global lost many good dealers that way, and now I could empathize.

Too bad, I thought. The company really could have been a success. If only the president hadn't been such a psychotic child. "Oh well, it's no longer my concern," I said, looking at the dazzling sky. Not a cloud was visible, and no whisper rustled, neither sage nor tree. Mother Nature was at peace and so was I. I took a deep breath, called my dogs, and headed back down the hill. "Thank you, Jesus," I breathed, as we descended. "Thank you for saving me."

I spent that week taking care of Jana and myself. I had started to cook, and we were eating nourishing and healthy meals. After she relaxed, but before night fell, we'd take long bike rides along the river. We were preparing for our four days in the mountains, but it was hard for me. My muscles were aching less, but I still tired easily. Rarely was I able to read at night, so I started looking at the book by day.

Dr. Scott Peck was addressing the issue of evil, and I found his work fascinating. He got my attention by immediately apologizing for the sins of the Christian church, saying great evil was and still is being committed by nominal Christians, often in the name of Christ. I flashed on the Crusades and the Inquisition and continued reading.

A convincing argument was made for the existence of human evil, real human evil, the stuff psychology books had, thus far, failed to identify. I saw bits and pieces of Rod's personality in the case studies, but Scott Peck's statement about a neurosis called "magical thinking" really hit home.

BINGO! That's Rod! He definitely thinks he can magically manifest his dream. Global had a business plan, but Rod didn't adhere to it. Business procedures and professional ethics could be set aside, and so could his partners, for that matter. Rod was divinely guided, so believe and it will be, he would say. And when something went wrong, he would shift the focus away from himself. It was never his fault, which Dr. Peck talked about, too. He called it scapegoating, which he said was another predominant characteristic of the behavior called evil.

Scapegoating! Rod could equivocate with the best of them. He was constantly passing the buck, and as of yet, he hadn't acknowledged his first critical mistake. Expanding into three new markets instead of two completely undid the organization. In my mind, that decision had been the beginning of the end. Cash flow problems arose, and as the company struggled, the dealers began to doubt. Of course, in his mind, the problem was all mine. I had failed to believe in him, and therefore, I had given rise to the takeover attempt. *What a crock!*

Thinking about those early days brought back a flood of memories. Rod and I had enjoyed a great deal of comradery, but when our friendship took an intimate turn, a giant red flag went up. On that first night, he imagined me a demon, not once, but twice. To me that was such a preposterous notion, I simply laughed it off. I should have questioned him further but didn't.

How scary, I thought, but it got worse. I learned the words "image," "appearance," and "outwardly" were crucial to understanding the morality of evil. Rod's behavior was a perfect example. He dressed to impress, and his watch, the coveted Rolex, was necessary to complete his persona. It was all about putting on the show, about demonstrating success. I thought about the Promotion, the Marathon, and the Premiere! They had been opportunities to grandstand. Even the Leadership conference was a tribute to his mightiness. Global had been cash poor, but Rod scheduled the expensive seminar anyway, and why? For no good reason, that's why. He said it was to increase the dealers' belief level, but now it appeared as one grand attention getter.

"Good Lord!" I cried. We were all fooled. He had every one of us under his ether. Yes, I had to give Rod credit. He was most definitely clever, deviously deceptive.

Rod had also gone to dramatic lengths to appear guiltless. When the takeover attempt occurred, he raised "holy hell," and his excessive behavior managed to cover his faults. Unfortunately, his tactics proved destructive. Had he applied the same energy in constructive ways, the conspiracy would never have gained power.

Stepping into his past, I recalled his childhood fear about being the Anti-Christ. No doubt this played into his adult agenda. He exerted a huge amount of effort to block this memory, always claiming to be a righteous leader, a God-fearing man, and a man of his word. I never understood why he felt the need to proclaim such a thing, but thanks to Dr. Peck, the fog was clearing.

It was part of his act, but the implications were frightening. Was it possible? Was Rod truly evil? I knew he was delusional, and I had witnessed acute states of paranoia, but I never thought of him as an agent for Satan. Within that shattered personality also existed a great capacity for good. In fact, by this time I had categorically identified five predominant temperaments in Rod, and all five of these characters were an apotheosis of God.

Only weeks before, when he came through my boarded-up window, I recognized him as the Warrior. There was no reason to fear him because the Warrior was an unwavering friend. He was also a "Servant to God," and he fought injustice tirelessly, always emerging victorious. I dearly loved the Warrior. He was my hero and he was a passionate, caring lover. He was also the man I had originally met, the man who once answered my ad for a roommate. No, the Warrior wasn't evil. He was good as gold, and he had filled me with hope.

As the Warrior became comfortable in my home, I was greeted by the carefree, innocuous man. The Innocent was a "Lover of God." He was childlike and curious, but he was definitely a believer. His unquestioning faith made him a perfect companion, and I relished in our playtime together. When Rod acted out this character, I would tell him he reminded me of a little boy sneaking down the stairs on Christmas morning. He was filled with confidence and that, too, had transferred to me. Because of the Innocent Rod I learned to trust—to trust my fellow man, to trust in God—and now I was learning to trust myself again. There was nothing evil about the Innocent. No, it simply didn't fit.

Now, the Victim ... that was a possibility. The Victim was unpredictable and guilt driven. He was a scared twelve-year-old boy—a boy who felt unprotected and helpless—and because of this, he was also a "Doubter of God."

I wondered, could this sense of aloneness open the door to demonic activity? Certainly this young man was practiced in the art of justifying. He was quick to cry and readily excused his behavior using the "poor pitiful me" routine. I feared the Victim, but not after I learned to manage him. Sex always took care of this doubter, and sex followed by prayer would put him to sleep. The Victim often called for protection, and he particularly liked that "hedge of thorns." Given that, I saw no way this man would ever forsake his Lord.

Oddly enough, the Leader would emerge after Rod shook off feelings of insecurity. This powerful personality was truly a "Man of God." He was devoutly reverent, and his self-sacrificing nature inspired others to greatness. He easily awed audiences, and he had the most beautiful eyes. They absolutely sparkled with a divine essence. I adored the

Leader, and in turn, he loved me. Actually, he loved everybody.

If it hadn't been for the Rager, Rod and I would have parted peacefully, but even this man had God in his life. He was fearful of God, but God was there.

When Rod raged, he claimed to be a banisher of evil, but now I knew better. There was nothing nice about this savage person. I had grown to recognize him as a dangerous enemy. This ugly partner was capable of wrapping his hands around my throat one day, and then lovingly laying them on my head the next. He was, in my opinion, a hypocritical fool, and also my most menacing companion. If there was a demon working in Rod, it would most certainly have found access here. In fact, I had seen a blood-red devil in the whites of his eyes the day he attempted to "save" me. A chill ran through me. 'Rod, Rod,' I'd cried. 'Don't you know we become what we hate? Evil makes us over into its double!'

I shuddered again and tried to recall more positive aspects of his personality. Reviewing Rod's performances made me feel a little better. He truly was magnificent on stage. When Rod was in the spotlight, it seemed like all five personalities merged, and I enjoyed watching him wow an audience.

Analyzing the circumstances made me feel responsible. I had effectively ignored his multi-faceted character, so didn't that make me his enabler? It sure seemed like it. Well, at least I was beginning to understand. Dr. Scott Peck was enlightening me, but I hadn't finished the book, so I asked Jana to ask if I could borrow it.

"Sure," she said, "Keep it. I think you need it more than I do at this point."

I laughed, but not wholeheartedly. "Thanks. So, are you ready?" I asked. "It will be dark soon. How many hours is the drive anyway?"

"Three, four at the most," she said. "Just follow me, okay?"

"Okay, baby sister. Lead the way. Let's get into those hills. I can't wait for you to torture me again."

"You got it," she said happily, as we loaded our dogs into their respective cars.

CHAPTER 24

A Week of Recovery

"HEY, JANA," I said on our second night. We were worn out from our mountain bike ride, and she was relaxing in front of the TV. I had been reading Dr. Peck's book.

"Sometimes, I think if Rod would just acknowledge his responsibility for what happened, I could rest easier. As it is, I feel so used. He really screwed me over."

"He sure did! God, Judy, please don't forget it. Please stay away from him. The man is nothing nice. In my opinion, he's pure poison."

"Yes, and I'm pure stupid. I swear I don't get it. How did I ever let it go so far?"

"I have no idea."

There was finality to her words, and she turned back to her program. The dismissal felt personal, but not surprising. If I couldn't understand it, how could anyone else?

The next day we went into the resort town of Glenwood Springs, riding that afternoon in the hills behind the town of Carbondale. The trail was a single track, but not overly tricky. With wildflowers blooming, the colorful array was a feast for my senses. Between rock and bush, blue burst through, then yellow, then red. Different plants swayed at different heights, but they all sang the sweet melody of life. At a particularly pretty area, near a babbling brook, we stopped to take it in. After catching my breath and gulping from my bottle of water, I commented on the landscape.

"This is incredible, Jana. God, I've never experienced anything like this."

"Kinda nice to get back into the wilderness, isn't it?"

"I'll say! And you can go so much farther on wheels. Just look at that valley. Have you ever seen so much green?"

"Yes," she said matter-of-factly. "That's why I love the sport."

"Well, I think you have a convert. I love it, too. I also like breathing the clean air. Gosh, you can smell the wildflowers."

"Better than any store-bought perfume," she said seriously.

"Sure is," I returned. Silence swept between us, and it was golden. After a few minutes, I said, "Thank you, Jana."

"You're welcome."

Simple words, but they spoke volumes.

The next morning, we took the dogs for a long walk and after they were worn out, we rode along the river. The paved path was busy with other riders and pedestrians as well. Even roller bladers stretched their muscles here, but we didn't mind. It was pretty enough to share.

We ate at one of our favorite mountain restaurants that night and then went for a moonlight swim in the huge hot springs resort pool. Steam funneled skyward as we soaked our sore limbs, but the twinkling sky kept our spirits afloat. I thought of nothing, releasing my mind to the tranquility of earth, moon, and stars. By the time we returned to our room, I was so liquid, you could have poured me between the sheets.

Our fourth day dawned, and it was time to go. We had

planned a final morning ride, but I no longer felt capable. Three days of high-altitude exercise had taken its toll. I knew I could not ride for four hours and then make it to Las Vegas. At breakfast, I broke the news.

"I'm going home, Jana."

She looked at me strangely. "Not before our ride?"

"Yes. I think I should get an early start."

"NO!" she cried.

I was taken aback by her response. I had not expected such a strong objection. "Jana, it's a long drive."

"Judy, I don't want you to go."

What she meant was "ever," and we both knew it. "Me, either," I said. "But I don't want to pay for a motel. If I don't leave now, I'll never make it."

There was a deep sadness in her voice. "Well, if you think it's necessary."

"Jana, you'll enjoy the solitary ride. You know you will. It's your form of meditation."

"I know," she acquiesced.

It wasn't easy to leave her, but we parted quickly and without tears. Once again, I was on the highway of dreams, but I had no idea what I might find when I got home. I had purchased the sound track for Evita while in Colorado Springs, so I listened to it intently as the miles clicked off. The lyrics were haunting.

I did not make it to Vegas that day. Physically I may have been capable, but emotionally I was not. Instead, I stopped in Cedar City, three hours short of my destination. The town hosted a world-renowned Shakespeare Festival, and it was a busy, cheerful place. Most motels had their "no vacancy" signs up, but I found one that was both affordable and willing to take my dogs. After settling, I called my daughter. "I'll see you tomorrow afternoon, Pam. I'm going to hang out here for a while, probably until check-out time, and then I want to hike Snow Canyon before returning to the big city."

"Sounds good, I'll see you for dinner then."

More than anything, I wanted to rest my mind, but that night I found television irritating. I tried to meditate, but thoughts were rampant. I kept returning to the possibility of Rod being inherently evil. Was it possible?

Scott Peck had explained true possession was extremely rare. He also said it was a process. I thought about Rod's strong Christian background and his evangelic preacher grandfather. No doubt as a child he had been scared out of his wits by the hell, fire, and brimstone. My hatred for organized religion renewed. Even if Rod wasn't possessed, he was most certainly wrestling with the demonic.

I worried, too, about the drug issue, for if ever there was something that could open the door to evil, it was drugs. Rod was fighting his addiction, but would he succeed without help? I wanted to return to my home more than anything, but I hated the thought of filing a restraining order and serving an eviction notice. I decided to call him.

"Hello, Rod," I said casually.

"Judy!"

He spoke in a surprised but defensive tone, angry and happy at the same time. I engaged him casually with the usual, "How are you?" and "How have you been?" I also asked him when he planned to leave, but I couldn't get a straight answer. My frustration mounted until I came right to the point.

"I want my house back, Rod. I had hoped it wouldn't be necessary to file a restraining order and have you evicted, but if that's what it takes, I won't hesitate."

The threat shook him. "Judy, you don't need to do that. Of course I'll move out, but I need at least another week."

"I'll be home tomorrow, Rod."

Another surprise. My return did not fit into his plans. "Judy, I'll try to make immediate arrangements. Sandy is selling some equipment, and I should have traveling money soon. Please, don't do anything without talking to me first."

"I'll call you from Pam's house." It was a curt "goodbye" which left him no room to maneuver. After that I was able to meditate, and I allowed the relaxation technique to carry me away. Rather than center myself, I simply drifted and woke well-rested. I did not stay until check-out time that next morning, nor did I take a hike. Rather, I left at the crack of dawn and drove straight through.

Those last few miles proved to be inspiring. After passing St. George and flying through the canyon near the Virgin River, I was struck with a thought. If Rod was possessed, then there was only one way to deal with him. Hatred would create power for the demonic, and it would also make a bad situation worse.

This was a battle for love.

Love was Satan's mortal enemy and truly the only thing he feared. Love, as the saying went, conquered all. Besides, crashing at Pam's house held no appeal, especially when I thought about the possibility of what might be running around in mine. Nope, I needed to confront Rod—or whomever—directly. It was not a time for either fear or cowardice.

And I did feel strong.

I had built a spiritual reservoir, and there was absolutely no doubt in my mind as to what I wanted. On top of that, I believed I'd have the financial means to make it happen. By now, my IRS refund would be waiting at my rented post office box. Remembering the windfall, I decided to make some of it available to fund his return to Reno.

It was only eight a.m. when I arrived in Las Vegas, and since that was too early to check my private box, I went to

Pam's instead. No one was there, so I had the luxury of a quiet coffee hour. I also unpacked, just in case, and then at nine o'clock, I loaded the dogs and took off again.

I was waiting when the attendant arrived at the small postal self-service station, who happily greeted me, apologizing for being late at the same time. Feeling empowered, I returned her cheery salutation and went straight away with my key. Relief flooded me when I saw the single envelope. It was indeed from the Internal Revenue Service. I snatched it quickly, gave the clerk a quick goodbye, and then returned to my car where I could open the envelope in private.

"An audit," I cried. "No!"

The news was devastating, and it completely thwarted my game plan. It also made me exceedingly angry. *How could they? Haven't I suffered enough?* Apparently not, but I had to acknowledge it was probably for the best. After all, money was never the answer. It hadn't solved any of my problems, and when it came to Rod, it had been the source of great aggravation. I spent a few minutes regrouping and went home to confront my nemesis.

Buster and Gus ran through the front door and bolted up the stairs as fast as they could. I went to the back door, slid open the slider, and sat down at the kitchen table. I figured that gave me two means of escape—if need be. I wondered who would greet me and would he be rational and reasonable? A voice answered from above.

"Is that Judy Burr down there?" he asked teasingly. "Is it really you?"

Nothing to fear. "Sure is," I responded to the innocent inflection. When he came downstairs, I kept my distance. We talked, but for a while our tone was guarded. He was most definitely straight, I decided, and he seemed to be in good spirits. At least he was until I broached the subject of his move. He tried to reason with me but ended up falling apart emotionally.

He wanted to divorce Mary Ann, he said. He could not live without me and knew it now. Before, he hadn't been willing to accept that fact but being without me had shown him the truth. He was ready to deal with the issues confronting us, and he said he hated drugs. "Never again," he proclaimed. He was clean, and he intended to stay that way.

"I'm glad," I said, altogether unimpressed. "You need to go home, Rod. You have two fine boys who need their father, and a beautiful baby girl who needs to know she has a father." I neglected to mention his wife because I thought that was treacherous territory. The kids would receive no objections.

It took some time, but when he realized I meant business, he tried a different approach. He agreed to leave but wanted to make love one final time. It was to be his fondest farewell. Inwardly, I smirked. Why do men always want to bid adieu in bed? With Rod, it was probably because he thought he could change my mind, but his technique backfired. I became hostile and stubbornly stood my ground. Much to my chagrin, the Victim emerged and Rod cried.

"Why do you always do this? Why do you have to hurt me?"

I said nothing but moved to the patio, trying to remember I needed to approach this devil with love, not fear. He followed and I watched him carefully. He tried to equivocate, but eventually the truth emerged. I discovered he truly wasn't capable of leaving. He was broke; so broke, in fact, he had been worrying about how to eat. The cupboards were nearly bare. He begged for my indulgence and asked if we could be roommates again. Sandy, he said, had sold a spa, and money was on the way.

"Okay, Rod. You can stay until Monday, but we cannot go back. I'll stay with the kids for the time being but come Monday I want to sleep in my own bed. You need to move on."

This brought on more tears. He was really laying it on thick and he begged me to stay. He didn't trust himself and said he needed a friend.

Whatever happened to the I hate drugs, Rod? I was also thinking of my own recovery. It had been tough, but with Jana's help, I had done it. Finally, I agreed to a compromise. I went back to Pam's and returned with my things. Rod begrudgingly moved into the downstairs bedroom. Well, that's a start, I said to myself. I had at least reclaimed the sanctuary of my master bedroom. Greatly relieved, I unpacked and then left for the grocery store. Stay strong, I said, traversing the food aisles. He'll be gone soon. Love will get you through.

CHAPTER 25

The Lion's Den

"TRUST ME, PAM, he's harmless," I said at the dinner table that evening. I had returned to explain, as if that were possible. "He has no money, no drugs, and no place to go. What do you want me to do? Throw him out on the street?"

That was exactly what she expected, but she did not speak the words. "Well, at least stay here then."

"Honey, if I do that, he'll never leave, at least not without a fight. Think about this. If Sandy sends him money and Rod is alone, the first thing he'll do is hit the streets for a fix."

Jason intervened. "Judy's right. Based on what I saw a week ago, Rod most definitely could use a hand. I can't stand the man, but I do feel for him."

Pam looked disgusted, but asked, "So, you don't believe Mom is in any danger?"

"I doubt it. Right now, Rod would probably have a hard time stepping on his own shadow."

I was thankful for Jason's support. "I'm guessing he's been clean for about ten days, but who knows how much he was using before then. My God, he didn't even go home for the birth of his daughter. Can you imagine?"

"No!" Pam said adamantly. "What in the world is wrong

with the man?"

"He's a two-time loser," I said. "He burned Coastline down, and now he's done the same thing to his own company. Since Global collapsed, he can't find the strength to face his own family."

"Coward," cried Jason.

"Yes, he's truly weak right now, but he's also an addict, and he could use some help. I only shot the stuff for four days, and that was enough. It took everything I had to leave town that day."

Pam brightened. "But you did. At least you had the guts to make a break."

"I also had a place to go. If I don't push Rod, he'll take full advantage. He'll stay simply because he fears going home. He's afraid of retribution. Believe me, I know the man, and I also know getting a restraining order is not the way. Just think about what Speicher did. Forcing him out of the business only caused him to retaliate. Now both Jason and I are facing possible incarceration. Rod's no different. He may be smarter, but he's every bit as sick as Speicher was."

"What a nightmare," she said.

"Pam, it's almost over. I really think this is the best way."

Jason helped me out again. "Call us if you need anything. I can be there in five minutes, and trust me, I will neutralize him."

I sighed but withheld comment. Rod, I knew, was a hurting human being. Using force against him would only serve to increase his anguish. I left without looking directly into my daughter's distraught face. I knew my situation was precarious, but it was my home and I wanted it back.

Pulling in the driveway, I was surprised to find my garage space occupied. Rod's giant truck was there, which I hadn't expected. I expected to put him on a plane, but now I knew things would be more difficult. He had wheels, and that made him mobile. *Trouble in River City*, I thought.

Inside, Rod was lounging on the couch. He seemed immersed in some program, so I attempted no contact. I checked the kitchen and saw that he had made a sandwich, so I went upstairs. He had eaten, which was all I needed to know. I did not say "hello," nor did I offer a "goodnight." I simply called my dogs and went to bed.

The next day he joined me at the pool. We engaged in some light conversation, and I learned, at some point, Sandy had brought his truck down. The master had been served, and then his servant flew back to Reno. Good old Sandy, he was still tending to business—Rod's business.

Later Rod and I ate some dinner together, but after cleaning up, I retreated again. This time we cordially called it a night.

It wasn't until the third evening I took him to my bed, but I did and I accepted full responsibility. The old friendship returned and it had been a good day. I stayed on the lower level to watch a movie with him, and when he cuddled up and put his head in my lap, I did not protest. Rather, I allowed the comfort, and I ran my fingers through his hair as though he were a small child. Words were not spoken, but when the program ended, I nudged him and extended a hand. Of course, he took it.

Life became a treasure after that, and although we knew our days were numbered, we basked in them.

On Friday, the money arrived.

"I want to take you camping," he said.

"Camping? Isn't it a little late for that?"

"Come on, Judy. Two days in the mountains will do us wonders. Let's leave in the morning, spend one night in the woods, and then on Monday morning I'll head back to Reno."

Reno? That was good news. "Promise?"

"I promise," he said.

"Okay then. Let's go pack the gear."

"We can do that in the morning. Let me take you to dinner and a movie. I've been in this house too long. Will you be my date tonight? I need to get out of here."

The preparation time for an overnight trip was minimal, so I agreed to the diversion. We had a wonderful meal and then purchased tickets for the movie, but the one we wanted to see was popular, so we had to wait until ten o'clock to get seats. We spent the extra time in the adjoining casino and Rod got lucky at the tables. He was back to his old self. Once again, he was seductively charismatic, and I enjoyed watching his flamboyant style.

After the show he wrapped an arm around my waist and we walked to the car. "I'm really wound up," he said. "How about you?"

"I feel great, but my bed is calling me. Let's get a good night's sleep, so we can start early, okay?"

"Okay," he agreed. "But I'd like to take some weed. Do you mind if we make a stop on the way home?"

My reaction was quick. "Mind? Yes, I mind. Rod, that's not a good idea."

But he thought it was, and I couldn't convince him otherwise. Finally, I made him take me home. I couldn't control him, but I wouldn't participate. He dropped me with a kiss and a promise. "I'll be home within an hour."

Two hours later he called. Rod was sorry, but he had trouble making a connection. He was leaving right now and wanted me to know. He did not want me to worry.

"Thanks," I said. "But hurry home. It's cold and lonely here."

"On my way," were his famous last words.

I returned to my peaceful slumber, but it wasn't long before my dreams were rudely interrupted. My subconscious jabbed me with something pointed and purposeful. Instantly, I was awake. With dread I turned toward the clock. It confirmed my suspicions. It was 4:00 a.m., which meant only one thing. Since it was impossible to sleep, I got up to write in my journal. When I turned off my computer, I spoke to the walls. "Too bad," I said. "What happened to the Soulmate Super Exchange? We once rode it regularly. This feels like Hell's Highway."

Not even love had managed to keep Rod's demons in check. He had gone to the other side and couldn't let go. Just like Pat Benatar's song—how did those lyrics go? Something about touching the devil. I was curious, but not enough to play the CD. Somehow, I thought it was better not to know.

Rod came in about seven with his tail dragging—tucked between his legs, actually. He confessed his transgressions, and then said something that made me even angrier.

"I wasn't with Mandy, though," he offered sheepishly. "I promise you, Judy. You are all I care about, and I never want you to think otherwise."

Mandy! Mandy hadn't even crossed my mind. I was pissed because he had forsaken himself, and I was angry because I had trusted him. He was tweaked beyond the point of understanding, however, so I held my tongue. Rod continued his justifying tirade. As far as he was concerned, he had hurt only himself.

I felt otherwise.

He was destroying so much, and many people were being affected. Still I remained silent. Speaking would serve no purpose. I stared for a few seconds and then turned toward my pups. They were playing, showing off in the backyard. I smiled as though I had not a care in the world.

Rod didn't know what to think and he couldn't tolerate my nonchalant attitude. He went off again, chastising himself and promising to get help. "I'll check myself into a care unit, Judy. I know it's the only way. Please, don't give up on me."

"I haven't given up, Rod."

My words encouraged him and then he came up with a whopper. He laid his greatest equivocation on me.

"I understand now, Judy. Without a doubt I know it was not your fault."

Oh brother. Let's pass the blame again. Whose fault is it now, Rod? I asked, without speaking.

"Don't you see, it's the principalities of darkness. It's been the band of black angels this whole time. They are the ones throwing me off balance."

I groaned. My worst nightmare was coming true. I had speculated about the possibility, but if Rod thought he was possessed, then it was as good as done. In fact, demonic possession was a perfect excuse. It would exempt him from the sins of an entire lifetime. The evil mask would also allow him to hide from himself, and if need be, hide from the entire world. It was the perfect disguise.

Realizing the incredible power of his statement, I wanted to scream, but I did it silently. Are you really, truly, deeply, and irrevocably evil, Rod? Are you that far gone? I pray to God you are not. You are clever, but are you really that weak—that stupid?

"I'm going to lie down for a couple of hours," he said. "But I still want to go camping. Okay?"

"Sure, Rod," I said, giving him permission to walk away. I knew camping was out of the question but allowing him room to retreat seemed like a good idea. I'll keep you in my prayers, baby. It was my only hope.

Three hours later, I packed a six-pack of beer, downed a shot of Jack Daniels, and headed to the pool with my cooler. Drinking, I knew, was the wrong thing to do, but it neutralized my immediate agony. I took my time, thoroughly tanned my backside, and when the brew disappeared, I went home to pass out. My only wish was to remain relatively comatose for the afternoon, but it wasn't to be. In my stumble bumbling way, I managed to stub my big toe and the resulting pain was excruciating. The rage hit me and I couldn't contain it. I presented my bloody stump to Rod.

"Kiss it, baby," I said, drawing him out of his stupor. Rod opened his eyes, but looked up, not down. I brought my foot closer to get the proper attention. "Come on, clean off the blood."

He was horrified, and his eyes went wide with shock.

"Do it, Rod. Do what you do best. Suck the blood from my big toe."

"What's the matter with you?" he asked, sitting up.

"What do you mean? Don't you like it? Aren't you excited? You are a vampire, aren't you?"

"Judy!"

"Well, you were out all night. Did you already fill up? Who did you bleed, Rod? Who was your victim this time?"

"You're drunk!"

"Yeah, and you're fucked up," I retaliated. "But I know you're capable. You're a seasoned vampire, Rod, so suck me dry, baby. Suck the life right out of me."

"That's it," he said, jumping up. "We're out of here."

"You going to drag me to your dungeon, are you? Want to take me down before the kill? Is that it? Well, okay, but you have to help me first. Come on, Rod, help me. I'd hate to leave a trail of blood."

Confusion engulfed him and I started having fun. I enjoyed playing the part of a looney-toon. The reversed role was quite satisfying. I began to pace, bouncing off the walls, and wailing like a madwoman. My insane act came easily. I had been taught by the best. When I raced down the stairs, Rod followed, but I would not allow him to calm me.

At some point, he threw up his hands and went to the garage.

Good, I thought, crashing to the couch. Get out and good riddance! I had worn myself out and I wanted to sleep. Rod had other plans. After a few minutes, he came back into the house.

"Come on, we're going camping."

He was tugging on my arm. "No! I don't want to go camping. I don't want to go anywhere with you."

He raced to the kitchen and came back with my purse. "Judy, we have got to get out of here. This whole house is under attack. Come on, honey. I've packed everything. All we have to do is stop at the store for a few groceries."

Shopping? In my condition? I didn't think so. I stood up, screamed, "NO!" and picked up one end of the coffee table. Then I dropped it. Glass went everywhere, and the sound was deafening. It even silenced me. Rod stood still for what seemed like an eternity, then swept me into his arms. I was bodily thrown into his truck, and since I was literally exhausted, I remained compliantly poised against the window.

We left the neighborhood, and he turned into a nearby shopping center. I thought he wanted food, but it was money on his mind. He got in line at the drive-thru for the bank ATM machine. While waiting, he rifled through my purse. Just take my last penny, jerk face. You really are a vampire.

"What's the code number?"

As he slid the card into place I told him. Rod programmed the withdrawal and I waited. "The transaction was denied," he said.

"How much did you ask for?"

"Just a hundred."

"I don't have a hundred, Rod. I've got about forty-eight bucks to my name and that's it."

He seemed horrified, but no more than me. Funding our excursion had not occurred to me, and now I knew he had blown every penny of his precious wad. The night before must have been quite a party. Rod jerked the card from the automatic teller and screeched through the drive. The truck skidded around the bank on two wheels, and then he drove around to the back side of the shopping center. I had no idea what he was doing, but he parked and I soon found out. The right jab to my mouth was vicious. I immediately tasted blood.

"Rod!" I screamed, but he slapped me. My arms went around my head as he flailed at them. Then he kicked out sideways. I took a kick in the shin and then the ribs. While I yelled in protest, his hands found their mark. No one could hear my cries for help, and I began to think he might kill me. Finally, the battering stopped. I drew a short breath and began to cry.

"Why?" he hollered. "Why did you provoke me? You know I can't take it. It's your damn fault. Are you trying to drive me insane?"

"No!" I screamed. More blows landed for my rebuke. I curled up and tried begging. I knew if I had any chance of escaping, I would have to reach him. I said I was sorry, I had been stupid, but it was because I was drunk. He of all people should understand. I went on and on, until I knew he was listening. I was no better than him. I had faults, too. We were both victims, both wounded and suffering. It was the abuse, the abuse we suffered as kids. That's what was causing our torment. We were warriors, and we were trying, but trouble followed us. He was quiet, so I professed my love. My reward came in the form of a rag.

"Clean yourself up," he ordered.

I swiped at my mouth, and wished I had a gun. At that moment, I could easily have pulled the trigger.

Rod watched, but I saw nothing kind in his expression. I forced the tears to a halt and controlled myself. He checked for witnesses. Since there were none, he put the truck in gear and slowly moved around the buildings. The diesel grumbled and I prayed. As we approached the busy street, I formulated a plan. As expected, he was forced to stop for traffic, and while he waited for clear passage, I jumped from his clutches. I slammed down on the door handle and practically fell out of his truck. Righting myself, I took off running. I also started screaming. "HELP!" I cried over and over. He was behind me and I could feel a hand. I dropped to the sidewalk, curled into a ball, and continued bellowing. This time I knew someone would hear. He tried to bodily pick me up, but I twisted away, screaming the whole time. Finally, fearing intervention, he made his break. The Dodge burned rubber for half a block, and I stayed on the cement, wondering what I might do next.

A red truck pulled up to the curb. "Are you okay?" she asked.

I looked up from my helpless heap. "I think so."

"Can we give you lift? Take you somewhere?"

There was a man in the truck, but he looked gentle. She looked like an angel. "Could you drive me to my daughter's house?" I asked through the tears. "It's not far."

"Come on," said the voice from heaven.

I directed them, and they did not leave me.

Pam and Jason were having a small party, but the voyeurs were kept at bay. The police came and my ministering angels stayed. We learned three people had called 911, and as it turned out, the man driving the rescue truck knew one of the investigating officers. He and his girlfriend had witnessed everything, which made things easier. The proper reports were taken, pictures were snapped, and then names and addresses were exchanged. Before everybody left, Pam took me to the bathroom, and we tried to doctor my wounds.

"Can I just lie down?" I asked.

"Of course, you can, Mom. You take yourself a nice long nap. In fact, promise me you won't leave, at least not without Jason. When you're ready, will you let him take you home?"

"Yes," I said quietly. "God, I'm sorry, Pam."

"I'm just glad you're okay. You will file that restraining order now, won't you?"

"I have to. He left me no choice."

"Good."

I tried to smile, but my mouth hurt, and the remembering made me wince. As she closed the door, I thought about what I had done. I had indeed returned to the lion's den, but it was my home. I was the Leo, and true to my nature, I remained stubborn to the bitter end.

PART IV

THE FAMILY

CHAPTER 26

Destiny on a Dime

AFTER THAT BEATING I was dysfunctional. Looking at my reflection reduced me to tears and caused me to wonder. What was wrong with Rod? And why in the world was I worried about him? I was the one with the bruised face and puffed lip. He had inflicted my wounds, created chaos in my life, and then left me in the worst way possible. So, why was my concern directed toward him? It was a conundrum. I had no wish to see him, and in many ways, I was glad for the brutal end. It left no possibility for reconciliation.

It was time to move on, but it was tough. I tried drafting a resume, but when I showed it to Pam, I knew my efforts were not good enough.

"I don't know, Mom. Maybe you should show this to someone else," she said.

She was trying to be kind, but the rendition was pitiful. I sighed and said, "My heart just isn't in it. I hate the idea of working. God, I wish that refund check was here."

"Maybe, but isn't that kind of a moot point? You can't afford not to work, can you?"

She knew my situation was bad, but she did not know it was desperate. I was down to forty bucks. "No, I suppose not, but I'm beginning to understand Rod's fifth ring."

She was befuddled. "His fifth key principle?"

"Yes, the one about sacrifice. He always said to manifest a vision, one had to be prepared to give up everything."

"Everything?"

"Yes, everything, including your life—if necessary."

"What? Isn't that a bit much?"

"I used to think so, but now I feel that way, too. I think I'd prefer losing it all rather than go back to a nine-to-five grind."

"Mom, you're grieving. You've been through an awful lot, but business has always been your middle name. You'll find a job, and once you do, everything will fall into place; you'll see."

After the fiasco with Global, I was sick to death of business, so I decided to see if there was another way. My neighborhood HOA was sponsoring a parking lot garage sale that next weekend. Participating in it would at least buy me some time. I went through my house with a pad and pencil, listing everything I might sell. Each room was inventoried carefully. I needed twelve hundred dollars to meet my immediate needs, and anything after that could be banked for the future.

I'll sell it all. Everything but the bare minimum. The list grew, and as I tallied the numbers, so did my hopes. I was at the four-thousand-dollar mark when I walked into my office. This was my favorite room and the furnishings were necessities. The desk had to stay as it housed my computer. My two favorite reading chairs were in there and giving them up was out of the question. Nor could I part with the beautiful world globe that had once been my father's. It was more than a family heirloom. It symbolized a small personal victory.

Rod had eyed it from the first day and had continually

asked me to part with it. He wanted my father's globe, or more specifically, he wanted me to leave my father's world and join his. I decided the globe would be a fine reminder of my hard-won freedom, so I left that room and traveled down the hall to another.

When I finished my tour, I called Pam. "Can I borrow Jason's truck on Saturday? There's a neighborhood garage sale and I want to sell some things this weekend."

"Sure, Mom. That sounds great. Can I bring some stuff, too? How about I help you get ready?"

"Are you up to it?" She was expecting any day, and I couldn't imagine her standing for any length of time.

"I'm feeling pretty good, but I'm bored. I need to get out. I'll come over Friday to get things marked, put clothes on hangers, do the light work. On Saturday morning, I'll have Jason come help with the heavier stuff."

"Cool. Thanks, honey." With that settled, I felt much better. I also became more pragmatic. Logic told me I would still need a job. I could not survive the duration of an IRS audit without losing the house, and even though it was my dream to write, I still wanted a roof over my head. I pulled at my word processor and tried again. This time my resume was good and my attention was on it when the phone rang.

"Hi!" he said.

Rod! I couldn't believe it. Immediately, I hung up the phone. *The nerve,* I thought. *How dare he?* The man was an enigma. Again, the phone rang, but this time I let the answering machine pick up. He sounded solid, not a bit sketchy, but there was no apology, not even a hint of remorse.

I called the phone company and had my number changed. I made sure it was unlisted and established a voice mailbox. That would ensure privacy and it would also prevent my nemesis from dislodging my momentum. I was on my way. On Saturday I would have emergency money, and then on Sunday I would start my search. "Goodbye and good riddance, Mr. Global. This girl has left the building."

What a weekend! It stirred us emotionally, and I was nearly overwhelmed by what occurred.

On Friday, Pam arrived as promised. She had taken Marie to daycare, so we could accomplish our mission, and we were bopping around to music when she doubled over.

"What's wrong?" I cried as she gasped and went down.

"My back. Oh my God, Mom. It hurts!" she cried.

As I reached for her, she righted herself and turned to stare. "Wow. S'pose I'm in labor?"

I smiled. "Maybe ... time will tell."

Twenty minutes later, it happened again. "You better call Jason," I said. "Give him fair warning. Looks like today may be the day."

She phoned his workplace but had to leave a message. Two hours passed before he called, but she hadn't experienced another contraction. "It was probably a false alarm," she told him. "You better phone once an hour, just in case."

I stared at her and wondered. Would this be the day? We went back to work, but intermittently the pain returned. After lunch, I began watching the clock. I didn't tell her when the pains steadied at ten-minute intervals, but Jason hadn't called either. I told her to leave him another message. She started to pace through the contractions, but when one sent her sprawling, I began to panic. They were more consistent and much more intense, but still her hubby failed to call. I was about to suggest we go to the hospital when he finally rang through. Pam was in the middle of a gut-wrenching contraction, so I told Jason to come and get her. "It's time," I said. "You are about to be a father again."

An hour later he still wasn't there, and she could sense the urgency. She left messages, and you could not mistake the meaning. "NOW!" she said.

Knowing she was worried, I tried to remain calm. I pretended everything was copacetic. "Don't worry, sweetie. He'll be here any minute. You'd be miserable at the hospital anyway; might as well hang out here as long as possible."

In my mind's eye, I was delivering a baby. I thought about the clean sheets, the scissors, the string, and the inevitable cry. God forbid it happened at my house, but a decision had to be made soon. We either needed to leave for the hospital without him, or we were going to need some hot water. I started rubbing Pam's back as the spasms came and went. Finally, Jason showed up.

"Thank God," I said.

"What?" he asked innocently.

"You're having a baby!" I hollered. "Now if you don't want to deliver it yourself, I suggest you get to the hospital."

"Come on, honey. I've got the truck running. Let's go." They left to bring another life into the world, and I left to claim my granddaughter, Marie. When I returned home, the phone rang.

"Your new granddaughter is here," he said.

"Big surprise," I chortled. "So how are my girls?"

"They're perfect. I couldn't believe it. Pam popped her out like a pro, and Hanna is too cute."

"The second one is always easier," I said.

"I thought we had all the time in the world. It took forever with Marie. This was great."

"Maybe for you," I chided. "For us it was scary as hell."

"I'm sorry, Judy."

"It's okay. Congratulations. Tell Pam I'm proud of her. She was a real trooper."

"Okay, I'll see you in the morning."

I was surprised. "You're still going to help?"

"Sure. I'll be over by seven. Will that be early enough?"

"Perfect. The sale starts at eight. That will give me an hour to set up."

"Okay, see you then."

"See you, 'Dad.' Don't party too hearty."

"I won't. Kiss Marie for me, will you?"

"You got it, Pops," I chuckled. I knew my son-in-law would soon be celebrating. Jason needed no excuse to drink, but when he had one, he took full advantage. In fact, I was pretty sure he had been drinking before he arrived at my house.

The next morning, he was late. By nine o'clock I was completely frustrated. I had been unable to get an answer on the phone, so I went over to his house. With the baby in tow, I barged into the bedroom.

"Jason," I hollered, shaking him out of his stupor. "Where are your keys?"

He rolled his eyes. "On the kitchen counter. Wait. Let me get a quick shower."

He smelled like a brewery. "I can't. If I don't claim a space, I won't get one. Just come help me as quick as you can."

By the time he showed up, I had made three trips. After that, he wanted to eat. I was left with my granddaughter and a parcel of goods to barter.

Men. They are so worthless.

Fortunately, I didn't miss much. The traffic thus far was relatively light. So far, so good. I wasn't sure how I was going to manage a toddler and still talk to people, but my mother showed up and made it possible.

"Thanks for coming," I said.

"Looks like you could use a hand."

"No kidding," I said, watching Marie run from one stall to the next. She delighted the participants, and I figured they would help take care of her.

"Where is everybody?" she asked. "I thought it would be busier than this."

"Me, too. I sure hope this wasn't a wasted effort. I was counting on it to generate some cash."

She tried to be cheerful, but before the day was over it looked bleak. Mom must have sensed my desperation because she offered to buy my pearls. I accepted, but I took the bare minimum, and said, "One day I'd like to buy them back."

For the balance of the afternoon, she encouraged others to buy. Unfortunately, the sale was a bust. The association, it turns out, had not advertised properly and the only traffic was drive by. I envisioned the day my utilities went off.

The prospect of living without gas, power, or water was daunting, but when Jason came by with Pam and Hanna, I put on a brave face for my new granddaughter. After a brief visit, Jason loaded up his truck with my heavier items and departed. Mom and I packed up the small things, loaded them in her car, and went back to my house to cool off.

"Disappointed?" she asked, sipping on a glass of iced water.

"God, yes. All that work for nothing."

"Will you manage?"

"Sure, Mom," I said. "I'll be fine, but I need to get serious about getting a job. I plan to start interviewing Monday."

This seemed to please her and she soon left without a worry. I took some aspirin and climbed into the tub. I wanted to forget about the disappointing and sweltering afternoon. After climbing from my calming waters, I went directly to bed. The next morning, I surprised myself. Determined not to get depressed, and in order not to be alone, I did the unthinkable. I got dressed and went to church!

Stranger in a Strange Land. I had read the book years ago, but it came to mind as I walked through those brass doors. I tried to be inconspicuous, but I was recognized as a newcomer and given a cordial welcome. The congregation assumed I was new to the neighborhood, and I didn't say otherwise.

Friendship stirred me and the hymns brought tears to my eyes. I had been away too long. Still, the remembering brought forward mixed emotions. I had once loved the Church, but the people in my congregation were another thing altogether. Had anything changed? Could I possibly trust this group? Would it be worth the effort or was I grasping at straws?

I listened to the sermon. There was nothing about guilt or fear, no mention of punishment or hell. In fact, the reverend offered nothing but encouraging words. I was moved. More tears, but these were the comforting kind. Suddenly I felt stronger and I believed things would work out with all my heart.

Pulling in my driveway, I realized I hadn't picked up my mail, so I parked the car and walked to the mailbox in front of my house. Mostly bills, I thought, flipping through the stack. By this time my creditors were numerous. I hadn't received a paycheck for months and I was deeply in debt. "Well, they can wait," I said, returning to the house. "Right now, there are more pressing matters—like buying groceries." I entered the kitchen, tossed the stack on the table, and poured myself a cup of coffee. With courage in hand, I returned to scrutinize the pile. One envelope came from my corporate attorney. Since I owed him nothing, my curiosity piqued. What could this be? I was almost afraid to break the seal. Surely it couldn't be good news. Timidly, I tore at the white parchment, and I pulled out a single piece of paper. It was a check, a check for a thousand dollars.

"What?" I exclaimed. "A thousand bucks! For what?"

I looked at the notation on the perforated lower half of

the voucher. Éclat! I had sued the company, but it had been three years. The court had ruled in my favor but getting payment for the breach of contract proved futile. I had given up, but now the first payment was in front of me. It was a godsend—literally! That money would keep the lights on. It felt like a miracle and I marveled at the fact I had just come from church.

I was willing to change and to grow and now fate was stepping in to help. It was dharma as opposed to karma. “Yes!” I exclaimed out loud. “Destiny really can turn on a dime. Belief is required, but with a little faith, the shift is possible. Ain’t it great!”

CHAPTER 27

The Flushing

AFTER THAT MINI MIRACLE, motivation became my middle name. By the end of the week, I had been on several interviews and nine resumés were in the field. Any one of those positions would have filled my needs, and in most cases, I was more than qualified. I felt positive for the future and was inspired to write. Bits and pieces were produced and then fine-tuned, but I was working on the final chapters, not the first. I had no idea where to begin. Feeling adrift, I changed direction and started to clean house. Rod had left a trail and I was anxious to get rid of the reminders. I began by changing the linens, disinfecting the bathrooms, and dusting away every flick of dirt. As I shifted knickknacks, took out trash, and pushed furniture around, I discovered evidence of his nasty habit. Hypodermic needles were everywhere, as if they had been deliberately placed.

Oh my God, what was he doing? I asked myself. The question really wasn't necessary, for truly I knew the answer. He had set me up for a fall. In case I came back and turned on him, he had left a trail of deceit. If my pretrial supervisor had come into the house and conducted a search, I would have been hauled away in handcuffs. The discovery was a low blow, and even knowing that Rod was sick, it still hit hard.

I found one used needle in the bedroom trash can and another in the bathroom vanity. When I moved the bed out from the wall, two were under the headboard. The more I cleaned, the more I worried. What if Rod panicked and called someone? What kind of trouble might he cause? I had no idea, so I went through that house with a fine-tooth comb.

In the attic I found his collection of pornographic movies. My Day-Timer and Rolodex were also up there buried under the layers of fiberglass. At least I have these back, I said, offering myself condolences. I put the calendar book and the phone index on my desk. The smut collection went into a huge black trash sack, along with the needles.

What else did you do, Rod? I felt like he could hear me, and it was spooky. His spirit was omniscient, and I turned quickly to see if he was behind me. For a moment I saw an aberration. It disappeared, though, and I wondered. Would he ever let go? Would I?

When I finished my sweep, I tied the lumbering bag and then placed it in another. Rather than set the contraband curbside, I stuck it in the trunk of my car. That evening, I drove out of the neighborhood and threw the paraphernalia in a dumpster behind a closed restaurant. So there, Mr. Steersman, you sick son of a bitch. You're out of here.

The shakedown shook me, so to escape what I was feeling, I turned to my word processor. I made several attempts at a beginning, but none of them satisfied me. I simply could not get in the groove. The fanciful fairy tale I had planned about angels, witches, and demons wasn't working. My story was real and needed to be told honestly. Trouble was, the truth hurt, and recalling it took me back to the days before my arrest. I began to plummet. The black hole was coming fast and there was no escape. If some compassionate employer had offered me a job, I might have climbed out, but no one was willing.

They could not see beyond my past. I had to be upfront about my legal situation and knowing that I had an impending court date didn't bode well. I did not get hired, which even I understood. Why take the time and trouble to train today if they couldn't count on the employee being there tomorrow? I wouldn't have done it. Of course, no potential employer had the courage to say this, at least not to my face.

"Damn you, Rod," I said, staring at the walls. "If only I hadn't gone to work for Global. If only I hadn't fallen in love with you."

As my despondency deepened, my daughter and my mother began calling. They tried to reach me and said lots of encouraging words, but I did not feel hopeful and couldn't pretend otherwise. The invitations came and I rejected them. I wanted to be alone. I thought about calling my counselor, but that was not possible. I could not afford her services and I wouldn't ask for a handout. Time moved slowly. To save myself, I went back to my computer.

I found focus, and within that iridescent screen the world slipped away. I couldn't create, not really, but I journaled like crazy and the days passed. The only thing I accomplished routinely was feeding my dogs. Feeding me required too much effort; besides, I wasn't hungry. Sleep was more comforting, so I sank dismally at the end of each day, thankful for the blackness.

Finally, one morning I woke up and everything changed.

After a fitful night, I staggered from my tousled bed. I was dreary-eyed and barely awake, so when I reached for my toothpaste, I managed to bang the medicine cabinet shelf. The impact jarred loose several items that fell to the counter below. While putting them away, I noticed my contact lens case, which reminded me of Rod. In the past he had hidden his drugs in the flat plastic case. Without really thinking about what I was doing, I unscrewed one of the lids. It was empty. Thank God. Just to be sure I opened the other side and low-and-behold, a small, crinkled plastic wrapper blinked up at me. Rod had forgotten his precious cargo on that fateful day of our demise. Camping had been on his mind, and in his haste, he had left his stash behind. I picked up the parcel and headed for the toilet. Tossing it, however, proved impossible. Instead, I started to justify. Maybe I'll do one line. One wouldn't hurt, would it? God knows I could use the lift.

I retraced my steps and brushed my teeth. As I washed my face, I anticipated the rush. The stimulant would kick me out of my doldrums and maybe, just maybe, I could find a creative spark. Attempting to rationalize my insane behavior, I decided to eat first. A good breakfast would naturally elevate my blood sugar, and the boost would last longer. I made myself ham, eggs, and toast. On the patio, I drank juice and watched my puppies play. They were excited. Must be in the air, I said to myself. I showered and dressed and then carried my small bindle into the office to turn on my machine. As the hard drive whirred, I tapped out a line. When the monitor asked for my password, I punched the proper keys. Keying down on my rolled-up dollar bill, I sucked up half the yellowish powder. Before the burn hit, I switched sides and pulled through the other nostril. The acid screamed into my sinuses, and I winced. Soon the pain lifted and the euphoria came. I centered my mouse on the rubber pad and requested the proper program. A blank page appeared, and I stared. How do I start? I asked. Where do I begin?

The answer was nondescript, but it was there. Anywhere, was the response. Begin wherever but do it now. Just go for it.

The word "I" came out, but that seemed scary. Was I really going to write this from my point of view? Suddenly I was thirsty. I gave up my chair and went back downstairs. I made myself a giant coke and did the dishes. After the kitchen sparkled, I threw in a load of laundry, reviewed my mail, and ran the vacuum cleaner. I was working through the initial rush while thinking about my manuscript. Where did it all begin? God knows it was long before Speicher, long before the federal raid.

I thought about the first man in my life and remembered how I hated his heavy hand. At the tender age of thirteen, I fought my father's lashing like a wild tigress and managed to kick him below the belt. The agony sent him sprawling, and he left abruptly. "Sorry, Dad," I said, as my childhood flooded back. I raced to the terminal. Just do it, I told myself. Begin anywhere but get started.

Something about soul shackles came out and before the day ended, I had a start to my story. I had also polished off the package of crystal methamphetamine. The experience was satisfying, but now I was wired. Knowing sleep would elude me, I made myself a downer drink. It helped, but one required another, and the ratios changed. The second one was nine parts liquor and one part water. I climbed into the bath, lit a candle, and put on some music. The glass glistened golden, and the warm water began to soak away the last of my chemical rush. After the water therapy, I clambered between the sheets. Amazingly, sleep came and when the morning dawned, I felt surprisingly good. I thanked my resilient constitution, because on that day I had an appointment with my pretrial supervisor.

"How's it going, Judy?" he asked nonchalantly.

"Oh, pretty good, Norman. Guess I can't complain."

Norman was a caring kind of a guy, but he was also a pro. His tall, good looks did not fool me. I was his responsibility and he needed to know what was going on in my life.

"Any luck on the job hunt?" He peered through his dark-rimmed spectacles.

I had told him about Global's relocation to Reno and he was concerned. My employment was of the highest priority. Being employed indicated stability.

"No, not yet. No one seems interested in hiring a convicted felon, especially one who hasn't faced the judge."

He was alarmed. "How are you managing?"

"I've sold my jewelry and my neighborhood had a big garage sale. I did okay, so far, so good."

"Do you have any leads?"

"A few," I encouraged. "I have several resumés in the field and I'm hopeful. I believe something will turn up. I'm also considering a roommate."

"I thought you had one. What happened to that other guy?"

He had met Rod, whom I'd introduced as a companion, not a roomer.

"We had a falling out. In fact, I've filed a restraining order against him."

Norman seemed relieved. "Is he leaving you alone?"

"Yes, thank God. He tried to call, so I had the number changed."

"Well, I wondered. I've been trying to reach you."

My alarm went off. "Gosh, I'm sorry. I forgot to tell you."

As he keyed in my new information, my heart skipped a beat. Why had he wanted to talk to me? If the Feds wanted something, they could have called my attorney, Karen. What was up with Norman?

He turned and said, "Judy, your probation officer from San Diego called. Apparently, someone told him you were using drugs. They've requested a UA."

"A UA?" I asked innocently.

"A urine analysis. Do you have a problem with that?"

"No, I guess not." I choked on my words, but I don't think he noticed.

"Good. That's what I told them. I said you'd be willing to comply, and I was sure we could quickly put this to rest."

Since he was reassured, I went into my act. "That jerk. He's retaliating because I kicked him out."

"Sounds to me like you're better off without him."

"No kidding, but I still can't believe he can reach into my life like this."

"You don't have to agree. We can't force you to give us a specimen."

He was so nice, so kind, so compassionate, I thought about confessing. I didn't, though. I was afraid of the consequences. "Really? Would you mind calling my attorney? I'd like to get her advice."

He didn't, and as he punched in the numbers, I prayed. God grant me a miracle. I cannot do this. This simply cannot happen.

Fortunately, Karen was out for lunch. He left a message and then turned. "What do you want to do?"

"Would you mind waiting? I'd really like to speak with her first."

"Not at all, just come back before five o'clock."

A reprieve! "Thanks, Norman," I said, standing up. "I'll see you later."

I walked to my car and felt the rush from the day before. I hadn't ingested drugs for approximately sixteen hours, but adrenalin was racing through my veins. I stopped at the first phone booth and made a call.

"Can I come over?" It was a coded question, and permission was granted. When I got to the house, I was asked another question.

"How much do you want?"

"None!" I said, "I need some advice."

"What's up?" he asked.

I told him what happened and asked how long the drug would be in my system.

"Forty-eight hours," he said flatly.

"Then I'm fucked." I was scared out of my wits. I had no idea what they would do, but I knew if the test results were positive, it would damage my credibility as a government witness. I saw my chances for probation going up in smoke.

"Don't go back today," he suggested. "Go to the health food store and get yourself some Clean Tea. Drink it all night and tomorrow morning. Then go test."

"But that will still be less than forty-eight hours."

"It'll be okay, Judy. You might even fly by today, but it's best to be sure."

I left the house and went to the store. After I purchased a double batch of the potion, I went home and began my cleansing routine. I drank the warm water and waited. I had no intention of rushing my attorney, but at four-forty-five she called.

"Your supervisor told me what happened. Why didn't you consent to the UA?"

"I was outraged. Can Rod really do this?" I had been under supervision for a year-and-a-half. No one had ever mentioned drug testing.

"Anyone can, Judy. I've seen anonymous callers stir up worse commotion. Who is this guy?"

"Just someone I was involved with," I said, downplaying Rod's role in my life. "I've been trying to break free from him, but he was obsessed. I filed a restraining order to get him out of my life."

"Regardless, I recommend you comply."

"And if I don't?"

"They'll assume you're dirty and will probably take action accordingly."

I did not want to ask what that action might be. It would imply guilt. "Okay, I'll take care of it."

"Call me if you need anything," she said congenially.

I called Norman. "I just spoke with Karen. She advised me to cooperate. When do you want me down there?"

I was granted a stay of execution. It was too late. They were getting ready to close. The next morning would be fine said the agreeable voice. I hung up the phone and drank the tea, relieved the pressure, and did it again. Over and over, I repeated the process. I felt like I was flushing all the way up to my eyeballs, but by noon the next day I would have logged forty hours. Somehow that had to be enough. Please let it be enough.

CHAPTER 28

A Crashing Reality

MY ARREST served as a hard lesson. It quickly taught me I was powerless against the Feds and I never forgot what my attorney said explaining my rights. Basically, I had none.

"You are persona non grata, Judy."

Less than a person. My status as a citizen had been downgraded to that of a dog. I had been outraged by the insinuation, but this was far worse. Not only did I have to submit to a drug test, but I also had to squat in front of an officer.

"I have to see the flow," she said.

"How embarrassing," I cried.

She was patient. "I don't like it any more than you do, but you'd be surprised what people try to pull."

"Really? Like what?"

I heard about hidden bottles, tubes that are switched on, and a whole lot of nasty stuff. I couldn't imagine being so addicted you'd go to all that trouble, but she assured me people did. Personally, the process was far too degrading, and I never wanted to submit to it again. Unfortunately, I wasn't that lucky. I passed the pee test, but they still wanted me down there for a weekly UA. I was really upset, but Norman reassured me.

"Judy, you have it made. I've got several people who come every day, and others are called randomly, usually at least twice a week. You have no idea how difficult they can make it."

"But they are taking the word of a lunatic. By now you'd think they'd believe me."

Norman acted in the same fashion as my civil attorney. I got a dull nod and one giant shoulder shrug. Basically, both men told me the same thing. My world was different now. Realizing the futility of my situation ignited my anger. I wanted to lash out, to hurt Rod somehow. Of course, that would only make a bad situation worse. My mood needed to settle, so I focused on my mantra.

If the whole world can turn on its axis in one twenty-four-hour period, then so, too, can I.

That tenet had saved my sanity on many occasions, so I took my bruised ego and returned to my work.

July passed into August, and with my birthday approaching, my family began to call. No, I don't want to do anything. No, not this year. I don't feel like celebrating. Please, I'm working. All I want to do is write.

My daughter was worried. I could hear it in her voice, but she tried to understand. My mother sent a card. It was a cutesy little thing from Hallmark, something about being the best of friends. Unfortunately, she didn't mean it, and she lashed out angrily signing it, Maybe in the next lifetime. It was a vicious strike, a real kick in the ass. I was already suffering, but my mother was unsympathetic, and true to her Scorpion nature, she stung me with that tail of hers. I went numb from her poison, and this time it took more than twenty-four hours to recover. Waiting for my emotions to clear, I considered rejecting the world. I wanted to hide out forever, just me and my dogs. The rest of society could take a flying leap.

About twice a week I snuck out to the mailbox, and one day there was an envelope from the IRS. 'Have been trying to reach you, please call.' It was signed Debbie Davis, Agent.

Debbie became my link to civilization. I was still hibernating, but she came over about once a week, and we worked through my records. I had expected a hard-nosed investigator, but Debbie was sweet. She was also sharp and went over my numbers carefully. My accounting system did impress her, however, and I was able to prove all my entries.

Silently, I thanked my assistant for having made that possible. If Marty hadn't secured my backup recovery tape, I would have lost the vital information. My corporate records would still be hidden in the FBI's treasure trove, and God only knew when they might release them, if ever. Because of Marty, my files were in order, and the audit was no problem.

Debbie took bits and pieces each time she visited, and she verified and cross-verified before she came back for more. She also took pieces of me with her. I had taken her into my confidence and she was outraged by my circumstances.

"It's really alright, Debbie. I am a different person today. My goals have completely changed and truly, I'm grateful for the new direction."

"What are you going to do?" she asked.

"I'm writing a book about the experience. I hope to inspire other women to follow their dreams. It's high time we stop doing what society mandates, and we need to stop serving our men, too. We must follow our hearts. That is where the joy lies."

She agreed, but suggested it was a difficult thing to do, then she changed the subject and asked if I had sent out any query letters.

"What's a query letter?" I asked.

She explained it was a one-page correspondence to a

publisher, agent, or editor, asking if they'd like to look at your manuscript. "You send it with a short synopsis and then they say 'yea' or 'nay.'"

"Really? I had no idea."

"I've got a Writer's Guide to Book Editors, Publishers, and Literary Agents at home. I'll bring it next time."

Debbie's nonjudgmental attitude stirred me. After she left, I called my daughter.

"Mom!" she exclaimed. "I am so glad you called. Is everything okay?"

"Yes, everything's fine. I've completed a first chapter, finally, and thought I'd take a break. Want to have lunch tomorrow? I could come over."

"Sure. Why don't you come early? We can sunbathe in the pool and visit for a while."

"Sounds good. I'll bring lunch. Don't bother making anything."

Pam knew I was practically destitute and she wouldn't have it. She said she had plenty of sandwich makings and told me to bring only my bathing suit.

The visit was cordial, and Pam listened as I expressed my annoyance concerning the weekly drug testing and my misunderstanding mom. Her heart went out to me, but when she became angry at her grandmother, I took a different stance. "Mom's just scared, Pam. She doesn't understand any of this and she hates the fact I haven't confided in her."

"Well, how could you? The whole crazy thing is far too complicated."

"I guess, but I don't think your grams is getting along with her boyfriend. She needs me to be a better friend."

"But we love you. We want to help you," she said, switching gears.

I was happy the focus was back on my transgressing nature. I did not want her to be angry with anyone else. After that, I kept the conversation light, and when I went home, I took Marie with me. Her parents were in dire need of a break, and my granddaughter needed some undivided attention. She had been the neglected big sister for too long, which had worn on her sweet constitution. I was just the person to restore the delicate young ego, so I took her home for the healing. She helped me as well.

Two weeks later, Debbie returned with the promised book, and I handed her a first draft of my synopsis. "Would you mind reading it?" I asked timidly. "I'd like to know what you think. See if I'm on the right track, will you?" While I left to go fetch us cups of fresh coffee, she sat down in one of my chairs, the one next to the globe. When I returned, she finished reading the last page and looked up. I held my breath.

"Judy, I think this is enough to get a contract. How do you write like that?"

I wanted to jump for joy. "I don't know. It just came. It took two weeks and several false starts, but when the flow began, it seemed easy. You like it, then? Does it sound like something you might read?"

"Absolutely. I think it's good."

That night I called my mother. She wasn't home, but I left a message. "I'm sorry I've been so neglectful, but I'm starting to feel better. Care to catch a movie this weekend?"

We did more than a movie that next Friday night. We also went to dinner and she paid.

By this time, my bills were mounting, so I wrote another ad. This time I specified "female only." I needed a roommate, but I didn't want a man in my house.

"I wouldn't touch one with a ten-foot pole," I told my sister Jana.

"Think so, huh? I wonder how long that will last?"

She was joking. She knew I was hopelessly addicted to

men, and although she couldn't understand it, she had come to terms with my need.

"You jest, little sister," I played back. "But I'm serious as a heart attack. I can't imagine getting involved at this point. I'm done with the opposite sex."

"Sure, Judy, sure. You say that now, but we'll see. How's it going, by the way? Sounds like you're climbing out of that hole."

"I am, but I'm broke. Can you float me a loan?"

I could feel her sucking air. My sister needed a good reason for most things in life, and lending money was not her forte. Still, I had nowhere to turn.

"Jana, I'm doing all the right things. I'm going to find a roommate and I'm applying for jobs. I don't know when I'll be able to pay you back, but worse-case scenario, you'll get the money when I receive the tax return."

"You still counting on a refund?" she asked incredulously.

"Well, of course. They may disallow some of the deductions, but I'm confident most of it will come. The audit is going well."

"Really?"

She needed clarity. Jana did not like going out on a limb.

"Yes, Jana. Debbie keeps coming back with questions, but so far, I've had the answers. She's pleased with our progress. She says I'm the most organized client she's ever had."

"Thank God for that. How much do you need?"

"Eight hundred will keep my utilities on; eighteen would catch up my mortgage as well."

This time I felt a shudder. "What about your car payment?"

"Mom's willing to make it this month."

"She is?"

"Can you believe it? Guess she's decided I'm not worthless after all."

"Judy," my sister admonished, "Mom's worried. She thinks you should be employed by now."

I became defensive. "I know. She believes my book is a pipe dream."

"No, but she thinks you could do both. You need to be pragmatic."

I was becoming teary-eyed. I needed my sister's support, but I wasn't capable of begging. "Whatever, Jana. Believe it or not, I am trying. If you feel uncomfortable floating me a loan, I'll understand. Just do what you can."

She sent me eight hundred and I kissed the ground she walked on. The mortgage could wait.

My efforts to secure work stagnated, but my writing kept me sane. It also helped when I found someone, rather someones, to share my expenses, and when they moved in with cash up front, I was elated.

Lester and Trish came as a package. I hesitated because of the "man" thing, but this man was attached to Trish and I liked her. She also needed a break. She had been in an accident the year before and was still recovering. Oddly enough, she was the one employed, had been employed, in fact, and with the same company for three years. They gave her a glowing recommendation.

Lester had given up his career to nurse her back to health, but at the end of the convalescent period, her job was waiting, his was not. He had been drifting but said that would change once they settled into a secure and safe home. I wasn't so sure, but I could not say no to Trish. Her scarred face and crooked smile gave her character, and my heart went out to her. She handled herself well in spite of the imperfections, and she appeared to adore her chubby chunk of a husband, so I told them they had found a home.

My puppies were especially happy because Lester and Trish also had a dog. Her name was Sugar, and although she was a sweet little thing, she was painfully shy. Buster and Gus immediately went to work on her, and it wasn't long before they had her bounding through the backyard. When the Yorkshire Terrier accepted her new friends, Lester, Trish, and I took it as a sign. Our union was meant to be. Lester and I needed jobs, but if we became employed, all would be well. He got lucky, but I did not. In fact, my hopes were suddenly dashed. Shattered actually. The call came from my attorney, and it was the worst kind of news.

"They want to move forward with your sentencing," she said in that ominous business way of hers. She was addressing me with her spike-heeled attitude.

"What! Why?"

"Your credibility has been challenged and they're worried about putting you on the stand."

"You mean I may be removed as a government witness?"

"I don't know."

"Well, if you don't, who does? How can they do this? All because of an asshole, a jerk I removed from my life." It was Rod again. He was entering my existence like an invisible thorn, twisting and turning to tear at my heart.

"That's just it. They think you're making poor decisions. The fact you filed a restraining order indicates as much."

"But he beat the shit out of me. He's the one using drugs, Karen. He wouldn't leave. I swear I tried everything, but he kept coming back."

"He beat you up?"

"Yes, and I filed a police report. Pictures were taken and everything. I promise, all this can be verified."

"I'll talk to them, but they're worried because you're not working."

There was the "they" again. They were the federal prosecutors, a group of attorneys who wanted to make their mark. These men and women wanted to fuel their careers by obtaining convictions. I was simply fodder for their fire. Karen's associate had once told me I had been caught in their crosshairs.

I began to cry, but through the tears I begged. "Karen, I'll find a job. It's been difficult, but someone out there will give me a break. You've got to do something. If I have to face the judge before the Pioneer trials, I'll be screwed. Unless I have a chance to testify against my former bosses, there is no hope for probation. The DA would never make that kind of recommendation."

"The trials are scheduled for November. It's not that far away. Maybe I can reason with them."

I took a deep breath. "Please try. I've been in full compliance. I make that trip religiously every week. Believe me, I am not a drug addict."

"I know, Judy. It's the fear factor. If the Feds think crystal meth is involved, even remotely, they get scared. People using that drug lose touch with reality."

"Well, I'm not, and I haven't. God, I wondered why they hadn't called. I was happy for the break, but I never suspected this."

"I'll see what I can do," she said. The call was abruptly terminated and the crashing reality hit me. I was going to prison. There was no way the DA would see daylight. Unless Karen talked some sense into the senseless power hungry Federalies, my days of freedom were numbered. How could this happen?

Please Karen, I prayed. Make it right just this once; make them listen.

CHAPTER 29

Resolution

IT WAS WISHFUL THINKING and I should have known better. I was interviewed, probably because of the pressure Karen applied, but my credibility factor had been called into question. Rod had been deposed, and he had blamed me for Global's demise. I was flabbergasted and initially at a loss for words. When I did find my tongue, I tried to explain but telling them Rod was retaliating didn't help.

The investigators pretended to empathize, but they were unflappable. The date had been set and it couldn't be changed. This meant, without a doubt, I would be doing federal prison time.

"Your sentencing date is set for September 15th, Judy, but we'll ask the judge to delay your surrender date until the Pioneer trials are over. That way a Rule 35 can be filed."

September 15th! September 15th was only days away. "What is a Rule 35?" I asked, trying to keep calm.

"It's a motion that will allow for an immediate reduction of your sentence," he explained gratuitously.

I couldn't believe it. They still expected me to testify, but after the fact. I would first stand before the judge, and then after the trials they would mercifully file a thirty-five something or other. I wanted to die, but I uttered two words instead, "September fifteenth?"

"Yes, the District Attorney in San Diego is retiring from public service on the sixteenth. She is the one familiar with your case. To get full benefit for your cooperation, it really is in your best interest to get this done before she leaves."

I thought otherwise, but it didn't matter.

"We need you back here on the sixteenth," he added. "The CPA assigned to the case will be reviewing Pioneer's financials that week and she has some questions. Do you think you'll be up to an interview?"

I was dazed. "The day after?" I asked, not expecting an answer. "I guess. What time do you want me?"

I was told to arrive by ten, and then I left the building.

If I had been alone, I might have starved to death, because I took to my room and rarely came out. Trish and Lester started to worry about me, and since Lester liked to cook, he began inviting me to dinner. I was reluctant, but he insisted. He had prepared too much food and said I needed to join them or it would go to waste. Each day my roommates tossed me this lifeline, and I gradually accepted the routine. The companionship also helped, maybe even more than the food. I did not discuss anything of a personal nature. I simply wasn't prepared to talk, but they were and I learned an awful lot during those days. I especially heard from Lester because he started to drink. Each day on his way home from work, he would stop to buy a twelve-pack and about halfway through it, he became quite talkative. He professed immunity to hangovers, but when he lost his job, it was no surprise.

Poor Trish. Looks like she's married to a beer-drinking bum. I was not happy about having him in my house, but if Trish wanted to support him, who was I to judge? He did cook and clean, and generally speaking, took care of us.

Debbie Davis completed her audit and announced she

was submitting the figures for final approval. When I wasn't jubilant, she asked why, and I laid open my heart.

"It may not matter, Debbie. I've tried to get out of this mess and keep a roof over my head, but nothing is working. They've moved my sentencing date up, and now I'll most definitely be going to prison."

She stayed and talked that afternoon and put a positive spin on my situation. The refund would be processed within the next month, she reassured. By catching up my mortgage and renting out my property, my home would be there when I returned. I would also be granted the gift of time.

"Just think, Judy," she said. "This could be a golden opportunity. You aspire to be a writer, so use the stretch to master your craft. Consider this a present."

Well, that's sensible, I thought, surprising myself. Without worldly concerns, I could concentrate on my manuscript. I might be incarcerated, but they couldn't lock up my mind. By the end of that afternoon, I had a different attitude and Debbie left saying she'd stay in touch and she'd hold me in her prayers. I was encouraged enough to tell my family.

"What!" screeched Pam. "No, Mom. They can't do that. What will I do without you?"

"Well, I haven't been much help, anyway."

"But the baby is young and it will get harder. Besides, Marie adores you. She's so attached to you, Mom. She'll be heartbroken if you leave."

"I love her, too, honey, but this isn't the end of the world. I'll be back."

She was not consoled. "Oh God, Mom. What if Jason goes to prison, too? What will I do?"

She was on the verge of tears. I attempted logic. "If he'd agree to a plea bargain, he'd probably get probation."

"Think?"

I didn't, but I wasn't going to say so. "Yes, I think. In fact,

I'll ask my attorney to mention it. Maybe she can talk the DA into leniency. After all, they're holding the prison card over my head now. If I fail them in any way, they'll forget I exist."

"I see what you mean."

"Look, I'll probably get a year, maybe a year and a half at the most. Once the trials are over, I'll be eligible for early release. Karen says at the most I might serve six months. I may even be released with time served."

"Really?"

"Yes, but talk some sense into that husband of yours. If he goes to trial, they'll crucify him. I swear he'll never see the light of day."

I explained why Jason didn't have a chance and patiently waited until she understood. My attorneys had done the same for me. I, too, had wanted my day in court, but I eventually came to learn that in the federal system there was no such thing as a fair trial. Conviction is usually imminent, and unless you cry "uncle" there is no hope.

The picture was clear, but her words were bitter. "God, you must feel like shooting Rod. He's sure a piece of work, isn't he?"

Her statement surprised me, and for a minute I had to think. "I'm not angry with Rod, Pam. He's a sick, hurting human being. How could I blame him? He's delusional. The man needs help."

"But you're going to prison because of him."

"No, I'm not. I'm going to prison, because long ago I chose to go after the almighty buck. I wanted to become a debt-free millionaire, and I was willing to compromise my values to make it happen."

"Mom!"

"I'm serious, Pam. I had never heard of telemarketing until Pioneer and when I understood what they were doing I was shocked by the nature of their business. Still, I stayed.

I was lured by the money and I internalized a false sense of security. After all, we were licensed and bonded by the state. Our operations were legal, and I believed the verification process protected us, but those tape-recorded conversations meant nothing. The federal laws are written in such a way that any embellishment is considered fraud. In one case a salesman jingled a set of keys in the client's ear, inferring he had won the car, and although that order was later canceled, that tinkling was enough for a conspiracy charge."

"But that's crazy. All salespeople exaggerate!" she said.

"I know, but truly, I wish to God I had used my talents in a different way. If I had chosen a different career path, I wouldn't be in this mess. I can't blame Rod for this, and it's not Speicher's fault, either. Each of those men played their parts, but I am ultimately responsible."

Pam gave me a look. She tried a different angle. "Well, if Rod had listened to you, Global wouldn't have gone down, and you wouldn't be facing the judge next week."

"Yes, you're right, but if I hadn't been weak and vulnerable, I wouldn't have let him walk all over me. I met Rod at the worst possible time and I was too tired to fight him.

"Think about it. I'm the one with business savvy. I should have resigned that very first time he deviated from our agreement. If he had launched the expansion with two cities instead of three, Global would still be in business."

"You couldn't do anything to stop that," she said. "He held all the power."

"He didn't hold the power. I gave it to him. I tolerated his insolence. I made a piss-poor decision and I was a weak-ass not to quit. From that moment on, we were scrambling, and things went from bad to worse. I should have cut my losses and got out."

"But it was your money, Mom. It was your investment. How could you abandon it?"

"I don't know, but I should have. Look how much worse it got because I didn't."

"I still don't know how you can forgive Rod. It's beyond me," she said emphatically.

Is that what I'm doing? Am I really forgiving Rod? It felt like it. "If I didn't, the past would trap me. It's hard and it hurts, but if I don't let go, I can never hope to move forward."

"Have you, Mom? Have you really let go?"

"Yes, honey. I believe it's possible to love someone with all your heart, and with all your soul ..."

She stared wide-eyed, waiting.

The words came smoothly. "You can love, yet leave and still continue to love."

"You love Rod?" she asked, incredulous. "After all he's done, you still love him?"

It was an admission of the worst kind and I was just as surprised as she was. "I guess I do. I suppose I always will."

"You need help, Mother."

I ignored her. "Rod and I are soulmates, Pam. It was our destiny to meet."

Her mouth was agape.

"I also believe our work together is done."

Relief.

"You know, I simply can't forget that day I called him Einstein. That was too weird and it came out of nowhere."

"Come on, Mom. You don't really think Rod is Albert Einstein, do you?"

"Not hardly, but I wonder why I said that? I really don't know anything about the man."

"It is odd Rod hung a poster of the genius," she said, remembering the day he told her.

"Yeah, and I had no idea. You know, I am curious. I think I'll go look up dear old Albert."

"What do you mean?"

"I'm going to check him out at the library. It will give me something to do until this sentencing thing is over."

"It must be hard," she sympathized.

It was difficult, but I was glad this chapter was finally closing. My life had been in limbo for nearly two years, and the thought of resolution was comforting. This, in many ways, signified a new beginning.

CHAPTER 30

Mileva Maric

THE LIST OF EINSTEIN references at the library was overwhelming. I spent a couple of hours pulling down books and poring through their table of contents. A few of the manuscripts offered clues to Albert's character, but most were heavily laden with scientific material. There was no time for quantum physics or his unified theory, so I put the books back on the shelves.

On the way home, I thought about facing the judge. How would I do it without collapsing? And how would I get through this next week without breaking? I knew writing was out of the question. I was far too worried, so I turned into a neighborhood shopping center and parked in front of the bookstore. As though hypnotized, I entered and asked where I might find books on Einstein. The clerk steered me to a shelf and pointed to a section. One immediately caught my attention: *Einstein, a life*, by Dennis Brian.

I was encouraged by the commentary on the back cover and decided to scrutinize the text further. I took it and sat down on one of the many comfortable couches scattered around the establishment. My mind reeled with excitement as I began reading. The preface alone was enough to move me to purchase. I discovered Einstein was loved and hated to excess. He was called a saint by some and a self-promoting fraud by others. He married twice and fathered two children. That meant other Einsteins might be running around. My intuition leapt, and I wondered if Rod might be related in some sort of distant fashion. Certainly he was genius lineage, a bit off the beaten track, but most definitely endowed with a superior brain. It was worth investigating, and if nothing else, the huge paperback would keep me busy for at least a week, maybe more.

EINSTEIN, a life, was a beautifully written chronology, and as I skimmed the pages, I was struck. "Déjà vu," I said quietly. I had heard it from Rod. Like Einstein, he expressed feelings of being misunderstood as a child and abandoned as a teenager. Then, too, there was the issue of school.

"There was only one more semester, but they wanted to expel me," Rod had said. "Thankfully, my math teacher saved me. Sometimes, I think he was the only adult who understood me."

"Why?" I asked. "Why was it so different with him?"

"He gave me a chance. I was cutting up in class, getting into the usual mischief, and he started yelling. I told him his numbers were as ridiculous as his clothes, and rather than send me to the principal's office he suggested if I was so smart, I should prove it. He told me to go to the board and demonstrate."

"Really?" I asked. "So, what happened?"

"I did it. I wrote the entire equation in a totally different way, cutting through the chase, and arrived at the conclusion in about half the time. I kept it simple and other students grasped the concept, too."

"Then what went wrong? Why didn't you finish high school?"

"Judy, it was too boring. I couldn't keep my mouth shut,

and the next time I stirred up trouble, I was expelled."

"But Rod, you were so close."

"I know, but by then most of the faculty hated me. I had made fools of them and they couldn't wait to see me bounced."

It must be something in the genius genes. In high school Albert was also told he'd never amount to anything. Like Rod, he failed to graduate. He also suffered feelings of abandonment, but in my opinion, Albert's emotions were warranted. He was only fifteen when his family moved to Italy and left him alone in Germany to complete his studies.

Albert left a trail of enemies, too. People of power did not appreciate his aggressive personality and many were jealous of his superior intelligence. Unlike Rod, Albert made it to Zurich's Polytechnic where he met Mileva Maric and was entranced by her intelligence. They became collaborators and lovers. Of course, they did, I said to myself.

Albert graduated, but Mileva did not. She became pregnant, and rather than take the final exams, she returned to her Serbian home to have the child. Ultimately, she surrendered her little girl, Lieserl, to some caring cousins, and returned to Zurich where she married Einstein.

Well, at least I didn't repeat that mistake. The words filled my mind, and I couldn't believe it. I had practically forgotten, but I, had almost given up my daughter. Not because I wanted a man, nor did I care about my career, but I sure coveted my freedom. I divorced Pam's daddy when she was six months old. He immediately remarried, while I stretched between the worlds of work, single parenting, and wild clubbing. I loved to dance, and I often left my sleeping child with a babysitter to engage in the night life. When my ex and his new wife wanted custody, I considered it. Not for long, though. Love prevailed and I refused to give her up. The request did serve as a wake-up call, however, and I became a better mother. Except for an occasional weekend date, I rarely went out.

Was I this woman? This Mileva? Her life was settling in my heart and it explained my deep connection to Pam. We were about as close as a mother and daughter could get. The men in my life often commented on our relationship; so did most of my friends.

I loved my son, Charles, too, but Pam and I were joined at the hip. We completed each other's sentences and in restaurants we'd order the same meal. Even our salads were the same, right down to the same dressing with no croutons, thank you very much. We were more like twins than mother and daughter, and I couldn't imagine living without her. How sad it must have been for Mileva.

Lord, I thought. That marriage was doomed.

She did bear two sons, Hans Albert and Eduard, so when her husband discounted her intellectually, she threw herself into the domestic role of caring for the family. I breathed through those opening chapters and occasionally angel bumps danced up my arms. If I wasn't Mileva Maric, then I was her twin sister. Our stories were amazingly similar, and it felt as though we were cut from the same cloth. The templates of time were practically identical.

Rod shared some of Albert's character traits, but still, I did not think he was Einstein. He had the same eyes, the divine, enrapturing deep velvety pools that could penetrate one's soul, but he did not have the wherewithal. Rod was easily distracted where Albert demonstrated remarkable concentration, even under great stress. They were both opportunists, but Rod was a showoff. He needed fine suits and Rolex watches to validate his existence. Albert needed nothing and rarely concerned himself with outward appearances. No, I did not think Rod was Albert Einstein's incarnate spirit, but he fit into the family somehow;

otherwise, I wouldn't have called him by the genius name.

I read about Mileva's tête-à-têtes with Albert, those magical shared times of conquered equations and mysterious scientific unveilings. It had been the same for Rod and me in that mini suite. We transcended time when I lifted my arm and pointed, "You are Einstein!" I said.

Now even that strange afternoon was beginning to make sense.

The declaration threw Rod. He responded, saying, "Hi," but it was in a little boy voice. The inflection was odd, but since Rod didn't believe in reincarnation, I discounted his tone to confusion. He didn't seem to know me. At least not like I knew him, so anytime afterward when we talked about the bizarre happening, I made light of it. I never forgot it, however, and now there seemed to be good reason for my exploration.

I wanted to know more, and in those days prior to my judgment day, I read voraciously. I couldn't get enough of Albert and Mileva. It was like they were a part of me.

CHAPTER 31

Elsa Löwenthall

I READ HOW MILEVA felt hopelessly alone and isolated because of Albert's extensive lecture circuit, but between the lines I also found his divorced cousin, Elsa Löwenthall. Albert's work took him to Berlin, and with Mileva back in Zurich, Elsa conveniently slipped in and filled the gap. Acting in friendship, the first cousin effectively terminated Albert's marriage to Mileva.

How convenient for Albert, I thought. Elsa Löwenthall made it all too easy. Was there always a woman enabler? Maybe not, but the circumstances were eerily familiar. Albert even treated his boys with the same kind of disregard. He missed his sons and wrote encouraging letters, but the support came from a distance and was ambiguous at best. Even the money situation sounded similar. Albert did send funds, but never enough, and Mileva made ends meet by tutoring math and giving piano lessons.

I had often wondered what Mary Ann had done to fill in the financial gaps. Probably her parents contributed heavily. Both men, however, conveniently preferred freedom to responsibility, and both formed attachments with women who helped them forget about their obligations at home.

Elsa made it easy for Albert, and I had done it for Rod. Weren't we a couple of love-struck fools?

Eventually Einstein asked Mileva for a divorce, causing her to break down physically and mentally. Again, my heart went out to her. It wasn't so much she needed Albert. By then she was relatively self-sufficient. Rather, she was devastated, because the divorce signified another failure.

This was something I knew intuitively.

Mileva believed she failed her parents by becoming pregnant, failed her daughter by giving her up for adoption, and now she was losing a husband. And she was suffering physically from a congenital dislocation of the hip, which made walking difficult. This pain, combined with the emotional loss, caused her collapse. Life was simply too difficult, too hard to bear.

"Isn't it?" I said, standing up to stretch. I reached for the ceiling and an electric shock rocketed through my lower back, right hip, and leg. Grimacing from the sciatic pinch, I quickly moved to relieve the pressure. I had been told I needed back surgery, but I was stalling. The pain was bearable, but when I stood the wrong way or for too long, it radiated into my hips with tremendous power. Another similarity—isn't it odd? I too suffer with pain in the hips?

Another sign. Mileva and I were one and the same.

I began to pay more attention to Mileva and all those around her. Albert went on to marry Elsa, but not before he became concerned about Eduard, his youngest son. Einstein feared he might be mentally disturbed, and the condition, he believed, must have been inherited from Mileva's family. Mileva had a sister, Zorka, who had been committed to a psychiatric hospital.

A rush of goose bumps covered my body. I was amazed by the parallel. The sisterly connection hit me like a ton of bricks. Mileva had a schizophrenic sister and I had Shirley.

Could Zorka and Shirley be incarnate spirits?

Over the years Albert became quite a philanderer. He was especially attracted to younger women, and amazingly, Elsa tolerated his affairs!

Just like Mary Ann. Two of a kind.

Mary Ann preferred turning a blind eye. In fact, at the end, she was my greatest supporter. Elsa, obviously, was of like mind, for she remained with Albert for the rest of her life. Albert's angel, Elsa, was Mary Ann. "Oh, my God!" I exclaimed. "Mary Ann is my soulmate, too. We were both 'married' to the great Albert Einstein!"

I thought about this and became more convinced. Rod's wife believed God had a special purpose for her husband. She repeatedly sacrificed her own needs and desires to love and support him. She also tolerated his affairs, especially the one with me. Believing I was helping him realize his goals, she encouraged him to remain my friend and roommate. She acted as Rod's guardian angel, and her life story was remarkably similar to Elsa's.

Both women were content to live in their husbands' shadows. History had proven Elsa's sacrifice a worthy one. In the case of Mr. Steersman, I wasn't so sure. I couldn't, for the life of me, understand why Mary Ann defended Rod. He hadn't created a new world order, nor had he successfully managed to restore hope of any kind, not to others, not to himself, and certainly not to his family. Why then did she remain the willing servant?

Was Rod perhaps Mary Ann's nemesis? Was he supposed to become her springboard to freedom? Or had she truly come to act as his perfect little Christian wife? Somehow, I doubted it and I suspected a deep lesson existed there.

My mind took me back to the day I met Mary Ann. She was pregnant, and she came to confront her husband—and me. Rod sent her packing, but I respected her courage. That day was a turning point for me and I worked diligently to cast the wayward husband out of my life. I hadn't recognized this on a conscious level, but my subconscious knew what was best. I needed to get away from the crushing presence of Mr. Rod A. Steersman, Sr., and he needed to return home for the sake of his wife and their children.

CHAPTER 32

Eduard

THE WEEK FELL AWAY and as judgment day approached, a strange sense of calm came over me. I had lunch with my daughter and told her she was my lost little Lieserl. Oddly enough, she did not think I had lost my mind. In fact, the story brought a tear to her eye.

I was called to testify at a grand jury hearing for one of the Pioneer cases and I stood on the truth. Afterward, I met with my pretrial supervisor, who, of course, asked me about my job search. I did not mince words.

"I've stopped looking."

The casual statement wasn't appreciated.

"I'm not exactly motivated. No one wants to hire me and, in a few months, I'll be locked up. I'm going to use this time to write."

The question was always the same with Norman. "But how are you managing?"

I explained about my roommates and told him the additional money was enough for food and utilities. I also told him about the IRS refund and justified my unpaid mortgage. Mom was making the payments on my Lexus, so my car wasn't an issue. "All's well," I said. "I just want to take advantage of these final days of freedom."

He understood, so I asked for authorization to make a three-week trip to Colorado. I wanted to say "goodbye" to my friends and family, spend time with my sisters, and visit my son who would be attending college. Permission was granted, and we slotted in the time after my sentencing, but before the big trials.

The day before I was to fly off to San Diego for sentencing, Karen called. She gave me a rundown of our travel plans but kept the conversation brief. "Is everything okay? Do you need me to pick you up tomorrow?" She was, obviously, afraid I might fly the coop.

"I'm fine, Karen. You don't need to worry. I'll meet you at the gate."

When my son, Charles, called, I lost my flip confidence and exaggerated my well-being.

"How much time do you think you'll get, Mom?" he asked. "I mean realistically. What do you expect?"

"Karen says there's no way to know, but it had better be at least three years. I'll need that long to finish my manuscript." It was a joke. I never expected to get more than a year. Worst case, Karen had prepared me for a year and a half. Still, I wanted to embellish for my son's sake. The exaggeration would give him reason to rejoice once I came back with the real news.

"May as well have the government provide room and board while I pursue my new vocation," I joked.

Charlie laughed and wished me luck.

I also heard from Rod. It was the last thing I needed, but thankfully, his greeting came from afar. It was delivered by mail, originating from Eugene, Oregon. Well, at least he finally went home, I said to myself, before tossing it into a drawer. Good luck, Mary Ann. He's all yours now.

Trish and Lester continued to feed me, and I swam laps

on occasion. My general health was improving, but my lower back and hips were giving me grief. Standing for longer than about five minutes was a real challenge. I wondered if Mileva's pain was similar. *Probably worse,* I thought. The night was encroaching, and to contain my nervous tension I escaped back into *Einstein, a life.*

I reflected on Einstein's relationship with his father. Sounds like Rod. He was always trying to impress his father. Too bad dads didn't get it. If Marvin had only attended Rod's championship karate match, things might have been different. The sensitive boy-genius might have found direction with a more supportive father. Why are men like that? I wondered. Why is it so difficult for them to display love?

A few more pages and I'll call it a night. I wanted to be well-rested for the plane ride, wanted to face the judge bright-eyed and bushy tailed.

Then a passage about Einstein's son Eduard unable to find his way home captured my attention.

"Oh, my gosh." He couldn't find his way back, I repeated. Rod suffered a mental breakdown, just like their son, and he never made his way back either. He repeatedly attempted to resume his role as president of Global Enterprises, but each time the paranoia paralyzed him. And like Eduard, Rod knew his mind was sick, but he, too, was unable to stabilize. It was eerily similar!

Now I understand why I called him Einstein. I was seeing Rod's spirit, and I recognized him as Einstein's son. *Oh my God. Rod was my son!*

No wonder Rod responded in that little boy voice. The moment was burned into my brain. I recalled it vividly, as though it happened yesterday.

And isn't it odd that Rod fell in love with me?

I was free-flowing and allowed the turn in time. The older woman in Eduard's life had jilted him, and now his incarnate spirit, Rod, was trying again. With me!

I remembered the day of my surrender. I had said, "I'll submit to your wishes until you feel safe. When you think you're strong enough to stand on your own, I need you to tell me, and then you must let me go. Promise me, Rod, when you are capable, you will release me."

He agreed, and now his past life obsession would be neutralized.

It was interesting, too, that Rod had little respect for women. He was like Albert in that way. Neither of them liked an intellectual challenge from a female, and especially not from their woman. Every time I disagreed with Rod's approach to business, he either ignored me or attempted to discredit me. He also blamed me for his personal failings, and in a way that sounded like Albert, too. When his son collapsed emotionally, it was Mileva's fault, not his. It was her family genes, after all.

I could see more parallels. Rod had put me through the same kind of pain as Albert, but I believed that was part of his divine purpose. It was his responsibility to challenge me, and thankfully, this time around, I rose to the occasion. I did not sacrifice myself to Global, and now I was on a path to realize my dream.

We hurt each other, but we loved, too. Because of me, Rod had returned to his family, and perhaps now, he would break the cycle of fatherly neglect. It was my hope he would discover the joy of sharing and caring with his children, something neither Albert Einstein nor Marvin Steersman had done.

It's kind of funny, too, I continued my train of thought. Just like his spirit dad, Rod was a womanizer, at least he was until he met me. Maybe he really will honor his wife.

The sins of the father are vested on the sons. Wasn't that what the Bible said? And the circle goes unbroken. At least it did until somebody deliberately changed it. Good or bad, cycles were repeated through generations and beyond lifetimes. Unless a caring individual stopped the insanity, the pain would continue. I felt like Rod and I had done that for each other. I was healing, and I hoped he was, too.

Conquer those demons, honey, I said affectionately to his spirit presence. He did indeed seem to be in the room. Mend that shattered soul of yours, Mr. Steersman. You can do it. You have the heart, the hope, and soon you will know the truth. In the meantime, you have a love freely offered. Mary Ann is your angel, baby. Guard her with care.

A deep abiding peace came over me, the peace that passeth all understanding. I read one more page and saw that Mileva had died in 1948.

1948! I exclaimed. I was born in 1948. If Mileva died before August 5th that would be another sign. I decided to quit and I ran a bath to calm my firing synapses. In the tub, I closed my eyes and began my relaxation mantra. Each time an Einstein slipped into my head, I caught the thought and pushed it into the recesses. Balance came and I allowed the flow. After several minutes, but before the water became cold, I pulled the plug, toweled off, and slipped under the bedcovers. I would bury the past for now, and tomorrow I would draw power from it.

CHAPTER 33

Tub of Tears

I AWOKE WITH A START. I had to know. When in 1948 did Mileva pass away? Without dressing or eating breakfast, I grabbed the book. Surely the month and day had to be there. I used the index and checked every page referenced—"Einstein, Mileva Maric—first wife," but I couldn't find it.

Time was running short, but I plowed through those pages again. Nothing! How could Dennis Bryan leave out such an important clue? But it seemed he had, and I had no choice but to stop my obsessive search. It was time to get ready for my day in court.

I dressed in a conservative business suit of dark forest green and chose the short-stacked heels that matched. It wasn't until I was racing to the gate that I realized my mistake. I hadn't worn anything but flats for a year, and now my back and hip screamed from the abuse.

"You made it," Karen said, obviously relieved.

"You had doubts?" I asked, teasing her.

"Not really, but you did cut it awfully close."

"Sorry, I got distracted this morning. Before I knew it, I had to fly out the door."

"Well, you look nice. So, what do you say? Should we

get out of here?"

"Let's," I said. "I need to sit down. My back is killing me."

Karen had a bad back, too. In fact, her doctors had recently recommended surgery. She could easily relate to my agony. She had chosen a more practical shoe, however, and I admired her sensibility. We boarded the plane, and once airborne, she told me what to expect.

"Your sentencing is scheduled for two p.m., but I haven't received anything in writing from the DA. We'll be meeting with her and the prosecuting attorneys before going to court."

"You still don't know what kind of a recommendation they intend to make?"

"No, I was supposed to receive the information Friday, but it didn't come until this morning. Unfortunately, I couldn't swing by the office to pick it up. I'll have to get it from them when we get there."

"That's ridiculous," I said. "What if we have objections?"

"There will be time to address them. We'll be clear on the issues before you go in front of the judge."

It seemed like a bad omen. Trouble was, it didn't matter. There was absolutely nothing I could do. It was simply another one of those times. They were in control. They held all the power, and we had no choice but to play by their rules. My silence must have been unsettling to Karen. She tried to reassure me.

"Judy, you'll get through this. Whatever happens, know that it's not over. You'll still be eligible for the Rule 35 motion. They've promised to shave time off your sentence, and after the trials, I'll work with the prosecutors to make sure it happens. You'll be out soon."

I did not like it, but right at that moment, prison was not my primary concern. I was thinking about the Einstein family and in particular, I was dwelling on Mileva's date of death. Of course, this wasn't something I could easily explain to Karen, so rather than try, I decided to reassure her.

"It's okay, Karen. I've had almost two years to prepare for this day. I never thought I'd be able to do it, but now I know I can."

"I bet you wish you had never been in the telemarketing business, don't you?"

That caused me some pause. "No. Actually, I don't feel that way. If I had to do it all over again—to get where I am today—even if I had to marry that renegade again, I think I would. I'm happier now than I've been for a long time. Well, maybe I should say I'm more content than ever before, more satisfied." I couldn't quite put it into words. What I was feeling seemed beyond description, so I gave up. "I know who I am today, Karen, and I understand my purpose. Many people go to their graves without that kind of insight, so in a way, I am truly grateful."

Her response was guarded. "Well, that's good, I guess. I don't know if I'd tell the judge that, though."

I laughed, imagining it. Nope, they wouldn't want to hear I'd happily repeat my crimes. It was my job as a government witness to be sincerely remorseful and full of guilt. "Oh, I know. Don't worry, I won't."

The rest of the flight was made in quiet contemplation. Karen, I was sure, was thinking about my fate. I, on the other hand, was thinking about Mileva's.

San Diego was dreary that day. There was a haze over the city and massive amounts of construction. The cab driver had to navigate carefully. *Another bad omen*, I thought, as we approached the Federal Building. I was beginning to lose confidence. I hadn't eaten, either and my blood sugar was plummeting. A headache was also settling. I was miserable as Karen led the way through those expansive halls. When we found the right office, we were told to return at one p.m.

"That's the Feds for you," I said. "Hurry up and wait. I've been through it before."

"Me, too," she said. "Want some lunch?"

"You mean my last meal?"

Her smile was instant and her green eyes lit up. She was enjoying my sense of humor. "What's your preference, Ms. Burr—steak or lobster?"

I watched her red crown of curls flash in the florescent lighting, and then said, "I don't care, but let's go somewhere close. I can't walk very far in these shoes."

We went upstairs to a coffee shop and I ordered something, although I didn't remember what. I was beginning to go numb.

~

"Six points," said the voice.

We were in court, and Karen was arguing. I wasn't sure about what. I had left the building—at least mentally. For the next half hour, I abandoned the field.

Point by point, they went over my presentencing information. Mistakes were corrected and then restitution was discussed.

A hundred and ten thousand dollars! Are you crazy?

The judge questioned my ability to pay, and the DA reassured him.

"Actually, your Honor, between Ms. Burr and her partner, I think that's a reasonable assumption. I don't think they have the money now, but unlike the other defendants, these are capable, intelligent people. Ms. Burr has tremendous ability, and I think she has already started a new business."

I would have started a new business if you had let me. I was coming out of my stupor, and her words were irritating.

"I really think it is, in fact, a manageable and appropriate remedy. She's obviously well-educated, articulate, and smart. She ran this business with a great deal of mastery. I mean, it was very well run, even though it was fraudulent. I think if anybody before this Court is ever going to have the future capacity to pay restitution, it would be Ms. Burr and her partner."

Well, of course! I exclaimed in my mind. Punish us for being smart enough to do it right. We stayed within the state's legal parameters. We delivered as promised and we paid through the nose for the license to operate.

Hearing how my efforts had ultimately led to my demise was aggravating. If only I had been a true scammer, a real criminal, one of those rip-and-tear owners, the 'don't give a damn' type ... maybe then I could accept what was happening, but to hear them talk about my expertise made me want to scream. Of course I didn't.

Karen was making a bid for leniency, and she was talking about the hundreds of thousands of dollars already seized, but they wanted more, another one hundred and ten thousand dollars. The judge asked me if I had anything to add and I found my tongue. I reminded the court about my personal cash the government had confiscated, another sixty-five thousand dollars. That was money I forfeited, but my partner had not.

A $60,000 restitution was levied against me, and the court's generosity caused me to gasp. I'm dead ass broke. I don't have a pot to piss in, and now they want me to come up with an additional 60K. *What is wrong with these people?*

My surrender date was established for November 24th. That would allow time for the Pioneer trials, but it would also put me behind bars before the holidays. *Thanks a whole hell of a lot,* I thought, walking out. In the hall, I abruptly sat down, or rather, I collapsed on one of the white vinyl couches.

"Are you okay?" Karen asked, taking a seat beside me.

I wasn't. "Thirty-three months!" I cried. "Karen, I can't

do thirty-three months!"

"It's an outrage. I can't believe it either," she said. "You did not get fair consideration for your cooperation and I intend to do something about it. I swear, you can't trust these federal people. They make all kinds of promises, but they rarely deliver. I've seen it time after time. They just don't care. That's why I hate to encourage my clients to cooperate."

That wasn't how I remembered it. It seemed to me she had done everything possible to dissuade me from going to trial. "How could this happen? God, I should have taken my case before a jury."

"Judy, it would have been worse. You were damned if you did and damned if you didn't."

"But what's the difference. It might as well be eighteen years. Karen, three years! Oh my God. I can't go to prison for three years. That's a lifetime."

"You won't be there three years, I promise. This thing is not over, and I'm with you until the bitter end."

I didn't feel encouraged, but I tried to be respectful. Karen was a professional, but her options were limited. "Okay, let's get out of here."

She stood up, but I couldn't. The pain of the previous hour shot through my hip, which caused me to fall backward. Karen extended a hand, and I winced as she pulled me to my feet. I was catalogued, fingerprinted as an official felon and prisoner of war. *This government is dirty,* I thought, wiping the black ink from my hands. Prosecutors hit below the belt. They can't make a case without using down-and-dirty tactics, so they find pawns to sacrifice. It wasn't right and if I had my way, the world would hear about it.

I was silent and sullen on the return trip home. Mileva was in the recesses, with three years stretching before me in the forefront. Be careful for what you wish. You just might get it. I had spoken the very same number to Charlie and I had created a self-fulfilling prophecy. Well, at least he won't be surprised, I thought. Some consolation.

When we deplaned, Karen walked with me to the parking lot, and before parting company, she spoke some encouraging words.

"Thanks for everything," I said, shaking her hand. "I know it's not your fault."

She was exhausted. I could tell. The day had worn on her as much as it had on me. I smiled and told her I would survive. "Just don't forget me," I joked. "When the time comes, I expect you to rally with the best of them."

"I will. I'll do everything possible."

I was sure she would. Karen empathized, and she understood the system, too. Trouble was, it was difficult to fight City Hall. I decided to put it out of my mind, and for the sake of my sanity, I brought Mileva Maric forward. When was it, Ms. Maric? When did you leave this earth? Was it before I arrived? Are we one and the same or am I off my rocker?

Remembering the hundreds of books at the library, I went back to the small neighborhood store. Surely, I could find it there. The selection was smaller, but there had been some good reference materials. It took about an hour, but eventually I found a passage about Albert's first wife. I reviewed it carefully, and then the date stood out. It seemed to be in bold on the page: "**August 4, 1948**."

"What?" I had spoken out loud and heads turned. I couldn't have cared less. "Oh, my God!" I cried. I couldn't believe it. I stared at the page, as if the date might change. It didn't. The image was fixed and burned an indelible impression into my mind. I was born less than twenty-four hours after Mileva passed!

"Isn't that wild?" I asked Jana. I had given her the bad

news and then followed it with the good. She already knew about my premonitions, but she found this information astonishingly coincidental.

"No kidding! That really is weird. And Rod sounds like Eduard. Before, when you said he might be Einstein, I thought you were delusional. Now the story seems plausible."

"Really? You don't know how much that means. If you can see it, then maybe I can make others relate as well."

She wasn't all that supportive. "You mean you intend to talk about this in your book?"

"Absolutely. Don't you see what kind of resolution this brings me? It offers insight as to why I've been in such a destructive cycle."

"Why?"

"I've been preparing for Rod. It's been my destiny to help him. He came to help me, too. Even Mary Ann is tied to this. I think we came as a family to help each other. We are soulmates and we came to evolve, to grow closer to God."

She was skeptical. "You waited all your life, suffered through several abusive relationships, just so you and Rod could unite and challenge each other?"

Put that way, with the delivered inflictive blow, my theory did sound preposterous. "Well, maybe not. I haven't completely figured it out." I decided to change the subject.

To keep things light, I spoke positively about the length of my sentence, saying something like I had to my son, Charles—something about being glad for the free room and board. After we disconnected, I managed to quiet my mind for the night. I did not have the heart to call either my daughter or my mother. They would be distraught and right then I could not deal with their grief.

The next morning my head was pounding. I did not want to get out of bed, but I had to. I was expected at ten o'clock sharp. The FBI wanted me to help them again. I was loathe to go, but I knew if I didn't, it would look bad. God forbid I failed them. God forbid I was too human or too hurting to come to their Godawful meeting.

Jerk faces, I said to myself. I wish I'd get in an accident or something. That would give me a good excuse. Instantly I regretted my words. "I didn't mean it, Lord. I take it back." With my kind of luck, I'd have another wish granted, so I wished that one away.

My thoughts were much the same as I drove toward the rendezvous, so I was distracted. I did not immediately notice the flashing blue light behind me. Quickly, I glanced at my speedometer. Fifty-five miles an hour. Thank God. I wasn't speeding. Still, the highway patrol car was right on my tail and it was obvious he had targeted me. I pulled over.

"License and registration please, ma'am."

I dug for both. One was in my wallet and the other in the glove compartment. He took his time, but I didn't mind. The diversion would give me an excuse to be late.

"Are you aware your registration has expired, ma'am?"

I hated that. Ma'am always made me feel old. "Yes. I've been unemployed and it's been difficult. I simply haven't had the money."

"Do you have someone you can call, ma'am? I have to impound the car."

"What? You can't be serious."

"Yes, ma'am, I am. I usually give a warning, but your plates expired six months ago. I have no choice."

I began to cry. I let out all the stoppers, and the horror of the judge's levy fell onto the pavement. "You have no idea what I've been through. Please, please," I begged. When he did not give way, I ranted and raved. "I'll go straight home. I'll never drive this car again, at least not until the plates are renewed. Oh my God, I cannot do this. I cannot take this anymore." I felt suicidal and my despair was on full display.

Finally, he relented, and I was allowed to return home.

"Don't go anywhere, ma'am. If I see this car on the highway again, I won't hesitate to take it in."

I promised, then drove home through the tears. Be careful for what you wish! Thank God I rescinded the one about an accident. "Thank you, Jesus."

At home I called to explain and promised to bring the ticket to validate my story, but I was told it wouldn't be necessary. Amazingly, the postal investigator, James Dominio, told me not to worry. He believed me and said they'd call later after another meeting was scheduled.

"Thanks," I had said, meaning it. At that point I was thrilled to hear a kind word, even if it came from a federal employee.

After being let off the hook, I went to take a bath. I desperately needed to calm my frayed nerves. The experience had rattled me and now I really felt trapped. No longer could I escape in my Lexus, for it had been grounded. What's next? I wondered.

Truly, I was concerned. I did not feel like I could take a whole lot more and I still had to get through the trials. How would I face those boys—my former employers? They had once been my friends, and if I received thirty-three months, they had to be looking at a lifetime. I began to question the sanctity of my situation. I believed in standing on the truth, but still, I did not like being a pawn and this cooperation thing ate at me. I considered the idea of bailing. After all, I had already been sentenced. What more could they do? And really, thirty-three months wasn't all that long. I could also use the time to my advantage.

I rationalized and attempted to justify, but it was a chore. The situation was hopeless and nothing would save me, or them, for that matter. We all decided to be in the telemarketing industry, and now we would face the consequences. Thirty-three months, eighteen years, or life—what was the difference? We were going to jail and our lives, as we had known them, were over.

The stark reality was slamming down hard, and I found little comfort in that tub of tears. The water was as murky as my mind, and the bubbles would not bring it clear. I had lost my greatest battle, with no hope of rescue, no hero on the horizon. I would soon journey into the unknown and I would do it alone. The thought was agonizing.

"Oh God, why?" I cried. "Why am I always so alone? And why Rod, Lord? Why did you bring him into my life only to take him away? Now I have known love, but I have lost that too. Why? Why is it always this way?"

I began to sink and the abyss was deep. The judge's gavel had slammed into my heart, and within one twenty-four-hour period, I had become the worst kind of prisoner. I was a prisoner of my own mind, and unless I helped myself, there was little hope of escape.

CHAPTER 34

Dark Night of the Soul

DEPRESSION IS an odd kind of illness. I thought I understood it, but no previous experience, neither mine nor my sister's, had prepared me for this. I cared not for an Einstein, nor did I care about my dream. If I hadn't already made plans to travel, I might not have survived those next few weeks. Literally, I could not stop the tears. I curbed the flow long enough to speak with my roommates, who promised to take care of the house and my dogs. I also managed a couple of chores. I got down to the Department of Motor Vehicles and obtained a temporary sticker for travel.

Jana was going to keep the Lexus while I was away, so Colorado plates would be purchased. We hadn't figured out how or when she would physically take possession, but this solved a couple of problems. Mostly the maneuver was a money-saver, and I was stretching a dollar every way possible. In fact, I was stretching almost everything, including my food intake. I barely ate; not even the enticement of a prepared steak could bring me to the dining room. I simply preferred isolation.

Lester and Trish were worried, but they did not become insistent. Lester continued to make me a plate and would remind me it was waiting in the refrigerator. That kept me alive, for when no one was home, I would venture downstairs for nourishment. Otherwise, I stayed to myself and continued to cry. I knew tears were cleansing, but this was ridiculous. After a few days, I began to wonder if they would ever stop. At the drop of a hat, my gut would wrench and the waters would flow. I was experiencing the dark night of the soul. I had heard of it and now, for the first time in my life, I understood why people commit suicide.

"Thank God I already have these plans," I said, on the day I was leaving. Thank God for the majestic mountains. I need them to restore my soul.

I left town hanging onto my last shred of sanity and gave myself a three-day head start. Jana was meeting me at our favorite hot springs resort, but before going into Glenwood, I needed some high-altitude healing. For two nights I stayed in Grand Junction and I hiked in Monument National Park. That brought me around some, but I was still a basket case by the time we met for our first swim.

When Jana found me, I was lying on a chaise lounge and I had no desire to move. She coerced me into the water and then told me massages were booked. Even that sounded like torture. It was too invasive; I simply did not want to be touched, especially by a stranger. She talked me into it, though. She talked me into a lot of things, including a fine seafood dinner. Little by little, she drew me out, and after a couple of days, we headed southwest.

We were planning to visit my son, who was in Durango attending classes, but we took our time getting there and visited my childhood stomping grounds. Cruising the streets in Montrose, we found the house where my grandparents had lived and around the corner, we discovered the park where we played as kids. It hadn't changed much, but on the street corner, I noticed something.

"Look, Jana." I pointed to the street sign.

"Nevada," she replied.

"Another divine coincidence," I prompted.

"Providence. You practically lived in this park when you were here and it was on the street of your future."

"And look where Nevada took me. I'm not sure I like the implication."

I started up again. It was those damn tears. They simply had a will of their own. Jana pulled me into a bear hug and held me until I was calm. When we found my aunt's ranch, it was much the same. The acres of pristine wheat were gone, replaced by tract homes, but the memories remained, and again they ripped me apart.

Poor Jana, I really wasn't very good company. For her sake I tried, and thankfully we were traveling in separate cars. This gave me lots of time to drown myself. Silence would send me plummeting, so would music, and a sad song would completely undo me. I found moments of respite, mostly times when a turn in the road would render a beautiful fall sight.

It was autumn. Trees and brush filled the valley with amazing contrasts of color. That essence of change helped soften my depression. When we stopped at a roadside apple stand, I got out of my car and listened to the trees. The sound of whispering leaves further woke me and I heard my sister. She was speaking to a country gentleman about a wide array of apple products. When she handed me a glass and pushed it to my lips, the lush flavor of cider burst forth. The taste was divine, something delivered by the Gods. It delighted my palate, and finally, finally, I smiled.

"Umm," Jana said, echoing my thoughts. "Isn't that wonderful?"

"That's the best apple juice I've ever tasted," I said.

"Should we buy a gallon?"

"Let's get two. One for the road and one to take home. Besides, it will give me energy for that bike ride tomorrow morning."

She was thrilled. Up until that point, I hadn't been interested in traversing a mountain path on two wheels. It sounded like too much work.

"Two," she said happily. "We'll take two, please."

Ouray was a quaint little mountain town. It looked like it belonged in the Alps. Nestled in a tight valley, it rested between Montrose, the town of my birth, and Durango. It was our last stop before my first official "goodbye" and was the perfect place to gain strength. Like Glenwood Springs, it had a hot springs pool, with waters known for their healing powers.

I took full advantage on that afternoon, floating myself into a tranquil state. Jana got another massage and offered to treat me, but I declined. A soothing soak was all I wanted. Looking upward toward the deep, rich sky, I thought about nothing, nothing but the drifting umbrella clouds that scattered to spread their protective veil. They danced around the surrounding mountain peaks and waltzed to a distant tune, teasing their way down to the treetops. I swayed in the water, and the quiet rhythm was comforting.

For the first time since Judgment Day, I felt a glimmer of hope, and by immersing myself in nature I began the process that would eventually lift the darkness. Unfortunately, the staying power came gradually, and the next morning I did not have the energy for a bike ride. Jana was disappointed, but knowing I was facing Charlie that day, she didn't fight me. She made the ride solo and when she returned to the room, I was cleaned up and ready to go.

"You're looking better," she encouraged.

"Think?"

"Yes. You don't look quite so gaunt."

"Charles won't care about that," I said. "He'll love the fact I'm skinny."

"Maybe," she said reluctantly.

"So, want to get some lunch?" It was the first time I mentioned food. Before that, she needed to twist my arm.

"Sure," she said. "Let's go to that cute little bar we saw in town. We've got time, haven't we? I mean before meeting Charles?"

"I told him we'd call after checking into a motel."

"Okay then, you ready?"

"Let's do it." I sounded more positive than I felt.

At the restaurant I ordered enthusiastically and ate most of what was on my plate. Trouble was, it didn't stay down. I was having problems with my stomach, and everything that went in either came up or raced out. On this day, the mountain curves were treacherous. I agonized around every turn, and we were constantly pulling over.

What a place to be sick. We were on the Million Dollar Highway. It was named such because of its original cost. Every linear foot required dynamite and the taxpayers paid dearly. Now I was paying, too. Maybe not a million bucks per foot, but the price to see my son was dear.

That evening I was feeling better so I made another good effort to eat, this time for the sake of Charles. He was, it seemed, worried about me after all. I was too thin, even by his standards.

"God, Mom, you look thin! Are you sick or something?"

"No. It's just been hard lately. I haven't had much of an appetite."

He had heard about Rod's antics and now he vented in anger. "I should have taken him out. I thought about it."

"Who?" I asked, pretending not to know.

"Who?" he echoed. "Rod, of course. I can't believe he did this to you."

"Did what?" I really wasn't sure what he meant.

"Hurt you like that. First, he stole your money and then he beat you up. Mom, you should have ruined him when you had the chance. Why didn't you?"

"Charlie! Rod didn't steal from me. I willingly invested in his company after we became friends. I could never have turned on him. No amount of money would have been worth it."

"Well, Global would still be doing great if you and those other people had taken over. It was a fun business, Mom. I don't see how you could let it go down like that."

Charlie had worked at several of the local sales promotions and made good commissions for his efforts. Naturally, he had hoped for a future with the company. I could understand his disappointment, but I did not like the reason.

"You may not understand, Charles, but if I had turned on Rod, it would have killed him. As it was, he still had an emotional and mental breakdown, but if his best friend had betrayed him, he might have jumped off a cliff."

"Whatever. I still think the guy's a jerk. He didn't deserve you."

The conversation was causing all sorts of unsettling, but I managed my emotions and said, "Thanks, baby. I love you, too."

"So, how long do you have? Before you surrender, I mean?"

After I told him, we talked quietly for the rest of the evening. When we parted, it was with plans to meet for breakfast. Thankfully, I was spared the "goodbye," at least for the time being.

Breakfast was a blessing. Charles brought friends and their congeniality was contagious. Before I knew it, the meal was over and we were on the road again. My first goodbye had gone off without a hitch, but two hours later my stomach was rocking and my head was knocking. I could not make it to Colorado Springs, at least not on that day. Jana followed me to a motel and made sure I was comfortable. Regretfully, she could not stay. She had to be at the office the next morning. I, on the other hand, had nowhere to go for the next few weeks. I took two aspirins and closed my eyes. *Help me, Lord Jesus*, I prayed. *I cannot do this without you.*

It was most definitely the dark night of the soul. I was fighting it, but the grayness was there. This time I did not sink into the abyss. Rather, I called on my twenty-four-hour rule again.

If the whole world can turn on its axis in one twenty-four hour period, then so, too, can I.

The next day I made it to my safe house. Jana's home was a place I could rest and rest I did. I tried not to think and spent the days in front of her television. That Saturday we took a long bike ride, but we were not alone. Some of Jana's friends joined us and there was a party afterward. No one spoke about my plight, although they had been informed, and the beer bash brought a pleasant relief.

On Sunday, we hiked the Helen Hunt Memorial Mountain, and I rather liked the idea of trekking after the famous female author. She inspired me. The incline was difficult, but I managed it better than my sister, who took notice.

"You seem to be doing well, Judy. Isn't your hip bothering you anymore?"

It wasn't. In fact, it hadn't bothered me in Monument National Park either. During those two days I had been too numb to notice, but now I was struck by the sudden healing.

"You know, it's odd, but it hasn't been hurting. Ever since I left Las Vegas, my hip has been fine."

"That's cool. Really, most times you had to stop and rest."

She was right, which gave me a thought. "I know, but now I know who I am. I no longer need to carry the pain of my past."

She had no idea what I meant, so I explained what I'd read about Mileva Maric's congenital hip dislocation.

"Judy! That gives me goose bumps."

"Me, too. Look," I said, extending an arm for proof. "I swear, Jana, I truly believe I am her. Our life stories are too similar."

"What do you mean?"

She knew my take on the abuse issue, but now I told her how Mileva had given up a child. I also reminded her how I almost gave up Pam. "It all fits and you know what, I even think I know who you were then."

"Who?" She was curious, oddly so. I found it strange she didn't debunk me.

"My arch enemy."

She stopped, abruptly turned, and looked down the hill.

Without pausing, I passed her with a smile. "You were Albert's little sister, Maja. Her name even sounds like yours. Maja—Jana. They sort of rhyme."

"Come on," she said, picking up the step.

"Really. You hated me. Well, you didn't really know me, but you didn't like the idea of your brother marrying someone like me. I wasn't perfect enough, and you took up sides with your mother. She hated me, too. You both tried to poison him against me."

"Why?" she asked.

"I don't know why ... because it was the thing to do. Or maybe because I wasn't a Jew. Who knows why? All I know is Maja didn't want Albert to marry Mileva and she let it be known. Now you've come back to make amends. Don't you think it's interesting we were once enemies and now we're best friends?"

I didn't get a direct answer. She skirted around the issue. "Thank God for that," was her response.

"Listen to this, Jana. You know how Shirley abused you as a kid?" I looked over my shoulder and saw her nod.

"Well, Albert did the same thing to Maja. You relived the same kind of childhood abuse this time around, too."

"What?"

"I'm not kidding. Everybody thought Albert was well-behaved, but Maja knew better. Her big brother was a terror and she knew when to run. He would turn yellow before a temper tantrum, and when that happened, she would take off. Once he hit her over the head with a garden hoe."

"Sounds like Shirley, alright."

"Yeah, but Maja sounds like you. She was extremely intelligent, Jana, and she excelled in math. Math! Can you imagine? That's your subject, little sister."

Jana stopped on the trail. She needed to catch her breath. The high altitude was causing her asthma to kick in. I backtracked and sat down on a log near her. The scent of pine penetrated my sinuses and suddenly I was glad to be alive. "Isn't this whole Einstein thing a trip?"

"Sure is. Makes me wonder."

"Jana."

"What?"

"Maja died in 1953. You were born in 1953."

"Wow," she said.

"She was a vegetarian, too. She hated the thought of hurting another living creature."

"My kind of lady," Jana said.

"I know. It all fits. I wonder why you keep getting attacked, though?"

"I wonder?"

"There must be a lesson there. I know Maja adored

Albert despite his antics. He loved her, too, and in fact, she lived with him for the last twelve years of her life."

"Did she ever marry?"

"Yes, but she separated from her husband to come visit the States. There was never a divorce, but apparently there was no great loss of love either. She simply never went back. That sort of fits your profile, too."

"Sure does. Take 'em or leave 'em. No big deal either way."

I laughed and we started up the hill again. It was getting steeper, so I conserved my breath for the climb. In silence we reached the peak, where the view was spectacular, too beautiful for words. The entire valley stretched out before us with the city off in the distance blending into the lay of the land. This was the view that inspired Helen Hunt, and it was so glorious that, for a time, it stilled us.

She spoke first. "So, you think we knew each other before? I mean even before Einstein?"

"Yes, but we were not always enemies. We've been together as friends, too. I'm sure of it."

"I think so, too."

She was buying into my theory. "I love you, Jana. I don't know what I would have done without you. No one else has helped me the way you have."

"Mom's been there for you."

"No, she hasn't. Not really." I told her about the birthday card and then we discussed how differently we had been treated as kids. Jana could do no wrong. I was the proverbial bad child, or at least they made me feel like I was.

"Mom and Dad were rough on you," she said adamantly.

"Especially Mom. She was probably my past life mother, too. I wouldn't doubt it."

Jana stared.

"Think about it. Mileva was a whiz kid and her parents must have had high hopes for her. They made sure she received a fine education, and more than likely they sacrificed dearly to make that happen, but guess what? She came home pregnant. Instead of graduating, she returned home to bear a child. Can you imagine their disappointment?"

"And what a scandal!" Jana chimed in. Then she laughed. "You did it, too. You dropped out of college because you wanted to get married."

"Yes, and the folks were pissed. Dad told me if I left the nest, I could never come back. I didn't care. I had no intention of returning. Later, though, there were times when I needed help, but it was like pulling teeth to get it. They floated me a loan to get away from Lance, and then again when I bought my first home in Vegas, but they never let me forget it. I heard about the debt continuously until every dime was paid back."

"Really? I borrowed money for my first house, but Dad told me not to worry about paying it back. I think I made a couple of payments, but that was all. He helped me get back into school, too. Even after I dropped out for a year, he made sure I had money to finish."

"I know. That's what I mean. They never did anything like that for me. Every hour of education after that first quarter I paid for myself. I think they were determined to stick to their guns, or maybe they simply believed I was capable, but you're lucky I was the firstborn. I paved the way for you girls. By the time you and Shirley needed help, they had a much softer attitude. I mean, think of the money they dumped Shirley's way. When she went through that divorce, it cost them a small fortune, and in a way, I think they did her a disservice. Now, she believes the world owes her. She never learned to stand on her own two feet."

"Well, you sure did."

"I had to, Jana. I had no choice."

I paused to reflect. The trees whispered softly. Most

certainly God was present. I could hear the divine rustling in the leaves. It was one of the reasons I enjoyed getting deep into nature. I was always filled with a great sense of spirit.

"Mom said she isn't going to make another car payment for you," Jana said.

I hadn't expected this. "You're kidding. Why?"

"She says you never had the courtesy to ask. She was angry when the late notice arrived."

"Oh God, give me a break. She knows I'll pay her back."

"That's what I told her, but she doesn't believe you about the refund."

"What!"

"I wasn't going to tell you," Jana said. "But I think you should know."

"What did you say?"

"I suggested she give you a break. I told her she should trust you."

"Thanks," I said, suddenly gaining insight. "She must be the incarnate spirit of Mileva's mother. She is still carrying the grudge from our last lifetime. To make matters worse, she was born under the sign of Scorpio. Good Lord, she had better forgive me this time around. God knows, I don't want to go through this again."

"Can't say I blame you."

Jana's support strengthened me and I had another thought. "She's still dealing with Shirley, too. Mileva had a mental sister. Her name was Zorka, and she was a real case. She was institutionalized most of her life, a true schizophrenic."

"And the plot thickens," she said. "So, are you about ready? It's cooling off. Maybe we should head down the mountain."

"Yeah, I guess."

The day had been a good one, and I was sad it was over.

I was looking forward to bed, however. I knew sleep would come easily and without nightmares. I was far too tired for any of the sinking grayness. On that night, the darkness would bring peace rather than sorrow. The dark night of the soul was slipping away. What would take its place, I did not know, but I was coming clear and I was grateful.

CHAPTER 35

Saying "Goodbye"

MY ATTITUDE IMPROVED after that hike. Traversing the same path as Helen Hunt increased my desire to become a published author.

"Judy?" The concern in my sister's voice spoke volumes. I waited. "Judy, are you going to be okay?"

"Yes, Jana. I'll make it. This has been hard. It's been a long two years, but I'm tired of the fight. God, I am so tired."

She was tearing, agonizing over the thought of losing me.

"It's not fair," she said. "You legitimized the industry and played by the rules. It isn't right they punish you when there are so many scumbags in the business. Why don't they go after the real rip-and-tear artists?"

"Because they are too hard to catch," I answered. "When the heat intensifies, the real crooks simply move underground. I, on the other hand, had property. I was stable and an easy mark; so were Rich and Chris. Why should the Feds do their job properly when they can make a case against us?"

"I've really lost faith in our government because of this."

"Me, too, Jana, but at least it's almost over and I'm a better person for the experience."

"I can't believe you mean that."

"Oh, I do. This happened for the wrong reasons, but I'm still happy to be where I am in life. Now I have a dream and that dream will sustain me. It will save me while I'm behind those walls."

The next morning, we had a farewell cup of coffee. Then it was time for me to head to Denver, time to visit Shirley and her son, Michael. Silence slipped between us because it was difficult to say goodbye. After a few minutes, Jana dug in her purse and handed me a check. It was made out for twenty-five hundred dollars. She had already helped me obtain Colorado plates and different insurance. When the time came for me to surrender, she would take possession without a worry, but this was different. This gift was out of the blue and extremely generous. Tears came, but they were quiet ones. The gesture filled me with relief. That money would most definitely see me through. I looked up and said, "Thank you, Jana."

"You're welcome," she said simply. Nothing else was required. She knew I would pay her back. I finished packing and left the nest.

Michael, my nephew, saw me enter the apartment complex and chased me through the parking lot.

"Judy!" he exclaimed as I got out of the car. "Are you going to stay with us?"

"Yep. For a few days. That alright with you?"

"You bet. Hey, want to throw snowballs?"

"Doesn't look like enough snow for a snowball fight."

"Up the hill there is," he said, taking off.

"Wait a minute. Come back here."

He turned around, but his body language was defensive.

"Don't worry," I said. "I'm not going to kiss you. Here, take this bag."

His relief was visible. Michael was not big on affection.

He hated to be hugged and he especially hated to be kissed.

"Maybe we'll shag snowballs later. Right now, I want to see your mom."

"She's making fried chicken," he said happily.

"Hi, Judy," Shirley said, as though my visit was an everyday occurrence. "How are you?"

"Fine, I guess. I'm hanging in there."

She went back to her work, so I found a corner to stash my bags. Michael had already exited the apartment.

That was life with my sister. She lived in her own little world, and I never quite knew what to expect. I sat down and waited. Presently she came out to take a better look.

Wiping her hands on the apron, she said, "You're skinny!"

"I have lost a little weight."

"A little? You're a rail. Why do you wear those tight pants? They're out of style. They make you look old."

My pants were not out of style. In fact, they were very much the vogue. I had no desire to defend myself, however. "Think so? Guess I never thought about it. Well, don't worry. They won't fit much longer. I've already started to gain."

This seemed outrageous to her. "You have? You were even thinner?"

"Some," I said casually. "Need help with dinner?"

"You can set the table." She stood up and opened the door. "Michael!" she screamed.

I jumped from the loud shock of noise and quickly moved to the kitchen. Three days and nights with Shirley would be plenty. She was not as easy to be around as Jana, who rarely raised her voice. Shirley, on the other hand, hardly knew another way, especially when it came to communicating with her son.

~

On the second night it began to snow and the dirty city streets looked more pristine. "It's beautiful," I said to Shirley.

"Yeah, but it's supposed to be a big storm. Something tells me you won't be leaving tomorrow."

My free days were up and on Monday, I needed to check in with my pretrial supervisor. I had allowed one extra day for travel, but that was because I could not afford to be late. "Oh, it'll stop. It always does. I'll get out of here."

But it didn't. It snowed all night and in the morning the cars in the parking lot were buried. I decided to dig into my nephew's room. It was a mess and I was bored. "Come on, Michael, I'll help you clean your room."

"Really! You'll really help?"

"Sure. It will be fun. We'll find all kinds of hidden treasure in there."

It took all day and we ended up with six large sacks of trash. I was exhausted, so I climbed into a bath.

On Saturday, the city shut down, and the storm made national news. "Guess my supervisor will have to understand," I said. "Looks like I'll be late."

"What will he do?" Shirley asked.

"What can he do? This was unavoidable. I simply had no way of anticipating this kind of weather. How about I clean your room today?"

She did not like my idea. "No, I'll do it. It's far too big of a disaster. You'd have no idea what to do with my stuff."

"Well, I need to do something. Can I work on the kitchen?"

This was acceptable, so I tore into it. That, too, took a whole day, and this time I needed a shower. The grime had to immediately go down the drain.

Sunday morning the promise of travel was in the air. I hired two teenage boys to dig out my car, and while they dug, I cleaned the main living area, tackled the bathroom, and then took a quick shower. When I finally left, Shirley had a spotless apartment, and she thanked me for the help.

"No problem," I said. "Just try to keep it that way, will you?"

She said she would, but Shirley wasn't much of a housekeeper. It was an eternal sore spot for the family. They hated the way she trashed a home. So did I, but I cut her some slack. I knew what depression could do, and my sister suffered on an ongoing basis. Even when she was manic, she wasn't prone to cleanliness. It was one of her flaws. We all had them. This one happened to be hers. I wished her and Michael well, and they waved as I drove away. The streets were treacherous, but I made it to the foothills and there the highway cleared. I was going home, and I felt more able to handle the weeks ahead of me. I had begun saying my "goodbyes."

One day at a time now, Judy. Just take it one day at a time.

A familiar song came over the radio, but it didn't tear at my heart. A few weeks ago the song instantly reduced me to tears. It was a Sawyer Brown tune reminiscing about hope and heartache.

I cried then and many times afterward, but today I was able to quietly listen. *Thank God this night won't last forever,* I thought as the tune went off the air. *Thank you, Lord.*

CHAPTER 36

Marie and Her Choo Choo

VAIL PASS SPARKLED in the sunlight on that afternoon. The crystal twinkling of the slopes should have created an easy mood, but as I dropped into the valley, I felt a restless stirring, a haunting of sorts. I was approaching The Crying Coyote where Rod and I had stopped for breakfast six months ago.

The memory chilled me. As I approached the West Vail exit, I thought about stopping and pulled into the right lane. When the time came, however, I did not exit. I flew past it, not feeling strong enough. When I was there before, I was filled with a newness of spirit. I was also in love, and Rod's Christian strength helped me bear the observation.

On this day I did not have Rod and I wasn't sure about my personal strength. After all, I was returning from no-man's land, from a spiritual depression. If I went in, and the people appeared normal, I would wonder if I had lost my power of observation. Certainly my divine essence had been strained. Was it still there? Could I still "see"? I didn't know and didn't want to find out.

I made it to Richfield, Utah, and the next morning I called my pretrial supervisor. "I'll be late," I said. "Did you see the news about the storm that hit Colorado?"

"Yes. It looked nasty. When will I see you?"

"Tomorrow. I managed to get on the road yesterday. I'm about halfway there."

I could hear the relief. His charge had not run away. "That's great, Judy. Come in at your convenience. I'll be here all day."

When I arrived at his office, Norman had a nice surprise for me. "The court has mandated more drug testing, Judy."

"What do you mean?"

"It's been written into your PSI. With the trials drawing closer, they want to be sure you remain credible as a witness."

I was more than aggravated. "What do I have to do?"

"Two UA's a week, every Monday and Thursday."

The thought of two pee tests a week was infuriating. One was bad enough, but two! He wasn't finished with me, however. He had more good news. "Make sure you don't leave town. I'll be doing more random checks at your home."

I should have left, I thought. I should still leave. These people are assholes. They do not deserve the time of day.

"I'm not going anywhere. For the most part, I'll be home getting ready. I have some packing to do and a lot of organizing. I'll keep myself out of trouble, don't worry."

"I'm not, but others are. They've put additional pressure on me, so I thought you should know. Sorry, Judy, but no overnight camping trips either—at least not without notifying me."

That was a low blow. Norman knew how much I needed the mountains. "No problem," I said. "So, when do you want me back—for the next test, that is?"

"Let's start next Monday. That will give you a week to settle in."

"Okay. I'll see you then."

I left that mighty federal building and went home

thinking about my check. If that refund came in, I might consider busting a move. I had just been shackled and I wasn't happy. It was the heavy hand of government authority, AGAIN. God, how I hated it.

Whether I went AWOL or not, preparation was required. The first thing I did was talk to my roommates. "I have something to tell you," I said after finishing dinner one night.

Lester was not surprised. "We've been waiting. We suspected something might be going on, but we figured you'd share in your own time."

"Yes, and it's time," I said. "I should have told you long ago, but I couldn't. I wasn't ready."

Trish looked concerned but said nothing.

Her silence prompted me. I didn't mention Rod or Einstein. Rather, I concentrated on my telemarketing career. I gave them the facts about Pioneer and explained how I had been targeted. It was my job as a government witness to help the Feds prosecute my former employers. For that, they had graciously reduced my sentence from eighteen years to thirty-three months.

"You're going to prison?" Trish cried.

"Yes, next month. I must surrender on the twenty-fourth."

Lester was shocked. "I knew it was bad, but I had no idea it was something like this."

"See why I've been so upset?"

Trish did. "You poor thing. This is awful. Oh my gosh, is there anything we can do?"

I hadn't intended to cry, but this confession reduced me to a blubbering idiot. I bawled like a baby. They wrapped their arms around me and soothed me with words and hugs.

"I was hoping you might stay," I cried, pulling away. "This is your home now and I thought you might move upstairs to the master bedroom. We could get you another roommate, and that way you could afford the place."

My offer made Trish cry. Offering my home was more than she expected. "Besides," I added. "We can't separate the puppies. They love each other now."

Lester agreed. "Sugar would be heartbroken. She's a totally different dog today."

"She sure is," said his adoring wife.

After talking for a while longer, I excused myself. I went upstairs and thought about the feds. It's my life and I do not appreciate being told how to live it, especially not in these last few days.

My rebel thinking was taking shape, but I did not let it consume me. I still had time, and I wanted to spend it with family. I headed to my daughter's house and asked if I could have Marie for the day. "I thought I'd take her for a walk in Red Rock Canyon."

"You think she's big enough?" Pam asked.

"Sure. She's two. I had you walking all over the hills of San Francisco by the time you were three. That walking helped shape your beautiful legs!"

She laughed and turned to her daughter. "You want to go with Choo Choo?" she asked.

My nickname was really JuJu. Pam, Jason, and I had decided on it when Marie was born. I wasn't quite ready to be called Grandma or anything similar, so we settled on JuJu. Marie, however, couldn't get the words right, so she called me Choo Choo.

"Me sleep at Choo Choo's?" she asked excitedly.

Pam looked at me.

"It's fine by me," I said. "I can take her to daycare in the morning if you like."

"Mom, that would be great. Let's go pack your bag, honey."

My dogs were waiting in the car, and their exuberance almost sent my granddaughter running back to her mother. She screeched when they pounced on her, but I quickly shuffled them into the back. I buckled her into the baby seat, and off we went.

In the canyon we took our time while Buster and Gus ran circles around us. Marie laughed and tried to keep up with the puppies. Her little legs were strong, but she rested them often. If a glimmering rock caught her attention, we'd have to stop to pick it up. I'd stash it dramatically in our day pack and then she'd take off again. After approaching what I thought might be a mile, I casually turned us around. She was still a bundle of energy, so I thought she'd be alright. I had pushed too far, though. About halfway back, she began to trip. One spill resulted in a skinned knee and a loud cry.

I bent down to comfort her. "It's okay, sweetie. You're getting tired. Those bad ole rocks are jumping up at you. Can you pick your feet up a little higher?"

She could and set off to prove it. Knowing I could not carry her, I began to pray. Lift her Lord. We're almost there. Give her little legs the strength.

I could see the parking lot the next time she fell. This time I pulled her into the shade. I distracted her by bringing out the water and I poured it into her little hands for the dogs. They lapped and she laughed. When they were done tickling her, they plopped down for a rest. I peeled an orange. We ate pieces alternately and then took up our march again. Gratefully, we made it, but before we were out of the park Marie was out cold. A picture of perfect innocence. Pink cheeks and long brown curls. I want to remember this for the future. I imprinted the image onto my mind.

I took Marie often after that day. Sometimes we'd go for walks and other days we'd go to the pool. She didn't seem to care what we did, so it was easy to spend time with her. One of her favorite games was tossing a ball. We had started playing it more than a year before, but we used imaginary spheres for a make believe game, since her fingers were too tiny for the real thing. Now at the age of two, she remembered our old routine. When she tired of the real thing, she'd toss the ball aside and pretend to throw me its invisible counterpart. I'd fall awkwardly to the floor, attempting to catch her wild throw, and she'd roar with laughter, loving it. I began to wonder what I'd do without her. What would she do without me?

One evening Marie and I retreated to my room to watch a movie. I chose the Disney channel, thinking the scheduled thriller would capture her attention. It did, but it also frightened her, and she moved closer for comfort. Another scene caused a whimper, so I snuggled her into me. With my arm around her, I could feel her body shake and decided it was time to end the distraction.

"I don't like this movie," I said. "Do you?"

A shake of her head told me she didn't.

"Should we turn it off?"

Her eyes were glued to the screen, but when a monster appeared, they went wide. She reached both arms around me and squeezed tight.

"Marie, look," I said, reaching backward and turning on the headboard light. "It's not real." I grabbed the remote and clicked off the terror. "Look, honey."

Her hands were in mine.

"Remember the ball?"

Curls bobbed.

"Can you throw it to me?"

She did.

"That ball is pretend, Marie. It's not real."

She stared. "Pretend," she repeated.

"Yes, for fun. We pretend, but the ball cannot hit us. It can't hurt us. Do you understand?"

"We play," she said simply.

I clicked the remote. The TV lit up, but the monster was gone. “The TV plays, too. It’s pretend.”

“Not real?” she questioned.

I turned it off again. “See it’s gone. It can’t hurt you, okay?”

“Okay,” she said happily.

“Okay, let’s go to sleep now.” She curled into me, and I was filled with a sad kind of tenderness.

“Bad TV,” she said, before leaving the field.

Her final words filled my mind with so many thoughts. I wanted to protect her somehow, to help her mother with the nurturing. Soon, little one, I said silently. I’ll be back, and I’ll be there for you. I will always be your Choo Choo.

CHAPTER 37

The Global Medley

I TRIED NOT TO THINK about the trials. Fortunately, my son-in-law, Jason, accepted a plea, and received a recommendation for boot camp. The judge waived his twenty-seven-month sentence and replaced it with a six-month stretch of military-like discipline. His surrender date was in January, which meant my daughter would have her husband through the upcoming holidays. It would be difficult for Pam, but now I knew she'd survive. Six months wasn't all that long, and Jason's extra two months of freedom would give her time to adjust to my absence. There were positives, so I focused on them while continuing my goodbyes.

Pam helped me throw a poolside barbeque bash, and we invited the close cluster of girls who once worked for me. I hadn't seen them for a long time, almost two years in some cases, but they were happy to attend, and it felt like a family reunion. I cooked hamburgers and hotdogs, while they swam, played with their kids, and hashed over old times.

"Look at you," Cindy said, as I returned bearing a tray of meat. "You're still taking care of us."

A year ago, Cindy was angry with me for not staying in touch, so I was pleasantly surprised she was there. I never told anyone, but one of my pretrial mandates demanded severing all telemarketing ties. For me that meant everybody, so I complied. On this day, however, I cared nothing about the rules. If the authorities came to haul me off, then so be it. Anyway, Cindy had a new baby, and she seemed to have forgotten my past transgressions. She proudly showed off her precious jewel.

"You're my girls," I said. "Of course I'm still taking care of you. All you need to do is have fun."

I was grateful they were all surviving. Despite the raids and government investigations, they were doing well, and life was improving for most of them. Only one friend concerned me. Before the day ended, and cranky children were carried away, I spoke to her privately.

"Corky, I still worry about you. When do you plan on breaking from that abusive husband of yours? I don't mean to lecture. Lord knows I've been there, done that, but you've got kids, girl. Aren't you worried for them?"

"Joe's always been a good father, and now that the kids are in school, I'll be able to make my break."

"It could get scary for you," I said.

"I know; I'll be careful. He'll be pissed as hell when I disappear with the kids."

I recalled my escape and wanted to help if possible. "I've told my roommates about you and your situation. If you ever need a place—even if it's for one night—you can go there."

"Thanks, Judy," she said.

"Don't worry about money or food or anything. Trish and Lester are prepared to help. Just remember one thing."

"What?" she asked.

"When you finally leave, don't look back. Run like hell and don't give him the time of day afterward. If you do, you may die."

"I know. He's crazy," she said.

"They all get crazy when we finally leave," I responded.

"I'll do it right, but what about you? We are all scared for you. This seems so unfair, but your attitude is incredible. I wonder though ... underneath it all, do you really feel so strong?"

I gave her my song and dance, much as I had the others, but at the end of the afternoon, I was mentally and emotionally whipped. When I went home and read the guest book, their salutations brought on tears. One of the girls had given me a farewell gift, so I reached for the tiny baggie.

I'll just do a flush of Clean Tea, I rationalized, sucking up the burning powder.

I believed I had gotten away with it until I got the call.

"What happened, Judy?" he asked.

It was Norman. I couldn't imagine what he meant. I had been down to pretrial services three times since the party. "Why? What do you mean?" My heart was racing.

"Your test was positive for crystal. Judy, you're jeopardizing what little freedom you have left. They could take you into custody right now."

"I'm sorry, Norman. My friends threw me a farewell party. We had a few beers, and then one of them offered me a line. I knew better, but I wasn't thinking straight. Really, it was a one-time deal. I promise it won't happen again."

"When?" he asked flatly. "When was the party?"

I told him, and he said he'd call back. I held my breath and eventually the call came.

"Okay, Judy. They said to give you a warning this time. For your sake, however, don't let it happen again. That stuff is bad news."

"I know, Norman. Believe me, I know—and thanks."

"You're welcome. So, I'll see you Thursday?"

"As always," I said. "Thanks again."

That was too close. Thank God, Norman was a tolerant man. He did try to help his people and he cared. I was grateful he was assigned to me.

November arrived and with it came the postponement. The trials had been set aside. No date was offered, but we were told they'd probably commence after the first of the year.

"I can't take this," I told my mother one evening over dinner. "This is getting too difficult."

"What do you mean?"

"You know how I am. I hate the fact they control my life."

"I'm sure you do," she said.

"Mom, I haven't told anyone this."

She sensed what was coming. Her oldest child wanted to break and run.

"What?" she asked hesitantly.

"I'm thinking of leaving. I have my surrender date, and there are things to do, places to go."

"But I thought you weren't supposed to go anywhere!"

"I'm not, but since the trials have been postponed, there's no reason to stay. They want to keep an eye on me, make sure I don't disappear or anything, so they are restricting my activities. No matter what I do, I'm going to prison. That's why I'm telling you. I don't want you to worry if I disappear. They'll probably question you."

"I won't tell them anything," she said indignantly. She hated the Feds almost as much as I did.

"You won't know anything, Mom. I would never put you in a position where you had to lie. I simply don't want you to worry."

"Thanks, honey. You don't know how much that means to me."

But I did. I knew taking her into my confidence would mean a great deal. I had kept too much from her, and really, it was the wrong thing to do. I wanted to protect her, but not sharing created a wall. More than anything, I wanted that wall to come down and there was no time like the present.

"I'm sorry I locked you out. I know it's been hard on you."

"It has. I knew you were hurting, but I had no idea how to reach you."

"Well, from now on, I'll tell you everything—well, almost everything. I am serious, though. If my refund comes, I may cut and run. I'll surrender on the twenty-fourth as expected, but I want those last days to myself. Can you understand?"

She said she could, and she also understood why I didn't want to give my daughter a farewell hug. We talked about the day I had left Denver for my move to Las Vegas. It had been a gut-wrenching experience for both of us, far too painful to relive.

One evening, Lester broached the subject of my impending incarceration. He was having a difficult time imagining I had done everything possible to fight the charges. Trish was there, too, and we were doing the dishes.

"Oh, believe me," I said. "I put up a pretty good fight. I was able to obtain a hefty retainer for counsel, and I had a team of three topnotch attorneys."

"Why didn't you go to court then?" he asked.

"Lester, even with my resources, it would have been impossible. The Feds have unlimited power, and you simply cannot beat them. My money was gone before I faced the judge. A court battle would have cost millions."

"What about a court-appointed attorney?" he tried.

"Not a possibility. Most of them are fresh out of college. They don't even know how to file a proper motion, let alone wage a war. My former bosses have paid four million dollars to their team, and it's still not over for them."

"Four million?" exclaimed Trish.

"That's what I've been told, and you know what? I hope they win. It's high time this witch hunt ends."

Lester seemed dubious. "I don't get it. If you were licensed to conduct business, how could they arrest you?"

I began to pace. I hadn't thought about this for some time. Lester and Trish continued with the chores, while I vented my anger.

"We followed the state regulations. I was licensed, bonded, and registered in twenty-two states across the nation. If we couldn't meet the state criteria, we didn't sell in that district.

"Problem was, the Feds didn't care. Apparently, the local laws mean nothing. They are essentially worthless. If the U.S. government wants to make a federal case out of something, they set aside the state statutes."

"They can do that?" he asked.

"Yes. I guess it happens all the time."

Before I escaped up the stairs, they offered more personal support, saying they'd always be there for me. I didn't need to worry about the house or the dogs. They would take care of everything. I even got assurances Lester would secure work. They had decided against a roommate, and for my sake as well as theirs, they intended to make ends meet.

I was skeptical.

During the second week of November, the refund still wasn't here and I began to panic. I had received a notice of foreclosure, and my mother had called the bank. Despite her verbal support, she refused to make another car payment. She told the loan officer to pick up my Lexus, as she could not honor the debt. I decided to call Debbie Davis, the IRS agent who was now my friend.

"I'm worried, Debbie," I said. "If the refund doesn't

come before the twenty-fourth, I'll lose my house and car."

"I'll call them, Judy. I'll find out what the holdup is."

"Thanks."

"How have you been?" she asked.

"I'm okay," I said. "I'm spending time with family, getting organized, working on my book, that kind of thing."

"You really are an inspiration, Judy. If you can convey that attitude to other women, your book will be a bestseller. Have you solicited an agent yet?"

"Well, no. I guess I should try. It sure will be difficult from prison."

"Do it. Your synopsis is good. I think you have real talent and I believe someone else will see it, too."

I thanked her for the encouragement, and she promised to call in a few days. While I waited, I drafted a query letter. Of the two hundred-some odd selections in the latest guide to "Editors, Publishers, and Literary Agents," one attracted my attention.

The Heart Sculpturing Agency beckoned me. It was owned by Joy Heart Hirschfeld and I liked the name. I wanted someone with a heart. Under Comments she said, "As our name implies, it is our desire to assist in sculpturing the ordinary writer into a literary success. We are willing to work with the authors to help them produce masterful quality writing."

"That's for me," I exclaimed. I drafted the letter, using my sister's return address and phone number. I licked the seal and prayed. As I dropped it in the box, I wished, Please Ms. Heart, have a heart. Help me make this happen.

After four days, Debbie finally called. "The check was held up for a final signature. I told the supervisor about your circumstances, and she has promised to overnight it."

"Thank you, Debbie. I owe you big time."

"Don't worry about it. I'm happy to help. Did you send

your query letter yet?"

"As a matter of fact, I did. Pray for me, will you?"

"You bet. Good luck to you, Judy. Stay in touch. Let me know where you are, and I'll send you some relaxation tapes. I've got some stuff you'll like."

"That would be great. I'll write as soon as I can."

Most everything was done, and the mention of tapes inspired me. I had been told music was allowed and a personal collection would be a great comfort.

My stereo component system was already in my office, so I was ready for the project. It filled the empty space where my father's globe once stood. That heirloom was packed away with other treasures, the sort of things I could not leave to chance. The world orb was highly symbolic, which I most definitely wanted around when I returned.

Albert Einstein also had a globe in his office, and since I was seriously excited about the Einstein family, my globe took on greater significance. Albert hated worldly attachments, but his globe was an exception. Mine would also remain a treasure, but thinking about it took me back to Rod. *What a wild ride.* Mr. Steersman, you were both the best and the worst. Life with you was never boring. I'll give you that much.

I wanted to remember. I wanted to recall every detail of our relationship, and I knew I could do it through tunes. Music had been a big part of our lives, and many songs were special to us. I decided to make a Mr. and Mrs. Global medley, something that would intimately represent Rod and Judy. I loaded my CD player, hit the auto programming feature, selected the first eight tunes, and started with my favorite song, "One Love," by Pat Benatar. I had nicknamed the tune "Lion Song," which described a golden dream, the kind of dream Rod and I once shared.

While our history played, I continued with the story. I

was writing the section called "The Roommate," and wanted to have it completed before my departure. The emotional pairing of musical notes and written words drove me on.

When the day came and I thought it was time, I walked to the street, praying. "Please be there. Time is running short. Please grant me a reprieve."

I pulled at the box and my heart skipped a beat. The envelope was not the official kind, but rather it was extremely personal. I recognized the handwriting immediately, and I nearly retreated. It had been one thing to hear the tunes, another to write the words, but now the memories were touching me. ROD!

"Dearest Judy," he began, "Being cut off from you is like losing a part of my soul."

The letter went on for four pages, and at the end he asked me to call him.

I felt his presence. He was right there in the room. It wasn't the first time I had sensed him, but on this day, I was overcome by synesthesia. The letter carried more than his message. I could smell him and I could nearly taste him.

"No!" I cried. "Leave me alone."

My words broke the spell. He was gone.

I thought about that tooth again. Would the remaining hole ever fill? Was it even possible to forget him? I felt our work together was done, but he was still on my mind every day. After all, I was writing our story. I decided that, no, I probably wouldn't forget him, not for a long, long time, maybe never actually, but I did not want to call him. That would be too painful. Still, if I didn't, would he show up? It would be just like him. *Good Lord. Please get me out of here.*

The day came, and the refund arrived. I was free. I only had to wait out the weekend, but on Monday, right after completing my banking transactions, I would leave. In two days, I would be a fugitive from the law. That meant I had work to do. I finished Part II of my manuscript and shipped the text to my sister. After that, I quietly began moving my clothes, either into a suitcase or stored in one of the two extra closets upstairs. The master suite was methodically emptied, making room for the new tenants. That night, I refused to join Lester and Trish. Talking might prove dangerous, and I could not afford a slip.

On Sunday I tended to details and then made a duplicate tape for Rod. I called it "The Global Medley," and added one brand new song for the grand finale. It was a beautiful tune by a rising opera star, which seemed perfectly appropriate for us. The words were an echo of my mind: "It's Time to Say Goodbye," by Andrea Bocelli. I let it fade quietly and then added my own subtle message, "I love you, Rod ... and I love you, Mary Ann. You take real good care of those beautiful kids, you hear?" Then I wrote Rod a letter and told him I was leaving. I told him to be happy, and said if he was happy, I would be happy, too.

On Monday I mailed the tape and left my mother a cashier's check. It was enough to cover the loan against my car and then some. Leaving the check on the counter meant "marker down," and maybe, just maybe, she wouldn't return to haunt me in another lifetime.

I took care of my mortgage and went home to load my car. Lester wasn't there, thank God. I finished packing and gave my dogs a final pat on the head. I was ready to walk out the door when the phone rang.

It was Pam, but I didn't answer. She left a message, and I deleted it before walking to my car. It was time for my new favorite tune: "It's Time to Say Goodbye."

PART V

SURRENDER

CHAPTER 38

Fugitive at Large

BEHIND THE WHEEL, I began to reflect on my situation. Where should I go? Where would I be safe? Not west. That would be the first direction they would look. Besides, I wanted no part of California, since I feared an earthquake and the resulting tsunami.

My attorney had told me about three prisons.

"You'll more than likely be designated to either San Francisco, Phoenix, or somewhere in Texas," she said matter-of-factly.

Texas held no appeal. It was too far from family. "Ask for Phoenix," I responded. "It's halfway between Denver and Las Vegas. If I'm assigned there someone might visit."

The judge agreed Phoenix was the best choice and entered the recommendation into the record. That did not guarantee placement, however. Once my documents left his courtroom, I would be the property of the Bureau of Prisons, and they could do anything. They could ship me to Timbuktu if they felt like it. Still, I wanted to believe the best, and although I knew the danger in assuming, I chose Phoenix and headed east.

Passing Lake Mead and crossing the giant Hoover Dam

brought forward J. Edgar Hoover. The gargantuan block of concrete had been named after him, a real blockhead, in my opinion. *You really did it to us, didn't you, Mr. Hoover?* You made a mockery of what this country stood for, and our government has gone steadily downhill ever since.

I no longer believed the FBI was there to protect the president or the people. It now seemed to exist for the sole purpose of gathering power and redistributing wealth. For the right people it represented a good future, but only if you were politically connected and corrupt enough to stay that way. After that, the agency was nothing more than a travesty of justice, or at least that's what experience had taught me.

Changing time zones sent my emotions reeling. I could not believe I was running from the law. I was once an upstanding citizen. I paid my taxes and tithed diligently every year. Now I was a felon and a fugitive. I was blaming my predicament on the corrupt judicial system.

I glanced at the speedometer and immediately let off the accelerator. I set the cruise control and eased back on my anger. In my mind, I created a space to feel free. I saw every detail, every dotted white line, all the highway signs, the scenery, and the cities along the way. I took it in, and the miles clicked off. Before I knew it, signage for Flagstaff appeared. I was getting close, but I did not want to enter a big city. I began to search for a wayside respite.

"Williams," spoke the white on green. "Gateway to the Grand Canyon."

That's for me, I thought. The idea of spending time at the entrance of the world's greatest gaping hole suited me. If the shoe fits.

The elegant hotel was nestled in the woods and seemed a perfect place to hide—off the highway, but not too far.

"How long will you be staying, ma'am?" asked the clerk.

"Three days," I said. I asked about the amenities and

then retreated to unload. Once I was comfortable, I started writing letters.

I wrote to Pam first. It was a long, tear-jerky kind of a letter, begging for forgiveness. "Saying goodbye was impossible. Please try to understand. I couldn't do it. I love you too much."

The letter to my mother was on the lighter side and filled with intrigue. I told her I was happily free and thanked her for helping me. My sisters received something ambiguous. I didn't want them to know my intentions in case the law came calling.

Finally, I wrote to Rod. I thought a second letter, postmarked from a different state, would further assure him I was really gone. That should prevent him from attempting a personal send-off. "Get on with your life. Be happy. And ..." I emphasized, "stay home with your wife."

When I was done, I went to the front desk. Momentarily I thought about the postmarks, but I decided not to worry. After all, I wasn't on the ten-most-wanted list, and I was no threat to society, not even close. I seriously doubted they would mount an effort to find me, so I left the stamped letters. They would be picked up in the morning.

What a relief. Now, it's time to take care of me. I went shopping and returned with plenty of snacks and drinks to hide from the world for a few days. I flipped on the TV, stacked pillows against the headboards, and laid back to relax.

Time to say goodbye, I said, thinking about the song and cracking a beer. The pillows felt good, and the drone of the tube lulled me away.

In the morning, I went to the dining room for brunch. Food was important, and I could no longer ignore the necessity. Before returning to my room, I picked up a handful of brochures about the surrounding area. I needed to relocate, so I took my pamphlets and went to check things out.

The food settled, and as my blood sugar rose, I made plans. Sedona beckoned me. I had heard of the community. A former friend and employee had raved about the city. Ben and his male companion traveled there every year for a week's vacation and always returned with wonderful stories. If it was good enough for him, it was good enough for me. I made some inquiries and settled on a resort/motel with a cluster of cabins. I tried to make reservations, but the manager required a credit card deposit. Since I no longer carried plastic, I called my sister.

"Hi, Jana. What's up?"

"Just working. How are things with you?"

"Great. I'm on the lam," I said casually.

"What?"

She could not imagine. Taking off like that was beyond her boundaries. I intended to explain, but before I tried, I needed to extrapolate a promise.

"I need you, Jana, but I can't tell you what's going on, unless you can keep my whereabouts confidential."

"No problem," she said.

"Are you sure? Because the feds might come knocking."

"I won't tell them anything—not unless I am called to court and sworn to tell the truth."

That was good enough for me. I explained my situation, and she promised to make my reservations. She also decided to join me.

"I'll fly into Flagstaff, and we'll do some biking together. When the time comes, I'll take you to your new home and drive your Lexus back to mine."

"Perfect," I said happily. That would solve the problem of my car. "That's great, Jana. It will be good to have company, especially for these last few days. I need you to see me, too.

I want you to know, I'm no longer sick with depression."

"Are you really okay?"

"I'm so much better, even I can't believe it. I've said my goodbyes and I'm ready to close this chapter forever. I just want to get on with it."

"Well, you sure are going out with a bang. God, Judy, the stress would kill me."

"I know, but for me it's all in a day's work." I chuckled at my rebellious streak and then broke our connection. Everything was falling into place, and it was time to enjoy. I did nothing for two days but read, eat and sleep. It was fabulous "me" time, and I had no regrets.

Sedona was everything Ben promised. The resort I chose was perfect, too. It was northwest of the main area, off the beaten path, in a beautiful canyon called Oak Creek. With the trees in full metamorphosis, their changing colors made the drive spectacular. *Just what the doctor ordered,* I thought, after unpacking and taking a short walk around the place. Nothing could be better.

I only needed supplies, so I left to buy groceries. Since I had a small kitchen, I was able to pick up more than snacks and drinks. I purchased wholesome foods and fine desserts. My appetite was calling, and I wanted to enter prison as healthy as possible. I also wanted my sister to know I could make the transition.

The next day, I went for a short walk, wrote in my journal, and called my daughter.

"Mom! What's up? Are you okay?"

"Didn't you get my letter?"

"No. What letter? Where are you?" she asked with concern.

"Damn," I said. I did not want to explain over the phone.

"Mom? What's wrong? Can I help?"

"Pam," I said. "The letter will explain everything. I'm

surprised you don't have it already, but I'm fine. It was just getting too difficult. I kept thinking about the day I would have to say goodbye to you and the girls and I couldn't cope. I was making myself sick, worrying about it. Finally, I decided to leave town. But I'm okay."

"What! Are you coming back?"

"No. I can't. There may be a warrant out for my arrest."

"Mom!"

"Don't worry. I still plan to surrender on the twenty-fourth. That's really their only concern. In the meantime, I want to do things my way."

After talking for an hour, she came to terms with her runaway mom. There were a few tears, but they were controlled. The conversation ended happily, and we released each other with love. *I'll miss you, Pam,* I thought after hanging up. Please, take care of yourself. And watch over those little girls.

The next day I took to the hills. I had purchased a small book titled, *Seven Hikes in Seven Days,* and I was determined to take the tour. The more I walked, the better I felt. Socializing was a pleasure as well, since trail talk was safe, and trekkers in the area loved conversing about the energy vortexes. Sedona, I discovered, was a New Age Mecca. The city was full of clairvoyants, Tarot readers, experts on astrology, Reiki masters, energy workers, and just about anything remotely related to New Age philosophy. I didn't want to dabble, but I explored the stores. I even bought a beautiful smoky-quartz crystal, a perfect addition for my collection. A well-grounded piece, I said to myself, holding it firmly. This will bring balance to my meditations.

I had brought stones and crystals with me, and now that I was welcoming a newcomer, I decided to purify the lot. I purchased a bag of sea salt and went home to give my charges a refreshing bath. Setting the colorful concoction on the outside table so it could bask in the sun, I thought about Rod. He did not like the fact that I was a collector, and we had argued about the sanctity of New Age practices. My thoughts on the subject had not changed, not even in my spiritually awakened state. *Check the intention, Rod.* Be aware of what you are feeling and understand your motivation. That is where the truth resides.

I looked fondly at my frequency enhancers and told them to enjoy. "Get rid of all that negative Steersman energy," I said to my stones. "Tomorrow we'll begin our work together."

When tomorrow arrived I hiked farther. Each day I grew stronger, and sometimes during my walks, I sensed a deep connection to nature. The environment was somehow sacred, and not because the days were growing shorter. It was more like my time in those hills was intrinsically spiritual. I never felt alone, and although I often passed strangers, there was a familiarity about them. I was keeping company with angels, beings filled with grace.

On Tuesday, I called Jana. "When does your flight land?" I asked.

"I took an extra day off. I'll be there Thursday morning at eleven."

"Cool."

"Judy?" Her tone was ominous.

"What?" How bad could it be?

"There's a warrant out for your arrest."

"Okay," I said quietly. I had called my pretrial supervisor, but only to leave a message. Assuring him I intended to surrender hadn't been enough. "How did you find out?"

My roommates Lester and Trish were questioned, and the officer told them a warrant had been issued.

"Well, I suppose my supervisor had no choice. Too bad. You didn't tell Lester anything, did you?"

"No, but he sure was curious."

"I bet he was. I slipped right out from under his busy-body bulbous old nose. He is such a know-it-all. That beer-drinking baboon is a piece of work. Gosh, I feel for Trish. Wish she would get away from that oaf."

"Look who's talking," lectured my wise sibling.

I laughed. "Yes, it takes one to know one. I'm a sucker and so is she."

Jana was silent. I knew her mind was reeling from the implications. "Don't worry, sis. They won't find me. I'll bend over real good when I get behind the wall. In the meantime, I want to enjoy. I'll see you Thursday, okay?"

"Okay. Love you."

I visualized her head shaking. Aiding and abetting was not exactly her thing. Fortunately, loving me was and she usually admitted I kept things interesting.

The trail I chose for the next day was a seven mile up and back. To do it would push my limits, but I believed I was capable. Since I expected to be gone for a while, I took a lunch and brought along my tunes. Pat Benatar's "You Touched the Devil and Couldn't Let Go," brought Rod to the forefront, and I half-jogged, half danced down the path. I also changed the words. "I touched the devil, but I'm letting go. He set the trap, but I said no."

If anyone was watching, they'd surely laugh. I was most definitely having a good time. Prison, I thought, would be my sabbatical. After serving my time, I'll fly from that world. Never again will I become captive to circumstance. Never again will a man control me.

"It's Time to Say Goodbye," came on again, and the significance sobered me. I slowed my pace and looked around. The ground was barely visible, for I was walking on a bed of new fallen leaves. Crimson shades of red predominated, but gold offered a softening contrast to the ever-thickening carpet. A cool breeze caressed my face, and

I lifted my eyes to search the trees. *So green, so thick*. This place reminds me of Christmas. Green, gold, and red. What a wonderland.

It was tunnel-like, too, and I imagined myself in a fairy tale. I was Alice, and she was me; we were walking through a magical looking glass. As the branches closed in across the sky, I fell through her mirror. The canopy thickened above me and the warming rays began to fade. It was chilly and I needed a wrap. Stopping to pull the jacket from my daypack, I was suddenly alert. Someone was approaching, coming fast from behind. I got off the path and sat down on a boulder.

"Good morning," said a young couple in unison as they passed me.

"Good morning," I answered, casually taking a sip from my water bottle. I was alone, and the presence of strangers reminded me of my isolated circumstances. Relax, Judy, I said to myself. This is God's country. I gave the couple time to draw distant and then resumed my walk.

The moss grew thicker and my feet sprang from the ground. I bounced down that trail like a flitting bird. Barbara Streisand was in the background with "The Wind Beneath My Wings," and again I thought of Rod. Will I ever get over that man? I wondered. Will I ever shed the attachment?

My emotions were running the gamut, and to rein them in, I thought about my immediate goal. At the end of the trail, I intended to meditate. The site was called Eagle's Nest, which sounded like a wonderful spot to merge with the universe.

Still, I was growing tired. I wanted to sit in the palm of a healing vortex, but fortitude was required. I decided to give it my all. Leaves began to fall like rain, and I grew wearier as nature's tears hit my face. Luckily, I saw a ray of sunshine. I had made it. I plowed on and trees gave way to cliffs. Finally, the canyon opened and the sun penetrated my heart space. I lifted my head to the warmth and as I did, the tape player filled with static. *That's weird*. I know the batteries are good. A few more steps and the sound cleared. Then I lost it again. Must be some kind of interference. I shut off the distraction and climbed to the sound of Mother Nature. Rod was forgotten as the hills challenged my burning legs. When the landmark appeared, it was high in the sky with a vertical climb. I would have stopped, but the young couple was there having a picnic. Not wanting to disturb them, I headed toward the Indian land marker.

The trail barely existed, so I picked my way through bramble and cacti. It was extremely difficult. Twice I slipped. A charge of adrenalin kept me going and finally, when I could go no farther, I looked out. A natural outcropping beckoned me, so I stretched a leg to reach the cliff overhang. Hugging the rugged rock, I pulled hard. With a deep breath I made it and the entire valley fell before me. I could see all the way to the city, a maze of cliffs and trees paving the way. *This is it*, I thought. *This has to be the place*. I looked down toward my companions and was shocked by their diminished size. Indeed, I had climbed into the nest. It was thrilling, but now I had a problem. How in the heck would I get down?

"Food," I said suddenly. The descent, I knew, could kill me. I blocked that thought. I was in way over my head, but I refused to surrender. Somehow, I would do it. I only needed to take my time. I practically swallowed my sandwich whole and then stood to face the mountain. My muscles were already stiffening but allowing them to cool would make things worse. I had to move, but I also had to pray. Help me, my friends. We got up here together, now help get me down. Please be the wind beneath my feet.

I made that giant leap and landed perfectly. Trust, Judy. Remember to trust and for God's sake, girl, take your time. When the mountain seemed to shake beneath me, I was curious about the quaking, but I passed it off to my nervousness. It was fear breathing through me. Or was it? I had just jumped from a giant nest. Didn't that mean something special? It did if you believed in the healing vortex theory, and as I made my way down, that mountain made me a believer.

I hit the bottom and didn't pause. I passed my friends without a word and trekked on as though nothing could faze me. When it got easier, I was almost afraid to stop. It was as though a miracle had occurred and I did not want to break the spell. Magically, I pushed through the tunnel of trees and did not slow down until the sun lit up my feet. When trail markers appeared, I finally stopped to rest. By then, every bone in my body was aching, and my hip was reminding me of its haunted past. I found a fallen log and crouched down for relief. Once comfortable, I began to meditate. I brought the Eagle's Nest to my mind and remembered the experience. My sensitivity was profound, but I didn't stay present for long. I recalled the moment and breathed deeply. I barely heard their approach, when a man's voice stirred me.

"Did you make it to the Eagle's Nest?" he asked.

I opened my eyes and tried to answer casually. "Yes. At least, I think I did."

"Could you feel the vortex?"

"I sure felt something. I lost my music up there, too. The vibrational shift must have interfered somehow," I said.

The girl was wide-eyed. "We couldn't get a station either. At first, I thought the batteries were dead, but my radio is working now."

"It has nothing to do with the batteries, believe me," I said. "I was listening to a tape and the same thing happened to me. All I got was static."

"Wow," said the guy. His eyes were slightly bloodshot. *Probably from smoking weed,* I thought.

"It's some kind of an electro-magnetic shift," I said, as though I had a clue.

"Far out," said the girl, turning toward her friend. "That's too weird."

They were moving away. "Well, have a nice day," he said. "Nice talkin' to you."

"You, too," I echoed, half laughing. They were high, and they were awed by the other-worldly interruption.

I stood up to move and felt the pain of centuries. My hip was tight, so tight, in fact, I couldn't walk without limping. "Sorry, Mileva," I said. "I pushed us too far."

That night I slept like a rock and woke up stiff. My muscles were loaded with lactic acid. I could barely move. Still, I knew a stretch was in order. I checked my seven-day adviser and chose an easy two-miler. Just enough to work out some of the kinks.

Since I was ravenous, I decided to splurge on a big breakfast. I went to the world famous Omelet House on the south side of town, and while waiting for a table, I looked through some tourist pamphlets. One brochure featured a beautiful cathedral. It appeared to be carved from the red cliffs, but windows adorned it and the glass formation looked like a cross.

"Your table's ready, ma'am," said the hostess.

I turned to follow her, and as she pulled out my chair, I asked, "Is this church in the area?"

"Yes, and you shouldn't miss it. It's spectacular." She gave me directions, and I thanked her, before indulging in my giant meal.

Maybe when Jana gets here, I thought. Maybe we'll go there.

I loaded up with enough eggs and potatoes for a week and waddled out to flop into my leather bucket seat. I was jubilant, and wow, what a beautiful day! The expanse of crystal-clear blue sky suited my mood. I didn't consciously do it, but my foot pushed, pedal to the metal. Almost instantly I was nailed by blue flashing lights.

"No!" I cried in terror. "Not now! Oh God, please don't let this happen."

I had forgotten my fugitive status, and in a moment of exhilaration, I had thrown my freedom out the window. I thought about speeding away, about racing toward the open highway. Surely, they couldn't catch me, not in my Lexus. But of course, that would be stupid. Nothing like making a bad situation worse. The moment of truth, I thought, pulling out of traffic. *Sorry, Jana. I know this one is going to kill you. Just hope they let me have one phone call before you leave town.*

"License and registration, please."

I dug. "Here you go, officer."

"Did you realize you were going sixty miles an hour?" he asked.

That's not so bad. "What's the limit here?"

"Forty-five."

"Forty-five!" I cried. "On a six-lane highway?"

"This is still a residential zone, ma'am," he scolded.

A residential speed trap, you mean. "Really? Gosh, I'm sorry. I guess I didn't see the sign. I was distracted by your beautiful town." I was pleading. Please don't put the cuffs on too tight. Really, I'm not as bad as you might think.

"Stay in your car, ma'am. I'll be right back."

"No problem."

The wait was interminable. My life flashed before me as cars whizzed past. It must be like this when you're drowning, I thought.

"Is this your car? ma'am?" His tone was suspicious.

I had forgotten that, too. "No. It belongs to my sister. I drove it down, but she's flying in tomorrow."

"You live in Las Vegas?"

"Yes, but I'm staying in Phoenix for a while. She'll be driving back to Colorado Springs."

It was the truth and I was prepared to say more. Fortunately, I didn't have to.

"Okay, ma'am. You watch for these speed zones, though. You wouldn't want to spoil your vacation, would you?"

He extended a pen and the ticket pad, but there was a friendly smile on his face. "No kidding," I said returning the happy-to-comply gesture. "Believe me, Officer, it won't happen again."

"You have a good day, ma'am ... and be careful merging. The traffic is unusually heavy this morning."

"Okay. Thank you." My heart soared as I pulled out cautiously. Norman, you are a good man, I thanked my pretrial supervisor. He had given me a chance. He must not have issued the warrant after all. Don't worry, my friend, I won't let you down. I'll be there with bells on.

I headed west and reflected on what had happened. My mind was wandering, so much so, I nearly missed the turnout. I hit the brakes and came to a screeching halt, skidding a bit in the process. It was time for the seventh inning stretch, and I needed to breathe fresh air. I gazed at the marker on the fence, but it was too far away. I needed to get closer, but in case I was at the wrong place, I left my boots and gear in the car. Nope, this wasn't it, I said ... Looks like private property.

Turning to retrace my steps, I wasn't alone. A white truck was in the small alcove. The owner was standing beside his door watching me; his beady eyes made my skin crawl. What was he doing? He didn't look like a hiker, he had no gear. Even his shoes were wrong. Hikers didn't wear steel-toed construction boots. They were too heavy, and his shorts looked uncomfortably tight. This guy is up to no good, said my intuition. I'd better be careful.

I returned to my car and nodded, then casually drove past him as he stared at me. I took a good look. *Nasty-looking dude*. He was tall and gangly, and his beard looked like his body—thin and dirty. I wondered how long it had been since he had bathed or even slept in a bed, for that matter. Probably a homeless bum.

My morning start had been an eye-opener, and I thought about going home. Maybe I should return to the safety of my cabin. Should I call it a day and forget about the highway patrol, forget about intruding strangers? I gave it serious consideration, but I didn't want to overreact. I moved toward the trailhead, but not right away. I waited a few minutes. No white truck joined me, so I began booting up. One shoelace was already tied when I felt him. His breath was on the back of my neck, making my hairs stand at attention. Out of the corner of my eye, I scanned the area. On the second sweep, my peripheral vision caught a glimpse of white. That's his shirt! It has to be.

He was in the trees, standing behind a thick trunk. That man is evil. He wants to roll me or rape me or something. God forbid, he may even want to commit mayhem or murder. A shadow crossed my mind, and the warning was distinct.

Not today, it said. Get away.

I casually took off my boot, trying not to tip him off. When my tennis shoes were on and laced up, I threw my boots in the back seat and jumped behind the wheel. I did not look in his direction, nor did I head back to town. I wanted to find his truck to be sure my imagination wasn't playing tricks on me.

It was less than a quarter of a mile down the road, but I spotted it. I knew it. I knew it was you! The white truck of doom was off the road, but when I flipped a U-turn, I was close enough to read the plates. I made a mental note but did not stop. I had no idea where he was and did not want a confrontation. Only after I was back in civilized territory did I stop to write the numbers down. You're mine now, you asshole. You picked on the wrong girl.

I sought out a ranger station, and even though I was reluctant to face anyone of authority, I had to report this menace. The next hiker might not be as observant or as intuitive or as lucky as I had been, so I faced my fear and made my report. I described the man in the truck and everything I could remember; everything, that was, except how I felt his hot breath on my neck. I neglected to mention the presence of evil and naturally, I dropped the description of his beady eyes.

"Thank you, ma'am," the forestry person said. "We've had a rash of burglaries in the area. Parked cars have been ransacked while the owners have been in the hills. I haven't heard of any physical assaults, but you might have been the first."

"Well, this man was up to no good. I couldn't let the incident go unreported. If I had read about a dead body or something, I would never have forgiven myself."

"We'll check him out. Thanks again."

"You're welcome." I was relieved but profoundly shaken. Two miracles had already occurred. First, I had not been hauled off to jail, and just possibly, my life had been spared in the bargain. Angels in the outfield, I thought. *Thank you.*

I drove toward town, wondering what to do next. I was wound up and not ready to retreat. I changed direction and headed for the chapel in the hills.

CHAPTER 39

Full Moon Rising

This place is spectacular, I thought, entering the abbey. It wasn't that the chapel itself was profoundly unique, for it was rather plain, at least on the inside. The pews were simply constructed and the altar was nondescript. A bank of candles was burning and I lit one. Sitting down, I observed nothing visibly impressive, but the place contained an aura of holiness. I was most definitely on hallowed ground. I could feel the spirit of Jesus Christ and the impression was more profound than my Eagle's Nest experience. It was stronger than my intuitive pre-hiking experience, too. God's house, I said, thoughtfully. The place radiated grace.

Quietly, I remained within those mystical walls and I simply allowed. When I felt content, I removed myself to the back of the church and looked up. The stained-glass windows reminded me of my little chapel in the woods, the one at choir camp where I had witnessed demons being expelled. "So much confusion, Lord," I said softly. "Man has wrapped society in a cloak of religious nonsense, and why? Why can't it always feel like this? Why can't life just be simple? And beautiful? And loving? Why must we distort your celestial purpose? Why not just let one another be?"

I turned with a thousand questions, then went out to read the inscription on the wall. The architect had seen the face of God within the red rock and had worked with the natural cliff formation to create a magnificent place of worship. From the valley floor, it molded perfectly with the landscape; the windowed giant cross was a tribute to its creator.

I was so affected and so empowered by the feeling of renewal, I dropped safely into the past. Not much more than a week before, I had been hiding at the gateway of a great gaping hole. Now, for some reason, I wanted to go back there. I hadn't been to the Grand Canyon for twenty-five years, and a week ago I couldn't face it, but now I was ready. I was still a fugitive, but the excursion no longer sounded like a journey into oblivion.

The drive was longer than anticipated, but two hours later, I was handed a map. "Welcome to the Grand Canyon National Park, ma'am. Have a nice day."

"Thanks," I said joyfully. "Is this a day pass? Or can I come back tomorrow?"

"It's good for today only, but I do have a three-day ticket if you'd like that instead."

I wanted to bring my sister here, but I wasn't sure when. If she was determined to spend her time mountain biking, we might not get back at all. "No, better not. Think I'll take it one day at a time."

The driving tour wasn't anything to write home about, but I stopped at all the major viewing points, which were spectacular. Rock gave way to sky and sky bored a hole into earth. Sparse vegetation lined the way, winding down the mountain to a trickle of water. The mighty Colorado River looked like a thread along the valley. "Unbelievable!" I had rafted down that river, and it didn't seem possible.

~

On the trip had been my sister Jana, my dad, and me. The five-day experience helped us bond. Jana and my father had always been close, but since I was the firstborn, he ignored me and waited for the proverbial son. Forty years later, we were getting better acquainted.

"I can't sleep," he said one night, as we stretched out on top of our sleeping bags.

"What's the matter, Dad? Too much fresh air?"

"Just look at that sky," he said. "Have you ever seen so many stars?"

I had, and I was sure he had, too. We were a camping family, and I was raised on the Milky Way. "It is spectacular, isn't it?"

"Look, Judy, there's the North Star," he said. "It's sure bright tonight."

I followed his arm, which I could barely see, but he was not pointing northward. "That's not the North Star, Dad. It's over there."

He stared and in his macho all-knowing way, chuckled. "You're turned around, Judy. That's south."

"No, Dad. You're the one who's lost. See the Big Dipper? Over there," I directed.

"Yes," he said assuredly.

"Well, follow the ladle down. Use the edge of the cup as a guide and come straight down to the nearest, brightest star. That's the North Star. You can always find it that way."

"Really?" he asked.

I could tell he didn't believe me. "Yes, really. Here, take these." I was handing him some vitamins. "It's calcium, a natural sedative. They'll put you out like a light."

"I doubt it. I'm really wound up."

"Trust me, Dad. Just take them. You'll see. Goodnight." I rolled over. Case closed.

"Goodnight," he said skeptically.

The next day he was slow to stow his gear. I found him looking at the clouds. "What's up, Pop?"

"You were right. I was completely turned around."

I laughed. "It's easy to get lost out here. Isn't that cool, though? If the Big Dipper is visible, you can get your bearings."

He looked at me with eyes of admiration. I had made an impression. "How did you sleep?" I asked.

He had forgotten. "Like a rock. I don't even remember zipping up."

I smiled. My father had a new respect for me. I wasn't so dumb after all. "Come on, get a leg up," I said. "They've got breakfast ready. We'll be breaking camp soon." I turned to give him some time. I knew he needed it, but after that, things changed between us. We talked often and about deep issues.

I was more than glad for the long-awaited approval, but later, when he passed, it was difficult. I love you, Dad, I said.

~

I took a break at the end of the Grand Canyon loop at the Angel Lodge, and a club sandwich helped replenish my diminishing blood sugar. It had been a long day, a good day, a day of inspiration, but it was time to go. I returned to my lap of luxury and took a shortcut home. I cut across the plains and went over Snow Mountain Pass heading directly toward Flagstaff. It was growing dark and as the evening filled with twilight, I noticed a flowing arch on the eastern horizon. That's right, I remembered, tonight is a full moon.

I kept a steady cruising pace and watched diligently, but before the orb crested the hill, my CD player made an unexpected random selection. Andrea Bocelli's, "It's Time to Say Goodbye," came on. I was moved by the divine coincidence, so moved in fact, that tears surfaced and my blue centers misted over. The rising globe seemed shrouded and glistening and huge. I had never seen anything so big.

Was it my blurry vision? I blinked, but nothing changed. Amazing. The image remained giant in stature. It seemed like another miracle, and I grew thoughtful as a spectacular harvest moon rose from the depths.

I was saying "goodbye" to my life as I had known it and goodbye to the canyon that had beckoned me, but I was also saying "hello" to a beautiful full moon rising. Earth's satellite lit up my heart, which I took as another sign. I was meant to see this, to be here at this exact spot, at this exact moment in time.

Higher and higher the moon climbed, and I was awestruck by its heavenly glow. Eventually, the elevation prevented a clear viewing, but when I did catch a glimpse, the size no longer seemed astronomical. As the moment shrank into perspective, so did my elation, and the emotions of the day tore into me.

I had been riding those winds, the roller coaster winds of life, and suddenly I was overwhelmed. When I returned to my cabin, I reached for some courage. I had purchased a bottle of Crown Royal to share with Jana, but I no longer cared to wait. I broke the seal, poured a glass, and raised my hand. "This one's for you, Mr. Man-In-The-Moon. I toast your magnificence, your rising spectacle of brilliance."

The sweet golden liquid slid down my throat, coating my belly and washing through my veins. In short order, I was feeling no pain. I was, however, wishing I was not alone. I needed company, so I made a call.

"Hi, Mom."

"Judy! How are you?"

"I'm fine. Feeling a little lonely, but otherwise, I'm okay."

"Jana's coming tomorrow, isn't she?"

"Yes, but I miss you. I miss Las Vegas and my family."

"Me, too. It isn't the same without you. I feel like I've lost my best friend."

We talked while I sipped my elixir. I didn't think she noticed, but I was becoming inebriated. I also started to sound pathetic, crying on her shoulder about my dismal fate, especially the prospect of surrendering to the authorities.

"Judy, when the time comes, I want you to imagine taking the hand of Jesus Christ. Let his strength carry you across that threshold."

"Okay, Mom," I said, thinking the idea was a bit much. "I'll call you as soon as I can. Love you."

"I love you, too," she said, tears trickling across her words.

That call served to increase my despondency, or maybe it was the golden demon, but for whatever reason, I wasn't satisfied. I needed more pain, so I called on the master. I rang up Rod and received exactly what I deserved.

I barely remember the conversation. We talked about evil and I told him about my experience with the man in the white truck. I admitted to my fear and the idea of self-surrendering and he suggested I return to the chapel in the hills. He wanted me to take communion on Sunday and said he'd take the sacrament as well. In that way, we would protect our union from demonic intervention. Something about angels came up, and then I guess I passed out. I woke up the next morning with the phone beside my pillow.

"Oh, God," I moaned, realizing what I had done. The words ripped through my skull and the pain was excruciating. I had a world-class hangover and regrets besides. I glanced at the clock. Two hours. Only two hours before I needed to be out the door. How would I ever make it?

I staggered to the bathroom and looked in the mirror. I did not recognize the reflection. The healthy hiker had disappeared and in her place was a bleary-eyed bag lady. "Oh God," I moaned. I took two aspirin, grabbed a Pepsi, and struggled back to bed. With the utmost care, I set the alarm clock. Leaving Jana stranded at the airport was not an option. Lord help me, I said, swigging at the fizzy brown drink. It sizzled all the way down and felt like it would pop all the way up. *Don't even move,* I thought. *If you do, you'll lose it. Lie still and go back to sleep. Let the medicine work.*

She was sitting curbside when I arrived. *Oh God,* I groaned. I hope she's not mad. I struggled out of the car and she wrapped her arms around me. I did not want to move, and for the longest time we remained entwined. Finally, I broke the spell. "Have you been waiting long?"

"Just got here."

Thank you, Lord. "Really? I was afraid I was late."

"You were, but so was my plane." She finished her matter-of-fact statement with the look.

"I'm sorry, Jana. I got wasted last night. It's a miracle I'm here at all."

She took a better look. "Want me to drive?"

"Would you? God, that would be great."

We stashed her bags and took our seats. "Where to?" she asked.

"Ever been to the Grand Canyon?"

"No, and I was hoping we could go, but are you up to it?"

I wasn't up to much of anything else. To me it seemed like the best option. "Sure," I said. "Besides, we'll never be closer. We're already halfway there. Take a right here."

She started to turn but stopped. "I have something for you," she said, pulling over. Rifling through her pack, she became impatient. "I know I put it in here, darn it. Where is it?"

Where is what? I wondered.

"Here." She turned with a smile and handed me some kind of a document.

I opened the envelope and read. "No way!"

Jana was merging onto the highway. "I thought that would make you happy."

"Happy? Happy? Are you kidding? I'm ecstatic. Jana, this has cleared my head completely. I could hike the Himalayas."

"It came yesterday on the last day possible. I thought about calling you but decided to save it for a surprise.

My foot hit the floormat and I arched back with a yelp. I felt like I had won the lottery. "She liked it," I exclaimed. "Oh my God, she wants to see my manuscript."

"I think you have an agent," Jana cheered. "Congratulations!"

I nearly went berserk in that bucket seat. I wanted to jump, to scream, to dance. I wanted to raise my arms and spin in circles. "Do you know what this means?"

"It means you're a writer."

"A writer? Jana, it means I am on my dream path. It means I have discovered my purpose. It means I have finally done something right."

She laughed. "What are you going to tell her? I mean you haven't completed the text. How are you going to explain?"

A minor detail. "Jana, I wrote to this woman because she said she was willing to work with new authors. As soon as she knows I'm committed to the project, she'll understand. She'll love the fact I'm creating from prison. It will be a good angle for PR."

"I guess."

"Not to worry, baby sister. Hey, take the next exit."

"We're going through Flagstaff?"

"Yes, I know a shortcut. And there's a McDonalds down this street."

"McDonalds?" she objected.

"Greasy French fries," I explained. "Made to order and perfect for a hangover. There it is. Just go through the drive through. Order me a giant coke, too, would you?"

"No burger?"

"Not yet. I don't want to press my luck. Wow! I can't believe it!"

"Believe it, Judy. You deserve it."

"Whoopee!" I said again. It was most definitely a full moon rising, a new day dawning, and in my mind's eye, I could see all the way to the stars.

CHAPTER 40

Divine Sparks

I BECAME THE HOSTESS with the mostest for the next few days, giving Jana the grand tour. I even took over the job of driving once we entered the park. Pointing out the best vantage points, my head began to clear, and I lined our day with my recent war stories. Jana was serious at first, too serious, but my good mood was contagious, and it wasn't long before she was laughing over my brush with the law. My encounter with Mr. Lawless was disconcerting, but she was glad to hear my intuition had saved me.

"Negative excitement," she said. "You're addicted to making waves." This started a discussion about another vacation we had shared, one where the phrase "negative excitement" had been coined and then, after we laughed some more, she turned the conversation. "So, did you receive word about surrendering in Phoenix?"

"Not yet. Can you believe it? My attorney has been calling, but I still have not been designated."

"That's terrible. What if they send you to San Francisco?"

"They won't," I said stubbornly. "Don't worry. Besides, Karen says I can turn myself in anywhere. If I can't make it to the specified prison, they'll transport me. Heck, I might even drive back to Colorado Springs with you. Maybe I'll surrender there."

This satisfied her, but it was frustrating when, by the close of business on Friday, I still did not have word. At four p.m., I spoke to Karen.

"Here's the number, Judy. I've explained the situation to the clerk. Apparently, they dropped the ball with your paperwork. You need to call first thing Monday morning."

"Oh, brother," I groaned.

"It's that federal quagmire," she said. "Nothing comes easily."

"Thanks, Karen. Thanks for all your help."

"I'll see you at the trials. Until then, you hang tight."

Hang loose, you mean. I was thinking about the noose around my neck, but the words were not spoken. For my sister's sake, I remained silent.

Jana was a planner and this news upset her. "You mean we won't know until our last morning?"

"Looks that way, but let's assume the best. Let's think Phoenix and plan something special for Monday."

"Like what?"

"Like a morning of pampering. I found this great day spa. I had my hair cut there last week, but they do massages and readings as well. How about we book back-to-back appointments? You can see the psychic while I get pummeled, and then we'll switch."

"Sounds good to me."

After I made the arrangements, we went to dinner. For two days, in between hikes and bike rides, we explored the finer dining establishments, sparing no expense. Fine wine and gourmet meals were made to order. Of course, for lunch we preferred funky, so we also enjoyed some beer and pizza. Occasionally we ate in, but being served seemed more appropriate, considering my circumstances.

"Wonder what prison food will be like?" Jana asked one day.

"It can't be good. I really hate thinking about it."

"Judy," she started, but the pause gave me a clue as to what was coming. "What's it like? I mean, how do you feel?"

It took me a minute to answer. "Now that you're here, it will be easier, but I think it might have been better if they had hauled me away in handcuffs. The concept of self-surrender is sort of like taking it in the ass. Bend over baby. You're getting it whether you like it or not."

The image was impactful. "Yuck. I'm afraid for you."

"I'll be okay. It's always the transition that's hardest. Once that first step is taken, things will get easier."

"I couldn't do it," she said.

"No, but you'd never put yourself in a situation where you might have to. I, on the other hand, have lived on the edge all my life."

"Any regrets?" she asked.

"Well, yes. I wish like hell I had never been in the telemarketing industry. Nothing good came from that, but the career path helped shape me. It made me who I am and I'm not unhappy with the result. It seems like I could have arrived at this place without having to go to prison, but it is what it is. Others have survived the experience, so I will too. Besides, now that I have an agent interested, I'm seriously motivated. I'll find a way to use the time effectively. All things happen for a reason, and really, we are who we are."

"Miss Abundance and Power," she said, referring to my numbers. We were both Leos, but numerology had revealed some idiosyncrasies. She was Integrity and Wisdom, while I was a three-slash-eight, which meant Abundance and Power.

I laughed. "Yeah, and remember how your book said I'd have to shed my attachment to material wealth before I could receive true abundance?"

"Yes, but that section also said you might go to prison before it happened," she said.

"Oh, my God! I forgot. You're right. Isn't that wild? Who would have ever thought?"

"Trippy stuff."

"To say the least. Let's hope abundance does come one day. Maybe I will make it, Jana. Wouldn't that be something?"

She was thoughtful.

"Jana, I saw the most spectacular sight last night. Have you ever watched a harvest moon rise on the horizon?"

"Umm, I'm not sure."

I tried to share the experience, but something was lost in the translation.

~

At five after nine on Monday morning, I hung up the phone. "She still doesn't know!"

"What in the heck are we supposed to do?" Jana asked.

"I have no idea. Let's go to breakfast and continue our day as planned. If we don't, we'll go crazy and besides, I don't want to miss our appointments."

She was dumbfounded. I wasn't sure which she found more credulous, the fact the Bureau of Prisons had still not assigned me or the idea that I didn't particularly care. Truth was, I did care. I found the whole thing annoying. I would have asked them to call me, but I didn't have a cell phone and I didn't want to involve Jana. I tried to reassure her. "I'll call from a pay phone, but now that you've decided to stay over, I don't see it as a problem. It's not like we have to check out or anything."

Silence. My suggestion was met hesitantly, so I prompted her by opening the door to the spa. "Come on; let's go have our fortunes read. I want to know if I'll become a published author."

As Jana went in a session with Sherril, the psychic, and

I waited for the masseuse, I finally got an answer on the second attempt.

"You're lucky," the officer of the court said sweetly. "They designated you to Phoenix. Looks like you won't have to surrender at a county jail. You need to be there by two."

I heaved a huge sigh and asked for directions. I got a phone number instead, and when I called, a very nice man named Bob was willing to speak with me from the prison. "You can't miss it," he said. "Come south on the highway until you pass the outlet shopping center. Take the second exit and turn right. We're just past the trailer court on the right. There's plenty of signs, not to worry."

He was casual about the whole thing, as if this was an everyday occurrence. I tried to sound nonchalant. "Okay, thanks. I'll see you at two." *And not one minute sooner,* I thought, shaking inwardly. "God, it's almost over," I said, after hanging up. In a few hours, I'd be locked up. *What then?* I wondered.

I wanted to tell Jana, but there was no time. I was whisked off for my massage. With my destiny determined, I let go of the past. My mind relaxed with each stroke, and it wasn't long before I was soaring.

Through the clouds and along warm currents, I floated without care or concern, releasing fully and content in the white light. Time fell away; the prospect of bars and razor wire no longer seemed threatening. Soon I would be hearing the clanging of iron, the slamming and locking of doors, but that prospect held no power in the moment.

Yesterday is gone, tomorrow may never come, think only of now, Judy, for this is your present. Gone. I was completely gone and fully balanced. Meditation was a great way to find peace, the best way to travel.

Even though Jana's session had started first, she was

second to finish. I was casually chatting with my magician in the front room when my sister and her soothsayer made their entry. They were laughing and I was amazed. I had expected my sibling to appear more skeptical. "You two look like you're having fun," I chided. "Cutting into my time there, baby sister."

"Not to worry," reassured Sherril. "You are my last appointment. We can take all the time you like."

"Cool, but I need to be in Phoenix for a two o'clock appointment. How long of a drive is it anyway?" I eyed Jana, who got the message. She was obviously relieved.

Sherril's cherubic face lit up. "It can't be more than about an hour and a half. You'll have plenty of time."

"Well, alrighty now," I said, using my daughter's favorite phrase. "Enjoy your massage, little sister. Watch out, though, she'll put you under."

"Really?" asked Jana.

The therapist laughed. "Your sister sure went deep. I never heard a peep from her."

When they disappeared behind a long velvety curtain, I turned toward my reader. What would she see? And would Rod be in the picture? Did I even want to know?

"I'd like to begin with a prayer," she said, with the innocence of a young child.

I was pleasantly surprised. I had not expected this from a card reader. I was even more surprised by the fact her solemn words were offered in the name of our Lord Jesus Christ. I was happy to know I was not in the hands of an avid New Ager. When she finished, I offered an "Amen" and looked up to reassess this woman before me. She was an enigma, a Christian card reader, my kind of lady.

Sweet-faced and mid-thirties, she was pleasingly plump with a personality that naturally attracted. You couldn't help but like her, and even her frizzy blonde hair was a sweet complement, sort of halo-like. Her smile radiated a well-balanced spirit and the soft grayness of her eyes mesmerized. If her voice had more of a drone quality, I would have remained in a trance, but she was vibrant, and bubbling words brought me to life.

"Draw," she said. "Take five cards, but don't rush. Feel for a connection."

I stared. She held a small deep purple silk bag with a drawstring dangling loosely. The opening was just big enough to accommodate my fingers. I reached timidly. What in the world? I wondered. What kind of cards can be in this tiny sack?

My first pick revealed a piece of white cardboard, white heavy paper with purple ink, maybe an inch square. Her hand was extended, palm up, so I made my first drop.

She laid it in front of her on the table between us as I read the upside-down letters. "Divine Spark."

"Another," she encouraged.

We repeated the process four more times and then she grew introspective. Her eyes closed for a moment and upon opening them, she said, "They want you to have another. This is rare. Usually I stop at five."

They? I wondered. Who's they? Sherril was receiving guidance from beyond.

"Okay," she said casually, setting the sixth spark in line with the others. "Now, we turn them over one at a time and see what happens."

I blinked. This was a new one for me. "Divine Sparks," I said. "That's pretty cool."

"Move with the currents of change," she said, reading aloud.

"Wow!" was my startled response.

"Your life is in a state of flux," she suggested. It was a statement rather than a question.

I smiled. "To put it mildly."

"This has something to do with your appointment in Phoenix?"

"Yes." I wasn't about to lead her. I wanted to test her.

"You shouldn't fear this change. It was meant to be. I'm told you will adjust quickly. You are supposed to be the student as well as the instructor."

Certainly, prison would be a learning experience, but who, pray tell, was I going to teach?

"Any questions so far?"

"No." Maybe later. Right now, I wanted her to tell me.

"Believe in your Vision. Joyfully awake." She read the words. The print revealed the message and VISION was capitalized. I became more attentive.

"That's nice," she said. "You must be doing something special. Do you feel positive about your future?"

"In some ways," I said.

"Judy, this change is an excellent opportunity for you. It will result in something quite unexpected."

"Really?" Like what, I wondered.

"You're an artist of some kind. What are you working on?"

"A book," I said, beginning to trust. "I'm writing a book."

"That's terrific," she said, and then listened. "You have the courage to complete, but you must not lose hope."

"No problem. I have every intention of seeing this to completion. It has become my purpose for living."

"They are very excited."

They? What did she mean?

The next divine message was curious, under the circumstances. "Open up your powers of observation and learn." I gulped and thought about the advice from my attorney. "Learn everything you can, Judy. They're building a new correctional facility here in Las Vegas. You never know, maybe you could gain employment there—when you get out, that is."

Sherril broke the spell. "This is very important," she said seriously. "You need to take a step back. You must allow. Allow others to lead. Let them be who they are. Even if they're not perfect, you must not interfere. Roll with the flow. Let go. Accept what is and understand some things are not meant to be changed, at least not by you."

My frown made her giggle. "Does this make sense to you?"

"Too much so," I said.

"Don't waste your energy. Choose your battles carefully and remember your goal."

We talked at great length about this, and it seemed like she was lecturing. Finally, she turned over another spark. "See what expectations are causing you to experience."

That was an eye opener, and I was more than curious. As far as I was concerned, the thing about expectations was a bit out there. I understood belief and faith, but this was different. Expectations implied creating your own reality, and the concept reminded me of Rod and his "belief" system, a bit too close for comfort.

"Before we discuss this spark," she said. "They want me to go back. For some reason they think this other message is important."

No! Not that again. I did not like the idea of surrendering control, and I wanted the subject put to rest. It rubbed my craw.

"Judy, others have work to do also. You need to respect their imperfections."

Keeping me under lock and key seems like enough. I would have no choice but to surrender, so what is she talking about?

"Keep judgment out of the way," she said. "Don't expect too much. Learn tolerance."

I was getting the message.

"Lose the animosity," she said. "Let go of the anger."

These were words I needed to hear.

"Any questions?"

I was about ready to ask, but my mind was reeling. I didn't know where to start. I shook my head.

"Okay. Expectations. You can make this experience anything you want, but if you think positively, it will become a time to grow."

My writing came to mind. I couldn't wait to get in front of a computer. Most definitely, I was feeling positive about that prospect.

When she turned another card, her attitude changed. Her voice became deep and the words reverberated in the room. "Give up the need to control. Flow."

"Flow," I echoed. "Didn't you just say that?"

"I did," she said, returning to her soft demeanor. "Do you have an issue with control?"

"Not really," I joked. "At least, not if things go my way."

Her smile bounced off the walls. "I believe this may be your challenge, but really, it seems you have no choice. This is a lesson you must learn. You must learn submission."

"Submission!" I cried. "I hate that word."

"Surrender," she tried again. "Only in losing can we expect to win."

Again, we discussed staying above the fray. Watch was the operative word. I wanted the session to end. Did I really have to hear this? Wasn't our hour about up?

"I need to show you something. Stand up."

I followed her words as well as her body language as she took me through a meditative exercise in observation. It was very intriguing. She had me open my arms wide, and then she rotated me in quarter turns, but my eyes remained focused straight ahead. I was seeing more than what was in front of me and I was feeling something, too. Somehow my mind remained behind with each turn and then before the next turn, I had a sense of great clarity. "Wow," I said, when my focus returned to her face.

"Practice that, and it will help you develop patience. You'll see things as never before."

I'm already seeing all kinds of new things. How much more is there?

"Any questions?"

"Yes." It was now or never. "I've recently separated from a man. What can I expect from him in the future?"

She closed her eyes and then opened them slowly. "This is not your lifetime mate. Your work together, however, is not complete."

Somehow that didn't surprise me. "Do you see any long-term relationship in my stars? Will I ever be loved? I mean unconditionally by someone very special?"

"Give me your hands."

I extended my arms across the table and she reached for my fingers. For a minute she drifted, and when she opened those sparkling grey orbs, I could tell the news was not good. "There is another entity out there waiting, but there is much work to do before you meet."

I sighed. The story of my life.

"Well, this is your last message, and I think it's the most important spark," she said, pushing the final spark toward me.

I turned it over and read out loud. "Know you are one with the Light."

"Beautiful," she said. "Your work is inspired."

"I often believe that's true. Sometimes my words amaze me."

"Well, hold the faith. You'll do fine. This sure has been an interesting morning," she said as we walked out. In the waiting area she saw my sister. "Enjoy your massage?"

"Oh boy," she said dramatically, practically collapsing with the words. "Did I ever."

Sherril laughed. "Come on, I'll walk you two out."

We paid the bill and then Sherril followed us outside. "I want to give you both a hug."

Jana opened her arms first. The embrace was sisterly, but when she turned to me, she had something to say. "I don't know where you are going, but I want to wish you luck."

I looked at Jana and then back to Sherril. "You want to know?"

"Sure, if you'd like to tell me."

More sisterly support, it came from both of them. I gulped courage and spat out the words. "I'm going to prison."

The pain fell visibly across her brow.

"It's okay, really," I said, trying to soften the blow. "I've had a long time to prepare and truly, those things you said in there, they were important words."

"When?" she asked wistfully.

"Now," returned Jana. "That's why we're going to Phoenix. She must turn herself in this afternoon."

Sherril looked at me incredulously. "No wonder you didn't like the idea of surrender. Oh my gosh, you poor thing."

I was embarrassed. "Yes, but you can also see why I am so determined about my book. For the next few years, that project will keep me alive."

"Years?"

"Thirty-three months," I said sadly. "Almost three years."

"Bless your heart. Wait a minute." She walked to her car and returned bearing gifts. I was handed one of the little purple bags. "Take this with you. Keep in touch with your angels. They will help you."

"And this is for you," she said, turning to Jana. "It's a

dream stick. It will guide you gently while you sleep."

"Let me pay you for these," Jana offered.

"No need," she said happily. "I feel fortunate to have met you both. And here's my card. Judy, stay in touch. Let me know how you are doing."

"Sure," I said. "I'll send you a Christmas card."

Jana began the process of saying goodbye. "We'd better be going."

"Yep. Can't be late for this date," I said. "They might throw me in the slammer."

Everybody laughed, and we waved our final farewells. Next stop, the Phoenix penitentiary. God help me.

CHAPTER 41

Pioneer Avenue

"JANA, LOOK," I said, as we approached the first exit past the outlet shopping center.

"Déjà vu," she said, reading my mind. "Pioneer Avenue. I guess we're getting close."

"Isn't that ironic? Pioneer Enterprises is the reason I'm going to prison and there's Pioneer Avenue. If I had never worked for Rich and Chris, we wouldn't be making this trip." Curious thoughts were racing. This chapter opened with Pioneer Enterprises and closes near Pioneer Avenue.

"What an odd coincidence."

Obviously, she wasn't nearly as affected as I was. Still, I had goose bumps. I thought about what Sherril had said, "This was meant to happen," and I was strangely silent as we drove past Pioneer Avenue and took the next exit.

~

My mind turned the pages recalling the day I had gone looking for work. I knew immediately after that interview that Rich and Chris would hire me. In fact, I hadn't bothered to continue my search after meeting them. Returning to the parked car, I made my confident announcement. "Okay, kids. Let's go on that picnic."

Charlie was only five years old. "You got the job, Mommy?" he asked.

"They're going to call tomorrow, but I'm sure they'll hire me. The rest of this week belongs to the two of you."

"Cool," chimed Pam. "When will you start?"

"Certainly not before you guys go home. I'll tell them you're only here for one week. Until your spring break is over and you go back to Denver, my new career will be on hold."

"Can I feed the fish?" asked my wiry tow-haired son. He couldn't wait to see the gaping mouths at the Lake Mead Marina. Those whiskered scavengers practically climbed out of the water trying to reach the tourists bearing bits of bread and popcorn."

"Sure, Charlie. Just don't fall in."

"Yuck," cried Pam.

Charles was so excited he turned a whole bag of popcorn upside down. The ensuing frenzy threw him slightly off balance, but he did not fall forward. I, on the other hand, fell hook, line, and sinker into that new job of mine.

"Gosh, how far out is it?" asked Jana, nearly thirty minutes later.

"Bob didn't give me the impression we'd be going far," I said. "It was supposed to be right past a trailer park."

"We're in the boonies. Not much chance of escape out here. You'd die from exposure before getting to the highway."

"No kidding, but why would anyone want to live this far from civilization?" I asked.

"Maybe the trailer park is for employees."

"There's something coming up, a big white building. We better stop for directions."

"Judy, it's a bar. Can you believe it? What in the heck is a bar doing out here?"

I saw two dark-skinned men and thought possibly we

were on an Indian reservation. If this was Native American country, then we were most definitely lost. "Beats me. There's a pay phone. Park over there."

I called the prison and discovered we had passed the proper exit. "Okay, but I'll be late," I said. "Who do I ask for?"

"I'll let them know you're on the way. Just get here as soon as you can, Ms. Burr."

"It'll take us about an hour to backtrack," I exaggerated. Forty minutes would have been sufficient, but I had a plan.

"Come on, baby sister. I'll buy you a beer."

"Judy!"

"We're cool. They know I'll be late."

She was looking at the men. I could sense her insecurity, but she followed me. "Okay, but just one. I have to drive back to Sedona, you know."

Inside, it was big and dark. The few patrons obviously thought we were a novelty. "Two shots of tequila gold and two Buds, please," I told the heavy-set, dark-eyed bartender.

My order received a big toothy grin, a spaced toothy grin, for a couple of those pearly whites were missing.

Jana gave me a dirty look.

"Come on, for old times' sake. Please."

The drinks arrived complete with salt and lime. "To you," I cheered. "My best friend in the world."

She followed my lead, and we slammed the jiggers. The salt doused the fire and then the limes washed it down. Finally, the beers cooled our throats. "Umm, nothing like it," I said happily.

Jana laughed at my last hurrah, but when I ordered another, she frowned.

"Okay, okay," I said. "I'll do this one alone. You're driving, but I'm bound for hell. I need one more to kill the pain."

"Go for it," she said.

~

Federal Prison Camp, the sign said. "This must be the place. My new home. How lovely."

From the passenger seat, I began to organize. I grabbed my bag and stuffed it with my books and research papers. I had been given permission to bring my project. I also had socks, underwear, and a few hygiene items.

"You'd better give me those," suggested Jana, when I picked up the unopened plastic package containing my Divine Sparks.

"Nope. I'm taking them. Religious medallions are permitted, and that's what this represents to me. If it's meant to be, there'll be no problem. If not, they'll be sent home along with the clothes on my back."

A raised eyebrow and a quirky brow told me I wasn't being practical.

I laughed. After two shooters, she could not dampen my spirit. Even the prospect of self-surrender seemed like no big deal.

Jana got out of the car and came around to accompany me through the doors.

"Go back to Sedona, Jana. You don't belong here."

"You sure?"

"Positive. Really, it will be easier to say goodbye right now."

"I love you," she said.

"Love you, too," I said, giving her a hug. "Oh, hey. I left you something. Play the last song on the last CD in the car. And don't cry. The tune is beautiful. It's meant to be appreciated."

"Okay," she said with a curious smile.

As she drove away, I could hear the melody. The words followed, soaring through my brain. Of course, I could also imagine her tears. I knew the song would make her cry, but that would be good for her. "It's Time to Say Goodbye," would effectively release her checked emotions. The words would cleanse her agony, just as they had mine. I turned to go. There were two heavy glass doors in front of me. I pulled hard and entered a large reception area. No one was around, not a soul in sight. Now what? I wondered. What kind of a prison is this anyway?

To my right was another double door. Beyond that was a large room with one lone desk. I could see chairs stacked around the edges, obviously some kind of meeting room, but it was empty.

On the left was a single door, which opened to an office area. One desk was in the center of the foyer, and then more doors lined the walls. "Hello," I called timidly, poking my head through.

A tall, thin lady, about fifty-something, came out from a side room. "Can I help you?" she asked sweetly.

"My name is Judy Burr. I'm here to self-surrender."

"Alright, dear, wait in the lobby. I'll tell them you're here."

"Thanks," I said, retreating. This is too weird. Nothing like I expected. Where was the manly matron? The bars? The razor wire? And for that matter, where in the heck was the fence? I hadn't seen one. Had I missed something, or was I just not remembering because of the shooters?

Maybe this is the administrative area, I rationalized. I'm probably in the wrong place after all. Oh gosh, she'd better hurry, or I'll really be late. They'll think I've run away for sure.

Sitting on one of the short side benches in the foyer, I surveyed the courtyard. Desert landscaping graced the area, with buildings of various shapes and sizes around the perimeter. Groups of girls were lingering on the sidewalk areas, and they, too, were of different shapes and sizes, and colors. I couldn't imagine who they were, but they were casually engaged in conversation.

They couldn't possibly be inmates, could they? Certainly, they didn't resemble hardened criminals, not the kind I had imagined. Various colors of sweatsuits adorned their bodies, and if not in sweats, they wore slacks and t-shirts. Most of the pants were green, but the shades varied and the shirts were different hues of yellow and gold. *Sunflowers*, I thought. They look like sunflowers. Since they were smoking and socializing, I even speculated they might be part of the administrative staff. Surely, they couldn't be prisoners.

"Okay, Ms. Burr. Follow me."

The woman reminded me of a grandmother, but she was about my age. It was her sweet demeanor that bowled me over. Her attitude said "Welcome," which seemed utterly ridiculous.

I followed her into the courtyard and down the sidewalk on the left. One of the girls smiled nonchalantly. *Oh, my God. This is it. These girls are prisoners.* I can't believe it.

Cement pathways were everywhere, crisscrossing the compound, but we didn't go far. Just past the mailbox was another glass door, with the words Receiving & Departure printed above.

"This is Ms. Burr," said my escort.

"You made it," came the friendly greeting from a short, balding man.

He smiled.

"You must be Bob," I said.

"That's me."

"Bad directions, Bob," I teased.

"I heard. Sorry about that. I always ride in with a friend. Guess I've never paid enough attention." He turned toward his co-worker, a black woman with tightly braided hair. "You start the intake, and I'll call her supervisor."

His back was turned to me, but I could hear most of what he said. “She made it. You can call off the dogs.”

Poor Norman, I had really taken him for a ride. Fortunately, I had not let him down, and now he could rest on his instincts. Maybe he would trust another one of his charges. One day I would personally tell him how much I appreciated the leniency.

“What’s this?” the woman asked as she chewed gum with relish. In her hand my Sparks were held high. While my bag was being severely scrutinized, a frown marked her popping lips.

“They are inspirational messages. Guess you could consider them my crucifix. A friend gave them to me. She said to draw one every day. They are supposed to assist me in coping.”

“What do you think?” She turned to Bob.

“The seal is still intact. Let her have them.”

And that was that. The purple silk bag was tossed in a pile with my socks and underwear. My angel messages had made it through, so they would provide inspiration after all. I could hardly wait to tell Jana.

“And these plastic folders?”

“They contain my notes and research,” I explained.

Once again, Bob spoke up. “Ms. Burr is writing a book. I told her she could bring the project. You’d better get her dressed out. It’s almost count time.”

“Back here,” said the black officer.

I followed her tightly stretched, gray polyester pants.

“You’re about a medium, I’d say. What size shoe?”

“Eight.”

“Okay, in here. She grabbed the clothes, and we went into a small bathroom. “Strip,” she said flatly.

“Strip?” I asked. “Now?” I had heard about strip searches, but in view of the lack of security, I was surprised.

"I don't like this any better than you, but it's regulation. You must dress out in front of me."

I stared at the clothes in her hands and gave thanks for the tequilas.

"Now turn."

With my back to her, she quietly spoke the next order. "Bend over and cough."

I turned to face her. "You're kidding."

"Sorry."

I could barely bark. The whole process was terribly degrading. They were beginning the transformation, stripping away my dignity and demonstrating their power. I decided I could probably expect more.

Don't let these friendly faces fool you, Judy. Remember, the feds are your enemies.

"Okay, Ms. Burr. Put these on."

Green and yellow. I was to join the garden, one of the many shining sunflowers. "Can't I put on my tennis shoes?" I did not like the blue floppy flight shoes. They were tacky and too big besides.

"Nope. They go back with the rest of your clothes."

"Oh," I said sadly. I had been told white tennis shoes were allowed, but not so, and the "bend over and cough" had taken the fight out of me. I did not argue.

There was a brief conversation about where my sleeping quarters should be, and then I was told to follow one of the officers. "That's your bedroll," she said, indicating I should grab it.

My arms were already loaded, so when I stooped to pick up the mesh bag, things started to fall. I dropped a book, my toothbrush, and a pair of socks.

"Here, I'll take these. We're almost late."

Late? Late for what? I wondered. What is the rush?

Another long sidewalk, more buildings, and then into

what appeared to be a dorm. More girls, two to a cubicle, staring as I came through. I felt terribly insecure, very much on stage, like a goldfish in a bowl, only I was on the outside, looking in.

We stopped in front of a cubicle. "I brought you a roommate," she told the girl.

"You did?" was the response, which rose an octave with the second word. My invasion was not appreciated, not by any means.

The officer dropped my notebooks on the desk and tossed my bedroll up onto the bed. Another surprise. I would be sleeping on a bunk, the top bunk, in fact. I had not done that since choir camp. Then I had fought for the lofty heights, but now I wasn't so sure. What if I fell out? Wasn't I a bit too old for a top bed? Shouldn't this younger girl be the one to go up? Apparently not. According to prison etiquette, "age before beauty" counted for nothing.

"My name is Debbie," came the crisp words. "This is your locker. Let me get my things out of here. I haven't had a bunky for six months." Her actions were a blend of frustration and animosity. She was stuffing shampoo, books, and other items into her own tiny storage space.

Well, at least she spoke. "My name is Judy. Sorry to encroach."

Debbie turned but didn't offer a hand or a hug. She gave me a shrug and her dishwater-blonde ponytail flipped as she flopped onto the bed.

Not much personality, I thought. I turned to shove things inside my locker. Shortly after stuffing folders, books, and socks, I climbed up to my part of the world. The mattress of thin plastic wasn't even remotely comfortable. Inwardly I groaned, but outwardly I began to pull bedding from the bag. Welcome to the Ritz, I said silently, tugging at the pillowcase. I was struggling and fighting back tears when an announcement over the PA blasted me.

"COUNT TIME."

Defensive words jumped from my mouth. "What in the heck was that?"

Debbie's dry lips cracked a smile. At my expense, she was having some fun, but no explanation was offered. "Count time," she echoed simply.

The tequila was wearing off, and I was fast becoming despondent. Prison, I surmised, would be a lonely, cold experience. Well, I'd survive. I'd figure things out by myself if need be. I was short on reassurance when another bark startled me. This one came from a live voice. "COUNT," said the man.

Debbie stood up and looked blankly at me. When I didn't move, she said, "Get down. Hurry. They're coming."

I threw my legs over the edge of my bed and jumped. My bunkmate was upset by this drastic move. *Well, you said hurry*. Hurry means now. No time for ladders. I was waiting for her to say something, but she didn't. I nearly spoke, but an officer came down the hall and his sudden appearance silenced me. Then another peered in, walking from the opposite direction. What the heck?

They were gone as quickly as they came, and then Debbie turned. "Don't do that. You'll hurt yourself. Get up and down like this."

It looked much easier her way, from the floor to the chair and then up, or vice-a-versa. "Okay, thanks," I said.

A little giggle, a flash of friendship. "You'll get it, don't worry. In less than two days, you'll have this whole place figured out," she said before disappearing.

Not knowing what else to do, I turned to make my bed.

CHAPTER 42

The Cricket Initiation

"WHERE'S THE BATHROOM?" I asked after finishing my housekeeping. There hadn't been much to it. My locker had four shelves and two drawers, but my worldly possessions were few. Space was ample. Laundry, I had been told, would be issued sometime in the future, presumably in the next day or two. Until then, I had the clothes on my back, and an ugly white nightgown. It reminded me of a hospital issue, but without the slit up the back.

My neighbor in the next cubicle was huge—a big black girl with a snarly mouth. "Down there," she pointed, attempting to curl her lips into a half smile. Her grin was less than cordial, and I decided that, in the future, it would be best to stay out of her way.

There were three sinks and four stalls. *Well, at least these are private. Thank God the toilets have doors.* The showers were individual as well, which thrilled me. It was bad enough our rooms were open, but if the restrooms had been public, I would have cried. Debbie and I were to share our time in a small eight-by-nine space, as were the other girls—two to a room, seventeen rooms to a floor, and two floors per unit. Each dorm had two sides, duplications of each other, and I later learned there was a carbon copy on the other side of the compound. Altogether, that meant two hundred seventy-two girls. I had expected more, but I also expected some degree of privacy.

I was bending forward at the sink, trying to scoop water into my hand for a drink, when I saw the thonged feet.

"Need a cup?"

I looked up. "Don't they supply glasses?' I asked, as my eyes swept the counter for paper towels.

The kind dark face responded with sarcasm. "Honey, they dun supply nuttin' roun' here. You got to drip dry all de way back to your room." Her words swung out, and her shoulders shook with a matching rhythm. As she turned to go, I smiled. She was an interesting character.

"Really?"

"Yeah, hon. De only thing in here is pads and toilet paper. We use 'em fer everything. One girl has a list of a hunnert-and-one ways to use sanitary napkins." She walked away, big hips swinging, but later returned to my room. "Here," she said, handing me a beige-handled plastic cup. "Pass it along afta you get one of your own."

"Thanks," I said, as she struggled away, bulk bouncing down the hallway.

The officer had told me commissary would be on Wednesday, and since I had brought cash, I would be able to shop then. Still, I wondered, how would I manage? I had no soap, no toothpaste, and no shampoo. Was I supposed to wait two days to take a shower? I returned to the bathroom and filled my cup with tepid water. The shooters had done their work, but their aftereffects were lingering. After cooling my thirst, I climbed back up on my bed to watch and wait. What next, I wondered.

It didn't take long. She barged in with a jar. "Dessert," she proclaimed, sitting the jug on the desk and asking me to deliver a message. "Tell Deb I got us a nice juicy one." Then she was gone.

Everybody in this place does a disappearing act. *What the heck was this?* I watched as a bug tried desperately to jump from his jar. The trapped insect was hopping frantically in his glass cage.

I was staring when another girl came in with a lid. She secured the trap, and said, "Vicky—she would forget her head if it wasn't attached." A smile flashed, and then she vanished.

I was still staring when Vicki returned. This time I watched her carefully.

"Got us another one," she said in a deep, gruff voice.

A bull dyke, I surmised. Must be retarded, too. She was a big girl, strongly built, and had a short stock of brown hair, cropped so close she looked more like a man than a woman.

"Hey, hey," came the demented laugh. "Tell Debbie it'll be a feast tonight. We won't even have to share."

"Okay," I said obligingly. "I'll tell her." When she left, I didn't know whether to laugh or cry. These tasty morsels were crickets. Were the girls really into eating the chirpy little critters? Lord help me.

The fiasco continued, and I took Sherril's advice. I became the observer. A bright-eyed blonde bounced in and asked, "Did she put the lid back on?"

"Yes, thank God."

"You never know about Vicki. She's unpredictable. We watch out for her in here."

I had no idea how to respond, so I didn't try. At least this girl appeared normal. She was young, about twenty-five, average size and rather pretty. Her long straight hair was pulled into a ponytail, and she wasn't even remotely mannish. She was cut out of a sixties cloth, but I liked her hippy look. The innocence of it made me feel comfortable.

Debbie, my roommate, had the same look. Flower girls who never grew up, I decided. Guess if they can tolerate Vicky, I can, too. Prison is obviously going to have its share of weirdos, just like the rest of the world.

Debbie returned and broke my train of thought. She picked up the jar and said, "Umm." Then she sat it down and took off again.

I wasn't sure whether she meant, "Umm, good," or "Umm, here we go again." As I was wondering, she bopped back in and began spinning the dial on her combination lock.

Vicki charged into the room, bellowing, "Debbie, Debbie, aren't they beauties?"

Calmly, my roommate turned. "Yes, Vicki, but you need to be cool. First supper, then dessert. Okay?"

"Okay," said the girl-man. "But we can hurry, can't we? We can come straight back, okay? Please, Deb, they look so good. I can't wait."

Straight from the funny farm, I decided. God, I can't get away from the loons. First Shirley, then Rod, and now this goofball. This time, I was relieved when the girls disappeared. I tried to read, but it was impossible. My eyes were glued to the crickets—a delectable delight, my eye. Yuck!

I was transfixed when the blast came. Another announcement: "Last call to main line," shouted the voice across the PA.

"Aren't you going to eat?" asked a passing girl.

Eat? It wasn't even five o'clock. What kind of a schedule did these people keep? Really, I had no desire to climb out of my nest, but the night would be long if my stomach started to grumble.

I stepped outside and looked around. No cricket-hunting mamas. Across the yard, girls were gathering in small groups. "That must be the place," I said, heading for the other building.

Following the example of others, I picked up my tray and utensils. There was a soda machine, so I chose Coke, hoping the caffeine would counter my plummeting blood sugar.

A woman behind the counter handed me a plate filled with beans and rice. This is it? I'm going to be eating beans and rice? Oh brother, it's worse than I expected.

As I reached for the cornbread the server barked, "Leave the plate."

I picked up the yellow cake with my fingers and moved on.

"Corn?" asked the voice.

Corn with all this starch? This was bad. If I had to eat a high carb diet every day, I'd be fat within months, and that kind of diet would wreak havoc with my hypoglycemia. I was a meat and vegetable kind of a girl.

"New here, aren't you?" asked the girl at my table.

"Yes. My name is Judy."

"I'm Debbie. Welcome to the camp."

Another Debbie. This one seemed nicer than my roommate. "Thanks," I said, trying to swallow the dry tasteless cornbread.

After a brief but pleasant visit, she excused herself. I couldn't stomach the food, so I left shortly afterward. The dinner was still on my tray, but the girl in the dish room dumped it nonchalantly. Into a thirty-gallon trash bag it went, along with others before mine.

What a start. On the way back to my dorm, a surge of loneliness hit me. Oh God, Jana, please come back. Get me out of this place. My eyes were on the ground, sort of like my feelings. More than anything, I wanted to throw off my fresh flower clothes. I was watching the sway of my green legs, and hadn't noticed the girls gathered around the table, just outside my door.

"There she is!" came the cry. The voice was loud and hostile. I looked up and saw Vicki. She was on her feet, leaning into clenched fists, supported by the cement picnic table. Her body language was intimidating. I got a distinct impression she wanted to leap up and wrap her hands around my throat, not the kind of thing I appreciated. "That's her," she exclaimed. "That's the lady who ate my crickets."

Oh, my God. This crazy bitch thinks I stole her dessert. I considered running, making a beeline for my bunk, but something told me to hold my ground. "That's right," I hollered back. "I need my protein. A girl cannot survive on beans, corn, and cornbread, for Christ's sake." I paused briefly to square off in front of the group. "I need meat in my diet." With that said, I turned and picked up my pace. I didn't race for my bed, but I didn't let the dust settle either. I reached my room, and climbed quickly to the top bunk, which now seemed like a blessing.

Surprisingly, I was not immediately attacked. "My name's Teresa," said the brown-eyed girl. "Where are you from?"

"Las Vegas," came my guarded response.

"Lynn's from Las Vegas. She picked up some kind of telemarketing charge."

"Yeah? Maybe I know her. That was my business."

Light banter continued, and then a girl named Nancy joined us. "I'm the jailhouse lawyer. Here, I brought you shampoo."

"Thanks," I said happily. "Now I can at least take a shower."

Teresa left and returned with a book of ten stamps. "If you need more, let me know."

Things were looking up. Someone else came in with soap and deodorant. Then lotion arrived. It wasn't long before I climbed down and began shaking hands. I couldn't remember names, but the faces were unforgettable. Eventually Debbie and Vicki returned with the other blonde-haired hippie. They, too, extended a warm welcome, and I discovered their cricket routine was an initiation joke.

I had passed their test, and now everyone was laughing, including me. Vicki was, I discovered, not the slightest bit retarded, nor was she mean, at least not to me. She was butch, but her sense of humor rendered her harmless. The evening quieted down, and I happily headed for the showers. The joke was on me, but it served a purpose. Even before the lights went out, I was welcomed. I was part of the gang. What kind of gang, I didn't know, but I belonged to something. That connection would help me survive, or at least that's what I thought. If I had only known. If only I could have imagined.

PART VI

PRISON

CHAPTER 43

Us and Them

IT TOOK LESS THAN FORTY-EIGHT HOURS. One day, in fact, was sufficient. Thanks to Laura, I was a seasoned inmate before the sun went down on day two.

"You want a tour?" she asked, after we finished raking our assigned square footage of rocks.

"Sure," I said, not knowing what else to do. Laura had arrived about two weeks before me but had not been allocated to any specific department. She was still taking care of the grounds, just like us other "new" recruits. She also seemed comfortable with her environment and her lackadaisical attitude attracted me. I welcomed a friendly face, one who didn't play practical jokes, and Laura filled that bill.

"Let's go this way. I'll introduce you to some of the girls."

Not exactly what I wanted, but an objection wasn't appropriate. I obliged by following, and we quickly encroached on a small cluster of girls. One of them was venting some anger.

"Hey, guys. What's happening?" Laura asked, ignoring the foul language.

"Fuckin' pig. Don't care if he does send me back. I'd rather be behind the wall, anyway. Goddamn son-of-a-bitch.

This place sucks if you ask me."

"Calm down, Rita," said one of the younger women. "It's not worth it. Let it go."

I stared at Rita, who was making a nasty racket. I fully expected her to be handcuffed and hauled away. Surely the officer in charge would do something to this disruptive Spanish fireball. I couldn't imagine the behavior being tolerated, but it was. Venting was an everyday occurrence, and so were other things.

I learned quite a lot from Laura that day, who nonchalantly turned from the next stream of obscenities and asked, "Hey, you got a light?"

"Matches are at a premium right now. Here, use my butt." One of the other girls offered her cigarette.

"Thanks, Carol," Laura said. "This is Judy. She got here yesterday. Judy, meet Carol."

"Welcome to Camp Fed," Carol said as she pushed out of the crowd. Rita was still raging in the background, and I was glad to be moving away.

"Thanks," I said, trying to mean it.

"How long you got?" asked Carol.

I cringed. Not a subject I wanted to discuss. By this time, I understood where I was. My new home was a minimum-security prison, a work camp of sorts. There were no bars, nor was there any razor wire. I could have, in fact, walked right off the property, and the highway was less than half-a-mile away. No doubt there were no major threats to society here. Probably just a bunch of girls getting their hands slapped. Surely no one in this place could be doing more than a few months. "Thirty-three months," I said, as casually as possible.

"Sheeit," Carol said. "I could do that standing on my head. Don't worry, it will go by fast."

Fast? I thought. *Is she crazy?* "Really?" I said. "How

much time did you get?'

"Nine years, but I'm almost done. I'm out of here in six months."

"Nine years!" I exclaimed. "What in the heck did you do to get nine years?" I couldn't imagine. This girl was young. I didn't think she could be more than twenty-eight or so, and I was shocked to hear she had spent so much of her life in prison.

"Drugs," she said flatly. "My ole man dealt. I went down with him on a conspiracy charge."

"Oh, my God. What kind of drugs?" I asked innocently.

"Cocaine."

I became quiet. Nine years was a lot of time. Laura saw my concern and changed the subject. "Lots of girls are here for a while, but not to worry. For the most part, they're harmless."

I turned to look back. Rita was still ranting. Her foul mouth carried across the courtyard.

"Rita's done some hard time. She just got here, and she's not adjusting. She wants to go back to Dublin. Thinks it was better there."

"Why?" I asked, trying to understand. 'Where's Dublin?"

"It's outside of San Francisco, and she's crazy, that's why. She probably had a girlfriend there or something. Who knows? This is the library," she said, dismissing the subject. "Let's go in here. Want to come, Carol?"

"No. Think I'll pass. I'll see you around. Nice meeting you, Judy. Be cool, girl."

"Thanks, you too."

The library wasn't impressive, but neither was anything else. Everything was substandard, but I did appreciate certain things. There were amenities—a church, various craft areas, a multi-purpose room with a widescreen TV. I learned movies were shown on the weekends, which surprised me. I had expected clanging iron doors. All things considered, I had to count myself lucky, and I was especially excited to discover a track on the property. "The girls call it The Angels Quarter Mile, and some of them swear they've had celestial encounters," Laura said.

I quirked a smile. "How about you? You ever seen anything ethereal?"

"Girl, not me. I never get near the place. This body is allergic to exercise, okay?"

She exaggerated the words girl and okay, and her inflection was infectious. I laughed at Laura's glib attitude; it was refreshing. In the center of an inhospitable place, I found a friend. She would have been enjoyable on the outside, but in here, she was a treasure.

Not only did I like Laura, but I also had a sense she could take care of herself. If push came to shove, I believed she would be a good person to have in my corner. I sensed this immediately, and eventually, time proved it true. Time also served to create a bond between us, for as it turned out, she needed me as much as I needed her.

"You do for me and I'll do for you," was the unspoken rule. *Cross me and your ass is grass*, was also part of the unspoken language, but for the most part camps were not violent.

The girls tended to form little cliques, but different as they were, they had one common theme. They all wanted to beat the man. It was us and them from the beginning, and an inmate did not play both sides, not if she hoped to survive. Finks or rats were hated by all, and I quickly learned who the would-be traitors were. "Watch out for her," Laura said. "She'll run to an officer at the drop of a hat. She'll fink for any reason, that one."

"Like what?" I asked.

"Like what we're doing. Technically, I'm not allowed to

help you with your manuscript."

I was shocked. "Why not?" There were no word processors or computers available to the general population, so Laura and I struck a deal. I was writing my story longhand. She took my pages and typed them. After that, I mailed them to Jana, where they were finally digitized for my agent. It worked for me, and I was buying Laura cigarettes as part of the bargain.

"No bartering. No trading of any kind. You either purchase shit from your prison paycheck or money must come from home," Laura explained.

"But some of the girls only make five bucks a month," I said, "and many of their families can't afford to send money. How can they possibly survive if they don't do things for other inmates? God, five dollars wouldn't keep you in hygiene. The commissary prices are outrageous, more like 7–11. If you ask me, it's a rip-off."

"I know, but those are the rules. That's how it is, so make sure you don't say anything about what we are doing."

Laura's typing wasn't the only trade I bartered. I was one of the few girls with a stream of money, so I helped whenever I could. Still, I had been warned and, in the future, would be more careful. It was us and them, after all, and what they did not know would not hurt them. Better yet, it wouldn't hurt us.

CHAPTER 44

Down and Dirty Dorn

I QUICKLY SETTLED IN, and by adopting the prevailing us and them philosophy, I made friends. My roommate remained tough, however. She was reluctant to let me in. Any attempt at casual conversation was brushed off, which I found frustrating. After all, we lived together in extremely close quarters. It seemed like we should at least be civil to one another. Finally, I decided on a different approach.

I had brought a novel with me, one I believed would be a good read, but for some reason I could not get into the book. Debbie, on the other hand, had several on the shelf that intrigued me. "Debbie," I said one day. "Would you mind if I read some of these?"

"No. Go ahead."

It wasn't much, but at least she was sharing. I pulled down a paperback by Dr. Wayne W. Dyer called, *You'll See It When You Believe It.*

Rod had often used similar words. "You'll see it when you believe, Judy."

"But, Rod, I don't understand. How can I believe in your business plan if you don't explain the long-term goals?"

"Just believe in me, honey," he would return. "Right now,

you need to have faith."

That attitude of his was a constant source of irritation. I found it frustrating not to be informed, and he found my lack of trust annoying. Now I was looking at a text mimicking his words. What can this mean? I wondered.

Fortunately, as I read I forgot about Rod. Dr. Dyer was speaking more plainly than my ex-partner and his message on transformation was like Shelia's. It was hauntingly familiar, more about accepting and observing than anything else.

That's why! I exclaimed silently. I needed this book to help me understand. Dr. Dyer was reiterating the words from my Sedona psychic. All the 'let go and roll with the flow' stuff was in those pages. I guess this was truly a lesson I needed to learn.

As I analyzed, the truth settled on me. I had been passing judgment left and right. My counselor's name was Ms. Fortune, and while I had decided early that it was my misfortune to make her acquaintance, there was no foundation for my assessment, for she had done nothing to either hurt me or offend me. In fact, she had allowed my sister, Jana, a special visit on Thanksgiving Day.

Jana had not gone home like I expected. Instead, she stayed in Sedona and returned to surprise me. Extensive paperwork was normally necessary before an inmate could have a visitor, but Ms. Fortune waived the requirement. She had effectively granted my sister and me a great favor. She did not deserve the criticism I was arbitrarily dishing out.

However, my work supervisor did, or at least I thought she did. I was assigned to the kitchen, which was the last place I wanted to be, and because I hated the job, I hated Miss Dorn as well. The girls warned me not to mess with her, as she was the epitome of Institution, but I did not listen. I tangled with her almost immediately, and if I hadn't checked myself, I might have been shipped out for disciplinary reasons.

"I can't unload the dock, Miss Dorn. Those boxes are too heavy for me," I said.

"You'll unpack them one can at a time then," she responded without sympathy.

I was outraged. My back, I knew, could not endure heavy lifting, and I did not want to undo the recent healing. It was wonderful to walk without pain, but my official job assignment was jeopardizing my health. I could not get a transfer for at least ninety days, and even then, I needed my medical records to prove my problem. I was about to quarrel, when one of the girls saved me.

"Come on," said Betty, the department's clerk, "I'll help you."

"Thanks," I said, turning quietly. These damn officers, I thought. They could care less about our challenges.

On another morning, Miss Dorn told me to put the milk on the cafeteria line.

"Okay, but you'll need to bring the crates out of the chill room. I can't lift anything more than ten pounds."

"Burr," she said harshly. She was using my last name in the coldest way possible. "Burr, you need a medical release for that."

I was ahead of her. "I got one yesterday. It should be in your office. Do you want me to get you another copy?"

She didn't and she didn't want me around either. "No, I'll do it myself."

"I can stock the coolers, Ms. Dorn. I'll be happy to if you'll just help me."

Not the right thing to say.

"BURR!" she screamed. "Forget it."

"But ..."

"I said I'd do it myself."

Fucking bitch. "Okay, then what would you like for me to do?"

"Go sit down."

That was it? Go sit down. The woman was an outrage. It was four-thirty in the morning, and no one else was there to help, yet she wanted me to go sit down. It was an easy request, however, so I obeyed. I went out to the eating area and took a seat by the windows. Minutes passed and my frustration mounted. After about half an hour, the rebel in me took charge. I returned to my bunk, climbed under the covers, and went back to sleep.

It was the screaming that alerted me.

"Where is she? Where is Yolanda?"

It was Down-and-Dirty Dorn. She was looking for one of the dishwashers; apparently the girl hadn't shown up for work. Quickly, I buried my head under the blankets.

"She's on that side, Miss Dorn. Second room, bottom bunk," said a familiar voice.

I heard my supervisor berate Yolanda for sleeping past the appointed hour, and her words scared me. I got down from my nest and went to the camp hospital.

"No," I said to the PA. "I have the restriction, but they haven't moved me. I'm still working in the kitchen. You've got to do something. I can't do that kind of work. I'll end up in a wheelchair."

"We can't reassign you. You'll have to see the warden. I'll call him and tell him you're coming over."

This was good. I was stepping through the hoops, covering my ass.

Mr. Strawhun was a taskmaster. He didn't like it when girls made waves, and he made that clear.

"With your disabilities, Miss Burr, I don't know what you can do around here."

The message was, If you can't work, I'll ship you out. I was aware of this unspoken policy, and the last thing I wanted was to be sent somewhere else.

"I have good office skills," I tried. "You could put me in a clerk's position."

"Those jobs are few and far between. You'll have to stuff napkin holders or something for now."

"Fine," I said, "But you need to tell Miss Dorn. No one has made her aware."

"Her boss, Mr. Jackson, is due in any minute. Wait in the lobby. Tell him to take care of it."

"Okay," I said, properly ingratiating myself. "Thank you."

When the officer arrived, I continued my act. "Are you Mr. Jackson?" I inquired politely.

"Yes."

"Mr. Strawhun asked me to speak with you."

"Mr. Strawhun?" he repeated.

The big guy had spoken. When the warden said "jump" the question was "how high?" Dorn's supervisor needed to check the schedule but said my job description would change.

"Great. Do you want to page me then? When you are ready, I mean?"

"Sure," he said, as if this was an everyday occurrence, which of course it wasn't. No one went over Dorn's head, at least not if she wanted to survive kitchen duty. I knew that, but by then I had already gone too far. I turned and went back to bed.

"BURR! Burr, report to the kitchen," came the cattle call over the PA.

"You're in trouble now," said one of my neighbors. "I heard Dorn's out to get you. Betty said she was all over the cafeteria screaming, 'Where's Burr? Where's Burr?' She's pissed as hell."

"Oh well," I said with a flippant attitude. I was worried, but I got dressed and went to work without giving anyone a clue. It worked out, but only because of my creative actions. For the most part, I stuffed napkin holders and occasionally washed dishes, and on those days, she made sure there was a steady stream. I hated her and complained often to the girls, but my venting accomplished nothing.

Reading Dr. Dyer, however, went a long way toward neutralizing my attitude. He said something about how he lost the ability to blame others for circumstances in his life, and his words rang true. Less than a year ago, I had said the same thing to my partner. "Stop blaming everyone else, Rod," I had cried. "It's not their fault. You created this mess and you need to fix it."

I had created my situation, and it wasn't Miss Dorn's fault. It was simply a lesson, one that was important for my survival. Down-And-Dirty Dorn wasn't so bad after all. She had her own troubles, probably a pack of them. It couldn't be easy feeding two hundred plus girls, and without a happy staff, it had to be nearly impossible. I began to empathize.

The doctor talked about how we are all connected and said it was imperative to give each other space. His passage on love, clarity, and codependence was profound. I needed to be less judgmental, more accepting, and recognize the good in officers and inmates alike.

It wasn't us and them after all.

They had a job to do and we were in this together. There was no one to blame, no one to hate, for in fact, neither blaming nor hating helped. The situation simply was and I could make it anything I wanted. To make it a more positive experience, I needed to become the observer. Just watch, learn, and listen, Judy, I told myself. It is the only way. And believe it! If you believe it, you will grow from this experience. You will be a better person for it.

Peace prevailed, rationalizing this way, and I stopped systematically categorizing individuals. I simply looked at others as connections of myself. We were human beings with faults. Not one of us was perfect, least of all me.

Debbie, I left alone. I decided she could have her space. Apparently, she needed it, and who was I to say otherwise. In the evenings, when she seemed to crave isolation, I went for long walks, and on one of those nights, I learned firsthand why that track had been christened The Angels Quarter Mile.

CHAPTER 45

The Angel's Quarter Mile

"HEY, JUDY. What's happening? You look like you've seen a ghost."

It was Diane. She lived across the hall, two cubicles down. She was offering the standard greeting. It was always "Hey!" Not "Good morning," or "Hello," but "Hey." Standard jailhouse lingo, I decided. It sounded strange coming from Diane, however. She didn't seem like the "Hey" kind of girl. She was too sophisticated, too classy, and too smart. She had previously done time for dealing marijuana, but she was at the Phoenix prison camp on a violation.

"You're kidding," I said. "They sent you back for seeing a boyfriend."

"It's okay," she responded. "We knew the risk. We just didn't believe they'd find out."

"How did they? Find out, I mean?"

"I think one of my competitors finked on me."

Diane was in the coffee business. She had a small shop in Jackson Hole, Wyoming, and her family kept the business going while she was imprisoned. Competitors moved into town, and her business floundered while theirs flourished. When she returned, the opposite occurred, causing the owners to "fink" on her. Unfortunately, her significant other was also an ex-con, which wasn't allowed. No association with other felons. That was the hard and fast rule. It seemed ridiculous, but Diane was proof the policy existed.

"Nope, not a ghost," I said, walking over to the cement table she was sharing with Sue. "Not even close. Hi, Sue. How are you?"

Sue was a quiet, mousey little thing. She wouldn't have spoken two words if we hadn't started playing bridge, but our games were loaded with conversation. She was of east Indian heritage and claimed to be a progressive thinker, a very modern American lady. Her husband also came from India, but his thinking was more traditional. Sue was only a woman. As a mere woman, she had little value, so when he was charged with a crime, he threw her under the bus. He told the authorities his wife was responsible. She was at camp Phoenix because she hadn't fought the bribery charges.

Not progressive or modern, I thought, but she had shared and now it was my turn. I didn't think either of my friends would pass judgment, but even if they did, I couldn't resist relaying my experience.

"What then?" asked Diane, as I flopped down.

The cement bench was cold, but I barely noticed. "Oh, my gosh. I've had the most incredible experience, a revelation of sorts."

As Diane leaned in, I focused on her curly brown hair. It encircled her pretty face, billowing in the breeze. A smile encouraged me, and I reached for the words. I couldn't tell them exactly what I had seen or heard. They would think I had lost my mind. Nope, I couldn't quite tell the truth, but I wanted to get close. Bursting to try, I began a bit emphatically.

"You know, I think this was meant to be."

"Everything happens for a reason," Diane encouraged.

"God's will," said Sue with her short stock of reddish-brown hair bobbing up and down.

"No, I mean, specifically. I believe it was my destiny to come to this prison, and I think I've known all my life."

They were silent. Diane was an open-minded person, but the prospect of knowing one was predestined for a jail cell seemed preposterous.

Sue turned up her lip. It nearly made it to her rather flat nose, and I laughed at the look. It especially seemed funny when she squinched her eyebrows together.

"Really, I'm serious," I said, trying to act the part. "Remember what I told you about my arrest? That I would have never been indicted if the Feds hadn't wanted my former bosses?"

"Well, yes," offered Diane. "But you weren't the only one arrested for that purpose."

"I know, but I am the only one who came to Phoenix. The other co-defendants are still in Nevada. I think some of them are in California, but to the best of my knowledge, I'm the only one here."

"So?" The question came from Sue, but what she really meant was, Well, whoopee-fizz, big deal.

"So," I exaggerated back in her face. "So, what is the only way into this place? What is the name of the exit off the highway? What path did we take to arrive at this lovely resort?"

Sue didn't remember.

"Pioneer Avenue," offered my bright-eyed, coffee-making friend.

"Right!" I exclaimed. "And what was the name of the company where I worked?" I paused to create the proper drama. "It was Pioneer Enterprises. Just think, if I had never gone to work for those boys, I wouldn't be here today. The name of their company was Pioneer Enterprises, and I entered this prison via Pioneer Avenue. Can you believe it?"

"Gosh, I got goose bumps," said Diane.

"Me, too," chimed Miss So.

They were warming to my story. "There's more. Get this. While I was walking tonight, I remembered something else. I've never told another living soul this."

"What?" came the collective question.

"When I was a little girl, about ten or eleven I guess, I had this chant. I took my initials and created a song, mostly during times of unhappiness, and sometimes just for the heck of it, but for whatever reason, I would sing my initials. Over and over again, I would repeat them. Judith Lynn Burr. I'd chant J-L-B, J-L-B. Then I'd sing, I'm a Jail Bee, I'm a Jail Bee."

My audience was captive.

"Don't you see? I was singing about going to prison, about living in a jail cell. Can you imagine? I repeated that chant for years."

"That's weird," said my greatest skeptic.

"I know and that's why I never told anyone, but tonight a little bird whispered in my ear, so I went back to those days. Subconsciously, I knew prison was in my future; even then I was preparing."

"Judy, that's amazing," said Diane. "I think you're onto something, but why, I wonder?"

"I'm not sure, Diane, but it may have something to do with the book I'm writing. I've often felt guided by someone or something."

"You're writing a book?" queried Sue.

"Yes, but there's more."

"More? You're kidding." Diane couldn't imagine what more there could be, which I was about to tell her when we were interrupted by Yvonne.

"Hey," came the greeting.

"Hey, girl," I responded. "Have a seat. Take a load off."

She joined us, flipping her long dark hair over her shoulder. Yvonne was a Puerto Rican beauty, younger than the rest of us, but she liked keeping company with girls who stayed out of trouble.

"I got too much time to do," she said one day. "My business is my business. These girls can kiss my ass. I want nothing to do with their bullshit."

I felt much the same way. Consequently we were hanging out.

"Anyway," I started, "when I was older, married and busy with the basic bullshit of raising kids, running a business, playing housewife, I resented the fact I never had time to read. I loved to read."

Yvonne was staring, so I tried to explain without starting over. "My intuition spoke tonight, and it told me this place was part of a grand plan. I was meant to come here, Yvonne. I knew it as a kid and I knew it as a young adult, too.

"When time became precious, I'd sneak away. Pat and I had this storage closet downstairs where I'd go to read. None of my family knew where I was, not even my husband. It wasn't exactly a comfortable place. I mean, there couldn't have been more than two feet between the shelves, but I'd go down there and lie on the floor with a book. It was my special place and I would wish for more of that kind of time."

"Yuck," said Yvonne.

"It gets worse," I said. "I'd wish for a prison cell. I wanted to be a jail bee, like my song. I'd wish to be locked up with nothing more than a huge library and bread and water. I used to think I'd be perfectly happy if society would go away and leave me alone."

"You wished to be locked up?" asked Yvonne.

"Isn't that crazy?" I asked. "Who in their right mind

would want to be stuck in a jail cell? But I did."

All kinds of speculation about my premonition occurred, and the conversation generated excitement. We were traveling in our imaginations when Yvonne stopped us abruptly.

"Who's the dark-haired guy?" she said, looking in my direction.

"What?" I asked, but I knew what she meant. Yvonne was a sensitive; she saw things the rest of us did not. She was referring to Rod.

"The tall, thin, dark-haired man? Who is he?"

"Young?" I questioned.

"About my age, nice looking. Is he a friend of yours?"

"Yes, I suppose."

"He wants to know if you're okay."

This unnerved me, what with my celestial viewings and the messages from beyond and all. "He's someone I worked with once," I said, getting up. "If he wants something from me, he can contact me personally, in the here and now, I mean. I'm beat. I need a shower. I'll catch up with you guys later."

"See you inside," said Diane quietly. She was filled with wonder.

I was in awe. The evening had been curious. What was happening? Was visitation part of the prison experience? Was there something mystical about Camp Phoenix?

That next week, a new kind of loneliness flushed through me. The revelation on the Angels Quarter Mile stirred me, as well as Yvonne's message from Rod, but the prison experience is one of contradictions, and I started to think about them. Friends abound, but they cannot make up for the loss one feels. Of course, we miss our loved ones, but the emptiness goes deeper. When you surrender to the authorities, they strip you of everything. You are told when and what to eat, when to sleep, what to wear, where and when to work, and how to behave. Nothing is left to chance, which leaves you empty.

There are constant reminders of the loss as well. We crave cards, letters, and the news from the outside, but they hurt, too. They remind us of our isolation. Visits are the best and the worst, because before we can see our friends or family members, we must first suffer humiliation. Strip searches accomplish this, and although we are only stripped of our clothes, the loss of dignity is profound. Prisoners have no value and we are reminded of our worthless existence. For this reason, many of us cling to the past. I was no exception. As the days stretched into weeks, I started to think about Rod more and more. I couldn't shake the memory of what we had shared, and really, I didn't want to. I blocked out the bad and brought forward the good.

I rationalized this retreat into the past by claiming him to be my soulmate. The Einstein revelation was real, just as real as the J-L-B thing. Rod may have been my son in a previous lifetime, but in this one he was my lover and I missed his love.

I wondered if he would write so I started to think about calling him. God, it would be good to hear his voice, the voice of the Preacher Man, as I affectionately called him. Maybe it was Yvonne's sighting that caused me to regress. Whoever understood these things? For reasons unknown, it finally happened. I received a message, but amazingly, it came not from the Preacher himself, but rather it was his Angel wife who called.

"Judy," she began quietly.

I gasped at the sound of her voice. I had called to check my voicemail messages, and usually these calls were cut short. Phone conversations were monitored randomly, and if an officer heard you trying to listen to a one-way conversation, you were abruptly disconnected. On this day, however, I was able to listen all the way through. Mary Ann wished me well and sent her love. It was a sweet voicemail, but I didn't like the poem she quoted. She prefaced the verse by saying it had been written by an Auschwitz victim and said she hoped I would find it inspiring. It went something like this:

Look around and be distressed.

Look inside and be depressed.

Look to Jesus and be at rest.

Quietly, I replaced the receiver. Why Mary Ann? Why couldn't Rod have reached out? Why did I have to hear from the wife?

My reaction was dumb. It was jealousy or something. And I was angry, not at Mary Ann, for I understood she was well-intentioned, but at her husband. He should have called. I decided to give him a piece of my mind. I returned to my room and took pen in hand. The note was brief but pointed. I told my ex-lover to let his sweet little Angel know I was doing just fine.

"Tell Mary Ann I look to Jesus every day. I look to Jesus, but I find no rest. Actually, he's got me working my ass off, but then," I joked, "I've got plenty to spare, so I really don't mind.

"Tell your wife that when I look around, I see a beautiful gift. It's the gift of time. I've never had it before and now I'm living my dream." Finally, I said, "And when I look inside, there's a new world, one filled with wonder."

Funny, isn't it, how we can make the "loneliness" disappear? We pretend everything is fine because we don't want the world to pity us. I especially didn't want Rod's wife to feel sorry for me. In my journal I wrote, "I am me, happy to be, and completely free."

Forget him, Judy, I said silently. Stay within the boundaries of your present reality. It's all you have now.

I posted the note and then went to call my sister. Jana, I knew, would ground me. Of course, I made no mention of the Steersman family. Instead, I told her about my celestial encounter.

"Dang, Judy, that's wild. And it's weird your counselor's name is Miss Fortune."

"For sure, more pieces of the puzzle are falling into place. I even knew how long my sentence would be."

"What do you mean? I thought you expected less than a year."

"That's what I told everybody, but the day before the judge leveled his gavel, I was on the phone with Charlie. He asked me how long I might get, and I told him three years."

"You're kidding? Why?"

"I don't know. I said it would take that long to complete my work. Isn't that wild? Jana, I said thirty-six months and I got thirty-three."

"Be careful for what you wish," she said.

"Exactly."

"By the way, how's your book coming along?" she asked.

"Good, I think. Laura can't keep up with me. I'm writing faster than she can type. She's found someone else to help us."

"Always the entrepreneur, aren't you?"

"I enjoy helping, Jana. Some of these girls get no outside support. God, who can make it on twelve cents an hour?"

"It is ridiculous."

"Slave labor," I said. "It's the government's answer to outsourcing. Manufacture in prison and make a bundle."

A clicking sound cut our conversation short. After fifteen minutes, all calls were abruptly terminated. It was another thing I hated about the system. "Well, better go," I said. "Love you. I'll call you next week."

"Love you, too," she said sadly. I knew she was missing me, as was the rest of the family. I was paying a high price for trusting my government. Too many disappointments had rendered me cynical, but wasn't this my destiny? If so, why? The million-dollar question ... *Why me?*

CHAPTER 46

The Eyes Return

MY CELESTIAL ENCOUNTER served as a catalyst for acceptance. Somewhere, long before coming to this earth, I agreed to live the prison experience. It was part of my purpose and even though I wasn't sure why, I believed, wholeheartedly. Believe and you will see. Those words were heavy on my mind.

Since I truly wanted to understand, I decided to seek the source diligently. Meditation became a serious part of my routine. I did not want to call attention to myself, so I pretended to nap twice a day, morning and night. For a time, the ritual was rewarding, but as I transcended deeper, the past returned to haunt me. I went all the way back, back to a time when I was twenty-four years old on holiday in Canada.

~

"That sounds wonderful, Phil," I had said to my neighbor's son. He had stopped by to see his dad and was telling me about his summer travel plans. "I really envy you. I wish I could do something like that."

"Come with us," was his casual response.

I laughed. "Oh, sure. Like how? I'm a mom, you know. I couldn't just pack up and go. I'd never leave Pami that way.

She's only three and she needs her mommy."

"Bring her," he invited. Phil and I were pals, but that was all. He was extending an invitation and I didn't know what to think.

"Phil! Your friend would pitch a fit. Besides, I couldn't be gone all summer. What would I do with this house?"

"Mitch wouldn't care. He's bringing a girlfriend, and I'm sure they'd love Pam. She's an absolute doll. Couldn't you rent your house or something?"

I was astounded. This sweet hippie acquaintance was serious! I was tempted, but what about Pat? Pat and I were dating, but he wanted more. In fact, he wanted marriage and had told me so. He hadn't proposed, but when he was in California, he wrote to ask if there might be a chance for us. At the time, this idea seemed preposterous. I thought of him as a brother and could not imagine being intimate. I wrote him back and said, "No. Go on with your life, because I'm not interested in getting serious. I like being single and need my freedom."

It was a curt reply, but I thought it would prevent him from doing anything rash. He had entered a new industry in sunny California, and from all appearances, he was doing well in the carpet-cleaning business. I did not want him to ruin his future, not on my account. Alas, though, it didn't stop him. He returned to Colorado and began seriously courting me.

I never looked at Pat the same way after that letter, and I started appreciating him more. Of course, I had always loved him, and we were good together. We enjoyed the great outdoors, water-skiing in the summer and snow-skiing in the winter. We were also white-water river rafting guides and we partied, too. People loved being around us, and we were having the time of our lives. It was time to take our relationship to the next level.

Now with Phil standing before me, I wondered why I was considering giving that up. How could I not? Never again would I have an opportunity to tour Canada and the Yukon Territory. And there were plans to build a raft! A raft! Can you imagine? Phil and Mitch expected to finish their trip with a ten-day float down the Yukon River. I could think of nothing more exciting and I wanted to go.

I wanted to go for the sheer joy of the experience, but I also wanted to go because I feared the lifetime commitment I was about to make. It took a few seconds, but I weighed the consequences heavily and responded.

"Actually, I could probably get my sister to take over the house for the summer. Shirley told me she hates the idea of going home for the break."

"Keep talkin," he encouraged.

"God, Phil, I'd really love to join you. Are you sure Mitch wouldn't mind? Is there room for all of us?"

"Sure. He's got a Land Rover, and my dad is loaning us his camp tent-trailer. It will easily sleep four, four and a half, that is, and it's big enough to store our gear."

My juices were flowing. I looked at Phil and wondered what he'd be like. Probably good, as I imagined most hippie types were. Not for one second did I think of traveling without engaging sexually. It wasn't practical and Phil was a cutie. His shaggy blond hair was beginning to thin, but he had the biggest, bluest eyes I had ever seen. And those lashes! They were longer than life, nearly as long as his beautiful thin limbs. No, sleeping with this man wouldn't pose a problem, but perhaps my schedule would.

"You know, I'm not much of a sleeper, Phil. I've been into yoga and meditation now for nearly two years and I function on less than six hours of sleep."

I was asking, What kind of habits do you have?

"I had no idea," he said, impressed. "That's great, Judy.

Mitch sleeps a lot, but once he runs out of dope, he'll be more active. Until he and his girl wake up, you and I can do long walks together. We'll explore while they sleep. How's that?"

"Sounds great." Could I really make this happen? "Okay," I said. "When do we leave?"

"Monday. We'll pick you up bright and early."

"Monday? Next Monday! You're kidding."

"Is that too soon? How about Tuesday, then? One more day couldn't hurt. Can you be ready?"

Tuesday was only four days away. I began to doubt. "Sure. Where there's a will, there's a way. Let's make this happen."

"Cool," he said happily. "Well, I've got to go. See you in a few days."

"See you," I said, barely breathing. "And Phil?"

"Yeah?"

"Thanks. Thanks for the invitation."

"Are you kidding? Judy, this will be great. Before I wasn't excited about the trip. I felt like the odd man out, what with Mitch taking his girl and all. Now I can't wait."

Phil left and I began to wonder. Would it really happen? I was not the kind of person to assume and I knew circumstances could change. Maybe Phil would have regrets. Maybe Mitch wouldn't like the idea of having a three-year-old along. Anything could get in the way; just in case, I decided to be cautious. I arranged for my sister to take over my home, the utilities and the mortgage, and I paid off my credit cards. After tallying up, I was left with a few hundred dollars, which was enough. If I was careful, I could pay some expenses and still come home with money.

Phil had already told me not to worry about food or gas. He was willing to foot the bill, so I was comfortable with my circumstances. I was also debt-free, the first time since my divorce. I had struggled, like all single parents, and after three years I was in the black. Ready, willing, and able—that was me. I did everything but quit my job and tell Pat. If it happened, I would do both, but if it didn't, I still needed a job, and I saw no reason to worry my would-be lifetime mate, at least not prematurely. Pat was far too practical. He would not like this adventure of mine, but if he didn't understand, then so be it.

Monday arrived, and I went to work as usual. Phil hadn't called over the weekend, so I assumed the trip was off. Surely, they wouldn't show up at my doorstep, not without making certain I was ready. Would they? It was the dawning of the age of Aquarius, but still, we weren't that free, were we? Not in my mind, we weren't. I was into the here and now, but I was a responsible young adult, a mother, in fact. Nope, something must have happened. Probably Phil and Mitch were already gone.

I wasn't upset for being abandoned, and it was sort of a relief, but relief is illusive. It skitters around the psyche like shadows dancing in the clouds, and such was the case for me. Just when I was resigned to my inevitable, predictable life, they showed up. On Monday night they were there at my doorstep for a Tuesday departure, as promised.

"Hi, Judy," he said, when I answered the door. "You ready?"

"Oh my God! Come in."

He came through the entry as though he had been there a thousand times. "Judy, meet Mitch. And this is Sally. You guys, meet Judy."

After greetings all around, Pam came running into the room. "Mommy, come look. I made a man in my coloring book."

"Pami, wait. Remember Phil?"

She stared. "Neighbor."

"Yes, and he's come to take us on a vacation. Would

you like to go bye-bye?"

Suddenly, Pam was shy, crawling into my lap to have a better look. "Come on," I prompted. "Let's go pack you a suitcase."

And so it was. I told Pat that night and the next morning I resigned from my job. My boss was more understanding than my beau, but then, who could blame him? He had returned from far-off places to claim me and I responded by running away. I rationalized if Pat truly loved me, he would wait. And if I truly loved him, I would want him to. This wasn't something I cared to analyze, but there wasn't time, anyway. I had things to do.

So there I was one morning out in a field, all alone. Everyone else slept the early morning hours away, Phil included. I ended up taking those walks by myself, and I always incorporated meditation into those times. On this day, I was sitting on a haystack, transcending time and space as the sun came up. I felt the heat on my face and saw red, orange, and yellow colors streak across the skyline.

It was awe-inspiring. If my eyes had been open, the vision couldn't have been more beautiful. Translucent dew tickled my nose, and then my fingertips began to tingle. The fresh, crisp air was bringing me to full alert. Bliss embellished my being and song erupted from my soul. I was bursting. Bursting with happiness and loving the moment.

This is it, I thought as the white light encircled me. *This is what it's all about. I have reached nirvana!*

I relaxed and allowed. Definition became elusive and I had a sense of floating. Floating? Am I really doing this? As soon as the question took form, so did the panic. Fear tumbled me back to the land and I opened my eyes. The horizon was exactly as I had seen it, and so was the field and its piles of hay. The tractor was there, too, and the edges of the field burst with alfalfa blooms, just like I expected. "No!"

I cried. "You can't do this. I will not be your pawn!"

I was speaking to the devil, of course. It was my Christian upbringing. Those images of dancing demons had returned. Without another thought, I terminated my spiritual journey and for the balance of that trip, I only took the walks. Meditation was out of the question, for I feared an out-of-body experience. I did not understand the phenomena, and I wasn't altogether convinced it was a good thing. Perhaps it was evil, for isn't that what the Christians proclaimed? Astro-projection would leave you open to any entity. You would never know whether the influence was good or bad. To be safe, one had to stay in control. Control was something I did understand. I liked being master of my own mind, so I abandoned the metaphysical realm and remained grounded for the summer.

~

Only after renewing my spiritual quest in that eight-by-nine cement cell did I remember that fear, but it surfaced. I wasn't leaving my body, but I was seeing the eyes. Demonic eyes had tormented me the night Rod laid hands on me, and now they were back. With them searching and staring, I began to question the sanctity of my practice. I stopped climbing into my repose, but when I didn't meditate, I became depressed and anxious.

Without my retreat it was difficult to cope, harder to hope, and nearly impossible to love. I stopped playing bridge and found no reason to either write or call home. Prison became a grim reality rather than the gift I had deemed it to be. Negativity engulfed me, and I needed something to restore my equilibrium. I wasn't quite ready to start meditating again, so I tried recalling Bible verses. I had learned enough over the years, and I remembered fear as the great enemy. Convinced angels were with me, I quietly told them I would like to read the Word. "Please find me a nice Bible," I said. "I'd like one that's easy to read, one I might understand."

It was a prayer of sorts, for my roommate did not have the good book on her shelf, and I was not sure about petitioning the chaplain. I did not want to seem "uncool," and no one I ran with had an affinity for the Church. I preferred playing it safe, so I simply made the request and forgot about it.

I returned to my quiet times of introspection, but I never completely released. When the eyes came, or the white light encircled me, I'd get up and go do something more mundane. Sometimes I'd make an effort to remain in the alpha, but trying didn't work. Meditation is one of those things—less is best. The more you tried, the harder it became, and I hated those eyes, those evil, staring, dark-seated pupils that came at me from every direction. They were frightening.

Finally, relief came and when it did, I felt joy again. The Joy of the Moment, I called it. Those times when something spectacular occurred, and you knew the mini miracle was meant for you. It was one of those divine coincidences, and I had no doubt it was an answer to my prayer.

CHAPTER 47

Judith

IT HAPPENED ON A DAY when one of the girls was leaving. Emotions run high during these exits. The releases were celebrated, but being left behind was difficult, especially if you were losing a friend. I didn't know this inmate well, since I was the new kid on the block, but I got a clear sense of the elation and the deflation. The mixture made my skin crawl; so much so, I decided to take a shower. On the way to the common facilities, I passed the ice machine and glanced up. Low and behold! I couldn't believe it! On top of that stainless-steel canister was a Bible! Hadn't I asked for that? Indeed! Apparently, the girl being freed had left it behind.

Ask and you will receive, I said in awed silence. It was a sign, another indicator I was not alone. Each time something like this happened, I felt closer to God. Of course, the lady probably left it out of laziness, but I didn't care. So what if she hadn't returned it to the chapel? At least she set it out on the machine, the designated spot for recycling. The girls put things there they no longer needed. Books, clothes, shoes, bags, rags, and now, a Bible! It was the way wealth was distributed since no bartering was allowed. At that moment I was happy for the "no asking, no thanking" policy. I forgot about my shower and ran back to my bunk.

Guide me, my angels. Help me understand. Rifling the pages, I slipped in a book marker. "This is where I'll start," I said, under my breath. "Let's see what you have in store for me."

Gently I pried at the text. The book opened to a chapter entitled, Judith. How ironic, I thought. Of all the books my marker could have selected, it managed to find the one with my name on it. *Isn't that wild?* "What do you want me to learn from this woman?" I asked. I didn't even know there was a biblical character named Judith.

My first read would be about a woman, and that made me happy. Maybe Judith would speak to me. Maybe she'd help me sort through my meditation mystery. God knew, I wanted answers. Opening my mind and my heart, I started the search. It was a quest of the most unusual kind, at least for me it was, so I investigated with as much mindfulness as possible.

As I read the hairs on the back of my neck stand at attention. I am there, back before the time of Christ, during the terrifying reign of Nebuchadnezzar. The King sends his sycophantic general, Holofernes, to the mountain pass outside Judith's village, Bethulia, and the city is laid to siege. Guards are posted in the mountains, blocking any means of escape, and then access to food and water is denied. When the Jewish people start to starve and fall ill from dehydration, they begin to talk surrender. Judith is upset with her countrymen for not trusting God, and she decides to act.

I felt steadfast reading the book of Judith, and courage filled me as her story unfolded.

She takes her loyal maid, and they head toward the camp of the enemy general. She slowly ingratiates herself to Holofernes, promising him information on the Israelites. Gaining his trust, she is invited into his tent. She is beautiful, and he vows to keep her safe from the ensuing wars.

Of course. He wants to possess her. If he saves her, then surely, she will revere him.

As Holofernes attempts to woo Judith, she charms him, but she refuses the drink he offers. He gorges himself on cheese and wine, and afterwards, falls unconscious to his bed.

My hand clenched as Judith takes sword from scabbard. She grabs his hair and pulls it. I held my breath and felt the strike. Intense! A bolt of electricity went down my right arm. Fear! I quaked as she hits him again. The head gives way.

In my mind's eye I held it triumphantly.

Judith wraps the tyrant's head in his jeweled bed-netting and hands it off to her servant.

My sister, Jana, appeared. *Of course; who else would it be?*

Work it, Judith, I thought. *You go, girl.*

The chapter continued, explaining how Judith inspired her people. She was a heroine and people sang hymns in her honor.

As for me, I decided if Judith could face down an entire army, then I can face my onslaught of eyes. After all, isn't fear the greatest enemy? I believed it was, so with Judith as my guide, I took the leap of faith. I began to meditate purposefully, and when the dark pupils pursued my psyche, I ignored them. Refusing to surrender my quiet times helped a great deal, and as the days passed, I was less depressed and more accepting.

Unfortunately, that level of comfort set me up for a fall, and I went down hard. It was a case of "open mouth and insert foot."

CHAPTER 48

A Birthday Celebration

PRISON IS AN INTERESTING PLACE. The shared experience causes inmates to fuse and attach to each other, but often for the wrong reasons. At least that was my experience. Women doing more time tended to bond and avoid associating with short-timers. That was me. I was a short-timer. Even though my sentence was nearly three years, I was still considered a little-leaguer.

When I sat down to have breakfast with Vicki and Nancy that day, I hadn't heard about this caste system, nor had I been informed the word "writ" equated to "rat." Rats, of course, were traitors, people who would testify to save their own anatomy. In a manner of speaking, they were people like me. I had agreed to cooperate with the government, but I believed my circumstances were extenuating. "Caught in the crosshairs, Judy," my attorney had said. "Don't you understand your status of citizenship has been seriously downgraded? Basically, you are Persona Non Grata."

I was outraged! Less than a person? Impossible! But alas, that was the reality, and I had no choice but to accept it. Prosecutors were never opposed to throwing away the key. It was either testify or rot in prison. It was only logical for me to agree to their terms, or at least that was what I believed. The problem was these two "long-timers" didn't give me a chance to explain. When I mentioned I would soon be going out on writ, their body language changed abruptly. Vicki was especially hostile. She decided to let me have it.

"Another one," she said, as I felt the knife go in.

"Yes, they're everywhere these days," returned Nancy.

I was alarmed. "What do you mean?"

"You've agreed to be a witness for the damn government," came Vicki's hoarse words.

I watched her big, broad, masculine shoulders pull back into a cat-like arch. I imagined her slinging forward, grabbing my throat, and pushing me onto the floor. The adrenaline rushed in and I retaliated with words.

"It's not like I had a choice."

Nancy's head dropped. She remained silent, but Vicki shot another remark. "I've seen too many families destroyed because of this plea-bargain thing. It's not like the old days, is it, Nance?"

"Nope, sure isn't."

How dare they judge me? I thought, holding fast in my chair. I wanted to leave, but I knew it was a bad idea. These women deserve no explanation. If they want to pass judgment without even considering the circumstances, then so be it.

"Hey, did you hear about Joanie?" Vicki asked, suddenly changing the subject.

"Yes, can you believe it?" Nancy asked nonchalantly.

Who is Joanie, I wondered, *and why had the intimidation stopped?* Nancy, I could understand. She hadn't been that negative, but Vicki ...? Well, Vicki was Vicki. "Tough" was her middle name.

The sandpaper voice got rougher and the bully returned. "Oh, I believe it. I don't think it was no suicide either. Somebody pushed her from that roof. She probably crossed her bitch or something."

"Dublin has a reputation for that kind of thing," returned Nancy.

"Yep, I'm still in touch with a couple of women up there. I'm gonna check it out. Bet Joanie gave someone up, though. Whadda ya think?"

"That would do it," said Vicki's comrade at arms. "Well, I'd better get to work. See you later."

The two judgment girls rose and left little ole me by myself. I wasn't on the floor, and I hadn't been choked, but they had subtly threatened to throw me off a roof. Amazing, I thought. *Wonder if they'll try anything? They wouldn't risk getting booted out of here, would they?*

I resolved to stay away from the duo and thought life would go on as usual. A bit naïve, perhaps, but I believed the prison's zero-violence policy would protect me, and besides, it was not the first time I had been threatened. Running for my life and hiding from my enemies had toughened me—or so I thought.

I was branded and ostracized, left alone in that forsaken place known as Camp Phoenix. I no longer shared any part of that intimate connection between inmates. The word got out I was a "rat," and that was that. No one would talk to me, and everywhere I turned, I got dirty looks. I began to experience morbid isolation.

Regret hit me like a ton of bricks, and even meditating couldn't keep the depression away. And the eyes! Oh my God, they were merciless. They charged at me day and night. I saw them walking, sitting, reading, and dreaming. They were everywhere, and I began fearing them again. Maybe these girls were right. Maybe I shouldn't have agreed to testify. Maybe I really did deserve this kind of treatment. Maybe, maybe, maybe. I was full of them, and life was miserable. Then one day, an angel stepped into my space.

"Hey, what's up, girl?" asked Laura at mail call.

Surely, she knew. The news could not possibly have missed her. Nothing got by Laura.

"Oh, nothing," I responded.

"You okay?" she asked.

"I guess, but I hate being hated."

"Judy, you can't pay attention to these idiots. Ninety percent of them are here on short sentences because they did exactly what you did."

"Really?" I asked hopefully.

"Really. Don't let these girls get to you. Believe me, they're not worth it."

"Thanks," I said.

"If anyone bothers you, let me know. I'll take care of it, okay?"

I laughed. God, it felt good. If anyone could "take care of things," Laura could. Having her in my corner made all the difference in the world. "No one has assaulted me. I've received nasty, threatening notes, but so far that's all."

"Well, be careful. Stay off the track for a while. And watch your back."

I told her I would, but later, back in the dorm, I started to wonder if I was even safe there.

My roommate had been standoffish before, but now when she entered our cubicle, a black cloud shrouded her. *Oh brother*, I thought. *How much worse can this get?* I swear, the air was so thick you could cut it with a knife.

Don't walk the track, watch your back, and sleep with one eye open. Anything else?

On another day at mail call, Yvonne tried to encourage me. "I want you to know," she whispered in my ear. "I know what these girls are doing, and you pay them never-no-mind. They're all bitches. If you have a chance to get out of here, you take it. Don't listen to any of their shit. They're all jealous anyway; most of them would jump at a chance to testify. I lost everything because I refused to cooperate. If I had to do it all over again, you can bet I would become a witness for the government. I've got three kids, and now, because I was a stubborn fool, they're growing up without their mom."

"I'm sorry," I said. My Puerto Rican friend was so sincere, I nearly cried. I could see her pain, and yet she was reaching out to me. It was heartwarming.

"Not to worry. I made my choice, and I must live with it, but you ... you choose freedom. Don't make this thing worse than it is."

And how do I do that? I wondered. "Don't worry, I won't. This is nothing compared to what I've been through, believe me."

Yvonne turned a brow. She was surprised by my "tough" attitude.

Things got better. I renewed my friendship with Diane, and although we didn't play much bridge, we did pal around together. She also got me out of the kitchen and into a clerk's position with the Water Operations department where she worked.

Thank God for friends. Even in prison you had to know someone. To get anywhere, you needed an "in," and for me Diane was that "in." I got off my feet and the physical relief made everything easier. Even the eyes began to dissipate. They didn't disappear altogether, but they ceased to haunt my dreams, waking or otherwise. If I could have stopped them in my meditations, I would have been happy, but so far, I hadn't developed the strength. Then one day, I got some advice.

Become empty so you may be filled, said the Divine Spark.

It was that "letting go" thing. I had a distinct feeling my angels were suggesting I forget my past and dump the baggage, eyes included.

Easier said than done, I thought, but the messages continued. I had a lesson to learn, and I couldn't pretend otherwise. Dr. Dyer's book echoed the spark. One passage said I needed to take responsibility for everything. That seemed logical enough, but accepting the idea we were waking dreamers was tougher. Still, with what I was experiencing, why argue?

The Messengers, which I had nearly finished, took the concept a step farther. Nick Burdick explained, in the words of the Apostle Paul, that we could not judge people for their behavior because, in all actuality, we created it.

"Bingo!"

It was a moment—one of those times when the hairs on your arms stand up, except for me the feeling swept through my upper body. It wafted across my neck and shoulders. Not like static, more like a fan of feathers sweeping slowly and deliberately. I shook with the sensation but marveled at it as well. It was pleasant and although I expected it to be a one-time occurrence, it was anything but. That light and airy feathery shaking became a common occurrence; eventually I decided the phenomena was a confirmation from beyond. It was angel wings sweeping in to say, "Pay attention."

Rod was calling regularly by then, leaving messages on my voicemail, and I began looking forward to the encouraging words from my "Son of the Son of a Preacher Man." I figured letting go of the bad and bringing forward the good was a positive thing. Surely it couldn't hurt.

That was another thing about prison. One looks for any way to stay attached. Touching someone, anyone, in any way, helps us feel connected, and we desperately need connection. Separating from society is gut-wrenching, and when the system makes you feel less than human, persona non grata, a lifeline is appreciated. Mine was family, a few close friends, and Rod. I still loved him, though without harboring any illusions about us getting back together, I attached myself in a remote way by phone and by note. I dialed my voicemail number to hear a message from him, and although he rarely wrote, I corresponded frequently. I figured my letters were good for him, and since they were therapy for me, I applied the pen often. Then, one morning it happened. I went to retrieve my lifeline and discovered the source had fallen into darkness. Rod's voice was heavy, and as I listened to his sinking words, I feared the worst.

"Why did you stop believing, Judy?" he asked. "Why?" It was more of a cry, a wail of anguish, a disembodied voice from a time long past. "I swear I could have pulled it off, if only you had believed."

I erased the message and slammed down the receiver. "God dammit, Rod, get over it. Accept responsibility and move on."

Dr. Dyer's lesson rang in my ears. "Indeed, we do create our own reality, don't we?" I hated Rod's splintering voice, but he was ill. He needed help, and unless he sought out a professional, those personalities would remain. The voice on the line had been the Victim, a paranoid and insecure grown up young boy-man.

Bingo! There they were again. Those angel wings fluttered across my back. "Okay, okay," I said. "I'm responsible, too. I see. If I think of him as weak, then that is how he will respond to me."

It was an epiphany, but I didn't like the implication. Had Rod been responding to me during the days of his delusions and paranoia? Surely not. I didn't think he was ill then, but others did.

~

"Do you think I'm crazy?" he had asked me one night.

"Crazy? No. Why?" The question was ludicrous.

"My dad said there are rumors going around."

I couldn't imagine. "Serious?" I asked.

"Yes," he said quietly.

"Rod, you're a creative genius. No one understands where you get those brilliant ideas. Saying they're from God probably causes people to speculate, but believe me, you are not crazy. Not even close."

He seemed satisfied, and I had forgotten about it, but now, looking back, I wondered. Could those rumors have led to Rod's breakdown? Had enough people believed him to be off balance—so many, in fact, that the illness manifested? Too deep for me. I dismissed the notion and went back to my room to write a letter.

It was a few days before I reached for the phone again, but when I did, the message was different. Rod no longer anguished over my betrayal, but he was still out of sorts. He told me it had been a "stretching" week and said he was enjoying the "battle."

"Lawyers are nothing more than paid whores," he exclaimed at the end.

Not my grounded Mr. Global. Worry consumed me and I suspected the worst. Could Rod be on drugs again? I tried to call him.

I had sent in the necessary paperwork to phone him directly, but up until that time, it hadn't been approved. On this day, I wondered if I really wanted permission, but I dialed the number anyway.

"Judy! Is it really you?" he exclaimed.

"How are you, Rod?" I asked.

"You wouldn't believe it! Everything is going great. I'm listening to your tape right now."

"Nice music, isn't it?" I asked.

"It's like reliving our time together. Every song reminds me of something we did."

"That's what I thought."

"Thank you, Judy. Thank you so much. The music has really helped me. It's been good therapy."

"Well, the tape must have been meant for you. I was going to bring it in here, but they wouldn't allow it."

"Really? You don't have any music?"

"Nope, just radios. You see, those songs are all yours."

"God is good," he said. "How are you, Judy?"

The conversation was inspiring, and for a while Rod sounded like his old self, the "Son of a Son of a Preacher Man." I learned he had organized a new "Vision Quest Assembly," and the dealers were now called "Patriots." That was well and good, but then the warning bells began to clang. It was the part about him acting as a conduit for Truth, mirroring the image of heaven that set me to worrying.

"It's so exciting. Remember the triangles?" he asked.

Of course, I remembered. How could I forget?

"Earth is a mirror of heaven, Judy, and I sit beneath Jesus Christ and the Holy Spirit. Isn't that cool?"

I tried to remain supportive, for the Preacher was most definitely on one of his creative waves. He declared he was the incarnate soul of Jesus Christ's little brother. The crucifixion had been harrowing. He had wanted to fight, but was helplessly small, far too young to wage a war.

Rod said his name in heaven was Valor and told me Christ once rocked him on his knee. Then the sadness came ... of course, it had to be there. The poor pitiful me person was alive and well.

"After Jesus died, nothing was the same, and everybody was mean to me. I'm still suffering from the pain. Judy, I understand so much now. I can't wait to talk to you in person."

"Me, too," I said, thankful it wouldn't happen.

We exhausted our fifteen minutes and the click, click, click saved me. Hang on, baby, hang on, I said quietly, after disconnecting. Widen your focus and heal. Shed that tunnel vision of yours and get on with your life.

Christmas came and I journaled a "Happy Birthday" to Jesus, but the words came hard. Not that I wasn't appreciative of the precious birth, but being joyous was impossible. Nothing felt right; even the weather was seasonably ugly. Dark clouds filled the landscape and the gloom penetrated the hearts and minds of everyone in the dorms.

Then the rain came.

Usually, rain brought cheer because it meant recall. Recall was "return to your room" and "get out of work," but on this day everyone was already off, so there was no elation. Girls simply dug in. The lucky ones had visits, but those left alone sank into their cubicles, either sleeping or hiding behind the pages of a book. The quiet was unnerving and I found myself wishing for the return of chaos. Make noise girls, get on with your gaggling, swear up a storm. Today I don't covet private space and time. Lord, give me something. Knock, knock ... Is anyone there? I left my cubicle, the one filled with mental muck and went down to Laura's room. She was chatting with her roommate, Maria.

"Come in, come in," said the pleasingly plump, middle-aged Spanish woman.

"What's up?" asked Laura.

"Not much. What's up with you guys?" I had overheard some of the conversation and knew they were talking about religion. My initial reaction was to walk away, but Laura's casual invitation warmed me.

"Oh, we were just reading some passages in the Bible. Come in. Sit down."

"Here," Maria offered, sitting up on her bed. "Sit here," she said, patting the mattress.

"Thanks," I said gratefully. "So, what were you reading?"

"Something about the second coming," Laura said.

"Do you believe?" asked Maria. Her affection for Jesus was pouring out, which was contagious. I felt lightened. Why doesn't my room feel like this, I wondered?

"Yes," I said. "I believe."

Up until that point, I hadn't really thought about it, but yes, I did think something was shaking in the heavens. I had experienced a resurrection of sorts. My life had changed dramatically in the last year, and no doubt my awakening had something to do with Jesus. I didn't really believe he would manifest in the flesh, but I did feel like a spiritual shift was occurring. I jumped into the conversation, and as we talked, the morning grew luminous. Soon other girls joined us and the shared camaraderie lifted everyone. We weren't in church, but it felt like a sanctuary. I found myself wishing it would never end, but the powers that be called "Count" and everyone had to return to their domiciles.

"Meet us for lunch," Laura said.

The chow hall was the last place I wanted to be. Too many people, too little joy. "Think I'll pass, but thanks."

Laura would not hear it. "Oh, come on. You can at least have dessert."

"Yes," echoed Maria. "If you don't want it, you can give it to me. Si?"

The Spanish vernacular was enduring. How could I say no? Begrudgingly I agreed, which turned out to be a good decision. Dinner was delicious, a veritable feast, and for the better part of the next hour, I nearly forgot where I was. I went back to my room to journal and began with an offering. "Thank you, Jesus, and really ... Happy Birthday to You."

CHAPTER 49

Blessings

IT TOOK THREE DAYS for the sun to come out, but when it did, attitudes improved. Holiday blues disappeared, and New Year good cheer flowed. If only I was included, maybe then I would have been happier. Unfortunately, the Vicki brigade remained unforgiving, and their scare tactics caused me some pause. They especially affected my meditations, and the eyes were driving me crazy. I started to believe demons were at work. They were hindering my growth, and I felt helpless against them. Needing inspiration, I drew a Divine Spark. "With Understanding the Fear Will Disappear."

But how? I asked. *How am I to understand?*

Ask, was the reply. It came from within, but it was a powerful suggestion.

~

I recalled another time. I was trying to clean my pool filter. At least I wanted to clean it. Trouble was, I couldn't loosen the nut securing the system. It was stuck and no amount of muscle would budge it, at least not my muscle. I tried pliers and then a wrench. Still, it remained fast. I refused to give up, but after about an hour my hands were cramping. I took a break and went in for some iced tea.

"I can't get it open, Mom. Looks like I may have to call a professional."

"There are things a woman can't do."

Fighting words. I went back outside and grabbed the pliers. Okay, my angels. I need you. Bust this loose for me, will you?

Granted, I had a firm grip, but I held tight before, and nothing happened. Then this! This was so easy! The bolt turned with ease. You're kidding! No possible way. I thought maybe my tool had slipped, but another turn confirmed the mini miracle. For sure, someone had helped. Not a neighbor, at least not the one who lived next door. My helper was the celestial sort, a helpmate from the other side. I laughed openly. Thank you, my friend. Thank you so much.

~

Funny how we forget. Even when we understand angels abound, we forget to call on them. It had been years, but here I was again—in need, but failing to call out. I thought of Maria.

"Do you believe?" she had asked.

"Yes, I believe."

I did believe, so why not? After all, it couldn't hurt. Okay, my friends. I need you. Protect me, will you? Guard me in my seeking? Give me a hand.

Maybe the results would be immediate, I didn't know, but at that moment I wasn't willing to try. It wasn't until the next morning I really made an honest effort. Waking at dawn, I decided to balance before crawling down from my bunk.

"Blessings, Lord," came the words. I was surprised. Never had I spoken such a greeting. I paused to reflect and then continued.

Emerging from the meditation, I knew something special had occurred. Peace had been plentiful and uninterrupted. There were no demonic glares, not even one! Not only did I enter that cherished space, but I also composed a prayer, a poetic one at that! That was something new and different. I wasn't a poet, not even close. In fact, as a kid I hated poetry. My mother had a talent for it, and she attempted to influence me, but I was inept. I simply couldn't understand the stuff. But this! This was a beautiful prayer, and I wanted to record my words for posterity.

BLESSINGS

(A Prayer for Meditation)

Blessings Heavenly Father, Earthly Mother, Eternal Light,
All that Is, Was, and Ever Will Be.
Blessings Lord Jesus, Son of God, Savior of Man,
Brother of Mine, Bearer of Burdens,
and Teacher Supreme.
Blessings Holy Spirit, Web of Life, Glue that Binds,
Breath that Connects,
Wind that Lifts and Tide that Ebbs and Flows for All Time.
Blessings All. Blessings on this wondrous and glorious day.
Blessings.
Blessings all my Angels, Spirit Guides, and Celestial Friends
as you help me along the way.
Glory Be to God on High, to All of You, and to All of Me.
Glory be.
Hold me tight. Hold me close.
Surround me with your Heavenly Host.
Protect me on this journey today.
Guard me and guide me, Oh Holy Ones.
Stand by me as I seek the essence of wisdom, peace,
and loving harmony.
Stand by me.
All of this I ask in the name of the Father/Mother, Christ
Child, and Holy Ghost.
All that I am, I offer. To serve is what I desire most. Amen.

To say I was lifted would be an understatement. On Thursday, January 1st, I drew four Sparks, one for each season of the year. "I Am Love. I Am Divine," said the first one.

Thank you. I needed to hear that. And it's good to know I am not alone.

"Believe in Your VISION. Joyfully Awake."

I wanted to cry. My VISION was keeping me alive, but the JOY was illusive. I do and I will. I'll embrace the goodness more every day.

"Remember, You Are Worthy to Receive."

The message humbled me, but hearing it made me feel love toward the girls, even those choosing to judge me or trying to hurt me. Feeling renewed, I turned over the last Spark. The final message was perfect.

"Be Open to New Beginnings."

Isn't that wild? So appropriate for the first day of a new year. In my journal I wrote, "I walk with God, and I talk with God. I am strengthened by his Holy Spirit, and I am loved by his Son, my brother, Jesus Christ. Miracles are occurring."

They say everyone gets religion in prison, but I didn't believe "religion" was something you acquire. It already resided within us, or at least spirit did. It is with us every day in every way. Most of us just forget or get too busy to pay attention.

The world catches us by the shirttail and flings us around until we are too dizzy to "see." If the pace was slower, the demands fewer, and the distractions less damaging, we would get it—religion, I mean. We'd start noticing divine coincidences and life would become curiously delightful. It would fill us with wonder and encourage investigation. Our eyes would open and then the world would be a better place.

As far as I was concerned, I was full of religion, always

had been. I had been on a spiritual quest most of my life. There were down times, but even experiencing the dark night of the soul had not been without reward. I had emerged from that depression with a new kind of awareness, more enlightened somehow. Now I was a ward of the federal government and although I wasn't happy about it, the pace had slowed and the lack of responsibility made it easier to concentrate on what was important—like the writing of my book. I was also noticing mini-miracles and those times were heartwarming. Of course, I had my ups and downs. And Rod, well, he made things difficult.

Messages were coming almost daily, and although I wouldn't always call him back, I did listen. One moment, he sounded perfectly sane, and the next I'd hear the opposite.

"I want to divorce Mary Ann, Judy. I need to stop living this lie," he said one day.

The message meant nothing. I had heard it before.

"Judy, the shareholders are vicious. They would hurt me if they knew we were communicating. It's spiritual warfare."

The implication was, of course, it was all my fault. Global had been destroyed because of me, because of my lack of faith. I ignored that one as well. Old news. The man was still equivocating. It was war alright, but he was warring with himself. He ran hot and cold, and then one day he cried in desperation.

"Isn't there any chance you could get out of there, Judy? I need you in my life."

This one I couldn't ignore and it made me angry. I wrote to remind him he was the reason we were apart. "You did this, Rod," I said. "When I locked you out of your gilded cage—referring to the restraining order—you turned tail and ran straight to the authorities. If you hadn't sung that bitter song of yours, I wouldn't be here." I called him a yellow canary and told him he went "tweet, tweet, tweet," all the way home. It was a mean thing to say, but he was oblivious. He barely mentioned it, and his messages continued, many of them becoming more than strange. One day he told me of a waking dream, a vision of some kind.

"I was standing on a precipice, Judy, a cliff of some kind, and I began to fall backward. I was losing my balance, but you swept in to fan your wings behind me. You were a giant white dove, and the warm rush of your love pushed me back onto the mountain. Isn't that cool?"

Sure, it was cool. So cool, it chilled me to the bone. No, Rod. I cannot be there to save you. Save yourself.

This kind of thing made prison difficult. I couldn't help. Not Rod, not my mom, not my sister, not anyone, and I felt their pain. I could hear my sister's desperation. It came through in her letters. Without me as a lifeline, Shirley was unraveling.

Jana missed me, too, and sometimes talking made us both sad. Mom was just angry; she'd rant and rave about the injustice of my situation. That gave me strength. I enjoyed having her take up for me, but Pam was heartbroken. She had lost me and her husband, and the weight of her responsibilities was enormous. She had a mortgage, two car payments, and all the things that went with them, not to mention her two little girls. No, it wasn't easy, not for any of us, but we reached out any way possible—them with cards and money, and me with positive news and encouraging words. Remaining upbeat lessened their worry, which was therapeutic for me. Effectively, I created my own reality and sometimes the rewards were good.

My agent wrote and her words were music to my ears. "Once I started your manuscript, I couldn't put it down." No contract was offered, but she encouraged me to complete the book. That, all by itself, was enough.

Another gift came from my psychic, Shelia, the Divine

Spark woman from Sedona. She sent me, The Celestine Prophecy and The Tenth Insight, by James Redfield—two novels in one binding—and I found the material intriguing. The manuscript outlined our spiritual quest, defining the journey as an enlightening process, beginning with the first insight and progressing to the tenth.

Shelia, you are a divine being, I said while reading. *Thank you for this perceptive book.* Redfield's contemplations were profound and they rang true! Had I taken time to analyze what was happening to me, I might have journaled the ten insights myself. Another mini miracle, I thought as angel wings swept through me.

I paused to reflect; the whole Pioneer Enterprises—Pioneer Avenue thing came to mind. So did everything that had anything to do with my coming to this prison, especially meeting and marrying Speicher and my subsequent association with Rod. Those relationships had sealed my fate, but there was more. An undercurrent was directing my play. *Angels in the outfield,* I thought.

"The Second Insight institutes our awareness as something real." Touché! I knew it!

What I was feeling and sensing and experiencing was most definitely real; so was the Einstein connection. Rod and I had joined forces for spiritual reasons and our experiences, however unpleasant, had helped us evolve.

Number three was more ambiguous, but still familiar. "The Third Insight begins a new view of life." It was that "believe and you will see" stuff. Amazing. Why am I hearing this everywhere I go?

This one set me to wondering. Could Rod have been right? Did Global go down because I failed to believe in him? I shuddered at the thought. Truth was, he failed to believe in himself. I shook off the negative introspection and moved on.

The Fourth discussed human nature's tendency to steal energy. Power was gained through mind control. The story of my life. Men always wanted to control me, especially Rod! Steal from me and see where it gets you. Unbelievable!

Where do we go from here? I wondered. How do we change this tendency?

I took a breath and continued. "The Fifth Insight reminds us that the universe can provide all. We only need to be open to the higher source."

Amen to that. Calling on angels and meditating for peace and balance sure helped me.

I couldn't imagine surviving my circumstances without connecting to a higher source. Not that I would have perished or anything, but using my time constructively would have been difficult, maybe impossible. Thank you, Shelia.

Even before finishing the manuscript, a hunger was ignited. I wanted a greater understanding, more knowledge, something tangible that would aid me on my path. Then one day it happened. I had asked and I was about to receive. An innocent invitation, perhaps, but the underlying intention was there and it did not go unnoticed.

"Want to go to Bible study with me tonight?" Sherri asked.

Sherri and I were about the same age, but thus far we had only engaged casually, usually in the cafeteria.

"I didn't know you were a Christian," I said, responding to the question.

"Yep," she said in her sullen way. She was a smoker and exuded a tough I don't give a shit kind of an attitude. Most people didn't approach her. "In fact, I do correspondence studies, too. The Bible really keeps me going."

"Really?" I said.

"Really. Why don't you come? The Tuesday night

group is terrific. It's led by a couple from Prison Fellowship, Ralph and Mary Lou. They are super nice. You'd like them."

"What are you studying?" I was dubious. I had little affection for the tenets of organized religion.

"We're starting a new segment tonight. It's on spiritual warfare."

Spiritual warfare! I couldn't believe it. What did these people believe about the battle between good and evil? Did Christians think devils manifest in the flesh? Did I? Had those dancing flames around my little chapel in the woods been demons? And what about The Crying Coyote? What about the eyes?

I recalled my Divine Spark, "With Understanding the Fear Will Disappear."

"You know what, Sherri. I would like to go. What time does the class start?"

"Seven. See you there?"

"Yes, and thanks. Thanks for inviting me."

She smiled and left. I was left to my inner rumblings.

"Blessings, Lord," I said later that night. My prayer was called up whenever I felt a need, and after that first lesson, I had a great need.

The entire group believed in a powerful Satan, but their dogma didn't align with mine. I didn't fear this ugly Lord and I didn't want to be brainwashed. I thought about my Sparks. This was a time to Allow and Observe. I wanted to understand these Christians and I thought their insight might help me deal with Rod. Help me understand my friends. Guard me and guide me, Oh Holy Ones. This one's a challenge.

CHAPTER 50

Spiritual Warfare

JANUARY WAS a most interesting "New Beginning." I wrestled with the Christian teachings and felt caught between the old world and that of a new order. Those lessons were difficult and depressing.

At first, my new job helped. I was working at the "Shit Ponds," which required a quarter mile walk daily. How I loved it. Leaving the camp offered the illusion of freedom, which made me feel less like a prisoner. And I was working with men! Civilian officers, real people, and good ones, too. I began to fantasize about having a little fun. After all, I was a sexual person, and it had been a long time. Maybe, just maybe, one of these guys would like to jumpstart my engine.

My boss was a cutie. His name was Mr. Gaukler, and he had a handsome face. He was taller than most men, and very much a 'take charge' kind of guy. I liked him. Trouble was, I liked him a little too much and knew the consequences if we were caught. I decided not to try—not to mention his wife! That was the last thing I needed, another man with a wife.

So, I waited and I kept looking. Each morning, I had to be there at 7:30 a.m., but since I couldn't access my office until the job assignments were made, I had ample time to observe. And look I did—Could this be what my angels meant about "becoming the observer"? I doubted it. The younger ones were appealing, but NO! I didn't need that either. God forbid! What then? Who then? I asked myself. More importantly, How? And was it worth it?

In the end, I decided it wasn't. I gave up and started looking at the sunrise and the ducks instead.

Rod, true to his nature, was also a source of delight and confusion. One day he'd enamor me, saying he wanted "us" to be together forever. I'd feel thrilled and loved and easily forgot the pain he had inflicted. Then he'd turn my joy to sorrow by saying something about how I failed to "believe" in him, and in the same breath, he'd tell me he understood that it was because of my "con" background. I'd go back to my room bruised from the verbal blow, and then I'd record my thoughts. I need to remember Rod carries a double-edged sword, lest I get cut again.

The biggest crusher came after he decided to change his business focus. He wanted to become involved somehow with the health-care industry.

"That way, Judy, I can save your life."

"What?" I asked, not understanding. He had talked about saving me, but it had always been my soul he wanted to save, not my body. This was something new.

"I had a vision you were ill and you weren't destined to live forever." Rod was sure the second coming was imminent, and he believed we would have an eternity together. At least he did until this vision of his. "It's going to be alright though, honey. We're going to find a cure for you."

Oh my God, I thought. It's that double-edged sword. He's imagining me sick so he can save me. Why was he saying such a thing? Was it in response to me? The answer came in a most unusual way. That night I failed to sleep.

Sleep is a precious commodity. It protects us

psychologically, and up until that point, I was a good sleeper. This night, however, was different. The entire night passed without one wink.

I slugged through the day, knowing the night would bring relief, but when the lights went out, it was more of the same. I didn't sleep that night either. Not at all!

"What's wrong?" Lori asked the next day.

"I'm not sure, but I haven't slept for two days."

"Worried about Rod, maybe?" she asked.

Lori knew about Rod because she was typing my story. She also understood because her boyfriend was nearly as outrageous.

~

After reading about one of Rod's escapades, she said, "Jeff did something similar to me. We had a fight, and I was running away from him. I left the house thinking he'd never follow me. He was on probation, you know, so I didn't think he'd dare."

Of course, he dared. Our bad-boy kind of men didn't live by the rules. Rules were for other people. "So, did he? Did he follow you?" I asked.

"Girl," she said. "Don't know how else he would have been right behind me at that traffic light. I couldn't believe it! I glanced in my rearview mirror and there he was! He was on his motorcycle, and I could sense the gun tucked tightly against his chest. The Harley Davidson jacket covered it, but I knew it was there. I just knew I was going to die."

Déjà vu. "What did you do?"

"I rolled up the windows," she giggled, "as if that would help."

I kept quiet and waited.

"Jeff came charging up to the car and busted the window."

"What?"

"Yep, he put his whole damn fist through my window.

Can you believe it?"

It was easy to see. "Oh my God."

"I'm tellin' ya. There were people everywhere, but he didn't care. You know what that fool did?"

I couldn't imagine. A faraway look glazed over Laura's eyes. What the hell? "What? What happened?"

"He was calm as hell. He reached through the window, unlocked the door, and pulled me out of the car. Then he kissed me."

"Kissed you! You're kidding!"

"Nope. He laid one on me, in front of God and everyone."

"How sexy!" I exclaimed. "How unbelievably hot!"

~

Laura did not leave her man, at least not that day. The experience, however, had prepared her for Rod. She didn't seem surprised by anything he did. She even empathized with him. "He sounds a lot like me," she had said. "Believe me, I can really get out there."

I didn't doubt it. Laura was medicated most of the time, but she was my friend. She understood the underworld and had plenty of experience with drugs. "I think he's using again," I said flatly.

She winced. "That would be bad."

"I know, but I can feel him. Laura, I feel exactly like I did when we were doing meth together. I must be having some kind of sympathy pains or something."

"Well, that fool. Let's go call him. I'll tell him a thing or two."

It was an idea, but not a good one. Rod knew about Laura and felt threatened by her. He even asked if we were lovers.

"Of course, we're not lovers, Rod. How crude."

"My brother said you'd come out of there hard as a rock and a dyke besides."

"I'm no lezzie, Rod," I exclaimed in defense. I decided to tease him, to rub him the wrong way. "She is awfully cute, though. Smart, too. Almost as smart as you."

I could feel him seethe. He was definitely jellybeans. I felt him then and I could feel him now. I knew the meth was coursing through his veins. It was that glue. Like in my prayer—the glue that binds. We were connected, and his abuse was making the small of my back knot. Only one thing made my back hurt that way, and the source was always the same.

"I can't call him right now. I've got to get to work. Maybe tonight, though," I said, making an excuse.

Laura didn't object. Laura was good at rolling with the flow.

On the third day, when I still hadn't slept, I called him. "Rod, I know you're using. I can feel it, and you're hurting me. You're hurting both of us, baby. Please stop."

It was a voice message. Of course, he wasn't about to pick up. Rod was good at hiding from the world, especially when he was in a chemically induced state of mind.

God help him, I said. God help me.

The quick prayer got me through my day, but I was desperately tired and needed relief. I headed for the sanctuary.

Not a soul was present, not even the secretary who usually sat at the front desk. No priest. No one in the video room. No one listening to music. I turned to my right and entered the small chapel. A soothing aura centered me as I assessed the room. Before I hadn't paid attention, but now I noticed the back wall lined with shelves of books. I went to look, trying to appear busy, acting like I had purpose, in case anyone invaded my space. Nothing. I took a seat on one of the red-cushioned chairs that accommodated the congregation on Sundays. They were arranged in three neat, perfectly straight rows across the center of the open space. Kinda nice in here, I thought after sitting for a while. There were tables in the back, long picnic-type tables, draped in white sheets, offering the illusion of holiness. Maybe I could write here. God knows there's no other place this quiet.

Lately, writing had become difficult. I was working the same hours as most of the girls, which meant less quiet time. At least in the kitchen I was home by noon. Now when I was off, so was everyone else, and that meant noise. It was tough to concentrate. I imagined myself working at one of those holy tables, bringing my God-inspired message to the page. Seems appropriate, I thought, before dropping into a trance.

I must have been under an hour or so. When I came back, I felt refreshed. That precious cosmic love restored me, and my heart space received a message with the renewal.

You can block him, the voice said. You can break the connection.

Of course! I was lonely at Camp Phoenix, and Rod's negative verbal battering was preferable to nothing. I had willingly listened, and now I was suffering for my complicity. I felt him, because I wanted to, but no more! I would let him go. Maybe I'd even stop writing to him. Maybe ... but for sure, I'd stop calling him. At least I could do that.

That night I meditated myself to sleep. I didn't wait for the vibrational shift; I simply prayed for protection and allowed my angels to take over. Thankfully, my efforts were rewarded.

"What did you do?" Laura asked, as she caught up with me on the track the next day. The evening before had inspired me, given me courage, and since the Vicki brigade had softened up, I ventured back to the Angel Quarter Mile.

"I called him," I said. "He didn't pick up, but I left a message and asked him to stop using the damn drug. Then I blocked him. I slept like a baby."

"I figured," she said, crinkling her blue-gray eyes into narrow bands. "You're not going to believe this."

"What?"

"He came to me."

I didn't really need an explanation. Rod couldn't connect with me, so he reached for my friend, his competitor and source of aggravation. "How?"

"I don't know how!" she wailed. "All I know is I couldn't sleep last night. Rod was in my head big time! And, Judy, I had leg cramps. The only time I get leg cramps is when I'm on a run. Only one thing causes those cramps!"

"Crystal!" I exclaimed.

"Yep. Crystal. I never got them otherwise, not ever. Had them all night long, too. God, they were bad. Will you tell Rod to leave us alone?"

"Laura, you know Rod will never do that. He's a controller. He'd love hearing this, but you can block him."

"Block him?"

"Yes, just like I did. Will him away. Ask Jesus to protect you and focus on the peace he offers."

She didn't seem convinced.

"Just do it," I said. "Trust me on this one."

It worked! The next day we were both rested, and I took notice. It worked for Laura and truly, it worked for me. I was most definitely onto something. Believe and you will see, said the metaphysical side of me. Unfortunately, that small revelation wasn't enough to sustain me. A change in weather turned the tide and I was nearly swept out to sea.

I had gone to work, waited the usual hour until I could get into the office, and then promptly got kicked out.

"What do you mean I have to go?" I asked Mr. Gaukler.

"We can't leave you alone in the office," he said. "It's against regulations."

Mr. Gaukler worked with two other officers, and one

of them had always been around. Now on this drizzly day, they were abandoning me.

"What do you want me to do?" I asked.

"You can pull some weeds or something. That front lawn area is your responsibility, too."

I knew that, but it was winter. The lawn needed little attending. "Okay," I said, leaving to go check my little yard. The grass was damp and getting wetter by the minute. Not a good time for landscaping. I decided to seek shelter. My picnic table, the one where I had once watched men and now watched ducks, had a sort of awning above it. The mesh netting wasn't much, but it offered some protection. I took my usual morning seat and tried to be happy about the landscape.

It is pretty here, I said, attempting to convince myself. The ducks were playing in the ponds, and there were lots of babies. They were frolicking, loving the light sprinkle and coolness of the day. I buttoned my vinyl brown army-issue type jacket, though it was not even close to being waterproof. When the rain came in earnest, my jacket grew dark. I huddled, tucking my arms down inside the coat, leaving the sleeves free to hang. God, it was cold. I began to shake. Where are they? Are they really going to leave me out here? I looked around. The next building was headquarters for the Lands Out department, and the girls were milling around. I went to join them.

"What are you doing here?" asked the brown Spanish-looking officer.

It was Santa, the girls liked this boss and spoke affectionately about him. Surely, he'd understand. "Just getting out of the rain," I explained. "Everybody left and I'm locked out."

"Well, you can't stay here. There's an inspection today. The big bosses could come any minute."

What big bosses? What inspection? I wondered. What was going on? "Okay, what would you suggest then?"

Santa shrugged. He didn't care. I wasn't his responsibility and he wanted me gone. Rain or no rain, I was out in the cold. I walked away, heading in the direction of my proper area, but when I reached the Water Ops building, I did not stop. I continued my stroll right past the guards and the gates. I was "out of bounds," and now I was the one who didn't care. Go ahead, you assholes. Write me up; see if I give a flip.

I expected to be confronted, but no one stopped me. I managed to get back to my bunk, and once ensconced in my bed, I was one of the many girls with a "lay-in." Girls laid-in every day. They'd go to sick call and profess the flu, or diarrhea, or cramps, or any number of things. Sometimes they had it all—cramps, headache, flu, the whole bit. Those were really sick girls! They got "lay-ins" for days. Because of them, I was invisible. The next day, I paid the price.

The sniffles started that night and the fever hit before dawn. I was sick, miserably so, down with a nasty cold or the flu. I skipped breakfast and went to sick call.

"Judy, you look awful," one of the girls said.

"I feel awful."

"But there's no sick call today."

Impossible! "What do you mean?"

"This is the day the dentist comes," she explained. "The PAs and doctors are off."

"What! But I can't go to work. I'm not capable!"

"Talk to the nurse," interjected one of the women. "Maybe she can write you a lay-in."

No such luck. She wouldn't consider it. It wasn't her place, and she let me know if I didn't go to work, I would suffer the consequences.

It was ludicrous. Who in the heck could control when

they came down with the flu? But of course, girls did. They controlled their illnesses all the time, and I would suffer because of their sham. Since ninety percent of the lay-ins were written to whiners, medical staff did not need to report every day, and since they were off, I was SOL. No lay-in for me.

I went to work, hoping Mr. Gaukler would take pity on me, but he didn't care and neither did his associates. Rules were rules, and the only person who could write a lay-in was the Physician's Assistant. *Damn,* I thought, sniffling. *This sucks.* Thank God I wasn't kicked out again. At least it was warm inside the office.

The walk back to campus at noon was torturous. It was raining, and for the second day in a row I got drenched. I couldn't even think about lunch. My bed was calling me, and when it was time to go back, the rebel in me stood tall. She was the only one capable. I was down for the count. This time I was the one who didn't care. Write me up if you want to. I need sleep.

My angels must have been standing guard because nothing happened. Mr. Gaukler didn't come looking for me and I never heard my name over the loudspeaker. I slept all afternoon and all night. The next morning, on Friday, I got a legitimate "lay in," which meant I was off for three days, one workday and two weekend days, all with Motrin. That was the cure-all. Motrin was the magical remedy. That and psyche drugs. Psyche drugs came easy. Lots of girls were on them, but Motrin was tough. You had to really be sick to get Motrin. You needed at least a temp of 102 to qualify, and that was me. I was burning up. I got my Motrin.

The experience made me feel like a persona non grata again, and I hated being less than nothing. I began to sink. I forgot about the good and got lost in the bad. I wallowed in my misery hoping somebody might notice, but no. The only person who paid attention was Debbie, my roommate, because my continuous hacking kept her awake. Poor baby. In the morning she went off with the appropriate dirty look, and I'd suffer some more. God, how I hated that room.

On Monday I was well enough to report to Mr. Gaukler and he never questioned me. Maybe he felt guilty. After all, he had thrown me out in the cold. He and Santa. God, how I hated them. I hated their condescending attitudes. I hated being treated like a criminal and I hated Camp Phoenix. I hated supporting their slave labor system and I hated Rod. I especially hated Rod. I hated him for loving me and I hated him for hurting me. And I hated myself for letting him.

To state the obvious, I was depressed. I stopped talking to the girls and started lying in my bed. Turning my back to the world, I counted the holes in my blocks of cement. Our walls were made of cinder block and painted a yellowish beige, the same yellowish color of crystal. I spent hours counting those holes. I didn't want to do anything and counting got me through. It helped me not to feel.

That was the prison experience. It was cyclical and inmates learned to cope. We'd keep starting over. We did the same things day and night, and then we'd start again, searching for something, anything that would make us feel less like a prisoner. When the depression hit, we had to get through it by ourselves. Unless you "bust a move," as Lori would say, you were left to your own devices.

So alone I was, locked in the tedious act of disappearing. I even missed the Superbowl! And it was my team! The Broncos were playing and I didn't even care. They'll probably lose again, I rationalized, counting and counting.

But they WON! Thank God. I heard about it and the news stirred me. This is stupid, Judy. This will get you nowhere. Get out of this room; it's killing you.

I busted a move and got out of bed. After circling the track a few times, I asked myself why. Why did I sink into those depressing, yellowish, crystal-like holes? My emotions ran deep, and I needed to root out the negativity. I decided to ring up Rod, who admitted to the drug use.

"You called it, Judy. You were exactly right."

"We're connected, Rod. We're soulmates. When you hurt, I feel your pain."

"But all this time I've been clean. How could you possibly know?"

"It's that glue, honey. We're stuck like glue. Be good to yourself, will you?"

I heard more about Valor, and then Rod talked about a psychiatrist he was seeing. "He's an Albert Einstein fan, Judy. Can you believe it?"

"Everybody is an Einstein fan, Rod," I said.

"I'm reading this really cool book, too," he said, ignoring me. "It was written by a lady from Sedona. Judy, I think we'll end up there. God has told me we will be in Sedona together."

Rod was invading my vision of retiring amongst the red rock. What else would he try to manipulate? "When?" I asked flatly.

"For the day of reckoning! Isn't that great?"

He was animated, but I was appalled. "Rod, you can't be serious?"

My question threw him, and instantly his voice changed. "Judy." The word was raspy. "Judy, don't you believe?" I was shocked by the deep, menacing tone.

I knew Rod was referring to the second coming, but I felt as though his words were meant to strangle me. "Yes, Rod, I believe. I have to go now."

"No, Judy! Please don't hang up yet. Please ..."

The Victim was back. His voice shifted, and the frightened man-child emerged, leaving me shivering. Rod's personality was splintering big time, probably from the recent use of crystal methamphetamines. "Alright. I have a few more minutes, but really, honey, I won't be able to call you anymore."

"Why?" came the cry of anguish. "I need to talk to you, even if it's only for a minute or two. Judy, I need to hear your voice."

"I can't afford it, Rod. Money is precious here. They've disconnected my voicemail number, too. Don't bother leaving any more messages."

"I'll send you money," he said, hearing only what he wanted to hear. "If I send you five hundred dollars, will you call me?"

"Well, sure. I love talking to my Preacher Man," I lied, thinking about the less-than positive conversations.

Rod didn't bother to read between the lines. He was too enamored by my Preacher Man tag. "What do you mean they disconnected your voicemail?"

I explained how the number was removed from my list. "Apparently, one of the officers was listening the other day. I was disconnected when I tried to retrieve your message. Now I can't access the number at all."

I wasn't sure why voice messaging was a no-no. It seemed like another stupid rule. Or maybe I did it to myself. After all, I did ask. I had wanted to block him. *Ask and you will receive,* I thought. *Be careful for what you wish.*

Regardless, Rod didn't seem to mind. It was speaking with me personally that made him happy. Well, no more. I knew the five hundred dollars would never come. After this conversation, it would no longer be an issue. I made the verbal break from Rod, and slept better because of it, but there were other things. El Niño was on the rampage.

Chapter 51

El Nino

IT WAS THE WINTER OF EL NIÑO. Literally, the tides turned and the Atlantic Ocean reversed direction, sweeping a dank foulness into the weather pattern. Tempest winds penetrated the plains and swept into hearts and minds at Camp Phoenix.

"It's Satan," the Christian girls declared. "El Niño is the work of the devil. It's a sign of the times."

I began to wonder. Maybe the atmospheric shift did have a negative effect on us. Certainly my little world seemed to be in an uproar.

"RECALL! RECALL!" resounded the commanding voice. Over the speakers, we were being ordered back to the barracks. "ONE WAY MOVEMENT BACK TO YOUR HOUSING UNITS! RECALL!"

"What's going on?" I asked.

My question was directed at Debbie. She returned to the room shortly after me, and I asked without thinking.

"It's the men," she responded casually. "They're staging a protest."

Camp Phoenix was next door to a men's federal correction institution, a real prison, one complete with guard towers, high fences, and razor wire. We, the women, supported the men. We tended the grounds, maintained the sewage system, ordered and stocked the food, and did numerous other things that kept the "real" prison functioning. I learned this was typical. Camps were always attached to FCIs.

"A protest!" I said. "What do you mean?"

"The men are pissed. There could be a riot!"

"What's that got to do with us? Why are we locked down?"

Debbie didn't seem to mind explaining. "They say it's for our protection."

I didn't get it. Surely no one could escape. We couldn't possibly be in imminent danger. "Well, what exactly are they doing?" I asked.

"They're striking. They've refused to work, and they are not coming out of their cells."

"That sounds kind of stupid. Why would the guards care? If the men are behind bars, what difference does it make?"

"Right now, none, but it could get nasty. They've been known to destroy property, instigate confrontations. Generally, they'll do anything to get attention."

It didn't make sense. Lock them up and let them starve, I thought. Eventually they'll come around. "What's the beef?"

Debbie wasn't sure, but after three days Laura told me. She and some other women were sent over for kitchen duty. They made sandwiches and performed other menial tasks.

"You were actually inside?" I asked. "What was it like?"

"Weird," she said. "Everything is huge. I had to climb inside a mixer to clean it. It was awful! And there are cameras everywhere. Every room is either barred or locked. It's totally spooky."

"Yuck. Did you see any of the guys?"

"Not even close, but the officers are talking. Guess they're worried the situation might escalate. They especially don't want the media to get wind of this."

"Why?"

"Because it will cost them. Public sympathy could sway things for the men. Right now, the authorities want the whole thing settled."

I learned the men were upset about the seven a.m. rule. All inmates, regardless of work duty, had to leave their cells by seven a.m. Monday through Friday. That meant those working on weekends never got extra sleep. No down time for inmates assigned to the kitchen, for example.

The men were angry about the size of their lockers, too. Apparently, they had the same tiny ones we did. Women had trouble cramming their possessions into those closets, so I couldn't imagine big burly men doing it. One coat would nearly fill the space, so where would the uniforms go? If the same rules applied, nothing could be left out. Cells had to be perfectly pristine, and not one piece of clothing could be visible. Boots and shoes could go under the bed, but that was it. No wonder the men were screaming.

Beds were also an issue. The mattresses, or at least some of them, were too thin. That was a beef I understood. When I first arrived, my bunk had one of those scrawny pads on it. I noticed other girls with much thicker mattresses; wider, too. Why did some girls have good ones when others slept on skinny sheathes of plastic? It was another one of those prison inequities. The only way to obtain a good mattress was to claim the object from a departing inmate. Fortunately, Diane had willed hers to me. She had received her walking papers, and although I missed her, I was more than happy to inherit her bed. Yes! My back had received a reprieve!

"I can relate to that one," I said. "They'd better not try

to confiscate my bed. I'd go on strike, too."

Lockdown was only three days for us, but staying inside those walls with the loud, obnoxious swearing drove me crazy; nearly got me killed, too.

The nights were the worst. You'd think when the lights went out, girls would quiet down, but no. Some women had no consideration for others, none whatsoever. Goldie was one of them, and unfortunately, she lived right next door.

Goldie was big and black, and attitude was her middle name. She ruled in Hopi B, and many girls followed her lead. Maybe it was her beautiful singing voice that attracted those drones. I didn't understand, but nevertheless, she had a fan club, and she was venting on the third night.

I had a bad case of cabin fever.

"QUIET!" I erupted. I tried to catch the word, but it spewed forth; out into the dark halls it went, ricocheting into the night. Where did that come from? I wondered.

"E-X-C-U-S-E ME?" Goldie said, exaggerating her disbelief.

I remained shocked by my utterance.

"Some people have no manners," she yelled. She was speaking to her clan, wanting them to know she had been grievously disrespected. "You could at least have the decency to speak to me in person."

I was still. Quiet as a church mouse.

"How RUDE!"

I nearly broke my silence. RUDE? You're the one who's rude!

Goldie raged for a few more minutes and then, amazingly, she shut up. I went to sleep.

The next morning, I was on my way out of the chow hall when Yolanda accosted me. "Hey, Judy!" she hollered.

I stopped halfway through the door. Yolanda was drying her hands on the apron that protected her from the filth of the kitchen. She had been washing dishes.

"What's up?" I asked, without feeling threatened. We were friends, or at least we were on friendly terms. We had worked together before my transfer, and she attended the Prison Fellowship Bible study. Her appearance was intimidating, but I knew her large mass and bulging eyes masked a caring heart.

"Was that you?" she asked. "Were you the one who told Goldie to shut up?"

I laughed. The look on her face was comical. I thought her big dark pupils might pop out. "Yes. Can you believe it? I stuck my foot in my mouth. It just popped out."

"Girl," she warned. "Don't you know where you are? This is prison, Girl. You're liable to wake up one morning with your hair glued to the pillow."

The image struck me as funny. Poor Yolanda, she was worried. I tried to appease her. "It's El Niño," I said. "The ole demon got to me. He's making us act stupid."

She seemed satisfied, and I sensed the information might get back to Goldie in the form of an apology, of course. Regardless, I refused to worry about it. I simply went about my business. Problem was, Laura wasn't taking care of hers. El Niño had gotten to her as well, and she had become complacent about typing my manuscript.

"I'm sorry, Judy. I've been sick. I'll get back to the book tomorrow."

"Laura, we've got to keep moving on this. I need to get something to my agent; otherwise, she won't believe I'm serious about the project."

"I know and I want to. Typing for you fills up my day. It passes the time and makes me feel like I'm doing something constructive. Really, I love it. I'll get a chapter back to you tomorrow."

But she didn't. It was one excuse after another and I

started considering alternatives. I needed a finished product. If Laura didn't want to help, I might have to type it myself. Now that I understood the rules, I was less willing to break them. Barter and trade were NOT allowed—God forbid!

By Sunday, February 15th, the day after Valentine's Day, the day after I got no card from my so-called soulmate, I was sick to death of El Niño. Wanting to be rid of the demon and the negativity, I reached for my little purple bag. "Face your fears," the spark said. "Feel it. Let go!"

What! But I am. I have been. I felt let down. I needed a lift, not a lecture. Besides, hadn't I been rolling with the flow? Hadn't I stayed away from those depressing holes?

Defiantly, I climbed up onto my bunk. I did not, however, turn to my wall. Instead, I pulled a light cover over me and crossed my arms. This was my posture for meditating. The blanket kept me warm and the prone position kept girls from wondering. Sitting up with my legs crossed drew too much attention. It made girls curious and I preferred being inconspicuous. I began with the prayer, and then, after calling for protection, I initiated my mantra. "God is love," I said in Sanskrit. "God is love." Over and over, I repeated the holy word. When I was deeply relaxed, I asked for guidance. "Lord, Jesus, help me. I don't understand. If it is not your will that I write this book, then give me a sign. If it is your will, then show me a way."

Call it a miracle, call it coincidence, or don't call it anything at all. To me it was a sign, and not to pay attention would have been blasphemous. It was the voice of God, or at least it was the voice of one of his servants.

"Ladies," announced the chaplain. "We have a clerk-typist position opening here at the Chapel. Anyone wishing to apply should do so within the next two weeks. Please submit your cop-out through proper channels."

Cop-out was a generic prison request form. Anything you wanted, needed, or disagreed with had to be stated on a "cop-out." Without a "cop-out" you were persona non grata. You, your request, or your grievance counted for nothing unless properly presented.

"Typist!" I said from the far reaches of my mind. "Did he say typist?"

I had spent many hours at the chapel of late and I had seen that typewriter. It was gathering dust sitting next to the clerk's desk. It was never used, and in fact, I rarely saw the clerk either. The chaplain wasn't even there. Except for Sunday services, he was pretty much invisible. Exactly what I need! A typewriter and an incognito boss. I decided to apply.

"Chaplain Borman," I wrote. "I am interested in your clerk's position. Currently, I am a grade two clerk, working for the Water Operations department, but my duties encompass maintaining a small yard. This concerns me, because the doctors ordered me to 'run from the sun' after finding skin cancer, a melanoma. I was lucky the first time, but I do not want to tempt fate. Perhaps, if you're considering another applicant, she could replace me. Mr. Gaukler is a fair man and a good supervisor."

Knowing a transfer would be nearly impossible, I did not go through the required channels. I bypassed my counselor and put the request directly under Father Borman's door. Then I prayed. I also kept silent. I told no one about my ambition.

Inmates were not supposed to transfer for the first ninety days. No matter how unsuited they were to that first assignment, they were stuck, or at least that was the premise. I already pulled rank once, and without even realizing it, I jumped two levels in pay. I went from a grade four to a grade two. We all started at a level four, which was twelve cents an hour. Getting a raise required time and a lot of sucking up. My Water Op's position was a grade two, a whopping thirty-five cents an hour. Wow! That was nearly enough to keep me in tampons and shampoo! Unfortunately, my newly acquired wealth made other girls jealous. Knowing they'd really hate it if I received a second new assignment, and especially this one, I remained quiet.

I returned to my bunk, took up my meditation pose, and considered the Spark, "Face your fears. Feel it. Let go." Just what did they mean? I was no longer intimidated by the girls and I was trying to break the ice with Debbie. Rod wasn't a worry, for I refused to listen. I transcended the depths and breeched the boundaries of space and time. There within the comforting glow, within the divine calmness, I found my answer. I was holding on to fear, and was, in fact, holding on to it for dear life.

It was the prospect of testifying! I feared it in the worst way, so much so I thought about not cooperating. I was considering saying, "No."

Three years wasn't all that long. Like Vicki said, "I could do that much time standing on my head." Of course, she got nearly twenty years.

Maybe it was El Niño, but I hated the idea of taking the stand. Those two men had been my friends. If Chris and Rich went to trial and were found guilty, which was highly likely, how many years would they face? A lifetime, maybe? God, I hated to think about it, and yes, I feared it! I feared for them and I feared for me. How would I handle this imminent situation? How would the Feds handle me if I dared say "No?"

"Okay," I said, coming from the depths with my acknowledgment. "I feel it. I feel fear and it's tangible. How do I let it go?"

"Trust."

A simple response, too simple perhaps, but it came from a source I was learning to recognize. The next day, I went to the phones and called my attorney.

"Hi, Judy," she said. "How's it going? Are you doing alright?"

I could sense she was busy. I envisioned her crown of red cropped hair, ear pressed to the phone, giving me a cursory moment, but no more. Fear gripped me. Was she trying to write me off? The retainer was long gone. "I'm fine, Karen. Have you heard anything about the trials? Are you still in touch with the Feds?"

"Yes, and they still intend to use you. The trials have been postponed again, but don't worry, Judy. We'll get you out of there. I'm on this until the bitter end. We've been through too much these last two years. I'm not going anywhere."

One question answered, thank God.

"Okay, thanks," I said, letting go of that portion of fear. I needed to place my fate in Karen's capable hands. The future of my former young bosses would be handed over to God.

CHAPTER 52

A Confirmation

EL NIÑO DID EVENTUALLY PASS, but not before calamity struck at my Las Vegas home. If I hadn't been distracted with work, I might have been more upset, but realizing my renters, my so-called friends, were screwing me over was only an annoyance. It didn't send me to the wall again.

I knew trusting my house and my worldly goods to Lester and Trish was a risk, but at the time, I was too weak to do anything else. Besides, I wanted to help Trish. Too bad she was married to that slob of a husband. Too bad for her as well as me. My mortgage payment had not been made and I needed to do something.

Lazy beer-drinking fool, I said to myself. Lester probably lost another job. Well, shame on me for thinking he might change. You could lead a man to hope, but you couldn't save his soul.

"Will you find me an agent, Pam?" I asked my daughter, knowing eviction was necessary. "I need a good leasing company, one willing to hire people and pack me out."

"Oh, God," she said sadly.

"What? What's the matter? You don't have to do anything. Just make the call. I'll cover the costs."

"Mom, I can't deal with this."

My daughter was on the verge of tears. "Pam, it's not that difficult. All you need do is make a phone call."

"No, I mean life!"

She started to cry. "Honey, you're stronger than this. What happened? Why are you so upset?"

"I'm such a bad mother! I can't do anything right with these girls."

My heart ripped. Pam was a terrific mother. Maybe she doted on her girls too much, occasionally she was overly protective, that kind of thing, but she never failed them, not even remotely. "You've got a tough job, honey. It's not easy raising two little ones alone, but don't worry, Jason will be home before you know it."

"I called Marie a hag!" she cried.

A hag? What an image. I pictured my two-year-old granddaughter with a hook nose and buck teeth. "You're kidding! Why a hag?"

"I don't know ... she was being a brat. I feel awful."

That I could understand. But a hag? I wanted to laugh. Of course, I didn't. This was serious stuff. "That's it, Pam? That's all you did? You didn't beat her or anything?"

"No," she said, beginning to calm.

I let go of a small giggle. "Well, maybe she deserved it. Maybe she was being haggy."

"You don't think I'm awful then?"

She was lightening up. "God, no! Are you kidding? Pam, none of us are perfect. The only thing we can do is give ourselves permission to make mistakes. Trust me, Marie will not hold this against you. She won't even remember it. In fact, she's probably forgotten already."

"Really?"

"Yes, really. God knows I made plenty of mistakes with you kids. You can't beat yourself up over this."

"Thanks," she said, sniffling. "I hate him, Mom. I can't help it. I just hate him."

"Who?" Was she mad at Jason now?

"That fat slob of a renter. Lester, that's who! He's such an ass. How can he do this to you?"

"Beats me. I'll bet his wife doesn't even know. Why don't you call Trish? Maybe she can get him to ante up. At least she might try."

"Okay; guess it's worth a shot."

It was worth the effort. They made the payment, but the whole sordid episode made me question other things.

Surrender ... give up control ... become the observer ... all those roll-with-the-flow sparks were giving me fits. Sedona Shelia had warned me, but having heard the message didn't make it easier. Rolling with the flow was becoming difficult, because I had a dream and it was dying. I was still producing handwritten pages, but they were going nowhere.

If it hadn't been for the job, I might have retreated to my wall, but I got it! God granted me favor, putting me in the most perfect place to continue my work.

"You'll be working weekends," said the Catholic priest.

Chaplain Borman was a tall, gaunt man. He looked like he had lived in a monk's cell most of his life, but I knew better. This man who was old enough to be my father had been a federal servant for a long time. He had eaten plenty of chow hall meals, probably lots of fattening wieners and such. Still, he appeared healthy for his age and his voice was soft. It reminded me of a light evening breeze, flowing without measure, without care.

My predecessor, the previous clerk, had called him condescending, but I didn't agree. He might have been too busy, maybe he didn't take enough time with the girls, perhaps he rushed through services, but condescending?

Never. He was far too saintly.

"Weekends are fine," I said, jumping for joy. That would mean I'd be off when things were quiet.

"The ladies will try to take advantage of you. They'll want you to play favorites, give them extra cards and yarn, that sort of thing."

Twice a week, each girl could order three greeting cards free of charge. Hallmark made this possible and it was a wonderful perk. As the chapel clerk, I would be responsible for delivering those orders. I would also be responsible for doling out the yarn. Yarn was donated by an outside group, and then girls made things for the homeless. It was another commendable enterprise, but in the past, it hadn't been controlled. The stockpile of yarn was diminishing, but completed items were not returning.

"I am not easily intimidated, Father," I said.

A twinkle appeared in his light grayish-blue eyes. "You can call me Chaplain, Judy. We're nondenominational here. No favoritism allowed."

I was tickled. The word allowed stirred me. "None whatsoever, sir. You have my word on that."

"It's probably best if you work evenings," he said. "You especially need to be here after dinner. Certain groups have been trying to take over the chapel. I've had complaints."

I had seen it. Goldie and her group used the place to practice their music. They called it choir practice, but I hadn't heard anything remotely religious. "Evenings are fine. I prefer having my mornings off. It gives me more quiet time."

"Good, but I'm flexible on that one. Let me know if you have anything special going on, otherwise, plan on one till eight p.m. You'll need to start disbursing the groups by 7:45, eight to eight-thirty is designated for quiet time, for prayer and contemplation."

"I can do that."

"I won't be here much. We're short-staffed. A new chaplain is due to start this fall, but right now the FCI requires most of my time."

Yes! Just as I thought. "No problem, Father—I mean, Chaplain. I'm not the kind of person who needs supervision."

A smile cracked the edges of his too-thin lips. "Yes, I can see that you're a cut above. I'll look to you for direction. You can create a system for sharing, so the ladies have equal opportunity. I don't want anyone dominating the audio or video rooms either. You put procedures in place and I'll back you up. Maybe we could start weighing and logging the yarn."

A cut above! Did he just tell me I might have value? I was thrilled! "Thank you, Father. I won't let you down. And weighing sounds perfect. Can you get me a scale?"

"Chaplain," he said. "Call me Chaplain Borman."

I never did get used to calling him Chaplain. It was that Episcopalian upbringing of mine. Our priests were called "Father" and "Father" he remained. After some time, Chaplain Borman gave up and I rather think he enjoyed being called Father. It made him feel more like a Catholic priest, less of a persona non denomina.

We set up a system and everything fell into place. Girls resented my control tactics for a while, but then everybody started appreciating my sense of fairness. Choir was allowed to practice, but only at specific times and never without their leader. Books were checked out, videos were reserved, and all sorts of services, including Bible studies were accommodated. Everybody learned that when yarn went out, it had to come back as a completed piece, otherwise I'd cut off the offender; no more free yarn. Knowing the project was the real deal, the girls got excited about participating. They couldn't wait to check out yarn, and they proudly returned with the cutest things imaginable.

I started producing typewritten pages and I was able to help others while doing so.

"How's the job?" Laura asked one day.

"I love it! I couldn't be happier."

"Really? Don't you hate working weekends?"

"God, no. What did I ever do on weekends except go crazy trying to find a place to write?"

"I suppose, but I miss typing for you."

I doubted it. "Well, if you need anything, if you come up short on cash or something, let me know. I'll still help."

"Thanks, Babe. That's good to know. How's Rod doing? I miss hearing about him, too."

Now that I believed. "I wouldn't know. I've totally cut him off. I still write an occasional letter, but I don't call him and I can't pick up his messages. Basically, he's out of my life."

"That'll be the day," she said, calling a spade a spade.

I looked offended, but she was right. I still missed my Rod. "He was screwing me up, Laura. I had to sever the ties. They were killing me."

"Me, too! Wow, I hope I never have leg cramps like that again."

"The man has power," I said. "I'm telling you he knows things, and he can do things like I've never seen."

"He'll be okay. He needs time, but he'll make it. Right now, you're right, though. You should stay away from him. He's most definitely bad for you."

"Rod is my demon."

Laura tossed her ponytail sideways and laughed. "And you are his," she said matter-of-factly.

"Hey," I said defensively, rising from the circular cement picnic bench. "That's not fair."

"Chill, child. You said it yourself. Rod thinks you are

betraying him with the book. He's scared shitless the truth will come out. Thinking about it is making him crazy."

"You're right!" I returned to my seat. "I swear, sometimes I think he's possessed."

I got the G-I-R-L look from Laura. She said nothing, but I heard it all the same.

"Honestly, Laura. I heard it in his voice. One time we were talking about the second coming and his tone changed completely. What came out was so menacing, so evil, it gave me shivers. I hung up as fast as I could."

"What did he say?" she asked, incredulous.

"He asked me if I believed. He wanted to know if I believed in Jesus Christ."

"You do, don't you?"

I was not getting my point across. "Yes, but not like other people. I don't believe Jesus died for our sins. I think he came to teach us, to show us the way, but I do not believe his sacrifice has freed us from sin.

"Don't you see? Rod had a problem with that. If he knew my basic ideology remains intact, then it would make the whole laying-on-hands thing a farce."

Laura looked fondly at me. "Well, why then would that bring out the demonic in him? Why wouldn't the devil be happy to hear your soul is still in jeopardy?"

"Because," I cried, "that is exactly what Satan wants! He wants us to believe we are free. He wants us to accept the idea of instant atonement. It makes his job easier."

"I follow. If you were quote 'saved,' then you would think your place in heaven was guaranteed, no matter what, right?"

"Sort of. The Church likes to promote that, doesn't it? Christian leaders bank on their flock not being accountable. It makes sin totally irrelevant, completely forgivable. People repent and then continue living the same old way. Now that's a sin! It excuses the worst kind of behavior and makes members of the church think they are impervious to universal laws."

"What laws?" she asked, taking a more serious interest.

"The law of karma, for instance. The law what goes around, comes around."

"I believe that," she said.

"Well, good, but it's easy to forget if you believe Christ died for your sins. That's why Rod's voice changed. Don't you see? That's why the demon emerged. Satan knew I hadn't been brainwashed and he was trying to reach through the telephone line to strangle me."

"Spooky."

"Seriously, Laura. That's exactly how it felt."

Sharing that story with Laura was cathartic, but it didn't spare me from further attack. Satan was busy and the more I learned about spiritual warfare, the more he made his presence known.

"Does anyone here watch Oprah?" asked Mary Lou one night at Bible study.

Hands shot up and I offered commentary. "She's terrific," I said. "Her show is one of my favorites."

The sugary-sweet voice of our Wednesday night volunteer was suddenly coated in grit. Her sandpaper rasp let me know I had committed a major faux pas. "Girls, we really need to pray for Oprah. I fear she's gone down the wrong path."

Why? I wondered. What could Oprah have possibly done to offend this Christian lady? I could think of no celebrity more vocal about Christ. She even cried crocodile tears because of His goodness.

"Have you seen this thing she does with her hands, holding them up for Spirit? That trance-like state she's promoting is dangerous!"

I had seen it, but my opinion was altogether different. I thought she was setting a wonderful example! Oprah was courageous enough to display her love for soulful prayer and I admired her effort. What could be wrong with that? Personally, I thought she deserved great kudos. Nothing wrong with nurturing the spirit, and if it caught on, the world might be a better place. Wasn't that the point? Oprah cared and she wasn't afraid to say so. Lord, there should be a thousand Oprahs—fewer Jerry Springers and more Oprahs.

The girls were nodding, bobbing heads all around, except for me. I was flabbergasted; this bobbing was a bad thing!

Ralph spoke next. "Yes, ladies, we must be careful. There are many false prophets."

Oh, my God! You have got to be kidding! I nearly got out of my chair and walked out. Calm down, Judy, I admonished. No church is perfect. You need to take the good with the bad. Practice discernment. Listen and learn, girl. Become the observer.

The conversation turned toward meditation and how it opened a door to evil. Fear is the greatest enemy, I thought. Fear opens the door, not meditation. Thank God these people didn't know I meditated daily, sometimes twice a day. I considered speaking but listened instead. Ralph and Mary Lou were entitled to their opinions, but I would not accept their dogma.

Another time, the round circle discussion turned to exorcism. Many of the girls seemed to be acquainted with the subject. Their experiences were nothing like mine, but I was still interested.

"But have you seen one?" I asked. "Have you attended an exorcism? Do demons manifest in the flesh? Can you touch them?"

My questions brought silence. No one could specifically

tell me how devils looked. *Figures*, I thought. *These people are clueless. They're no help at all.* One woman finally recommended a book. At least I got that.

"If you're really interested, Judy," she said. "If you're serious, then read *I Come to Set My People Free*, but be prepared and pray. Pray before you read it and pray each day it's in your possession."

"Yes," echoed another voice. "That's an incredible read. Very scary stuff!"

What in the hell could be so scary? Didn't these women know demons were the world's greatest cowards? Those tortured souls are afraid of us! And claiming victory sent them running; even witches could be conquered in the blink of an eye, literally. I knew. I had done it.

"Thanks," I said. "I'll ask my mother to send it."

She did mail it, but the book never arrived. I waited and waited, but it never came.

"I don't know what happened, Mom, but I never got it. Maybe I'm not supposed to read it."

"Maybe not," she said.

But why? And who was waylaying the source of information? Was it my angels? Or was Satan involved? I started to believe it was the demon, for why would my celestial friends care? Knowledge is power. It leads to Truth and isn't that a good thing?

Thinking I might meditate on the subject, I climbed up to my bunk. It was a quiet morning and my day off. I had all the time in the world.

"Blessings Heavenly Father, Earthly Mother," I began. I always started with the prayer. I believed in asking for protection, but by now I was also donning the "full armor of God." The concept had been taught in Bible study and it suited me. I often felt like a soldier, so in my mind, I began looking like one, too.

"Bless this belt, oh Lord. This belt of truth, bless it, lest I stray."

After the belt, I put on the breastplate, imagining myself tying up the laces. When I was righteously secured, I strapped on the helmet, protecting myself from guilt, fear, and doubt. The shoes of readiness came next, PF Flyers. They had to be fast. Like a kid, I wanted to be ready. I was a Warrior, standing for Jesus, and fully armored. Finally, I took up the sword of the spirit and the shield of faith. I loved the image. Proud and tall, regal in my gear, and invincible, nothing could interfere with my meditation now. On this day, it was remarkably easy. The halls were quiet, and I soon transcended.

In the background, I was aware of activity. Someone had entered my space, but departed quickly, probably checking to see if I was asleep. Well, whoever it was would come back. I repeated my mantra and went further. Quiet. Quiet. I felt the vibration, the cleansing of the soul. It was perfectly divine.

"She's in there," said the voice a little later.

I paid no attention. Deeper, deeper. Relax, Judy. Let go. Roll with the flow.

"BURR!"

The powerful voice startled me. In my face! I began to emerge.

"BURR, MS. JUDY BURR!" the officer yelled.

I opened my eyes and turned slowly toward the obnoxious interruption. A uniform greeted me, a woman in gray. Behind her were two girls, one black, one white, and they looked like they had seen a ghost. The black girl's eyes were wide and staring.

"Are you alright?" asked the woman wearing the uniform. "These girls thought you were dead."

"I'm fine," I said. "I was meditating."

"You sure?" she asked, as the girls backed out of my cubicle. They were visibly upset.

"Yes, I'm sure. Thank you for your concern, though."

"She's fine," the short, squatty officer told the disbelievers. "She was meditating."

I was slow to get up, but when I passed those two in the hall, they reminded me of Lazarus' kin. Dead man rising—or dead woman, in this case. *Great. Now the whole camp will know I meditate. Just great.*

I was worried about the possible ramifications and needed to vent, but when I called my mother, she wasn't much help. She thought it was hilarious and laughed till she cried. "Judy, that is too funny! They thought you were dead?"

"Yes, they were ready to claim my damn mattress. Can you imagine! I know meditation slows the metabolism, but I never dreamed someone would think I was dead."

She couldn't stop laughing, and finally she got me laughing, too. It was funny, and as to the consequences ... there weren't any, at least, none that bothered me. Fully armored, I was comfortable with my spiritual practices. I knew God and I was growing fonder of Jesus. The Bible study had done that for me. I hadn't internalized the doctrines, but my respect for the Christ child was on the rise. I'd follow you anywhere, Jesus, I said, thinking about my prayer. I had called him the "supreme teacher," poetic words, rising spontaneously. As I was remembering, my angels swept in for confirmation, tickling my neck and fluttering through my chest. I smiled. The sensation was divine. Thank you, my friends. Thank you.

CHAPTER 53

The Remembering

IN THE BEGINNING, God created the heavens and the earth. In the beginning, I had been told it would get easier. Those words hadn't done much for me in the early days. I simply couldn't imagine. But as time passed, it was getting easier, remarkably so. Each morning I'd sit at my desk and draft a new chapter, and each afternoon I'd type it. In the evenings I was a peacemaker; sometimes I'd attend the various classes, other times I'd listen to audio tapes.

Lessons were still coming, which I was happy to share. I'd talk to the girls and they'd tell me their stories, some of them heavily laden with sadness. I did my best to focus on the positive and often I'd succeed, other times I wouldn't. If tears started to flow, that was okay. A stream of tears could heal. It was that connection thing, clearly an example of Redfield's last insight. People in our lives are probably souls from relationships over many lifetimes, souls who need help, souls who compel us to be courageous and to act.

So true. We helped each other any way we could, and we compelled ourselves to be courageous. It was that prison mentality, the us against them theme, except I had gone beyond the camp definition. I was hooked up to some of my camp sisters in a very special way, but I was also able to empathize with staff members. And what a burden they carried! I did not envy them, not in the least. By day they were responsible for our welfare—totally responsible—and at the end of their shifts, they had to face family and finances. Nope, I did not see their jobs as easy. At least the world of inmates never changed, it was completely predictable, so maybe we were the lucky ones.

You might say I was "seeing" in a whole new way. There was a kind of transparency to people, as though I could feel them, sense their joy, their sorrow. And that Angel's Quarter Mile ... why, it began to shimmer. On many occasions, that black concrete disappeared beneath my feet. I couldn't understand it, but these were times when I felt airborne, light as a feather. Other times, the asphalt appeared wave-like, rolling into hills and valleys. I'd soar ahead, but always climbing, never falling. Of course, it was my imagination, as our track was completely level.

I knew athletes sometimes called this euphoria "the zone," and maybe it was the endorphins, I didn't know. What I did know was the track was magical and I had marvelous revelations while walking it.

One day I was giving thanks, generally being grateful, and as an afterthought, I thanked God for my mother.

Wow! What a shock! I had really hit on something. Those angel wings nearly knocked me off my feet! The waves were profound and lasted a long time, longer than any of my other featherings. I nearly dropped to my knees.

Yes, I said quietly. I am grateful for my mother. Thank you, Mom. I couldn't have done it without you.

More tickling. It was kinder, gentler now, but it was still there.

I recalled the times my mother had hurt me, the times she spoke harshly, and the time she sent me that hateful birthday wish. "Maybe in the next lifetime," she had written. Those words had ripped at my heart, but now I could see her wisdom. Without her powerful lessons, I would not have toughened up. I would have faced this prison experience unprepared and until this last angelic shaking, I had not understood.

Mom knew, I realized. She knew all along. It was a subconscious knowing, but she knew I would be doing some time.

Oh, my gosh. She's been preparing me.

My mother had, in fact, always provided, sometimes kindly, sometimes harshly, but she had always been there and with love.

She had loved me in the last lifetime, too. I had disappointed her, grieved her tremendously by bearing a baby out of wedlock, and then marrying the man who made me give up that child. "What a waste of a college education," I imagined her saying. "What a waste of intelligence."

Yes, I had hurt her, but she was still with me. She came to share another earthly experience, and we were learning together, growing together. God, how I loved her. My heart filled with admiration and respect. Again, I wanted to drop to my knees.

On another day, I hit the track shortly after reading the introduction to yet another book that had magically surfaced. It was entitled, Awakening to Zero Point, and Gregg Braden's words quickened my spirit. So many thoughts rang true.

I had been lost! I had no idea who I was or for what purpose I had come. Thank God for Rod! Thank God for all that grief he gave me. At least he shocked me into remembering.

I was recalling all sorts of things. I was especially seeing into a lifetime that predated Jesus Christ, and I was pretty sure I was this Judith character, the one who chopped off the enemy's head.

Even James Redfield, the author of The Celestine Prophecy, had talked about the remembering. It was in relationship to prison reform, but the insight had been inspiring.

Amazing, I thought. This process is incredible, fascinating. Thank you, my angels. I love these divine coincidences.

Most definitely, that quarter mile was a good place for illumination, but my most profound experience came when I wasn't trying to remember anything. Rather, I had been thinking about Rod.

By then, he had started to write and was making a noble effort at being positive. Mary Ann, his wife, was also corresponding, and I was getting a clear sense of her happiness. In some ways I was jealous, but I was a realist. Rod and I were not meant to be together, not permanently, not in this lifetime anyway. I believed we had joined for good reason, but I also thought our work was mostly done.

I had successfully assumed the role of the older woman, and somehow, despite all the abuse, I had not failed to love him. I would always love him, in fact, and now, because of me, he would heal from old wounds, wounds that had once sent him to an institution. He, in turn, had set me free. Because of Rod, I renewed my spiritual quest, and I was pursuing my dream, my purpose in life. Mary Ann played her part as well, and I was thinking about this when it happened. It was an epiphany, not one induced by angel wings, but one that came straight from my heart.

"Oh my God," I said. "I have done it! I finally made it!"

Tears! Tears of joy! They were streaming down my face. All that pain, all that sacrifice, had not been for nothing. I had not joined the conspiracy and because of my sacrifice, a friendship had been saved. Love, not money, had triumphed, and, yes, it was worth it.

Suddenly, I wanted to celebrate! I wanted to jump for joy and there was a special date approaching, one that provided the perfect excuse. It was nearly March 9th. One year had passed since our infamous Day of Reckoning. In my mind, it was our anniversary, an anniversary of soulmates.

A day to remember.

I picked out a special card, one covered in symbolic pictures, stars and stripes, lots of fireworks, that sort of thing. Then I composed a nice long letter to Rod, wishing him a happy celebration and offering my heartfelt thanks. "Thank you for setting me free, my friend. Thank you for saving my soul."

In my private journal I wrote, "We are entering the Age of Accountability, a beautiful age, and a new age indeed, one of many Uncommon Partnerships."

When March 9th, the Day of Reckoning, arrived I pulled down my Bible. I turned to the place where it all began and there—preserved forever—was a verse I would never forget, Proverbs 9:1-6.

I had read those words shortly after Rod had laid hands on me. Amazingly, they had made sense! Now, one year later, the meaning was clearer yet. I had built that house. It was the house of belief and because I "believed," I was secure in my relationship with God. Those seven columns sounded like my flower: Love, Heart, Hope, Forgiveness, Truth, Trust, and Faith.

Remarkable.

Furthermore, I had killed an animal. The beast of greed had died at my feet. Yes, my spices were mixed, and the table was set. I wanted to shout it to the world. "Come people. Leave your dogma! Open your minds and hearts and follow the way of knowledge. Believe and you will see!"

Miraculous? I thought so. At the very least, a divine

coincidence. "Wisdom has built her house and made seven columns for it." March 9th was most assuredly a day worth remembering.

CHAPTER 54

Wings

MOUNTED ON THE WINGS of an eagle, renewed in strength and spirit, that's how I felt after that powerful revelation. I had believed before, but now my faith went beyond the sublime. Forgiveness became unnecessary because I no longer harbored grudges. My once-upon-a-time enemies were anything but. They had played their parts, but that was all. I couldn't even blame my ex-husband, Speicher. He had called out the federal dogs, but that was part of the divine comedy. He had also suffered horribly before his death, which I decided must have been intended as well, probably some serious karma. It was a mystery, yet it was not. I labeled my history intriguing, and as I settled into that attitude, confirmations came.

"Hi, Judy. Got a minute?"

It was the voice of my Hindu friend, Sue Sharma, the lady who had made a bleak attempt to learn bridge. She had not been adept, but we remained friends. I looked up from my typewriter, momentarily regretting the interruption. "Sure, what's up?" I asked. "Grab a chair from inside the chapel. Take a load off."

Sue smiled shyly, obviously needing some reassurance.

"You sure? I can come back later."

"No, no," I said, stepping out from behind my desk, retrieving the chair myself. When she sat down, I noticed her hair, it was getting thinner and grayer. The auburn pageboy had lost its luster and was hanging drearily at the collar, a sad complement to her drab green uniform shirt. "What's the matter, Sue? You look tired."

"I haven't been sleeping. I don't know what's wrong."

Old news. Sue went to bed late and got up early. She preferred stewing and brewing to sleeping and complained readily to anyone who would listen. On this afternoon, I was reminded of an old teakettle, one left to burn low, whining the day and its contents away. I wondered if she'd start complaining about her husband again.

When I had learned of his betrayal, I felt outraged. What kind of a man would make his wife a scapegoat? But, like her lack of sleep, it was old news. She obviously had no intention of leaving her betrayer, so why talk about him? According to her, she was the business wizard. She was capable of rebuilding, so why rehash the tired story?

"I'm sorry," I said, trying to be sympathetic. If only she'd trust herself. If only she'd divorce that asshole. "Have you talked to the PA about it? Maybe they need to adjust your meds."

"Yes, and yesterday I got a double dose, but now my dreams are waking me up."

Sue scrunched her brows, causing deep caverns to spread across her dark-skinned forehead. Relax, Sue. You are growing old before my eyes. "What was it? What did you dream?"

"It was the strangest thing. I was an ice cube. Isn't that weird?"

A shiver passed through me. I was relieved hubby wasn't involved, but amazed, because I, too, had been dreaming about cubes, not ice cubes, but cubes, nonetheless. Those visions started after Rod rehashed his triangle theory, the one about earth mirroring the heavens and him being the conduit to truth. Somehow the concept captured my imagination, and one night I went to bed thinking about the geometric design.

Triangles attached themselves to one another and the diamond design created a cataclysm of color, casting rainbows into the universe. Father, Son, and Holy Ghost, I thought. *But you, Rod, are not the conduit. You are not the earthly messenger, my friend. That position is held by angels.*

The image was spectacular, and as it traveled through space and time, I was calmed by the white light. My mind's eye enveloped the sight, but amid my seeing, something went wrong. There was a sudden thrust, and the celestial body rocketed away, threatening a nearby star. I watched, expecting a calamitous collision, but there was no show of fireworks. Rather than burst upon the neighbor, the night diamond simply fell from grace. It lost its luster and sank toward oblivion, leaving me in utter darkness. "No! Come back! Don't leave now!"

My cries were unheeded. The mirroring triangle was abandoning my dreams. "Balance!" I screamed. "Seek balance."

Far away I saw a glimmer, an iridescent glow, rising on the horizon. *Thank God.*

Tears came and I brushed them away, clearing a path to my guiding light. Good. I can see again. But the shape was different. Amazingly, the celestial body had changed. It was no longer triangular, nor was it a diamond, but it had moved into another dimension. I was viewing a cube! A beautiful, radiant, perfectly balanced cube!

~

"Wow!" I said, startling myself into consciousness. With my mind on alert, I searched the recesses. This is very significant.

The cube is symbolic somehow.

I thought about that dream for days, toying with the idea of a divine, six-sided symbol. It suited my personal philosophy far better than that of the holy trinity. First, the triangle shape didn't include the essence of female—a major transgression as far as I was concerned—and furthermore, where were the angels? Why weren't they included? Weren't angels our guides, our helpers? Didn't they serve as the conduit between heaven and earth? Surely it was plausible.

For sake of clarity, I decided to map out my thoughts. Roughly outlining a cube, I filled out the sides. The utopian design manifested before my eyes. God, the cosmic birther, father and mother to all, claimed one side of the cube. Jesus Christ held another as the Son, but represented all humans—mother, father, sister, and brother alike. Angels held their position as entities of the spirit world, and I saw the Holy Ghost, too. Effectively, I labeled four sides of that cube. Two were left, but that didn't bother me. I didn't expect to completely understand. Still, together we were one. One for all and all for one. The omnipresent essence, traveling, learning, and growing together, within and without the ethers. Now, sitting with Sue, I felt the shaking, the angelic confirmation. She, too, was receiving dimensional messages.

"A cube! How intriguing!" I said. "What else?"

Sue was surprised by my positive reaction. Expecting some sort of condemnation, she hesitated. I waited patiently.

"I can't remember much, but I melted! Isn't that awful? I simply became a puddle of water. Maybe it means I need to be more firm, stronger somehow."

I smiled. I didn't think so. Sue's dream had been different from mine, but in some ways, it was the same. It was about change, and in fact, I had recently read about this melting phenomena. “No, Sue, I don’t think this is about you being weak. I think it’s about your awakening!”

“What? What do you mean?” She scrunched the furrows even deeper.

“Sue! This is about Rapture! It’s about the dawning of the Age of Aquarius.” I was ecstatic, but she needed an explanation.

“I’ve been reading this book called Awakening to Zero Point. It’s all about an atmospheric shift that is occurring.” I paused to collect my thoughts. How could I explain this scientific material? I had found it confusing, but the author’s analogy of an ice cube had helped. Now it seemed perfectly appropriate for Sue.

“You see, the earth is in a state of flux. Our electromagnetic fields are changing. Scientists are studying the phenomena, much like they study shifts in weather patterns. The high and low fields can be observed and measured as they move around our planet.”

More scrunchies. She was confused, probably feeling exactly the way I had when first reading about the phenomena.

“It has to do with the density of matter, the vibrational patterns of our material existence. We are moving toward a lighter alignment, one in which the elements will become more transparent.

“Like your cube, Sue. Depending on temperature and pressure, water shifts. It becomes dense, like an ice cube, then melts—your puddle vaporizes, and then solidifies again. From ice to liquid to gas. Isn’t that simple?”

A nod. She wanted to grasp the concept but couldn’t quite get there.

“The shift is a molecular one, a vibrational one, and one of form to formless. Like Rapture, like traveling from an earthbound existence to the spirit world. Don’t you see?

You are ready!"

Sue brightened. Like all of us, she appreciated flattery. Hearing that she was ready was music to her ears. She was a ready kind of a girl.

"Sue, you are a spiritual being, probably an old soul. Heck you've seen what's-his-name, ole Ali Baba himself." She had told me about a spirit visitation and without a doubt, in her mind, the blue entity had materialized. I jokingly referred to him as Ali Baba because I could never remember what she called her God-like friend. "Sue, this is why we've come to earth. We are here to witness, experience, and forge a new tomorrow. Ain't it great!"

A warm smile spread through her thin lips. I wasn't sure if she was happy because she thought I was insane or if she was pleased by the idea of being an old soul preparing for a new order. Whatever reason, she was feeling better, and she left thanking me. I was left to wonder. Was I on track? Did all this tie together? Was the cube truly significant? What did that passage say anyway? I could remember the gist of it, but I needed clarity. I left my important typing project and returned to my cubicle. I wanted to reread the last paragraph of the first chapter of Zero Point.

The words hadn't changed, but on this day, shivers went through me. The profile fit. I was awakening and I felt an urgency. And yes, I had been "lost," but no more. That doorway of experience was real, and within the remembering I came to terms with the past.

"They that wait upon the Lord shall renew their strength; they shall mount up with wings as eagles; they shall run, and not be weary; and they shall walk, and not faint." (Isaiah 40:31)

CHAPTER 55

This Too Shall Pass

ANALYZING SUE'S DREAM set my wheels in motion. I wondered about the validity of the Rapture phenomena; might it be achievable? Could we transcend this low-density existence? If the earth's electromagnetic field did change, would elevating one's state of awareness be possible? The author of Zero Point, Gregg Braden, explained the process logically, and I was excited by his blend of science and religion. His explanation of how the seen and unseen worked in tandem and could not be separated sounded familiar. I had read about it before in "Einstein a life."

I pulled the book from my shelf and began rifling the pages for anything that referenced God. Bohr's explanation about the dual wave-particle nature of the electron jumped out at me, much like the book of Judith had. Providence was in the making; Braden's electromagnetic theory was like Bohr's scientific explanation. Two truths exist rather than one, and furthermore, those two together offer science and man a more complete view.

Sounds like God to me, I thought. God and science; one in the same. Now, what did Einstein say? He was an agnostic, but he changed his mind as he got older. A shiver ran through me. If Einstein had become a believer, then anything was possible. Maybe a Zero Point Awakening would occur, and if it did, that might mean the Christians were right about the Messiah returning. If matter were less dense then transcending would be more common. Of course, we would need educators, and who better to teach us than Jesus.

The prospect settled on my spirit, but it also prompted a question. If this was true, then how did Satan fit into the scheme of things? Did he even exist? Could evil truly manifest in the flesh, and if so, how would that affect us? Would some people fall during the awakening? Would non-believers fail to ascend? Maybe. Transcending would be difficult without a strong belief system. Without faith, it might not even be possible.

I thought about my Bible studies, but some of the doctrines seemed ridiculous. The idea of being instantly "saved" or "reborn" was ludicrous. Water couldn't do that, nor could a priest. Spiritual rebirth was a process, and it required effort, dedication, and practice.

Rod had laid hands on me to save my soul, but my belief system remained the same. I was more committed to my spiritual growth, and my love for Jesus Christ was profound, but many questions remained, especially the ones regarding Satan. I had confronted demons, but were those dancing images manifestations of evil or had my imagination gone wild?

My mind went back to the day of the crystal chalice, so beautiful, so richly laden with deep red wine, so full of cavorting imps, drunken fools waiting for me to drink their lusty bounty. I had watched them revel and then swept them away. Down into a torrential river of doom they had gone. In my vision, I had willed the witch and her entire evil entourage from my view.

Now my meditations were peaceful and nurturing, helping me grow and increasing the creative flow; did that mean the New Agers were right? Was Satan imaginary? Did evil exist only in the psyche? I needed more information. More than ever, I wished for the book, the one about spiritual warfare, the one that, if it were in my possession, I would need to pray about every day. I decided to call my mother.

"Yes, I have it," she said. "The package came back marked Unacceptable."

Unacceptable! Goose bumps crawled up my arm. Who thought it was unacceptable? God? My angels? Some dumb guard who didn't like the idea of an inmate reading such material. An agent of Satan? "Well, isn't that strange? I wonder what in the heck 'unacceptable' means?"

"I have no idea, Judy, but there's a big red stamp on the box, and that's what it says. Do you want me to send it again?"

"I guess. I'm really trying to understand, Mom. He Came to Set His People Free is about demonic possession, and one of the gals in my Bible class recommended it. She said to read it if I truly wanted to understand spiritual warfare."

"Well, I think it's Satan," she said. "He's waylaying the text because he doesn't want you to understand. Ignorance is bliss, you know."

"So, they say, but the mind is a powerful thing. This devil business has been part of the dogma for so long, it's accepted without question. Personally, I'm not so sure. As far as I'm concerned, it's a convenient form of control."

"Do send it but package the book by itself. Send some other novel at the same time but wrap them separately. If one comes, and the other doesn't, then I'll really be curious. Right now, though, let's consider it a fluke."

"Okay," she said. "So, how are you doing? Been sick anymore?"

"Nope. Not since I got out of the rain. God, this system sucks. It's awful how inmates are treated. We are chattels, nothing more than slave labor, if you ask me."

My mother's next words came seething across the wire. "I hate those bureaucrats. I really hate them."

"It's all about money, Mom. I'm convinced of that. Prison is big business today."

"I wish there was something I could do."

"Maybe that's why I'm here, to figure out what's going on and write about it."

"How's the book going, anyway?"

"Great. My agent has lined up an editor here in Phoenix. Jana is going to finish up the first book, but when I start the second one, those pages will go straight to a professional. Ain't it great!"

"Sure is! That's super, Judy. Congratulations."

"Thanks, Mom."

By focusing on the positive, the call terminated without harsh words, but within the prison population, anger was not so easily defused. Sometimes it would come in monumental waves, like the negative yuletide that had occurred last December. I had suffered dearly during that time, but now I was more resilient. I had trained myself to observe and to accept, but the seeing could be unsettling.

Oh sure, I had asked. I wanted to know, once and for all, if demons were real, but this ... this slam of reality hit hard. I was trying to believe evil existed only in the mind, trying with all my might to deny the existence of Satan, but it was not meant to be. Once again, I was born on the wings of an eagle, and this time it was not a pretty sight.

I was aware of the arguments. They were interminable and spreading. Initially, the inmates were complaining about officers, but then quarrels between friends began erupting. Stupid, petty issues were eating away at the "Us and Them" foundation, leaving women with no sense of unity. No one was immune and no place was safe. Maybe it was because Easter was approaching or maybe girls were restless because of spring fever. For whatever reason, a nastiness permeated the camp, and it lasted for three days. I witnessed it sweep into Camp Phoenix and I could see the difference when it left.

It was a repeat performance of what had happened at The Crying Coyote. I had observed the demonic at work that day. It had been an unworldly and frightening experience. Now at Camp Phoenix I was living the scenario for a second time.

Thankfully, I understood evil was powerless against love, so love I did. I loved every cruel word directed at me, and I remained neutral in the face of opposition. In a sense, I stayed above the fracas and reminded myself not to be afraid. Whatever was occurring, I had no intention of fueling it, so I prayed for grace. I prayed and I watched and I waited.

On the second day, I was sitting alone eating my lunch when Sue joined me with her friend Ida. They were quite a pair. Neither was over five feet, reminding me of Frick and Frack. They simply belonged together. They were the same age—somewhere around fifty—and both had been wounded by a man and wronged by the system. Since Ida was an attorney, she made a terrific sounding board for Sue. Sue loved to sing her sorrow, and Ida's trade had taught her to listen. *Better her than me*.

"Hi, Judy. Have you met Ida?"

"Yes, we've met. How are you, Ida?" I asked, watching her take a seat, and praying for peace.

Sue plopped in a third chair and the bitching began. I was about ready to escape when Sue abruptly excused herself and left me alone with Ida. I groaned. Now I was stuck. Leaving would be far too rude, but etiquette demanded dialogue, which presented a challenge. Could I engage in a tête-à-tête without sinking into the mire? Would the negativity drag me down? This will test you, Ms. Burr. Just remember your lessons.

I mentioned the weather, but Ida drifted toward sex. Sex could be an entertaining subject, but little ole Ida was bent on the obscene. She said something odd, something out of character, and then she stuck out her tongue! The words were bad, but this—why, it was just plain disgusting! It wasn't a b-l-a-h kind of tongue, but rather a cunnilingus kind of lashing. Totally gross!

I was repulsed and turned away. Was she gay? Her gesture hadn't been inviting, not even remotely friendly, far too dark and barely human. Was I imagining something? I looked up to check my reality.

My God! Ida had disappeared, and in a flash some devilish ghoul had taken her place. The soft Asian slant of her eyes was gone, and now round, dark, marble-like orbs stared back at me. Her tongue still protruded, but it was skinny and slit. And the nose! It was large, pointed, and flaring. I was reminded of a horse, one breathing hard, frothing from the bit. Nothing remained of the quiet little listener. Her demeanor was completely foreign. Even her dyed black hair had changed. It was more raven-like, feathery and greasy. I imagined her lifting from the chair, flying toward me, and pecking at my head.

I blinked hard and looked again. Ida was laughing. At what, I had no idea. I couldn't think of anything except that lizard-like tongue! I was expecting it to dart out again, slash at my face, and whip a bloody line across my cheek. I ventured a prayer, then begged her forgiveness, but said I had to go. Maybe I managed a degree of politeness, maybe I didn't. In that moment, I didn't care. I wanted out of there.

Granted, that was an up front and personal experience,

but it was the sort of thing that was happening, and few of the girls were exempt. To some degree most were tormented; I could see their unhappiness, and my vision was profound. Thankfully, The Crying Coyote had prepared me. If not for that experience, I might have thought I had gone wacko. I might have run to the doc, begged for psyche meds, and confessed my craziness. As it was, I rolled with the flow. I accepted the phenomena and found it fascinating. I also refused to exude fear because I understood this was Satan's work. It could be nothing less.

Ask and you will receive. I had wanted to know, and the veil had been lifted, but on the third day I was growing weary. The fascination was abating and I was becoming angry instead. I started a silent vigil against my enemy, declaring him to be a weak fool. Satan, you're wasting your time. Why don't you move on to riper territory? These girls can't help you. They're already prisoners. Go pick on somebody else, you coward.

It was spiritual warfare, but I knew where to turn for help. Lord, grant me the strength to endure. Send warring angels to this camp. Save us from this band of demons.

That prayer was offered at my desk, and I didn't really expect much, but it was only moments before Dorothy came through the door. Whew! Her presence lifted my heart. She was there to lead a Bible study, for she loved leading others to the Lord, but more importantly, she was unaffected! Her deep black skin was as smooth as silk and I saw no signs of anguish. What a beautiful robust body! She was a feast to my eyes. Thank God, there is at least one free soul. Thank you, Jesus.

"Hi, Dorothy. What's up, girl? How've you been?" I asked casually.

"Mahvelous. Just mahvelous. Come to get ready for my girls."

“Mahvelous,” was Dorothy’s canned response. She was a Billy Crystal knock-off and loved making others happy, yet there was an underlying current of concern in her marvelous attitude. Could she see it, sense it? I wondered. Her confidence was missing, and that “follow me” charisma seemed to have fallen into shadow. Would she lead the “Happy Am I” hymn tonight? That song had a way of getting things going, and on this evening, I was considering joining the group. I wanted to be near her, within her space, safe inside her circle. “Here, let me help you set up,” I said.

“No, girl, you keep at that typewriter of yours. It’s music to my ears.”

Dorothy also aspired to be a writer and she was moved by my dream. She shared some of her stories with me and we joked about our sordid pasts. I was the telemarketing queen of fraud and she was the welfare queen of fraud. Neither of us was proud of our tag, but we were happy in our evolution and that attitude augmented a bond. We respected one another, could understand each other, and on this night, I knew she was asking for time alone. She obviously wanted to pray before the girls arrived and of course I understood. “Well, alrighty then,” I said, turning toward my typewriter. “You go, girl.”

“Bless you, dear,” she said.

Dear? Dorothy never called me dear. She was not the sweet-old-lady type. Not a Dear kind of girl. Something is wrong. Dorothy is out of sorts. Maybe she does feel it. Maybe she can ‘see.’

The girls filtered in and I could hear the chitchat, nothing too angry, not loud, but still ... the conversation carried an edge. Dorothy would have her hands full tonight. I was about to pray for her when something extraordinary happened. My spirited friend left her ladies-in-waiting and came out of the sanctuary. She closed the doors behind her and began browsing the leaflets on my desk. I kept typing. Minutes passed, and since Dorothy never—and I mean never—left her Bible circle until after closing prayers, I was moved to speak.

"Are you okay?"

My words startled her, and she was tongue-tied. I noticed droplets of sweat on her brow, also unusual. Dorothy was a cool cookie.

"Dorothy, do you feel alright?"

She told me she was fine, then turned to enter the chapel.

After the final hymn the space emptied and Dorothy came back to the pamphlets. Since most of the information was either for the Indian population or the Jehovah's Witness group, I found her body language curious.

"Dorothy," I said cautiously. Without thinking about what I was doing or how she might react, I reached for her hand. "Dorothy, you feel it, don't you?"

She said nothing, but her eyes spoke volumes.

"I want you to know," I said, still holding her hand. "I want you to know you are not alone."

Where those words came from, I did not know. Why I braved them was a mystery, but she appreciated the gesture.

"Thank you," she said, "But this too shall pass."

"Yes. Yes, it will."

"Bless you," she said, before leaving. As she turned to go, I could see the change. Those pamphlets were still in place, but they had served a purpose. They had connected us and that was enough.

I closed the chapel and walked back to my cubicle. Without even brushing my teeth, I went to bed. I wanted to avoid all contact, avoid being confronted by anything remotely devilish. Stay out of my head, I thought, climbing onto my bunk and rolling onto my back. It was a time for contemplation, not depression, and the prayer for protection began in earnest. "Blessings Heavenly Father, Earthly Mother, Eternal Light, all that Is, Was, and Ever will Be. Blessings."

I woke to the sound of singing birds and sensed a change. Maybe Dorothy called it. Maybe it's over.

I had to know, was excited to see, and soon left my room. The chow hall was clear! Thank God! Plenty of girls were eating, but there were no tortured souls. No visible attacks from the underworld. Yippee! I wanted to shout. This too shall pass indeed. The evil band of renegades is gone! Yes! Elvis has left the building. Ha, you didn't get me, not even close. I no longer fear you, you devil, so you can just go to hell. My soul is my own, and no one will ever steal it. Never again!

That afternoon, Dorothy stopped by to thank me. "I wanted to thank you for praying with me last night," she said with a smile.

I was animated, feeling glad to be glad. "You're welcome. Pretty negative sweep here at the Camp Phoenix, don't you think?"

"Yes, but things seem more normal today, thank the Lord," she said.

"Praise God," I returned, laughing. Praising God was NOT my style, sort of like Dear was not hers.

It was an interesting moment, sort of holy, but hilarious at the same time. Dorothy seemed at a loss for words and I had no idea what to say. Finally, she offered a "God bless you," and left.

I turned to my typewriter and began transposing my handwritten scribble. My mind hummed with another thought, and this too shall pass. It was my twenty-four-hour rule. Words to live by.

CHAPTER 56

A Golden Dream

WHAT IS IT ABOUT LENT? Is it the sacrificial lamb or the remembrance of him that makes us so emotional? Why does the season leave us feeling either full or empty? Easter is a reminder of the cycle of life, and thinking about death and rebirth makes us question most everything.

Such was the case for me. I was suddenly wondering what I would do with these recent revelations. Would I put this knowledge to good use or would I allow it to fall by the wayside?

"Are you Miss Burr?"

The voice was booming, which shook me even before I discovered its source. I looked up to discover an officer at my desk. Oh my God. *What have I done?* Are they mad at me for using the typewriter? Has someone reported me? "Yes," I answered simply, responding to the woman in uniform.

"You need to come with me. Do you have your ID?"

"No, do you want me to get it?"

The response came with a slight smile, a hint of kindness. "I guess they know who you are. Let's just go down there."

I nodded, feeling nervous and trapped. Down there

meant down to administration, and girls had disappeared after such a journey. They'd get called "down" and transferred "out" to who knows where.

Sensing my panic, she tried to reassure me. "Don't worry. You're not in trouble or anything. You have visitors, that's all."

Visitors! Who could be visiting in the middle of the week? We weren't allowed visitors except for the weekends. Has somebody died?

I pulled the paper from my typewriter, pressed it between the pages of my yellow pad, and pushed it into a drawer. I was typing a sex episode, a highly erotic section, and only moments ago my heart had been racing from the scene. Now the beat was erratic, pulsating with the flight or fight hormone. I wanted to run, but since that was impossible, I rose to follow. What in the world? Who wants to see me? And why all the drama? Why not page me?

"Here's your girl," she said, opening the door to a small office.

"Hi, Judy. How are you doing?"

Doing? I'm in prison, you fool. How do you think I'm doing? The adrenalin high was replaced by feelings of quiet contempt. "Fine," I said, addressing the lead prosecuting attorney. "I'm doing alright, all things considered."

So, this is it, I thought. *They want me to be their rat.* No wonder I wasn't paged. I took a good look at the man who had moved up my sentencing date. I was in prison because of him. His elegant, distinctive features were no longer reassuring, no longer trustworthy. How dare he act like a friend! How are you doing? What kind of question was that? And his associate, the postal investigator, was no better. He knew I had been treated unfairly, they both did, and their bleeding-heart attitudes sickened me. I wanted to spit, to scream in their faces, to say "no dice." No, Mr. Conrad Baker, chief liar for the government, no, Mr. Dominio, postal executive of the highest inequity, I will not testify. I will not play your game. Get out of my face!

I wanted to say it, but I knew better. I had been forewarned. Karen and I had already discussed the matter.

"You can't do that, Judy," she said. "You cannot rescind your promise."

"But I've already been sentenced. I'm already serving time. If I'm willing to stay here for three years, then why should I help them?"

"Because they can pull your plea. If you fail to cooperate, everything could revert to square one. You might end up serving the original eighteen to twenty-five years."

I was not happy with the news, but it was out of my control.

"Are they treating you alright?" asked James, the postal investigator.

Come rain or shine, James Dominio was always there. He was the first person to question me after the Pioneer raids, the only person to confront me after my arrest, and now he was here with the chief prosecuting attorney. Probably came to play golf or something, I thought. *Getting off on this, aren't you James? Feel like a big important bureaucrat?*

"Can't complain," I said, trying to be polite. "I'm making the most of my time."

There was some cursory conversation, but while we discussed the weather, my mind went into overdrive. If I had to do this, had to testify, then I wanted something in return. I wanted my freedom. I wanted them to honor our original agreement, but would they? Perhaps if I ingratiated myself to them, maybe then. Certainly it was worth a try.

Yes, I wanted out, but not so much that I would commit perjury.

No, I wasn't bitter, not at all. Prison hadn't soured me. In fact, I was writing a book. Of course, I'd be happy to take the stand. Truth was truth. Why not testify?

This was the attitude I put forth, not in those exact words, but I was agreeable and credible. What more could the government ask?

They coached me, gave me the questions, and implied what my answer should be. An improper response drew an eyebrow, and I caught on quickly. Yes, indeed, I was trainable, highly pliable.

When it was nearly over, I got straight to the point. "Just get me out of here, would you?"

"We can't promise anything, Judy," said Mr. Baker. "I'll present the judge with a Rule 35, but that doesn't mean he'll grant you time served."

"But you will ask, won't you?" These guys didn't get it. They were oblivious, as were most of the court officers. To them it was all a game. A win at all costs game. Wake up! I wanted to scream. I am a real person! So are the others. We have lives, families, and children. What about the children? What happens to them?

"Absolutely, of course I'll make the recommendation. "You've honored your end of the deal, and Judy, you've been a great help to us," he said.

Yes! That's all I needed to hear. I knew the process; if the DA made a recommendation, that was usually enough for the judge. It was a done deal. I was going home! "Thank you, Conrad. I truly appreciate that," I said, trying to contain my joy.

"You're second on the roster, so you shouldn't have to spend too much time in the county jail."

That meant I'd be returning to Camp Phoenix. Not a good thing. I needed to stay in Vegas to make sure they delivered. God, if I testify and then come back, they'll forget about me. All this will have been for nothing.

I tried again. "I don't care how long I'm there. Leave me in Vegas until you petition the judge. At least I have family there."

Dominio interjected. He was trying to be positive, but in a backward sort of way. "North Las Vegas isn't anything like this, Judy. It's an entirely different world."

"I don't care if it's a hellhole. I don't want to come back."

Both bureaucrats were surprised.

What in the world is so shocking? I wondered. Seems perfectly logical to me.

"Well, if you're sure."

"Sure, I'm sure. I can endure anything if I know there's light at the end of the tunnel. How soon before I'm transferred?"

"We don't have a definitive date, but as soon as we do, the marshals will be notified. It could be tomorrow; it could be six weeks."

Six weeks! Mentally I began to prepare. I had nearly completed the first draft of my book. Now I would race to finish it, race to send it to Jana, so she could have it put on a disk and sent to my editor. With any luck at all, a polished product would be in my agent's hands even before my release. I would move back into my house and let Lester and Trish pay the mortgage until I got published. Thank God they had made good on the rent. Thank God they would be there for me. Things were looking up.

When it was over, I went straight for the phones.

"Mom! I'm coming home. The Feds were just here, and they're pulling me out for the trials! Can you believe it?"

"Really? When?"

"Soon, Mom, soon. Maybe within six weeks."

"Great! Should we cancel our visit then?"

Mom and Pam were planning a trip to Phoenix. They

were bringing my granddaughter, and my sister Jana was coming, too. I was looking forward to the visit. "Please don't. I need to see you. I need to draw on your strength before taking the stand. God, do you know how hard that's going to be? Mom, those boys were my friends."

"Yes, but this isn't your fault. It is what it is. Remember that!"

Of course, but still ... "Okay, but you will come, won't you?"

"You bet. We'll be there."

"Thanks, Mom. Thanks for everything. I couldn't have done this without you guys. God, I feel sorry for the girls who have no support system. How in the heck do they make it after release?"

"Some don't," she said flatly. "You hear about it all the time. The residual rate is at an all-time high."

Unfortunately, she was right. Even the Phoenix girls came back. I was shocked the first time it happened, but parole violations were common. In some cases, simply having a six-pack of beer was enough. Amazing! One girl was violated because her parole officer found a couple of beers in the fridge, and those cans weren't even hers! How do you control that? You don't, of course, but the officers didn't care.

They expected inmates to return and there's a term for it. It's called the "revolving door policy," and it kept going and going, sort of like that Energizer bunny. Most inmates would leave with a two-to five-year probationary term, but even one year could turn into a lifetime sentence. Sounds radical, but it happens.

I vowed to never violate, not for any reason. Nope, Phoenix had seen the last of me. I would make it, but I had advantages most did not. I had family, some money, and good prospects for the future. I was the exception, not the rule. Unfortunately, most of the girls were not so lucky, which made me wonder, could I help? Maybe I could do something for my friends, assist them with their transitions. After all, I fully expected success, so why not share?

It was an epiphany! That's why I'm here! That's why I'm in Phoenix. Even Laura said I only stopped by to pick her up. And there were others, people like Yvonne and Dorothy, people I considered my friends, intelligent ladies with a lot to give. I began to count them. There were at least ten, maybe as many as fourteen. Why, we could make one hell of a team. If we joined efforts, we might show the world that felons were not necessarily felonious. Wouldn't that be wonderful?

A seed was planted and it immediately took root. I did not have time to dillydally. If I wanted these women to join me in business, then I needed to act. I formulated a business plan, one complete with dates and numbers. Our foundation, I decided, would be called Lion Song. Lion Song was my name for Pat Benatar's "One Love." The lyrics spoke about a man with a 'golden dream,' but in this case, it would be a woman with a golden dream.

We would work together and seal our success by becoming a mastermind, a team. I could see it clearly and I had a way to fund us. The royalties from my trilogy would capitalize us and our combined talent would do the rest. We might become leaders of a new movement—one to put ex-cons back to work. We would succeed by standing in our own power, not falling to some predisposed label. I was excited and my enthusiasm could not be contained.

I called a meeting. I was already teaching a class in creative writing, and I expected most of those ladies to be receptive. They had, for the most part, gravitated toward me because of something deeper than a desire to write, but there were others. Altogether, I sent out fourteen invitations. Eleven came.

Eleven! Including me, that made twelve! What a magical number! I was moved. I explained my plan and told them to consider it.

"Ask this question," I said. "If a genie suddenly appeared and offered to grant you one great wish, what would you request? If you knew for certain it would be impossible to fail, what would you aspire to do? What would you choose to give the world? What would you dare to dream?"

Until that moment, the response had been lukewarm. Maybe I had frightened them, suggesting destiny brought us together, or perhaps they didn't understand my "web of life" theory, or maybe they just couldn't imagine themselves as winners. It was a lot to assimilate, but the genie query threw them into a frenzy. That question unleashed something spectacular and the room reverberated with ideas.

"I've always wanted to open a shelter for the homeless," one woman said.

"I've had a dream to promote reading among impoverished children," came another voice.

"Start a foundation to assist people on probation, help them reenter society."

"Offer a free drug rehabilitation program, base it on people helping people, using those who have been there, done that, sort of like Patch Adams, similar to AA, but more intense."

It was a magical hour, a synergistic experience that reminded me of the early days with Rod. Inspired by their enthusiasm, I chalked the numbers on the board and illustrated the basics of my business plan.

Finally, I suggested we commit the plan to secrecy. "Keep this quiet," I said. "We are a closed group. There are twelve of us, and that is a good number. No one else is invited, at least not for now."

"Watch for the release of my third book," I said. "When

the trilogy is complete, I will have the funds to launch us. In the meantime, dream the dream, see the vision, and create your plan. We can do this. We can make this happen. I know it and so do you."

Again, the group erupted, but this time everyone spoke at once. Like a smoldering volcano, excitement burst forth, bringing buried thoughts from the recesses and expelling the imagination of a collective mind. The energy lifted me, and as my emotions soared, I noticed something else, something alarming. Other women were curious, gathering to look through our windowed wall. They wanted to know what was causing all the commotion.

Trouble.

My meeting was strictly against prison policy. I was organizing and promoting a cause, which was not allowed. Another rule. If I wasn't careful, someone would report me and the dream would end. I better get this under control. If I don't, there will be hell to pay.

"Quiet! Everyone, QUIET!"

A soft hush fell into the room, and as it did, their crushed expressions made me laugh. I was thrilled by their disappointment. It meant we were one, unified by like-minded thinking, a rare event between inmates. "Remember what we're supposed to be doing here," I said. "What could possibly be so exciting about a creative writing class?"

Giggles erupted and the message was received. Like me, they did not want our efforts thwarted. Everyone was happy, and I ended the session by quoting Dr. Dyer. "Believe. Believe and you will see."

"Did I sound crazy in there?" I asked Laura as we walked back to our unit.

"Not to me, girl. I think it's a terrific idea. I'm not so sure about some of those women, but for sure I'll be there. You can count on it. Will you organize in Las Vegas?"

"Initially, but eventually I'd like to move to Sedona."

"Why?"

"I'm not sure, but I feel called to the place."

"That's cool. I've been thinking I might end up back in Arizona. Isn't that weird?"

It didn't seem weird, not to me. "Land of the rising sun," I said nonchalantly. "I heard those lyrics just the other day and they spoke to me. I was on that track, but the song sent me scrambling up hills of red rock. God, it's beautiful in Sedona, Laura. You're gonna love the energy there. I swear it's sacred ground."

"I'm going to miss you, girl. You have a way of firing me up. I can be in the pissiest mood and after only a few minutes with you, I change completely."

"I feel the same way about you, but you won't be far behind. I'll get things started and then you can join me when you're ready. God, this is exciting," I said. "I just pray it's all real."

"Oh, it's real alright," Laura said. "Better believe it."

And I did, but someone else wasn't so sure. There was a Judas in my group, and I heard about it from Yvonne. "They're saying you've gathered your disciples. Some of the girls are wondering who in the hell you think you are. Better watch your back."

I had done it again. Drawn attention to myself, attention that wasn't necessarily good, but I didn't really care. It was nearly over and soon I would be out of there. In the meantime, I would keep a low profile. Maybe then the rumors would subside, maybe my Judas would forget the whole thing.

On a deeper level, I was inspired by the negative feedback. No, I was no savior, not even close, but I sure felt close to another biblical character. I was walking in the historical shoes of Judith. She had struggled to save her people, the Israelites, and my mission was funding a nonprofit to curb the rising residual rate. If my plan didn't work, then our tribe would scatter to the four winds. On the other hand, if it was a success, a golden dream would be born.

CHAPTER 57

Fellowship Down

TO SAY I WAS FLOATING on a cloud would be an understatement. I would soon be a free woman and I had a plan, one that would benefit more than just me. I was feeling secure, nurturing my hopes and loving my world when, once again, it was shattered. Well, maybe not shattered, but certainly shaken. It happened at Bible study, an unlikely place considering my new respect for the Christians.

I was beginning to appreciate studying with Ralph, Mary Lou, and Darlene. Ralph and Mary Lou were kind, compassionate people. They were senior citizens, married for too many years to count. They told us divorce nearly separated them but turning to the Lord saved their marriage. In fact, everything about their lives improved after joining the Christian Fellowship. I was listening.

Darlene was also a volunteer who had a similar tale, but she was closer to my age. She was a single parent and career woman, so I related to her, but I especially appreciated her open mind. I could speak freely with her about things like reincarnation and not feel judged. If it hadn't been for her, I might have lost faith in the Fellowship group, but because of her I stayed.

With Easter approaching, ascension was on my mind. More than anything, I wanted to discuss the scientific relevance of the "cube" thing. If nothing else, the theory would spark a lively debate and presenting it to the group seemed a good idea. At least it did until the lesson began.

We were still studying spiritual warfare and the session started with a videotape. The short docudrama set the theme for the evening and was historically informative, in a Christian sort of way. On this night, it set the stage for me to "Shut Up." I heard the directive loud and clear.

The narrator and lesson-giver mentioned meditation and proceeded to tell his listeners how dangerous the practice was, saying it opened a door to evil. Fighting words, as far as I was concerned, nothing but narrow-minded thinking. Exactly what the world doesn't need! I thought.

Darlene was sitting next to me and seemed to sense my anger. She reached over and patted my hand, as if to say, "Don't worry about it. It's only one man's opinion."

The video ended and Mary Lou took over. She looked directly at me and said something about losing one's will to Satan. Someone must have told her I was a practiced meditator.

Ridiculous!

I wanted to open my mouth, but speaking would serve no purpose. The church had control of her belief system and arguing would bring attention to me, serve as fodder for my enemies. I remained silent. Up until that moment, I had considered joining the Prison Fellowship group. Now I wanted to run.

The next week it got worse. We were watching a movie about the crucifixion, which was beautifully inspiring and tragically terrifying at the same time. I was filled with emotion, as were others. Trouble was, my feelings came from the collective "we," not the single act of adversity. I silently wept for all of us, not just Jesus. Why? I wondered. How can people be so cruel?

Ralph was the first to comment after the lights went on, saying something that echoed my thoughts, but when the group—Mary Lou in particular—started going on about Jesus, and how he had suffered to save our souls, I got angry.

He's not the only one who has suffered! I wanted to scream. What about the Spanish Inquisition? The Crusades? The Holocaust? Don't you see? It's not just Jesus! Millions have died because of their differences. It's greed and bigotry that's killing us! Man sits in judgment, and Christ's great teachings have been for not!

I was conflicted. On one hand, I wanted to tell them it was their tunnel-vision thinking that caused atrocities like the crucifixion. On the other hand, I had worked hard to become an observer and I did not want to lose ground. Still, it was difficult, so difficult, I could not stay. Without a word, I got up and walked out.

The night air was a refreshing contrast to the stifling environment inside, but getting away was not enough. I needed solitude. I walked to the back of the campus and sat down on one of the cold cement benches. Reflecting silently, the tears began to flow, and within minutes, control was impossible. I looked around. Nothing. I could see no one in the darkness. Knowing I would not be confronted, I let go. The floodgates opened, and the atrocities, both past and present, were swept away. Finally, I made a proclamation. "Never! Never will I join. Down with your Prison Fellowship! Your group is not for me!"

CHAPTER 58

The White Horse

I DID NOT ATTEND BIBLE STUDY that next week. I was still trying to deal with my anger and disappointment. Thoughts of persecuted individuals filled my mind and I wondered at the ignorance of people. Socrates had received a death sentence because of his progressive thinking. Joan of Arc had been burned at the stake and Martin Luther King had been assassinated, as had Ghandi. All free-thinking beings. All persecuted because of prejudicial attitudes. Jesus Christ may have died on the cross, but it seemed like his message died with him. At the very least, it got distorted. What happened to love thy fellow man? Judge not, lest you be judged. Why were these so-called followers of Jesus caught up in their personal righteousness?

The question brought a chill across my shoulders. I recognized the signal and realized I was being reminded to pay attention. If you are unhappy with something, take a closer look. What you see is usually a reflection of self.

It was an "aha" moment, one I shall never forget. I had cast the stone, but not without guilt. I had become the essence of what I abhorred. Realizing that great truth, I returned to class.

"We missed you, Judy," said Darlene. "Were you sick? Is everything alright?"

Darlene's words were insightful and I read between the lines. "Be patient," she said. "We are not perfect, but our intentions are good."

"I'm fine, thanks. That movie was too much for me."

"I know what you mean. The first time I saw it, I bawled for days. But you're okay? I was worried about you."

I looked into her blue eyes and saw the softness. Suddenly I was glad to be back. Darlene was reminding me of the goodness within that tribe, reminding me of why I was there in the first place. "Yes, I'm okay. Sure was one heck of a reminder, though; tough lesson, that one."

I turned a corner that night, and once again I was at peace with myself and my surroundings. I also stopped worrying about upcoming events or the fact I would soon be shackled. That was the procedure. Inmates did not leave the camp without being bound by chains and cuffed at the hands and feet.

When my family arrived, I nearly bowled them over with enthusiasm. The first day I described my business plan and told them they would all be officers. "Pam, you'll be secretary. Jana, I'd like for you to be treasurer, since you're Ms. Integrity and Wisdom," I reminded her jokingly. "And, Mom, I'd like you to be the vice president."

Everyone seemed to enjoy being included, so I went on. "Pam, I need you to contact my attorney. Have him file the corporate papers right away."

Until this moment, my family had been listening. They were fascinated but not convinced. Jana was the first to interject. "Don't you think you're moving a little fast? Why don't you wait until you're out?"

"Jana," I said. "That could take a few months, and I could

get an offer before then. It's important Lion Song owns the book rights from the get-go."

The second day, I calmed down. My behavior had been off-the-wall as far as my family was concerned. My project was dubious and their "goodbyes" reflected those feelings. I felt it in their gestures and I heard it in the tone of their voices. In their eyes I was crazy. I had to prove otherwise. I never mentioned my business plan again. Instead, I engaged in things they could understand. I spent a good deal of time playing with my granddaughter, Marie, and I did all the things "normal" people did when receiving a visit. We cried when the appointed hour arrived, but they left believing I was sane.

Finally, I began saying goodbye to a handful of selected friends. Yvonne was one of them. "No! You can't go," she said. "You are one of the only people I trust."

I reminded her of the business plan and told her I needed to get started for all our sakes. "Yvonne, remember you are always welcome. When you're ready, come and join us. Lion Song will help you realize your greatest dream."

She was not soothed. "Judy, I don't understand these ladies. Why do they go pray at the chapel and then pass judgment on me?"

Yvonne's Puerto Rican background caused some people consternation. Her talent for reading cards didn't help, but when word went out that she saw spirits, judgments were made. It didn't matter that she prayed every day and her kindness and compassion wasn't a factor. Yvonne saw things others could not, and that meant only one thing—Black Magic. It was voodoo. Had to be. She must have learned it from her ancestors.

The night she saw Rod, I was surprised, but not for a minute did I think something evil had occurred. I simply recognized her gift and appreciated it for what it was. Others were not so sure. Even Laura's roommate, sweet Maria, had insinuated Yvonne was into black magic.

"You know where her father comes from," she had said. "Bad religion, that one. No get near."

I was not surprised, given Maria's serious romance with the Bible, but still, the ignorance amazed me. "Yvonne, don't worry. Those women don't know any better. They believe what their priests tell them, and because of that, they assume all kinds of stupid things. Remember who you are and stand in your personal power. Don't let them get to you."

Thinking about Yvonne's challenges reminded me of Rod. He, too, was gifted, but he abused his talents and suffered because of them. The misuse of power nearly cost him his company, though Global was making a comeback. He had sent pictures to prove it. In fact, I had received a whole package from Rod, complete with product slicks and business cards. He also sent a picture of his new team. They were proudly standing in front of a jet, holding a giant Global banner. I was impressed. The picture seemed an indicator of success. Knowing I'd be leaving soon, I decided to call him."

"Judy! Judy, how are you? Oh my God, it's good to hear your voice. I can't believe it! I was just thinking about you."

Rod was animated. I knew it would be difficult to get my two cents in, especially since I only had fifteen minutes.

"I had a vision yesterday. You were in it."

"Really? And what did you see?" I asked.

"I saw a giant white cloud and it took the shape of your face. Then you spoke to me. Know what you said?"

I couldn't imagine. "What?"

"You said, 'My Son.' You called me your son! Isn't that funny?"

He was amused, but I was amazed. "No, Rod. It's not funny. It's real. You are my son."

"Oh, right," he said, ignoring me. "Judy, everything is going so well! God, I wish you were here to share in this. I miss you so much."

I was glad for him, but I wanted no part of his business. Never again! Global had nearly destroyed me. For certain it had destroyed us and I couldn't imagine touching it again. Not with a ten-foot pole! "I'm happy for you, Rod. Looks like you'll be inheriting my father's globe after all."

"Really? Would you really let me have it?"

"I told you I would. I promised you the globe when Global became a success. Sounds like you're on your way."

He took off on another tangent. "Judy, my Angels have told me how to discover the Beast."

Oh, brother, here we go again. "How, Rod?"

"They said when you and Mandy and Mary Ann agree, that will be my signal. That will confirm the identity."

Mentioning Mandy affected me in a negative way. I hated the fact she was still special to Rod. I had grown to love Rod's wife, Mary Ann. She was my respected soul sister, but Mandy ... well, Mandy didn't fit into the picture. "R-e-a-l-l-y," I said, drawing out the word.

"Yes, really. What's the matter? Jealous?"

"No, I'm not jealous. Just curious. Why Mandy?"

"She's working here with me. Didn't I tell you?"

I hadn't talked to him for some time, and even if I had, I doubted he'd give me this detail. Eventually, I worked my departure into the conversation, and then he forgot about the beast and Mandy.

"That's wonderful! That's the best news I've heard in months. When?"

"Soon," I said. "I'll have to testify and then the motion will be filed. I'm not sure how long it will take, but I am on my way. This nightmare is nearly over."

"Judy?"

His voice had an odd inflection, one I didn't recognize. Who might be speaking now? "What, Rod?"

"Judy, you are the White Horse."

"What?" I asked again.

"Look it up in Revelations. I am Valor, Faithful and True, and you are the White Horse."

"Rod, what in the world are you talking about?"

"You don't understand, but you will. Let's talk about you. How can I contact you? Can I meet you in Vegas? God, I miss you, honey. I can't wait to put my arms around you."

I was stirred, but seeing Rod was out of the question. Yes, I missed him, but I couldn't forget those hands around my throat. Until he was well, completely and totally, fully healed, I had no intention of getting near him. Fortunately, I was saved by the click, click, click. We said goodbye and I promised to write. That was the best I could do.

Back in the barracks, I had plenty to cogitate. True to form, Rod had given me an earful. He had mentioned this name, this Valor, before, but I hadn't paid attention. At the time, I thought Valor was an alter ego, some personality that came out to protect Rod. Valor was old news, but what was the White Horse? I decided to look it up.

"Then I saw heaven open, and there was a white horse.

Its rider is called Faithful and True."

Faithful and True! Rod believed Valor was the Faithful and True of Revelations! Oh, my God. And I am the white horse? He thinks I am the white horse! Good grief! I read on:

"His eyes were like a flame of fire,

and he wore many crowns on his head."

Now that sounded like Rod! I had seen those flame-red eyes. They had confronted me in our mini-suite ... and those crowns! They reminded me of his alter egos. I had identified at least five of Rod's personalities. They were all different, and as they emerged, I adjusted my response tactics. It had been an experience, but nothing I'd call divine, not even close.

Well, at least this time he has a positive image of me. I am still a horse and still carry a rider, but that rider is no longer from the pits of hell, thank God.

I was recalling the day Rod laid hands on me. We had just finished an exercise in introspection, and the horse represented his lover, which was fine, but then he put a rider on my back. I was carrying a dark rider, a figure cloaked in black. His subconscious had spoken, and the message was, Judy's possessed. With that confirmation, he attempted to expel my demons. That had been an "other" worldly experience, one I would never forget.

Now it was the same, but different. I was still the horse, but the rider was no longer from the pits of hell. Or was he? Rod saw himself riding the white horse—that was me. Did I still carry the damn demon? Was it him? I shut the good book and took to the track. Clearing my head was a primary concern. Good God, what was up with my Rod?

Days passed and I began to settle. I decided no damage would come from Rod's illusion. If he wanted to believe he was the Faithful and True character of Revelations, then so be it. Worse things could happen. And I didn't mind playing the part of the white horse either. The white horse represented Truth, and more than anything, I wished Rod could climb into the saddle. I had to wonder, though, could he stay there once he took the reins?

If that magnificent animal bent low and asked him to get on board, could Rod do it? Could he assume the role of Faithful and True, and if he did, could he remain seated? Could he stay on the back of Truth or would he, once again, fail miserably?

I was fascinated by what Rod read between the lines of the Good Book and I continued to delve. The Beast, I decided, was organized religion, and I proceeded to tell him so. In a letter I suggested he wouldn't have to kill it, for it would die a natural death. Finally, I said "Goodbye," and explained why we could never be together.

I love you dearly, Rod, always will, and I'm sure we are soulmates. Maybe there was a time when we were husband and wife, I don't know. What I believe is you were an Einstein. Remember that day I recognized you? I didn't understand what was happening, but I do now. You were Eduard Einstein in your last lifetime. You were the genius son of Albert and Mileva. I was your mother. That is why we were drawn together. That is why I could never abandon you. A mother never stops loving her son, after all.

I know this sounds incredible but hear me out. There's more. Your wife, Mary Ann, was there too. She was Albert's second wife, and she helped him realize his great dream. She acted as his protector while he worked on the mysteries of science. Mary Ann was Albert's angel, Rod. She was his then, and now she is yours. Isn't it fitting? She is perfect for the part, I think. No woman could serve a man better.

In some ways I'm jealous, but still, I could never do that "submission" thing. I follow no man. Never did, never will. I will say you had a chance, but truly, it was not meant to be.

We came together for a reason, but it wasn't to marry. This time I played the part of the older woman, the love of your life. For me, you played the part of dream weaver. Because of you, I am living my dream. For that, I thank you.

I have recognized so many members from our soul family. You would be amazed and one day when we have lots of time I will share more. For now, I need to tell you I seek another. I have found a daughter and one of my sons, but their father eludes me. In many ways, that shouldn't be a surprise, since the world now calls him the Father of Relativity. Doesn't that just figure? My kind of luck. Anyway, all kidding aside, I must tell you we can never be together, at least not as lovers or business partners. We must separate and travel our own paths. Go preach those Five Golden Rings, my love. You speak it and I'll write it. We'll make it our legacy. In that way, our love will live forever.

The Five Golden Rings

HOPE FOR ALL MANKIND rests in the HEART,
and the heart is nourished by LOVE, a love freely offered.
Such freedom is found in TRUTH,
but truth does not come easily.
There is a price to pay. A lesson must first be learned.
We must first learn to FORGIVE.
Without forgiveness, truth remains buried,
and the freedom to love cannot be found.
Without love, our hearts harden
and no longer have strength for hope.
Without hope, we will most certainly perish.
Learn the lesson of FORGIVENESS
and embrace truth.
The TRUTH will set you free.
In that newfound freedom, you will discover LOVE.
The HEART, nourished by love, will grow strong
and provide sanctuary for HOPE.
With a place of perpetual rest,
HOPE will finally Spring Eternal.
Learn the lesson of forgiveness.
Begin by forgiving yourself.
It is a small price to pay.

About the Author

JUDY BURR is originally from Colorado, where she raised a family and started a bookkeeping service. She now resides in Las Vegas, NV and continues her career in the field of finance. She is the owner of an accounting firm, but her love of "numbers" has been replaced by a love for writing.

Judy's debut memoir *Lion Song* was published in 2020. *Five Golden Rings* is her second book in the Uncommon Partnerships series, with the third installment of the trilogy outlined and waiting in the wings.

Judy maintains a balanced life by water walking, stretching daily, and playing bridge. Bridge is a competitive game, but she plays to nurture her friendships, of which she has many.

www.ingramcontent.com/pod-product-compliance
Lightning Source LLC
LaVergne TN
LVHW040824090826
845145LV00001BA/37

* 9 7 8 0 9 8 9 7 7 8 8 1 7 *